ISSA

INFORMATION SYSTEMS SECURITY & ASSURANCE SERIES

Access Control and Identity Management

THIRD EDITION

Mike Chapple, PhD, CISSP

JONES & BARTLETT
LEARNING

World Headquarters
Jones & Bartlett Learning
5 Wall Street
Burlington, MA 01803
978-443-5000
info@jblearning.com
www.jblearning.com

Jones & Bartlett Learning books and products are available through most bookstores and online booksellers. To contact Jones & Bartlett Learning directly, call 800-832-0034, fax 978-443-8000, or visit our website, www .jblearning.com.

Substantial discounts on bulk quantities of Jones & Bartlett Learning publications are available to corporations, professional associations, and other qualified organizations. For details and specific discount information, contact the special sales department at Jones & Bartlett Learning via the above contact information or send an email to specialsales@ jblearning.com.

Production Credits

VP, Product Management: Amanda Martin
Director of Product Management: Laura Pagluica
Product Manager: Edward Hinman
Content Strategist: Melissa Duffy
Content Coordinator: Paula-Yuan Gregory
Project Manager: Lori Mortimer
Senior Digital Project Specialist: Angela Dooley
Marketing Manager: Michael Sullivan
Product Fulfillment Manager: Wendy Kilborn

Composition: Exela Technologies
Project Management: Exela Technologies
Cover Design: Briana Yates
Media Development Editor: Faith Brosnan
Rights Specialist: James Fortney
Cover Image (Title Page, Part Opener, Chapter Opener):
    © fandijki/ShutterStock, Inc.
Printing and Binding: LSC/Harrisonburg

Library of Congress Cataloging-in-Publication Data

Names: Chapple, Mike, author.
Title: Access control and identity management / Mike Chapple. Description: Third edition. | Burlington, MA : Jones & Bartlett Learning, 2021. | Revision of: Access control, authentication, and public key infrastructure / Bill Ballad, Tricia Ballad, and Erin K. Banks. 2014. | Includes bibliographical references and index.
Identifiers: LCCN 2020008013 | ISBN 9781284198355 (paperback)
Subjects: LCSH: Computers–Access control. | Public key cryptography.
Classification: LCC TK5105.59 .B353 2021 | DDC 005.8–dc23
LC record available at https://lccn.loc.gov/2020008013

ISBN: 9781284198355

6048

Printed in the United States of America

24 23 22 21   10 9 8 7 6 5 4 3 2

Contents

PART I   **The Need for Access Control Systems and Identity Management   1**

CHAPTER 1   **Access Control Framework   2**

Preface

Purpose of This Book

This book is part of the *Information Systems Security & Assurance Series* from Jones & Bartlett Learning (*www.jblearning.com*). Designed for courses and curricula in IT Security, Cybersecurity, Information Assurance, and Information Systems Security, this series features a comprehensive, consistent treatment of the most current thinking and trends in this critical subject area. These titles deliver fundamental information-security principles packed with real-world applications and examples. Authored by Certified Information Systems Security Professionals (CISSPs), they deliver comprehensive information on all aspects of information security. Reviewed word for word by leading technical experts in the field, these books are not just current, but forward-thinking—putting you in the position to solve the cybersecurity challenges not just of today, but of tomorrow, as well.

The goal of *Access Control and Identity Management*, Third Edition, is to provide you with both academic knowledge and real-world understanding of the concepts behind access controls. These are tools you will use to secure valuable resources within your organization's IT infrastructure. The authors' goal was to provide you with a book that would teach important concepts first and act as a useful reference later.

Access control goes beyond the simple username and password. This book approaches access control from a broad perspective, dealing with every aspect of access controls, from the very low-tech to the cutting edge.

Part 1 of this book defines the components of access control, provides a business framework for implementation, describes the impact of human nature and organizational behavior on access control systems, and discusses the risk assessment process.

Part 2 focuses on implementing access control systems in enterprise environments. It includes a discussion of mapping business challenges to access control types, the technical details of implementing access controls, and a review of access control issues specific to physical security and teleworking.

Part 3 provides a resource for students and practitioners who are responsible for implementing, testing, and managing access control systems throughout the IT infrastructure. Use of public key infrastructures for large organizations and certificate authorities is presented to solve unique business challenges. This part also includes a review of the legal issues surrounding access control and a discussion of security breaches.

The book is more than just a list of different technologies and techniques. You will come away with an understanding of how and why to implement an access control system. You will know how to conduct an effective risk assessment prior to implementation and how to test solutions throughout the life cycle of the system.

Learning Features

The writing style of this book is practical and conversational. Each chapter begins with a statement of learning objectives. Step-by-step examples of information security concepts and procedures are presented throughout the text. Illustrations are used both to clarify the material and to vary the presentation. The text is sprinkled with Notes, Tips, FYIs, Warnings, and sidebars to alert the reader to additional helpful information related to the subject under discussion. Chapter assessments appear at the end of each chapter, with solutions provided in the back of the book.

Chapter summaries are included in the text to provide a rapid review or preview of the material and to help students understand the relative importance of the concepts presented.

Audience

The material is suitable for undergraduate or graduate computer science majors or information science majors, or students at a 2-year technical college or community college who have a basic technical background, or readers who have a basic understanding of IT security and want to expand their knowledge.

New to This Edition

The third edition of this book reorganizes the content to better fit modern discussions of access control systems. It also includes technology updates to bring the content in line with current best practices. The book includes more detailed discussions of the government certification process for access control systems and the technologies used to provide assurance in government computing environments. This third edition includes updates on wireless technology and the use of NIST Special Publication 800-48 to implement wireless security standards.

Cloud Labs

This text is accompanied by Cybersecurity Cloud Labs. These hands-on virtual labs provide immersive mock IT infrastructures where students can learn and practice foundational cybersecurity skills as an extension of the lessons in this textbook. For more information or to purchase the labs, visit go.jblearning.com/chapple3e.

Acknowledgments

The production of a book is a complex effort involving many people. I would like to thank everyone involved in this project, especially those whom I never had the opportunity to meet. Special thanks are due to Jeff Parker, who served as an excellent technical editor; Kim Lindros, our developmental editor; Melissa Duffy and Ned Hinman, who managed the project; and Carolyn Cohn, our copyeditor. I would also like to thank Carole Jelen, my literary agent at Waterside Productions.

Mike Chapple

About the Author

Mike Chapple, PhD, CISSP, is teaching professor of IT, analytics, and operations at the University of Notre Dame's Mendoza College of Business. In the past, he was chief information officer of Brand Institute and an information security researcher with the National Security Agency and the U.S. Air Force. His primary areas of expertise include network intrusion detection and access controls. Mike is a frequent contributor to TechTarget's SearchSecurity site and the author of more than 25 books including: *CISSP Official (ISC)*^{2} *Practice Tests*, the *CompTIA CySA+ Study Guide*, and *Cyberwarfare: Information Operations in a Connected World*. Mike offers study groups for the CISSP, SSCP, Security+, and CySA+ certifications on his website at www.certmike.com.

This book is dedicated to the memory of Dewitt Latimer, my friend, colleague, and mentor.

—Mike Chapple

PART I

The Need for Access Control Systems and Identity Management

Access Control Framework

ORGANIZATIONS RELY UPON ACCESS CONTROLS to grant and restrict user access to information, systems, and other resources. Access control systems, when properly designed, implement business rules and often direct implementations of policy in such a manner that individuals have access to the information and resources needed to perform their responsibilities but no more.

The consequences of weak or nonexistent access controls range from inconvenient to downright disastrous, depending on the nature of the resources being protected. For the average user, it may be a personal invasion of privacy to have someone else reading your email. On the other hand, without strong access controls, companies could lose billions of dollars when disgruntled employees bring down mission-critical systems. Identity theft is a major concern in modern life, because so much of our private information is stored in accessible databases. The only way that information can be both useful and safe is through strong access controls.

Chapter 1 Topics

This chapter covers the following topics and concepts:

- What access control is
- What the principal components of access control are
- What the three stages of access control are
- What logical access controls are
- What authentication factors are

Chapter 1 Goals

When you complete this chapter, you will be able to:

- Identify the principal components of access control
- Define the three stages of access control
- Choose the best combination of authentication factors for a given scenario

---

Access and Access Control

There are two fundamentally important concepts you need to know before diving into the content for this chapter:

1. What does "access" mean?
2. What is "access control"?

In an ideal world, you wouldn't need to control access to what's important to you or of value—you wouldn't even need to lock your doors. Unfortunately, that's not reality—at home or in the business world. In the real world—especially in business—there is a need to protect precious data, systems, network bandwidth, and other assets from a variety of threats. This chapter will help you understand how to lock your virtual doors and secure your information assets from unauthorized access, modification, and disruption.

What Is Access?

Fundamentally, **access** refers to the ability of a **subject** and an **object** to interact. That interaction is the basis of everything we do, both in the information technology (IT) field and in life in general. Access can be defined in terms of social rules, physical barriers, or informational restrictions.

For example, consider a busy executive with an administrative assistant who serves as a gatekeeper, deciding who will be allowed to interact personally with the executive and who must leave a message with the administrative assistant. In this scenario, the visitor is the subject and the executive is the object. The administrative assistant serves as the access control system, restricting which individuals (subjects) may access the executive (object).

Consider another scenario that is a bit closer to home. When you leave your house, you lock the doors. The locked door physically restricts access by anyone without a key to the assets stored inside your house—your TV, computer, and stereo system. When you come home, you unlock the door and replace the physical restriction of the locking mechanism with a human gatekeeper who decides whether or not to let someone enter the house.

What would happen if data were freely available? After all, open source software has certainly made a convincing case for open information. What if the data in question is your company's payroll file? If that file is unsecured, anyone could open the file and obtain sensitive information, including your Social Security number and annual salary. Think of the chaos that would ensue if a disgruntled employee decided you did not deserve the money you made and reset your salary. Data is one of the most valuable assets an organization possesses. IT professionals must invest time and energy into appropriately securing it.

What do executives, deadbolts, and payroll have to do with IT? They are physical counterparts to the technical access control systems that we use to protect digital and electronic resources—sensitive files, servers, and network resources. You might not have specific, documented rules for access when it comes to which visitors you allow into your home, but information systems use formalized systems to grant or restrict access to resources. Computers are not very good at making intuitive decisions, so you have to lay out specific rules for them to follow when deciding whether to grant or deny access.

What Is Access Control?

Access control is the formalization of those rules for allowing or denying access. Access controls define the allowable interactions between subjects and objects. It is based on the granting of rights, or privileges, to a subject with respect to an object.

What Is Identity Management?

Identity management is the process of creating, maintaining, and revoking user accounts and providing the mechanisms used to authenticate users. Theoretically, identity management allows you to confirm that a person is who they claim to be (authentication), and access control allows you to restrict his or her activities to authorized actions (authorization). In practice, the concepts of identity management and access control are interwoven and are difficult to separate. For this reason, many people refer to both fields together as **identity and access management (IAM)**.

Principal Components of Access Control

There are three principal components of any access control scenario:

- **Policies**—The rules that govern who gets access to which resources
- **Subjects**—The user, network, process, or application requesting access to a resource
- **Objects**—The resource to which the subject desires access (e.g., files, databases, printers, and physical facilities)

Any time you have to decide whether to allow or deny access by a subject to a resource, you have entered the access control problem domain.

Access Control Systems

A well-defined access control system consists of three elements:

- **Policies**—Clear statements of the business requirements regarding access to resources
- **Procedures**—Nontechnical methods, such as business processes and background checks, used to enforce policies

- **Tools**—Technical methods, such as file system access controls and network firewalls, used to enforce policies

Organizations typically use **procedures** and **tools** together to enforce policies. For example, most companies have strict **policies** to determine who has access to personnel records. These records contain sensitive and confidential information that could be used to inflict serious harm on individual employees and the company as a whole if those records were compromised. The policy may state that only employees within the human resources department, with a specific need for the information contained within a given record, may have access to it.

To enforce this policy, the company has procedures that state that a record can be given only to employees with the proper credentials (the authentication process) who fill out a form stating their specific need for the information contained in the record they request. When the request is approved, the employees may be given a username and password to access the employee records' Intranet site (the authorization process). The Intranet site, along with the username and password, is the tool required to grant access to personnel records.

Access Control Subjects

The subject in an access-control scenario is a person or another application requesting access to a resource such as the network, a file system, or a printer.

There are three types of subjects when it comes to access control for a specific resource:

- **Authorized**—Those who have presented authenticated credentials and have been approved for access to the resource
- **Unauthorized**—Those who have presented authenticated credentials but are not approved for access to the resource
- **Unknown**—Those who have not presented authenticated credentials

Every individual who initially approaches an access control system is unknown until he or she attempts to authenticate. For example, someone might be asked to provide a username and password. If the user does not provide the correct password, the system still does not know who the user is and he or she retains unknown status. On the other hand, if the user's password is correct, the system now knows with certainty who the user is and must check to see if the user is authorized to access the requested resource. Someone allowed to access the resource moves to the "authorized" state. Otherwise, the user is still known, but now moves to the "unauthorized" state.

This process is known as AAA (or "triple A") security and involves three components:

- **Authentication**—Ensuring users are who they claim to be
- **Authorization**—Ensuring that an authenticated user is allowed to perform the requested action
- **Accounting**—Maintaining records of the actions performed by authorized users

Users are not the only subjects in access control systems. Technological resources may also serve as subjects. For example:

- **Networks**—A network is a subject when a resource on one network requests access to a resource on another network. A firewall rule that authorizes access to the Internet might use the internal network as a subject, with the Internet as the object.

- **Systems**—A system is a subject when one system requests access to resources on another system or on the network. This usually happens when a PC attempts to access a printer across the network.
- **Processes**—A process is most commonly a subject when an application process requests low-level access to the file system.
- **Applications**—An application can be a subject when it attempts to access other resources on the same computer or over the network.

Technology subjects may use password authentication or may rely on other forms of identification and authorization. For example, a network may be authenticated by its IP address.

Access Control Objects

There are three main categories of objects to be protected by access controls:

- **Information**—Any type of data asset
- **Technology**—Applications, systems, and networks
- **Physical location**—Physical locations such as buildings and rooms

Information is the most common asset in terms of IT access controls. You put passwords on databases and applications to ensure that only authorized users can access the information they contain. Technology objects are just as important because a malicious user can easily compromise the integrity of data by attacking the technology that stores and uses it. If an unauthorized user gains access to a file server, that user can easily steal, delete, or change the data stored on the file server.

 NOTE

Consider an automated teller machine (ATM) in a mall. That system deals with highly sensitive data, but in order to fulfill its purpose, it must be in an open, easily accessed area. In this type of situation, information and technology-based access controls become doubly important.

Physical security is the process of ensuring that no one without the proper credentials can access physical resources, including hardware and physical locations. If all of the servers require a password to log on, why bother restricting who can enter the server room? The answer is simple—if a malicious user's goal is to bring down a server, he or she doesn't need to log in. All the person needs to do is unplug it, steal it, or destroy it.

Most server and network systems have "backdoors" that are available to anyone with physical access to the machine. These backdoors allow system administrators to take control of a server that has been corrupted. For example, an individual who is able to gain physical access to a network router can almost always take control of that device, even without knowledge of the correct password. Some locations, such as a server room, are controlled-access locations for the reasons just described. Others must have uncontrolled access in order to be useful.

Access Control Process

There are three steps to the access control process:

1. **Identification**—The process by which a subject identifies itself to the access control system

2. **Authentication**—Verification of the subject's identity
3. **Authorization**—The decision to allow or deny access to an object

The second step usually happens behind the scenes, so the subject is really only aware of two stages: He or she enters credentials and is either given or denied access to a resource. **FIGURE 1-1** illustrates the access control process using human interaction as an example.

Identification

The first step in any access control process is **identification**. The system must be able to apply labels to the two parts of the access equation: the subject and the object. In this case, a label is a purely logical description that is easy for the computer to understand. A human might easily recognize that "Beth" and "Elizabeth" are the same individual, but a computer cannot necessarily make that logical connection.

To make things simpler, you can assign a universal label to each subject and object. That label remains with that individual or resource throughout the life cycle of the privileged interaction with the object. The object also has a label to distinguish it from other resources. For example, a network might have six printers available, labeled "printer1," "printer2," and so on. A person's label might be a user ID, his or her email address, his or her employee ID, or some other unique identifier.

The key is that each label must be unique, because it also provides accountability. When combined with the authentication system (which correlates the identified subject with the resources he or she is allowed to use) and system logging facilities, unique labels correlate subjects with their actions. This becomes especially important when trying to track down the cause of a system

> **NOTE**
>
> Trust is a two-way street. The system must trust that a subject has not falsified his or her credentials, but at the same time, the subject must be confident that the system will store those credentials securely. If a system stores usernames and passwords insecurely, they can be stolen and used to impersonate legitimate users. This destroys the integrity of the entire access control system.

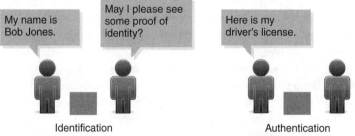

FIGURE 1-1

The access control process.

failure. This correlation relies on the trust between the subject and the access control system. If you do not trust that subjects are who they say they are (and this trust is predicated on proof), the use of a uniquely identifying label is pointless.

Authentication

Authentication builds upon identification by requiring that the subject provide proof of identity. There are many ways to authenticate a subject. The most common ones are:

- **Password**—A secret word or combination of characters that is known only to the subject. A good password is difficult to guess but easy for the subject to remember.
- **Token**—Something the subject has that no one else does, such as a **smart card** or a challenge-response device.
- **Fingerprint scan**—Optical analysis of a person's fingerprint compared with a recorded sample to verify identity.

The key to both a **password** and a **shared secret** is secrecy. If the subject shares its password or shared secret information with someone else, the authentication system becomes less secure and the ability to correlate an action to a subject becomes less precise. Many companies regulate this problem with a policy that an employee is personally responsible for anything done under his or her credentials. If an employee shares his credentials with a friend, for example, he is personally responsible for anything the friend might do.

Most authentication systems require only a single authentication factor, but those protecting highly sensitive assets might use multiple factors. The three most common factors are:

- **Something you know**—Generally a password or shared secret
- **Something you have**—A **token** or smart card ID badge
- **Something you are**—Fingerprints or other biometric factors

The last two factors are often used to provide or restrict physical access to secure buildings or rooms within buildings, although they can be used in access control systems protecting data as well. You will learn more about all three authentication factors later in the chapter.

Confidence in any authentication system can be measured by two components: the confidence in the accuracy of the authentication mechanisms and the number of authentication factors. An iris scan, such as the one shown in **FIGURE 1-2**, is a biometric authentication technique that is inherently more secure than a simple password because it is much more difficult to copy or steal an eyeball than it is to guess or steal a password. Using more than one authentication factor increases the security of the system, because if one stage of the authentication system is compromised, the second can still restrict access to those who do not have the proper credentials. This is referred to as "two-factor authentication."

Authorization

Once a subject has identified him- or herself and the access control system authenticates the subject's identity, the access control system must determine whether the subject is authorized to access the requested resources. **Authorization** is a set of rights defined for a subject

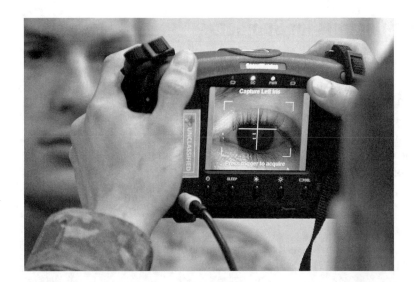

and an object. They are based on the subject's identity. For example, a manager in the human resources department might be authorized to view personnel records but not authorized to edit the year-end financial report.

Authorization rules can be simple. For example, a corporate e-mail directory might allow access to any employee with a valid user account. Authorization rules can also be complex, depending on the value of the resources being protected and the number of people needing access. For example, a file server might limit folder access by an employee's role and membership in a particular department.

In a small organization with a high level of trust among the users and resources that are not sensitive, a simple authorization system is reasonable. An enterprise system with a mixture of highly sensitive data and open printers on the same network needs a more complex authorization system. In this case, you might design a system with multiple levels of authorization—a low-level employee might be given rights to the printers, while a manager would have rights to the printers and some areas of the file system. High-level executives might have all the rights of a manager, as well as rights to view sensitive information. How you define your authorization rules depends on business needs and the sensitivity of the resources.

The bottom line is that organizations must perform a balancing act when designing their authorization systems. The more complex the approach to authorization, the more secure the environment. However, more complex authorization may cause user inconvenience and require more administrative work by IT staff.

Logical Access Controls

Most IT professionals spend their time focusing on logical access controls: the tools used to provide identification, authentication, and authorization for computer systems. While they may be involved in other areas of access control, the nature of logical controls requires a good deal of IT attention.

Logical Access Controls for Subjects

Logical access controls can be based on one or more criteria, including:

- **Who**—The identity of the subject, proven by a username and password combination or other authentication technique
- **What**—The type of access being requested
- **When**—The time of day or day of week the request is made
- **Where**—The physical or logical location of the user placing the request
- **How**—The context of the access request

You should take each of these criteria into account when designing an authorization system.

Who

The "who" criterion is the most intuitive, as discussed above. One subject may be given access while another is denied.

What

The decisions made by authorization systems must also factor in the type of access being requested by the end user. The object of the authorization request is significant. For example, you might create different access controls around a customer price list on one hand and a listing of your top 10 accounts and the revenue generated from each on the other.

When

Time profiles can be a useful way to prevent an authorized user from using resources for unofficial purposes. For example, an employee may be legitimately authorized to use a network printer, but it should raise questions if that employee begins to print jobs outside of normal business hours. This could mean that the employee is working overtime, or it could be an indication that he or she is using company resources for personal projects. Time profiles are also used when a user has a limited amount of time to perform an action. For example, a journalist may only have until 1 p.m. to submit his or her story for the evening newscast. Restricting the journalist's access to the story submission system after 1 p.m. prevents the journalist from turning in the story late and forcing the editing staff to scramble to fit the story in.

 TIP

If you must use time profiles to meet business needs, design the system to be easy to modify for special cases such as overtime or a breaking news story.

 TIP

"Why does this user need access to this resource?" This is a question you should ask every time you design a set of access controls. Every user should have a well-defined purpose related to his or her job function in order to gain access to resources.

Where

Location can be another way to ensure that only authorized users access resources, and that those users are performing legitimate tasks. You can determine location either logically or physically.

"Logical location" refers to the Internet Protocol (IP) address or **Media Access Control (MAC) address** a user connects from.

"Physical location" is more obvious—within a certain building or secured facilities. If a user attempts to access resources from his or her corporate laptop on the company network, the system grants access. The same user could try to access those resources from his or her home PC and be denied. This type of restriction is often used with highly sensitive information. If an employee decided to work from the local coffee shop and accessed a confidential file, another patron at the coffee shop could "sniff" that transmission and gain access to confidential information. Restricting access by location ensures that sensitive data is sent only over trusted, secure networks.

How

Once you evaluate all of the above criteria, you can determine how the user will access a resource, that is—what type of access you need to grant. There are four basic access levels:

- **Administrative**—The ability to read, write, create, and delete files
- **Author**—The right to read and write his or her own files
- **Read only**—Can read but not edit files
- **No access**—Complete denial of access

In some systems, you can define these four access levels with more granularity, but every system includes them.

Group-Based Access Controls

Access controls may often be more efficiently managed through the use of role-based groups. This is especially true in large organizations. Rather than deciding and assigning rights to each individual within an enterprise, you cluster individuals into groups based on department, job title or role, or some other classification.

> **NOTE**
>
> Granting access by groups rather than individuals does not reduce individual accountability for activities. An individual still needs to log in with a unique username and password, and the log files catalog actions by username, not by group.

You can assign individuals to several groups. For example, every person within an enterprise may be a member of the Employees group, with read access to the company Intranet and an account on the time card system. A manager might also be a member of the Managers group and have write access to his or her department's page on the Intranet as well as read access to each of his group's time card reports. Employees on the corporate retreat committee would have their normal levels of access as well as access to files related to the corporate retreat, regardless of their other job functions. A manager might not have access to those files, despite the fact that employees below him do.

Group access rights are a way of simplifying the management of the rules. When an employee changes roles within an organization, you merely have to change his or her group membership rather than altering the employee's individual access rights. Similarly, when you create a new resource and want to grant access to a particular role, you can do that using the group mechanism and you don't need to list all of the individual employees.

Logical Access Controls for Objects

So far, you have focused primarily on subjects and access controls. Now you will examine how objects fit into access controls. The biggest difference between a subject and an object is passivity. A subject is active—it acts upon a passive object. An object must contain something of interest to the subject. This is usually information, but can be noninformational as well. Consider a printer. It is passive in that it is the target of a print request and does not generally initiate new contact with the subject after the print job is complete. It contains, or rather produces, something of value—a hard copy of digital information. Printers, however, do not usually have a high level of granularity. They receive a print request and process it. A server, however, can have many elements that must work together to supply the subject with the information it requests.

You can define objects at many levels, depending on your business needs. Some examples of objects include:

- **Data element**—This is the lowest level of granularity for information-based assets. For example, if a database table contains a Social Security number, you may need to place special restrictions on that data element.
- **Table**—You may also define a database table as an object. You could grant users access to tables containing employment information, order information, or other types of information based on their roles in the organization.
- **Database**—You can also define an entire database as an object. For example, you might grant all employees read-only access to the entire product information database and give product managers write access to certain tables or rows within that database.
- **Application**—An application is also an object. You might wish to grant some users the ability to run an application while denying it to other users. Applications may also implement their own access control systems that restrict use of individual components of the application. For example, an administrative user within the application may see a menu that allows them to add or delete other users. A basic user would see this menu and would not have access to that functionality within the application.
- **System**—A system is also a security object. For example, you may restrict access to the CEO's laptop so that only the CEO and his or her administrative assistant have permission to log on to it.
- **Operating system**—This provides various user modes, such as privileged or superuser mode, user mode, and guest mode. It also governs configuration files and log files. The operating system also provides write protection on files, subdirectory permissions, and restrictions on the ability to create, delete, access, or execute new files or directories.
- **Network**—This provides access restrictions for resources stored on the network or on a subnetwork. It provides the ability to traverse network connections and restricts external access, either inbound or outbound.

In real-world applications, these levels may work together or separately to provide access rights to resources. A simple example is an application (in this case, the application is the subject) that needs to work with data stored in the database (the object). It makes a request through an application programming interface (API), which handles the communication between the application and the database.

A more complex example is that of a user who needs to modify a data file stored on a file server across the network (**FIGURE 1-3**). In this case, the user (subject) logs into the operating system (object 1) and requests access to the file server across the network (object 2). The system layer on the file server (object 3) checks the user's credentials against its rules

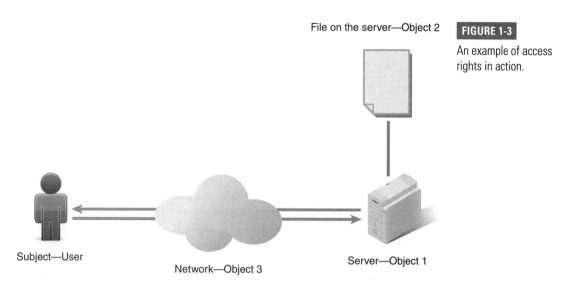

File on the server—Object 2

FIGURE 1-3

An example of access rights in action.

Subject—User

Network—Object 3

Server—Object 1

to determine if the user has no access, read-only, read/write, or administrative access to the particular data file requested.

Authentication Factors

As described earlier in the chapter, an **authentication factor** is a way of confirming the identity of the subject. The three primary authentication factors are:

* **Something you know**—Secret knowledge, such as a password
* **Something you have**—A token or device
* **Something you are**—Unique physical characteristics of a person, such as those that can be detected by a retinal or iris scan, fingerprint scan, or voice analysis

Most authentication systems rely solely on the first factor, implemented as a username and password combination. For access to highly sensitive data, you might combine the first two factors, requiring a token just to access the login screen, where the user would enter his or her username and password. The most sensitive data are protected by all three factors. For example, the United States military uses Sensitive Compartmented Information Facilities (SCIFs). Just to walk through the door of a SCIF requires recognition of identifying characteristics such as a retinal or fingerprint scan (the "something you are" factor), swiping an ID badge (the "something you have" factor), and typing in a PIN (the "something you know" factor).

Something You Know

A password is the most common authentication tool. Many people use passwords every day to check email, log into online banking, and use the ATM. The biggest challenge facing administrators of password systems is convincing users to use strong passwords. Users are primarily concerned with convenience. Ideally, you would prefer to have a simple,

> **TIP**
>
> One solution to the password problem is the use of a **passphrase**, such as "INeedToRememberASecurePassword." It is longer than a typical password, but easier for a human to remember. In systems with maximum password lengths, you can use a passphrase as a mnemonic device to remember complicated passwords. For example, the passphrase "Anyone for some tennis?" could be a reminder for the highly secure password "ne14+10s."

easy-to-remember password. However, simple passwords or ones based on your name or a dictionary word are also easy for malicious users to guess. An easily guessed password is almost as unsecure as no password at all.

To address this problem, you need to set password requirements on length and composition. For example, you could require that a password have at least eight characters, and that it must contain a combination of uppercase and lowercase characters, as well as numeric or punctuation characters. This system ensures strong passwords, but you might have difficulty remembering them. Because users are primarily concerned with convenience, not with the security of the system, they often write down difficult passwords and post them in obvious locations. A malicious user with physical access to your work space can easily find the desired password.

In addition to addressing password complexity, it is also important to remind users that they should use a separate password for their work account and any personal accounts they may have. One of the most significant security risks facing organizations today is the risk that *another* website, not associated with your company, could be compromised and the attacker could gain access to an improperly protected password list. The attacker may then try logging in to *your* site with the usernames and passwords on the list. If users have used their work password on other sites, chances are that, with a big enough list, an attacker will stumble upon an active account.

Something You Have

Used alone, a physical token or device is generally used to provide physical security. Think of a smart card ID that you wave in front of a reader to gain access to specific floors of an office building. Tokens are also used in conjunction with passwords to provide logical access controls. Tokens can take a variety of forms such as the smart card or a time-variable token such as RSA's SecurID. **FIGURE 1-4** shows an example of the smart card authentication devices used

FIGURE 1-4

Smart card authenticator issued to U.S. government employees.

© United States Department of Defense

by the U.S. Government, known as the Common Access Card (CAC) in military organizations or the Personal Identity Verification (PIV) card in other government agencies.

Time-variable tokens change users' passwords at regular intervals, usually every 30 to 60 seconds. Users have a physical device that tells them what their password is set to at the moment they need to log in. This two-stage authentication process ensures that passwords are not guessed or stolen—and if they are, damage is limited because the password is valid for only a brief period of time. This token may be a separate device or, more commonly, an app running on a user's smartphone. **FIGURE 1-5** shows the Google Authenticator app configured to work with the multifactor authentication systems of a variety of services.

Possession of the physical device or token is the only way to retrieve the current password. Because the token could be lost or stolen, this type of authentication requires a two-stage login process. For example, a user activates the token to find his or her active password. She enters the password, along with her username, and is granted access to a secondary login prompt. At this second prompt, she enters a conventional password that does not change. In this way, if the user's conventional password is guessed or stolen, a malicious user would not have the token and would not be able to access the secondary login prompt to enter the stolen password. If the token is lost or stolen, a malicious user is stopped at the secondary login prompt because he or she presumably does not also have the user's conventional password.

Challenge-response tokens are similar to time-variable tokens. An authentication system using this type of token will begin with a code (the "challenge"), which the user enters into the token device. The token provides another code (the "response"), which the user enters into the authentication system. Assuming that the response code is correct, the user will be granted access to the secondary login system, where he or she enters a conventional username and password. The challenge is chosen randomly and the token must provide the correct response. This reduces the possibility that an attacker will be able to predict a challenge and generate a response in advance if he or she has temporary access to a token.

FIGURE 1-5

Google Authenticator app configured to work with a variety of services.

Google, Google Authenticator, and the Google logo are registered trademarks of Google Inc., used with permission.

FIGURE 1-6

Push authentication request from Duo to a user's smartphone.

Courtesy of Duo Security.

In some cases, the challenge-response can be even simpler. For example, **FIGURE 1-6** shows an example of the Duo smartphone app for multifactor authentication. In the approach used by this system, the user first completes the normal password-based authentication to a web application or other system. After successfully completing this knowledge-based authentication approach, the Duo system then pushes an alert similar to the one shown in Figure 1-6 to the user's registered smartphone. The user simply taps "Approve" on the smartphone app and the authentication sequence is complete.

Something You Are

This is the most advanced as well as the most time-tested of the three primary authentication factors. It relies on either physical or behavioral characteristics. Humans have been using characteristics to authenticate each other for millennia. Consider an infant who recognizes its mother or other primary caregiver. The infant uses visual cues, scent, and the sound of the caregiver's voice to authenticate the caregiver's identity and determine whether to settle or scream.

Biometrics is the study of physical human characteristics. Access control systems use biometrics to accurately identify and/or authenticate an individual. There are two primary types of biometric authentication systems: physical and behavioral. Physical biometrics read physical characteristics, such as fingerprints, retinal scans, hand geometry, and facial recognition. Physical biometrics are highly reliable because they measure characteristics that are unique to each individual. Even identical twins do not have the same fingerprints or retinal scans.

 NOTE

Biometrics, which includes fingerprints, retinal scans, and so on, is an important "something you are" authentication factor.

Fingerprints are commonly used to authenticate access to physical devices or facilities. **FIGURE 1-7** shows an example of the use of fingerprint authentication by military troops in the field.

Facial recognition is also growing in popularity because of its ease of use. Some smartphone models offer facial recognition to unlock the phone, make purchases, and perform other authenticated actions. One common example of this is the FaceID technology used on some Apple devices. Airports are also now using facial recognition technology for security screening, as shown in **FIGURE 1-8**.

Behavioral characteristics may include tempo or speed of typing (or keystroke dynamics), writing rhythms, and voice recognition. Behavioral biometrics requires a significant "training period" for the system to "learn" a legitimate user's behavior patterns. They are also much more subject to error than physical characteristics.

CHAPTER SUMMARY

In this chapter, you learned the basics of access control. The purpose of access control is to regulate interactions between a subject (such as a human user) and an object (such as data, a network, or a device). The key difference between the subject and the object is passivity: The subject acts upon a passive object. There are three key components of access control: identification, authentication, and authorization. First, both the subject and object must be identified. Second, the subject's identity must be proven or authenticated. Finally, the authenticated subject is authorized to act upon the object. You can establish logical access controls for individual subjects, groups of subjects, and objects.

Authentication methodologies are based on three factors: something you know, something you have, and something you are. Once the subject is identified and authenticated using one or more of these factors, the authorization system grants access to an object based on a specified rule base.

KEY CONCEPTS AND TERMS

Access
Access control
Authentication
Authentication factor
Authorization
Biometrics
Identification
Identity and access management (IAM)

Identity management
Media Access Control (MAC) address
Object
Passphrase
Password
Physical security
Policy
Procedure

Shared secret
Smart card
Subject
Token
Tool

CHAPTER 1 ASSESSMENT

1. The three principal components of access control are _____, subjects, and objects.

2. The subject is always a human user.
   A. True
   B. False

3. Which of the following describes technical methods used to enforce policies?
   A. Access control
   B. Procedures
   C. Tools
   D. Physical security
   E. Authentication

4. An organization typically uses procedures and tools together to enforce policies.
   A. True
   B. False

5. The three states of a subject in an access control scenario are authorized, unauthorized, and _____.

6. Physical security is typically the responsibility of the IT department.
   A. True
   B. False

7. What is the first step in the access control process?

   A. Logging in
   B. Authorization
   C. Authentication
   D. Identification
   E. Access

8. Which of the following is an example of the "something you know" authentication factor?

   A. Username
   B. Token
   C. Password
   D. Retinal scan
   E. Access control list

9. Which of the following is an example of "something you have"?

   A. Username
   B. Token
   C. Password
   D. Retinal scan
   E. Access control list

10. Which of the following is an example of "something you are"?

   A. Username
   B. Token
   C. Password
   D. Retinal scan
   E. Access control list

11. Authorization rules can be as simple or complex as business needs require.

   A. True
   B. False

12. The four basic access levels are _____, author, read-only, and no access.

13. Assigning group access controls eliminates individual accountability.

   A. True
   B. False

14. The two types of biometric authentication methods are _____ and physical.

Business Drivers for Access Controls

A WELL-THOUGHT-OUT APPROACH to access control implementation advances the goals of an organization. In this chapter, we will discuss the reasons behind access controls in both the public and private sectors. In the public sector, access controls and the information they protect could save a soldier's life or keep the public infrastructure running smoothly. In business, or the private sector, access controls help protect valuable assets such as trade secrets from unauthorized disclosure and keep business systems running efficiently. This chapter covers how organizations can determine the value of their information assets and the role that secrecy and access controls play in protecting valuable information systems and assets.

Chapter 2 Topics

This chapter covers the following topics and concepts:

- Business requirements for asset protection
- How information is classified
- How information can be used competitively
- Business drivers for access control
- How access is controlled and value-protected
- Some examples of access control successes and failures in business

Chapter 2 Goals

When you complete this chapter, you will be able to:

- Identify business requirements for asset protection
- Explain how and why information is classified
- Understand the competitive use of information
- Identify various business drivers for access controls
- Control access and protect value internally, externally, and with respect to third parties
- Give examples of access control successes and failures in business

Business Requirements for Asset Protection

In business, it is essential to protect the assets that make doing business possible. Inventory and raw materials are kept in secure locations to avoid theft or damage. Information assets are no different—they must be kept secure to avoid compromise.

Importance of Policy

In our knowledge-based economy, many organizations place intellectual property among their most valuable business assets. Firms seeking to ensure their competitive advantage must control access to information to ensure their ongoing survival. Protecting **confidential information** involves more than just technical controls. It also requires clear policies and sound business processes that allow those policies to be implemented. Developing and implementing these policies and processes can protect an organization against security incidents.

For example, a chemical company may have a policy that states that only those employees with a legitimate purpose can enter the laboratories (labs). This policy should ensure that secret chemical formulas are not leaked to unauthorized personnel. For this policy to be effective, it must be enforced by a combination of controls. The firm may use technical measures such as a radio-frequency identification (RFID)-enabled badge reader, combined with administrative measures, such as training employees to scrutinize the identity badges of people they don't recognize. A policy cannot prevent an information leak if employees regularly hold open the lab doors and allow each other to enter without swiping their ID badge, a threat known as **piggybacking**.

Senior Management Role

As with any policy-based initiative, access control policies will be effective only if they have the explicit and implicit support of senior executives. When organizations first issue access control policies, they should consider asking a very senior executive to send the message communicating the policy. This is especially important if the policy requires employees to engage in unpopular or inconvenient behaviors. Similarly, senior managers must serve as models of policy adherence. If the CEO is seen holding the door open for other people, rather than expecting them to swipe their badge, or asking that policy be implemented differently or waived for him due to his position, line staff will assume that this is acceptable and will do the same thing. Before you know it, piggybacking will move from being a security risk to a standard practice.

Classification of Information

Information classification assigns information to different categories based on its sensitivity. Both nations and many major corporations have **sensitive information** that gets classified, limiting its availability both to the organization and to the outside world.

Classification Schemes

A **classification scheme** is a method of organizing sensitive information into various access levels. Only a person with the approved level of access is allowed to view the information. This access is called **clearance**. Every organization has its own method of determining clearance levels. The methods usually include a background check, interviews, and a determination of the user's need for the information. Most nations and many corporations have classification schemes set up to handle the organization and access of sensitive information.

Need to Know and Least Privilege

"**Need to know**" is a major component in accessing sensitive information. The requester should not receive access just because of his or her clearance, position, or rank. The requester must also establish a justifiable need to see the information. Access should be granted only if the information is essential for the requester's official duties. This further secures the information and reduces the risk of one rogue official with security clearance compromising sensitive information. This concept is also seen in computer access controls with the principle of least privilege.

Following the principle of least privilege, a computer user or program should have only the access needed to carry out its job. For example, a web server service may run as a nonadministrative user with access only to the web directories. If the program is compromised, the **attacker** has access to only a limited part of the system.

National Security Classification

The United States government classifies sensitive information into four main categories based on the degree of damage that would occur to national security if the information were disclosed in an unauthorized manner. Individuals cleared for a particular classification level may access information at that level and below, provided that they have a specific need to know the particular information in question. The four classification levels used by the U.S. government are:

- **Unclassified**—Information that has not otherwise been assigned a sensitivity level under the national security classification scheme. Generally speaking, **unclassified information** is subject to public release under the Freedom of Information Act (FOIA). Under certain circumstances, government agencies may designate unclassified information as **Controlled Unclassified Information (CUI)**. CUI information is exempt from disclosure under FOIA.

- **Confidential**—Information that, if disclosed, could reasonably be expected to cause damage to national security.
- **Secret**—Information that, if disclosed, could reasonably be expected to cause *serious* damage to national security.
- **Top Secret**—Information that, if disclosed, could reasonably be expected to cause *exceptionally grave* damage to national security.

■ NOTE

Unclassified information is included here for completeness of discussion. However, it is important to note that "unclassified" is *not* technically a classification level. It is a term used to describe information that does not meet the criteria to be classified. This may seem like a semantic nuance, but it's an issue that often pops up on security certification exams.

Information may change classifications at any time, as circumstances warrant. Information that may have been deemed confidential in 1992 may be considered **Secret** or even **Top Secret** today. Likewise, information that was of Top Secret importance in 1939 may no longer be sensitive enough to be classified at all.

Corporations

The classification schemes used by private organizations vary widely but often share some elements with the government scheme. One commonly used approach to corporate classification has the following classification levels:

- **Public**—Information that the company freely releases to the public. This category would include information that is published on the organization's website or distributed in sales materials.
- **Internal**—Information that is not normally released to the general public but may be disclosed without damaging the company. This may include information about product road maps or pricing that is released to customers but not widely published.
- **Sensitive**—Information that, if disclosed, could cause serious damage to the firm. This may include new product development plans or internal marketing strategies. Sensitive information is often not released outside the company except under the terms of a formal nondisclosure agreement (NDA).
- **Highly sensitive**—Information that, if disclosed, would be extremely damaging to the company. This may include customer Social Security numbers, credit card numbers, or other very sensitive information. Highly sensitive information is often encrypted at all times and requires special permission to access.

Reasons for Classification

Information is generally classified if disclosure could harm the controlling organization. Corporations classify information to try to keep a competitive advantage over other companies. A soup company, for example, may want to keep its recipes as **trade secrets**. A company that tests the strength of materials may want to keep its testing methodology proprietary. Governments want to classify any information that would damage their security, such as troop locations and movement, facility locations, and so on.

Declassification Process and Policy

Declassification is the process used to move a classified document into the public domain. Every country and organization that classifies documents has a method of declassification. Let's look at the U.S. model as a baseline.

There are four ways a U.S. government document can become declassified:

- **Automatic declassification**—**Automatic declassification** happens with any document over 25 years old. Unless it meets strict criteria, the document is automatically declassified after the department that owns the document reviews it. It is then moved to the publicly accessible shelves of the national archives.
- **Systematic declassification**—With **systematic declassification**, any document that is under 25 years old but of significant importance to the historic record of the United States is reviewed for early declassification. Once identified, these documents go through the same procedures as automatically declassified documents.

- **Mandatory declassification review**—A **mandatory declassification review** is instigated when an individual attempts to get a document declassified. After the review request has been filed, the owning organization must respond with approval, denial, or the inability to confirm or deny the existence or nonexistence of the document. If the request is denied, the requester can appeal to the interagency security classification appeals board.
- **FOIA request**—A **FOIA request** is an attempt by a member of the general public to get a document declassified. The act allows for full or partial disclosure of the document; if the owning organization refuses the request, the decision can be appealed in a judicial review.

Personally Identifiable Information (PII)

The U.S. Department of Commerce defines **personally identifiable information (PII)** as:

> *Information which can be used to distinguish or trace an individual's identity, such as their name, social security number, biometric records, etc. alone, or when combined with other personal or identifying information which is linked or linkable to a specific individual, such as date and place of birth, mother's maiden name, etc.*

This is usually sensitive information for a corporation and must be safeguarded. It is also information that is targeted for theft, as it is the key to identity theft. Protection of this information is mandated by numerous federal and state laws, and any security breaches must be disclosed in a timely manner. It is especially tightly controlled in the healthcare and financial industries.

Privacy Act Information

This is any information that is covered by the Privacy Act of 1974. The act covers the collection, maintenance, and dissemination of PII inside the federal government. Information covered in this act includes Social Security numbers (SSN), payroll numbers, information on education, financial transactions, medical history, criminal history, and employment history. This information can be disclosed only with the written consent of the subject or if the use fits into one of the following exceptions:

- By the U.S. Census Bureau or the U.S. Bureau of Labor Statistics for statistical purposes
- Routine use within a U.S. government agency
- A document with significant historical value for archival purposes
- For law enforcement
- Congressional investigation
- Other administrative purposes

It is important to remember that this act applies only to organizations inside the federal government. State government and private entities are not governed by the Privacy Act of 1974.

Privacy Controls Catalog

The National Institute for Standards and Technology (NIST) produces standards that are not only binding on U.S. government agencies but also useful to others designing and implementing cybersecurity programs. NIST Special Publication 800-53 (SP 800-53) is a lengthy document providing a set of security and privacy controls for protecting sensitive information.

Appendix J of that publication provides a robust look at privacy controls, organized into four major areas of concern:

- **Authority and Purpose:** Does the organization have the authority to collect PII, and is the purpose for that collection clearly stated?
- **Accountability, Audit, and Risk Management:** Has the organization implemented privacy governance, detailed privacy requirements, and created the support structures to ensure that employees are properly implementing the privacy program?
- **Data Quality and Integrity:** Is the organization taking appropriate steps to ensure the quality and integrity of PII that it collects and maintains?
- **Data Minimization and Retention:** Is the organization retaining only the minimum amount of information necessary to carry out the stated purpose, and are data being promptly and properly destroyed when no longer necessary?

For more information on these controls, refer to Appendix J of NIST SP 800-53.

Competitive Use of Information

Obtaining information about a competitor or its products can give an organization a significant competitive advantage, if it is used strategically. For example, if a firm obtained surreptitious access to a competitor's customer list, they could use that list to try to lure away the competitor's customers. If that list included details about a customer's contractual relationship, the competitor could use that information to craft an irresistible offer that would increase the likelihood of closing the deal. That's why it is vital to keep information, like formulas and recipes, secret—ensuring customers can get the information from only one source.

Valuation of Information

The value of information depends on both its strategic and tactical importance to the organization and the impact on the organization's business if that information were disclosed, changed, or destroyed without permission.

Some information, such as federally protected health information, if improperly disclosed, can cost an organization millions of dollars in fines, and even lead to prison sentences for those responsible for the disclosure. Other information, such as trade secrets, will lead to lost profits if it is leaked to competitors.

For example, the United Kingdom's Information Commissioner assessed British Airways with a £183 million fine in 2019 after a data breach affected the personal information of 380,000 British Airways customers. The commissioner's office alleged that British Airways failed to implement appropriate security controls and put customer information at unnecessary risk.

Information as a Competitive Advantage

Information provides almost every organization with its competitive advantage. From financial firms with proprietary trading strategies to e-commerce behemoths with confidential models of consumer behavior, information provides the key ingredient that allows most firms to differentiate themselves from their competitors. Securing that information is paramount to a company's success. Loss of that information can lead to a company's decrease in market share and reduced profits.

Case study. The 1971 *Data General Corporation v. Digital Computer Controls, Inc.* case is an example of insufficiently secured trade secrets and the penalties for misappropriating them.

Upon request, Data General Corporation would provide customers with the design documents for its Nova 1200 computer system. This was done to allow customers to maintain and repair their own computer systems. The drawings were marked as confidential, and customers signed a confidentiality agreement when they received the documents.

The president of Digital Computer Controls purchased a used Nova 1200 through a third party in March of 1971. Digital Computer Controls requested the design documents as part of the purchase and were supplied with a copy from the seller. Digital Computer Controls then developed the D-116 minicomputer from the design drawings, ignoring the annotation on the drawings that they could not be used to manufacture similar items without written permission.

Data General Corporation eventually won a permanent injunction barring Digital Computer Controls from selling the D-116, but it took 5 years. During that time, Digital Computer Controls sold many D-116 computers and had time to develop its next system.

Penalties for Improper Disclosure

A lot of information that a corporation collects is legally protected sensitive information—for example, PII, financial information, and in some industries, classified government documents. Although this information might not have an intrinsic value, there are severe penalties for improper disclosure, both official and in the market. The following are some examples of what a company faces for improperly disclosing information.

Below are penalties for disclosing medical/patient information in violation of the Health Insurance Portability and Accountability Act (HIPAA):

* **Unknowingly disclosed**—$100 per violation or record affected
* **Reasonable cause to disclose**—$1,000 per violation or record affected
* **Disclosure due to willful negligence situation that is corrected**—$10,000 per violation or record affected
* **Disclosure due to willful negligence that is not corrected**—$50,000 per violation or record affected
* **Disclosure due to criminal intent**—up to $250,000 and 10 years in jail

These HIPAA fines can be substantial when many records are involved. The maximum fine that may be assessed for a HIPAA violation is $1,500,000 per year that the violation occurred.

Organizations involved in credit card transaction processing must comply with the **Payment Card Industry Data Security Standard (PCI DSS)**. This contractual obligation requires that companies comply with a rigid set of security controls, including specific provisions surrounding access controls. Organizations that fail to comply with PCI DSS are subject to fines that may range up to $200,000 or more per quarter.

In addition to these financial penalties, organizations that suffer data breaches also often suffer reputational damage that is more difficult to quantify. Consumers who know that a company has suffered one or more data breaches may be less likely to trust that organization with their personal information and may choose to take their business elsewhere.

The Business Drivers for Access Control

There are obvious business reasons to secure information. To determine whether or not there is a clear business reason to secure a specific piece of information, consider a cost-benefit analysis, the results of your organization's risk assessment, and various other factors.

Cost-Benefit Analysis

A cost-benefit analysis is essentially a pro-and-con list that helps businesses make decisions. To decide whether a given piece of information justifies the effort and investment of access controls, consider two factors: the advantage gained from keeping the information secret and the risks avoided by controlling access to the information.

Some information is not usually worth the effort to secure. The date of the company picnic is a good example. There is little to be gained by keeping this information secret, even externally. There are few risks associated with releasing the information; it is highly unlikely that a competitor will try to disrupt your company picnic if the competitor knows the date.

Other information may be worth expending significant effort, depending on the level of sensitivity. For example, it may be desirable to protect an employee telephone directory to prevent competitors from easily soliciting your staff with job offers. Protecting proprietary machine learning models may be much more important and worthy of a higher level of security control.

Advantage Gained

One consideration of access control is that of advantage. Does a company gain an advantage from securing its information? Could its competitors gain a similar advantage if they had access to the information? Is the information already secret?

Consider a proprietary recipe developed by a food manufacturer. In testing, the company realizes its new recipe is popular with customers. In fact, since releasing the new product, its sales have tripled. If sales levels hold steady, the new item will become the best-selling product of its kind within a year. Holding the recipe for such a popular product clearly gives the company an advantage over its competition.

Would a competitor gain a similar advantage if it had access to the same recipe? The competitor would probably release a similar product at a lower price point because it did not have to invest in research and development. Once customers realize that the less-expensive product is very similar to the original, sales of the more expensive original product could decrease.

Risk Avoided

Another consideration of access control is **risk**. As you read earlier in this chapter, there can be significant penalties for allowing sensitive information to be disclosed, even if the disclosure is purely accidental. In the preceding example concerning a secret recipe, the company might not risk fines or jail time by sharing its recipe, but it does risk being undercut by the competition.

This is where the asset valuation portion of a risk assessment (covered next) becomes important. Every organization should know what information it possesses and how important that information is in terms of access control. Organizations should also be aware of negative consequences that could arise if that information is not adequately secured.

Risk Assessment

After you've performed a risk assessment, how do you use the information that it turns up? One of the deliverables from a risk assessment should be a prioritized list of threats and vulnerabilities, as well as a complete inventory of assets, including sensitive information.

The inventory of information assets (also called "intellectual property") can help you determine what should be classified and what information is not important or advantageous enough to warrant access control resources.

The list of threats and vulnerabilities is another guideline you can follow when deciding what to secure. When taking this approach, you might choose to secure the most vulnerable assets first. For example, you know that there have been concentrated efforts to obtain the personal cell phone numbers and vacation schedules of senior U.S. executives, probably as a precursor to a social engineering attack at a later date. This information makes it more crucial to secure information that may not otherwise be considered a top priority. The fact that it can be used to obtain more critical information makes it critical itself.

Business Facilitation

Information is the backbone of many business processes. In manufacturing, inventory and order numbers determine how productive the assembly line must be in any given week. In the financial industry, constantly changing stock prices dictate buy and sell decisions. Controlling who has access to this information, and at what level, is critical for facilitating the day-to-day operations of a business.

> **NOTE**
>
> Modern operating systems implement access rights in a more granular way, giving users read, write, and execute privileges. Some operating systems combine these three basic privileges into other combinations.

Access Levels

In terms of business facilitation, there are essentially three levels of information access: no access, read access, and read-write access.

Understanding access levels: A newsletter example. To understand access levels, let's use a corporate newsletter as an example. A corporate newsletter is a tool used to distribute important information to employees, such as the dates for open benefits enrollment. All employees have permission to read it, but only a few are entitled to write and publish information in the newsletter. This one-to-many scenario—or few-to-many, depending on how many people are involved in writing the newsletter—is used to carefully control the flow of information to the average employee. If the enrollment dates are published in the newsletter, every employee receives the same information and is expected to abide by the published deadlines.

The newsletter is also a tool for creating corporate culture and supporting employee morale. You will rarely find a negative article in a corporate newsletter, because that would be damaging to morale. Likewise, the tone of the newsletter is indicative of corporate culture.

In a traditional financial firm, the employee newsletter is likely to be straightforward and data-heavy. In a technology firm, the newsletter is more likely to be written in a fun, slightly irreverent tone. It might include trivia, news oddities, and other "fluff" that would not be included in a financial firm's newsletter.

Both newsletters support and reinforce the firms' corporate cultures. This does not happen by accident, but is carefully constructed to meet a goal. This goal is met by carefully restricting who can publish information in the company newsletter. By restricting write access, the organization maintains a unified voice.

Understanding access levels: An order process example. What about other information sources within a company? Consider a single order for an herb garden kit from a mail-order nursery. A wide variety of people have access to that information throughout the life cycle of the order, as shown in **FIGURE 2-1**.

Mike, the customer, is the first person to have access to order information. When he places his order via the company's website, Mike has read-write access to the order data. Once he submits the order; however, he is restricted to read-only access. He can track the status of his order but can no longer change the data.

When the order is placed, the data are stored in a database, and notifications are sent to Mike (confirming the order) and to an employee in order processing. This person collects the pots, seeds, and peat pellets necessary to assemble the herb garden kit, and passes the kit

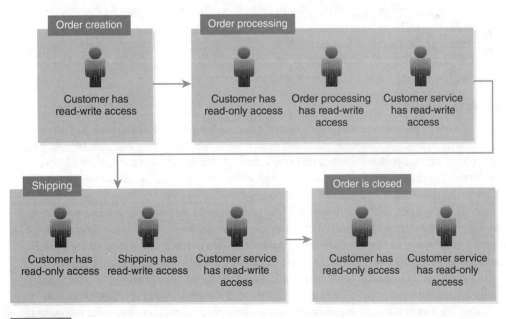

FIGURE 2-1

Access to information through the life cycle of an order.

to the shipping department. At this point, order processing updates the database to reflect the new status of the order. The order processor may also update the inventory database to reflect the fact that items were removed from inventory to assemble the order. The person in order processing has read-write access to the order information, *at the point at which he or she needs it.* The order processor has no access to the information during order creation, has read-write access while fulfilling the order, and has no access once the product is sent to shipping.

The shipping department schedules a pickup with Mike's preferred carrier and receives a tracking number from the carrier. This tracking number is amended to the order information and sent to Mike. When the shipping carrier picks up the package, the order is closed. The shipping department may have read access to the order information while the order is in processing, and has read-write access during the time the order resides within the shipping department—after it leaves processing—but before it is picked up by the shipping carrier.

Customer service has read access to the order data throughout the entire workflow, so that representatives can give Mike an up-to-date order status. Customer service representatives may even have read-write access, if the business allows customers to modify orders or make special requests during the life cycle of an order. For example, the business may allow customers to call in and request an upgrade to priority shipping, as long as the order has not yet been sent to the shipping department. To facilitate this business need, customer service representatives must have read-write access to the order data throughout the order life cycle.

Customers themselves have read-write access only at the point of order creation. Once they submit their order, they are restricted to read-only access for the remainder of the order life cycle. This is done to avoid crisis. If a customer had read-write access—that is, the ability to modify his order at any point in the order life cycle—the order processing department could assemble the order, only to find that the customer has changed his mind and now wants a different product. The time and effort expended in assembling the first version of the order would have been nonproductive.

Controlling who can modify order data at any given point in the process is the only way to ensure productivity. Without this type of access control, order processing could go into an indefinite loop trying to assemble one customer's order.

Restricting Access

As shown in the previous examples, restricting access to information can be a way to ensure productivity in business processes. Access restrictions to information can also be a way to ensure that a consistent message is conveyed throughout the organization. When information has one author—one individual with read-write access—you can easily verify that the information is accurate and has not been changed.

Consider the open enrollment dates discussed earlier in this section. If those dates are published in the corporate newsletter (an information vehicle with restricted read-write access), employees can be confident that those dates are correct. What if open enrollment dates were distributed by word of mouth (essentially, without any access restrictions at all)? If you ever played the game "telephone" in kindergarten, you can imagine the chaos that would ensue. No one would really know which dates were correct and which were not.

These are all simple examples of the need for access restrictions to facilitate business processes. However, there are more serious reasons that businesses need to restrict access to information. Internal business policies should not be shared with customers or competitors, for example. In addition, there are situations in which commonly known information within one part of the business cannot be shared with another.

Consider a large financial firm with two divisions. One division handles client investments while the other is involved in banking and insurance activities. On the banking side, everyone may be talking about an upcoming acquisition of an insurance carrier. Many of the details of the acquisition are common knowledge. However, employees on the investment side are not allowed to know those details because they could influence, even subconsciously, their buy and sell decisions. In this case, strict physical access limitations to data are necessary. An employee from the investment side of the firm, which has offices on the second floor of the building, would not be allowed on the third floor, where the banking and insurance division is located. Smart card ID badges and other physical security measures would generally be used to enforce this access restriction.

Cost Containment

What would it cost a company if a given piece of information were released to the public? This is the essential question to ask when determining whether to secure information from a cost-containment perspective. In some cases, there may be actual monetary fines for releasing information. A more likely scenario is that the cost to the company would be measured in terms of a competitive advantage or lost productivity.

Consider what seems like a trivial piece of information: a memo from the chief information officer (CIO) asking IT to research and make recommendations for a new customer relationship management (CRM) software vendor. The memo states that recommendations should be made by March 1 because the CRM project must be started by April 1.

On the surface, this does not seem like critical information. However, if a CRM vendor were to find out that IT must choose a preferred vendor by a certain date, the vendor could delay a price reduction until after the contract is signed, thus costing the company more for the CRM product than it otherwise might.

Simple physical access restrictions may be enough to keep this memo out of most unauthorized hands. After all, unless the CRM vendor physically walks into an IT manager's office and sees the memo tacked to a bulletin board, the vendor would have no way of knowing the memo even existed. If the memo is sent in electronic form, as most are in modern businesses, the process of restricting access becomes more complicated. If hard copies of a memo are physically distributed to recipients, the only access control concerns are who has physical access to those documents. As long as the IT managers in this scenario don't leave these memos out where unauthorized people could read them, the information will not get into the wrong hands.

If memos are sent out electronically, access control becomes both simpler and more complex. It is more likely that a paper memo will be left lying out on a desk (or tacked to a bulletin board) than it is to have an electronic memo left visible on a computer screen for someone to walk by and casually read. On the other hand, it is very easy to accidentally or deliberately email that memo to 100 or 1,000 people.

One of the IT managers in this scenario reads the CRM memo and decides to delegate the task to one of his lead developers. He begins to forward the memo via email when the phone rings. While he answers questions on the phone, he completes his email and sends it.

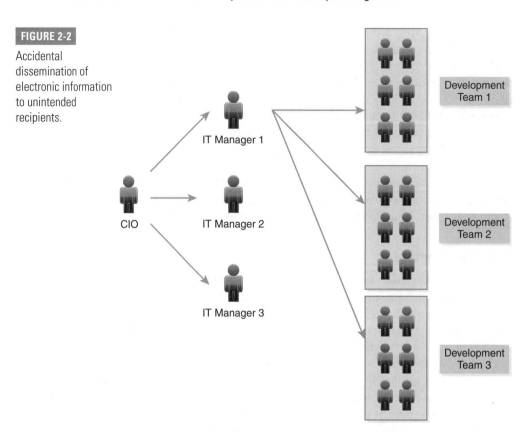

FIGURE 2-2

Accidental
dissemination of
electronic information
to unintended
recipients.

Unfortunately, because he was distracted, instead of sending the memo to one developer, he sends it to all development teams. Now the memo that was originally given to three IT managers has been distributed to dozens of developers, as shown in **FIGURE 2-2**.

What if one of those developers plays golf with a college buddy every Saturday? While they walk the golf course, they vent about work, and the developer mentions the hunt for a new CRM vendor and the fact that he has had to put his other work aside in order to research CRM vendors and make a recommendation before next Monday. The college buddy mentions this to his wife, who has lunch with a friend who works for CRM First, Inc., one of the vendors under consideration. Knowing that the topic is something her friend might have an interest in, she mentions the big decision deadline coming up next week. Suddenly, an outside vendor knows about the internal deadline.

This simple scenario, of course, does not delve into the realm of corporate espionage and deliberate passing of internal memos to outside vendors. The scenario does, however, highlight the importance of employee training in restricted information and the ease with which information can be disseminated throughout an organization, especially when it is in electronic form.

The cost containment benefits of access controls must be balanced with the cost of those restrictions. There are overhead costs involved in any effort to restrict access to information. It does not make sense to spend large amounts of time and money developing a customized access control system to protect information with little or no value.

Operational Efficiency

There is such a thing as too much information, and too much of the wrong information. The key to operational efficiency is in giving the right people the right information, at the right time. The following factors are discussed in this section:

- The right information
- The right people
- The right time

The Right Information

If a warehouse manager comes into work on Monday morning and finds the quarterly financial report on her desk instead of the inventory report, she cannot do her job. She has to track down the necessary information, costing her valuable time. The warehouse manager has no immediate need for the financial report (although if she is vested in the company, she may be interested in the information), so having access to the report does not increase her efficiency. The inventory report, on the other hand, is information she has a direct need for.

In IT, it is your job to ensure that the warehouse manager has the inventory report on Monday morning and has access to the financial report only upon request.

The Right People

As shown in the earlier example of an order life cycle, if the wrong people have access to information, productivity can come to a halt. If a customer can change the details of his or her order after it has already been assembled, there can be a breakdown in processes and efficiencies.

The same thing can happen if too many people are brought into a decision-making process. Consider the CRM vendor example in the previous section. Management and select experts from the IT department should be involved in that decision process. What would happen if the entire assembly line from manufacturing were invited to comment on each CRM choice? The decision process could be slowed down or even halted because the wrong people were brought into the process.

The Right Time

In the CRM vendor example, sales might be the driving force behind the initiative. The company has determined that a CRM solution will increase its ability to serve customers and make sales. This determination is made within the Sales department before it is brought before senior management for approval. Senior management must approve the initiative before it is sent to IT for research and before the contracts are requested from the legal department. Much time would be wasted if someone in Sales were to send a memo directly to a manager in Legal asking for a contract to be drawn up for a new CRM vendor. That work would have to be redone later because requirements would inevitably change during the requirements gathering and research phases.

In the warehouse example, if the manger has the quarterly financial report on Monday morning instead of the inventory report, she loses efficiency because she does not have the right information at the right time.

IT Risk Management

The risk assessment itself can be considered sensitive information. The risk assessment report contains a number of pieces of information that could have a devastating effect in the wrong hands:

- Full asset inventory
- Vulnerability assessment
- Threat assessment
- Mitigation plans

 TIP

The asset inventory should also reference intellectual property assets such as customer records, trade secrets, and business plans. This information is even more useful to an attacker than the existence and location of physical assets. The risk assessment report would not contain the information directly, but it would note where that information is stored and who is authorized to access it.

Full Asset Inventory

The asset inventory contained within a risk assessment report should contain a list, along with location information, of every major resource within the IT infrastructure. However, if an attacker learns that the company's customer database is located on Server A5 in the third rack on the northwest wall of Server Room 12, the task of stealing or disabling that server is a lot easier. Once the attacker is past physical security measures, he or she has a short amount of time to get in, do the job, and get out without being caught. Knowing exactly where to find resources helps to get in and out more quickly.

Vulnerability Assessment

For a risk assessment to be useful, it must look at the weaknesses in the infrastructure. Every system has weaknesses. They are an unavoidable fact of life. The point of a risk assessment is to look honestly at those weaknesses and determine how to eliminate them or minimize their impact.

If an attacker were to obtain a copy of the risk assessment report with the vulnerability assessment, he would have a customized manual for attacking the resources he is most interested in. Instead of trying dozens of possible vulnerabilities until he finds one that hasn't been patched, he knows exactly what has been done to strengthen the system and where the weak points can be found. This information makes attacking a system trivial.

Threat Assessment

A **threat assessment** is similar to a vulnerability assessment, with one slight difference. While the vulnerability assessment looks at weaknesses within the existing infrastructure, the threat assessment deals with the potential for those weaknesses to be exploited.

An attacker with access to a threat assessment knows what attacks the company's security team has already considered and may have begun to mitigate. He also knows which attack methods the company has overlooked or did not realize were possible. This saves the attacker the trouble of attacking in ways that the security team has already anticipated. Depending on how recently the risk assessment was done, the attacker could assume that the threats described in the threat assessment have already been mitigated, or that they are open doors. If the risk assessment is relatively recent, the attacker has a list of attacks that are known to be effective. If the risk assessment is several months or years old, he knows which attacks he shouldn't bother with.

Mitigation Plans

A risk assessment usually has a section that details plans to mitigate the vulnerabilities and risks described in the previous two sections. If an attacker has those **mitigation plans**, he knows how much time he has before a given attack is no longer effective. He can also pick apart those plans, looking for new vulnerabilities that may be introduced in the course of mitigating older vulnerabilities.

A particularly sophisticated attacker who is skilled at social engineering could even pose as a vendor or consultant selling threat mitigation services. If he can convince the company that he is legitimate, the company could face a situation where the attacker is the same person hired to "fix" IT security problems.

Risk-Assessment Policies

The final section of a risk-assessment report is usually a description of the company's policies governing how often a risk assessment should be carried out, what methods should be used, and who should be involved. It also contains a list of individuals who will receive a copy of the report.

An attacker can use this information as well. If he knows that a risk assessment is carried out every 2 years, and the report he has is 18 months old, he may decide to wait 6 months to attack that company because he knows that in 6 months, a newer risk assessment will be available. Like everyone else, an attacker is interested in the most up-to-date information available. He also knows what the risk assessment team is looking for, so he can figure out where to hide the evidence of his activities if an attack is already in progress. For example, if the risk assessment policy states that employees should be secretly tested for vulnerability to various social engineering ploys, an attacker might choose that time to attempt social engineering. He knows that if someone catches on, he or she is likely to assume he is just a member of the risk-assessment team. The attacker has a built-in story to cover his actions if someone begins to suspect something.

Controlling Access and Protecting Value

Confidential information is the most common asset that is devalued by a failure in access control. In this case, information is valuable only if it is hidden. If confidential information becomes common knowledge, it ceases to hold special value.

Importance of Internal Access Controls

Some information is confidential internally and externally. Salary and benefit information is a classic example of privileged information that must be controlled internally. Certain employees have a right to salary information, while most do not.

 NOTE

It is more effective and less expensive, both in terms of time and money, to prevent a security breach than to fix one after the fact.

2

Business Drivers for
Access Controls

For example, a manager might have access to salary information for her direct reports but not for other managers or employees who report to someone else. Implementing internal access controls to regulate which employees have access to confidential information is costly in terms of time and resources, but the risks associated with unauthorized disclosure of that information justify the costs. Unauthorized disclosure of sensitive employee information could cost the company millions in fines and legal fees. There would also be less tangible consequences from lowered morale and resources funneled away from primary business activities into rectifying the root causes of the information breach.

Importance of External Access Controls

Trade secrets and business plans are some of the information that should be secured from external disclosure. You learned earlier in this chapter the consequences of failing to secure that type of confidential information, but it is crucial enough to warrant repeating it. In most cases, the cost (in time and resources) of implementing access controls to protect confidential information is justified by the penalties for failure to do so.

Implementation of Access Controls with Respect to Contractors, Vendors, and Third Parties. It is usually straightforward to implement access controls to safeguard internal information and to control what information is released to the public. When businesses begin to work with contractors, vendors, and other third parties, the access control puzzle gets significantly more complicated.

Access Controls with Respect to Contractors

When outside contractors are hired to provide products or services to an organization, they often require information that could be considered confidential. A good example of this is an external consultant. In many cases, external consultants are either self-employed or employed by a consulting firm and work on an hourly basis for the client company. They are generally highly skilled professionals who are brought in to work on a specific project. When the project is finished, they move on to the next client company. Some client companies hire contractors indefinitely, so in day-to-day practice, they are just like regular employees of the company.

This assumption, that a contractor is "just like a regular employee," can be useful when building team coherence, but it can also be dangerous. The contractor's primary alliance is to the consulting company, which provides payment. If a conflict of interest arises between the consulting company and the client company, the contractor is likely to side with the consulting company.

 TIP

In addition to NDAs and user access rights, when dealing with outside contractors, it is important to restrict which outside equipment can be used on the corporate network.

Contractors often supply their own laptop computers and other equipment they need to perform their jobs. This can be problematic, because those laptops may or may not have the same security safeguards in place as corporate laptops. To illustrate this risk, consider a programmer who is brought in to create a specific application for a company. One of the terms of the contract states that the contractor will supply his own laptop. The contractor agrees and does the work on his personal system, which he also uses to play online games and download music from various sites. At some point, he downloads a file infected with a virus. Because his virus scanner is out of date, the virus goes undetected and infects his system. When he connects his laptop to the corporate network to view design requirements for the application he is developing, the virus uploads itself and infects the file server, quietly sending information from the file server to the hacker who originally created the virus.

Access Controls with Respect to Vendors

When a company contracts with a vendor to manage confidential information, the client company is responsible for ensuring that the vendor has stringent access controls in place. This is especially true in regulated industries such as health care and finance.

A good example of this scenario is an insurance company that outsources its claims management application to a third-party vendor. The vendor runs the application on its servers, allowing the insurance agents to access it from any browser. This is convenient for the agents, who can submit a claim report directly from the site of the incident. It is also convenient for the insurance company because it no longer has to maintain and update its own servers. Unfortunately, the insurance company is still legally responsible for the information contained within those claims— including personally identifiable and sensitive customer information such as addresses, telephone numbers, and mortgage or auto loan information. If the vendor does not implement stringent access controls to protect those data, the client company is legally responsible for the disclosure as well as the vendor.

The most common way to safeguard confidential information that is processed or stored with a vendor is through contractual obligation. Before a vendor-client agreement can be reached, specific access control requirements should be laid out that describe what the vendor is required to do to safeguard any confidential information received in the course of dealing with the client company.

 NOTE

With the increasing popularity of cloud computing and software-as-a-service (SaaS) applications, vendors are becoming more and more responsible for information that was once strictly controlled internally. Unfortunately, many of these applications are seamlessly integrated with applications that run on corporate servers, so there is a danger of complacency.

Access Controls with Respect to Other Third Parties

As business needs evolve, so do the partnerships that meet those needs. In the realm of access control, the key thing to remember is that the owner of the confidential information—the client company—is responsible for ensuring that it is handled securely. If the client company fails to do due diligence and hires a third party without investigating the third party's access control policies, the client company can be held partly responsible for the inevitable disclosure of confidential information.

Case Studies and Examples

Access control success stories are hard to find because they are unremarkable. When access control works, no one really thinks about it. When access control fails, everything is thrown into crisis. In this section, you will discover both success stories and case studies of access control failures.

Case Study in Access Control Success

Acme Insurance has a complicated information access requirement. All customer data are held in an information store. Various entities need access to parts of these data, but not all of it. In fact, sharing the data incorrectly could violate federal law or expose proprietary information to Acme's competitors.

Some parts of the customer information need to be shared with industry groups, which include Acme's competitors. If too much information is disclosed, competitors can derive an advantage over Acme.

All of the customer information has to be shared with the agent who signed up the customers. That agent should only have access to his or her own customers. If a customer is linked to the wrong agent, Acme could get into legal trouble, as well as have to resolve the issue with the agents.

Claims inspectors need access to all customer information attached to customer claims they handle. Various third-party vendors need access to some or all of the customer data for claims appraisal purposes, but only for customers on which they have claims.

The solution to this complex problem is a multilayered access control list. Various groups can access what data they need when they need it, not at other times, and only the part of the information they need.

Case Study in Access Control Failure

Access controls are not just a computer issue; they can also come into play in the physical realm. Due to lax security, Company X almost lost invaluable trade secrets.

Company X is a major beverage company that relies on trade secrets to protect its drink formulas. The company usually makes sure its trade secrets are secure, but this time, physical security was easily breached. An executive administrative assistant gained access to the company's trade secrets. He copied the formulas and took two samples of a new experimental drink.

He brought the formulas and samples to a pair of accomplices to sell. They presented the samples and formulas to Company X's top competitor, Company Y. This is where the scheme fell apart. Company Y had no interest in the documents and instead alerted Company X to the theft. Company X and Company Y then worked with the FBI to set up a sting to arrest the thieves.

In the end no damage was done, because Company Y was not willing to buy the stolen trade secrets and instead notified Company X of the breach. However, you can't rely on luck and trust every competitor to be honest. Good access control policies, including physical access control, would have prevented the theft in the first place.

CHAPTER SUMMARY

In this chapter, you read about the ways that information can be classified, and why businesses and governments go to great lengths to keep certain information secret. You looked at several business drivers for access control to protect the value of information that can be used in the competitive environment of business.

KEY CONCEPTS AND TERMS

Attacker
Automatic declassification
Classification scheme
Clearance
Confidential information
Controlled Unclassified
  Information (CUI)
Declassification
FOIA request

Freedom of Information Act
  (FOIA)
Mandatory declassification
  review
Mitigation plan
Need to know
Payment Card Industry Data
  Security Standard (PCI DSS)
Personally identifiable
  information (PII)

Piggybacking
Risk
Secret information
Sensitive information
Systematic declassification
Threat assessment
Top Secret Information
Trade secret
Unclassified information

CHAPTER 2 ASSESSMENT

1. Just like governments, corporations need to restrict access to information.

  A. True
  B. False

2. The national security classification scheme includes the levels Unclassified, _____, Secret, and Top Secret.

3. PII may or may not be considered sensitive information.

  A. True
  B. False

4. PII may be disclosed without the written consent of the subject under a few specific circumstances, including law enforcement or congressional investigation.

  A. True
  B. False

5. A company can face fines for disclosing sensitive information, even if the disclosure was accidental.

  A. True
  B. False

6. All information is potentially sensitive, so you should secure all of it.

  A. True
  B. False

7. The findings of a risk assessment are sensitive and should be protected.

  A. True
  B. False

8. There are situations where information that is common knowledge in one part of a business should not be disclosed to another part of the same business.

  A. True
  B. False

9. A company can be held responsible if a third party, such as a vendor or contractor, discloses sensitive information owned by the company.

  A. True
  B. False

cooperate with an expert or an executive without question. The delivery person example used earlier in this section is an example of an assumed identity.

- **Believability**—The social engineer is careful to inject as much truth as possible into his or her story. Social engineers use insider jargon, names of actual employees the victim is likely to know (but not well), and other information. They often use a technique called **pretexting** where the attacker lies about his or her own identity or intent in order to persuade the victim to reveal sensitive information.

- **Multiple contacts**—The more contact a person has with another individual or group, the more likely the person is considered "trusted" or a part of the group. A skilled social engineer makes one or two preliminary calls to the victim, each time gathering a little more seemingly innocuous information. The social engineer weaves this information into his or her story and request for help, increasing the believability of both.

- **Request for help**—Once a social engineer gains the trust of a victim, the social engineer asks for help. Typically, he or she has a serious problem that could be easily solved if the social engineer only had a certain piece of information (that the victim has). Because the victim has already identified the social engineer as one of "us," the victim is predisposed to be helpful and solve the fictitious problem by providing the crucial information.

Social engineering works only when employees are trusting and complacent. If employees are trained to recognize social engineering tactics and know how to respond appropriately, the social engineer will usually fail. Unfortunately, most employees are not alert to the possibility of social engineering. They assume that because they are required to show their employee ID to enter the office building, anyone they meet inside must belong there.

The Unintentional Threat

Human beings make mistakes. When employees have access to data they don't need, the data is at risk of accidental deletion. Another common problem is the employee who inadvertently shares sensitive data with someone who shouldn't have access to it.

Many employees don't understand risks from viruses and worms or sophisticated phishing attempts. An employee might open an infected email and forward it to coworkers without realizing the danger. Another source of malware is universal serial bus (USB) flash drives. Employees often use them to transfer files back and forth from their work and home computers. If an employee's home computer is infected with malware, he or she can transfer that malware to his or her office computer via the USB drive.

Laptops and other mobile devices are handy to use but are easily stolen. When users don't exercise physical control over their laptops or smartphones, the devices often disappear. The larger issue may be the data on the device. Are the data confidential? Can someone with malicious intentions access the data? If inadvertently exposed, could it be used against the organization or perhaps people the organization deals with?

Training employees and controlling their actions with access controls reduces a significant number of these incidents.

Hackers and Motivation

There are two primary elements to every malicious access control story: the attacker who seeks to break into a computer system and the resource owner who needs to protect the confidentiality, integrity, and availability of resources against the attacker. What motivates certain individuals to try to gain access to resources to which they do not have a legitimate right?

A hacker usually has two primary motives to break into a computer system: wealth and status. Very young hackers, at 12 or 13 years old, usually begin by defeating copy protections on video games. They desire games but don't always have the resources to purchase legitimate copies. Instead, they borrow games from friends, make copies, and study the protections until they determine a way around them. It's possible that what they learn through these efforts might help them defeat more stringent access controls later in life. They might use their skills to access information with a higher monetary value. They could either sell the information for cash or use stolen credit card and bank account information to purchase items they want.

The status motivation is less obvious than the wealth motivation, and more powerful. A hacker generally does not gain positive status in mainstream society for hacking efforts, although he or she may gain notoriety. At the point that the hacker is engaging in illegal hacking activity, he or she has already rejected the possibility of mainstream status. Instead, the hacker works for status within the hacker subculture. There are two main keys to status in the hacker subculture:

- Esoteric knowledge of computer systems and networks
- Hacking into desirable targets

A **target** is a system or network that contains valuable data and has attracted the attention of the hacker. A target is considered highly desirable if the government, and specifically the military, owns it. A corporately owned target is considered highly desirable if it is protected by particularly strong access controls. By understanding the psychology of the hacker, you can more effectively design access controls to dissuade or prevent him or her from hacking your systems.

Pre-Employment Background Checks for Sensitive Positions

Hiring a new employee is a serious decision for an organization. In addition to the significant financial investment the organization is about to make, the new employee may have access to sensitive information during the course of his or her duties. Organizations need to know if individuals they are about to hire can be trusted and will not harm the company and its assets.

That's why most organizations perform pre-employment background checks before hiring job candidates. Employers want some assurances that information provided by applicants is true and complete, and they want to know if an applicant has a personal history that may conflict with the goals of the organization. For example, a financial firm would not want to hire (and in fact, would be legally prohibited from hiring) someone with a history of embezzlement and fraud to be an investment fund manager.

What Information Can Be Considered in an Employment Decision

A wide variety of information can be obtained through a pre-employment screening, done either by the hiring company or by a third-party firm. Examples of pre-employment screening information includes:

- Driving records
- Credit reports
- Criminal records including arrest reports, incarceration records, and court records
- Medical records
- Bankruptcies
- Military service records
- School records
- Worker's compensation records
- Character references
- Neighbor interviews
- References from previous employers
- Drug test results
- Sex offender listings

> **NOTE**
>
> Under the Health Insurance Portability and Accountability Act (HIPAA), medical information can be used only in determining an applicant's ability to perform a job, with or without reasonable accommodation for disability.

Much of this information is publicly available, but some information such as medical and school records, credit reports, and permission to conduct interviews with neighbors and other personal associates requires special permission from the applicant. Laws that restrict the use of such information are HIPAA (for medical records), the Family Educational Rights and Privacy Act or FERPA (for school records), and the Fair Credit Reporting Act (credit reports).

What Information Cannot Be Considered in an Employment Decision

In general, according to the Fair Credit Reporting Act, negative credit information over 7 years old cannot be considered in an employment decision. In addition, although an employer can investigate an applicant's bankruptcy history, that information cannot be used to make an employment decision.

Applicant's Rights

If an employer uses information obtained in a credit check to deny employment, the employer must notify the applicant of the decision and provide the name and phone number of the reporting agency that performed the background check. Applicants generally have 10 days to dispute the negative information used to make the employment decision.

Consequences of a Bad Hiring Decision

At best, a bad hiring decision can lead to lowered employee morale, failed projects, and the expense of hiring someone else to replace the unqualified employee. In the banking industry, hiring a prohibited person can lead to fines of up to $1,000,000 per day for every day the individual remains with the company or up to 5 years in prison for the hiring manager.

These penalties may seem unreasonable for simply hiring an unqualified person to do a job. They are assessed when a bank hires an individual who has been convicted of a violation under Section 19 of the Federal Deposit Insurance Act. Section 19 deals with criminal offenses involving dishonesty, breach of trust, and money laundering.

Ongoing Observation of Personnel

After a hiring decision is made, and perhaps an initial probationary period expires, it may seem unnecessary to continue to observe employees. However, where ongoing observation is a part of standard procedure, many organizations are able to prevent incidents of workplace violence, employee embezzlement, and avoid other forms of risk associated with hiring employees.

Identify Potentially Disgruntled Employees

A **disgruntled employee** is a person who is angry or dissatisfied, usually with some aspect of his or her employment. Disgruntled employees often believe they have been unfairly passed over for recognition or promotion, or that they are expected to accomplish more than is reasonable.

Some disgruntled employees are easy to spot—they complain loudly to anyone who will listen about the unfair treatment they receive. Others are more difficult to identify. Some things to watch for when identifying potentially disgruntled employees are:

- **Work that is consistently below average**—Not bad enough to warrant termination, but below average. This can indicate a person who does not care about his or her work.
- **A pattern of coming in late and leaving early**—This can indicate a person who simply does not want to be where he or she is.
- **The loner**—Someone who does not join in normal workplace socialization may not identify with the organization.
- **Displays of passive-aggressive behavior**—This can denote someone who is dissatisfied with his or her situation.

Most disgruntled employees do not show up for work with the intention of causing harm to coworkers, but they still represent a significant risk to the organization. In 2019, a disgruntled contractor working for Siemens pled guilty to planting a logic bomb in spreadsheets used by the company. The malicious software broke the spreadsheets periodically, requiring the firm to hire the contractor to "fix" them repeatedly. At the time that this book went to press, the contractor faced a $250,000 maximum fine and up to 10 years in prison.

If managers at Siemens had identified the contractor as potentially disgruntled, the situation could have been diffused and his frustrations dealt with in a more constructive manner. At the very least, his activities could have been more carefully monitored and his logic bomb found earlier.

The Proper Way to Terminate Access on Termination of Employment

Termination of employment is a sensitive issue that should be handled carefully. On one hand, the soon-to-be former employee should be treated respectfully and with understanding—after all, losing one's job is a traumatic event that can have a significant impact on one's life. On the other hand, the organization must protect itself from any negative actions on the part of the employee. When an employee leaves the organization, administrators should undertake a formal offboarding process that includes the following steps:

- Lock the terminated employee's workstation and network accounts and back up data prior to the termination meeting. This will prevent the employee from causing damage after receiving notice of the termination decision.

- Lock or remove accounts on databases and file servers prior to or during the termination meeting.
- Change all passwords, especially those to online accounts that the terminated employee could access from outside the organization, prior to the termination meeting.
- Arrange for company property to be returned. This may include a corporate mobile phone, tablet, keys, a company car, an ID badge, a parking pass, a laptop computer, client files, and contact lists. A terminated employee could use these items to gain unauthorized access to facilities or data.
- Consider how the terminated employee will be allowed to retrieve personal belongings after the termination meeting. After the meeting, the employee should be considered a potentially hostile visitor to the facility and appropriate physical security measures should be taken. The employee should not be allowed to return to his or her office or another area of the facility unescorted.
- Consider whether security should be called to escort the terminated employee out of the building after the termination meeting.
- Change the locks on the terminated employee's office door and change keypad codes as needed.

 NOTE

The timing of these actions must be well-planned. If an employee comes in to work in the morning to find that all of his or her accounts have been locked, he or she might suspect the termination.

- Lock or remove the terminated employee's email account. If the email account is left active, the employee could use that account to send seemingly official emails containing sensitive information to clients or members of the media.
- Change the terminated employee's voicemail message and forward his or her office phone to another employee or to a manager. Change the personal identification number (PIN) on the voicemail system.

The majority of security breaches do not come from hardened criminals or teenagers looking for something to do, although those types of breaches do happen. As a security professional, you should be aware of them and mitigate those risks. Most security breaches are performed by disgruntled employees and former employees. These employees have intimate knowledge of the organization and its systems and may have friends and allies in the organization willing to help. One way to reduce the risk of employee retaliation is to perform thorough background checks on hiring candidates. However, because you can't always predict human behavior, access control techniques such as those discussed in this section minimize the risk of retaliation by removing a disgruntled employee's opportunity to do harm.

Organizational Structure and Access Control Strategy

Most organizations are structured as a hierarchy composed of senior management, operational management, and staff. In terms of access control, this hierarchical structure implies that a higher-level employee should have all the access rights that a lower-level employee has, plus some additional rights. A skilled social engineer can exploit this assumption by posing as a high-level executive and then target a lower-level member of the support staff. Support staff members are trained to be helpful, and the target may be intimidated by someone he or she assumes is a high-level executive. These natural tendencies represent an easy opportunity for a social engineering attack. All the social engineer has to do is call the help desk and claim to be the executive or the executive's assistant and ask the support person to create an account on a sensitive system. Assuming the executive must be authorized on any system, the help desk employee creates the account without question, and the attacker has all the access he or she needs.

An access control model based on organizational structure is designed to prevent social engineering attacks. Rather than giving high-level employees high-level access to sensitive resources, employees are given access based on the tasks they must complete as part of their job. Access rules are based on the balance of confidentiality and necessity. In this sense, an organizational structure model is similar to the role-based access control (RBAC) model.

The organizational structure model adds consideration for the two-way flow of information in an organization. Managers communicate information downward to their departments and teams, and employees communicate information upward to their managers. Unfortunately, if all members of an organization are not well trained in information security, this two-way communication can result in unintentional breaches of confidential information. For example, a manager who was not aware of information flow might mention to employee A that employee B is highly favored to receive a promotion because of B's excellent productivity. On the other hand, employee C, who knows that employee D is planning to leave the organization, might mention during a project planning meeting that they'll need to be sure that D's replacement is up to speed before the project launch, inadvertently informing the entire team and the manager that employee D is planning to resign.

Job Rotation and Position Sensitivity

For the most sensitive positions, especially those that are directly responsible for crucial information and assets, job rotation is a way to minimize the effects of dishonesty. Take, for example, the responsibility of signing checks and reconciling an organization's bank statements. If a single individual holds this responsibility for several years, that person could embezzle significant amounts of money from the organization. However, if the responsibility rotates among half a dozen managers, a manager could embezzle for no more than a few months, knowing that the next manager who checks the bank statements against approved expenditures would probably catch any fraudulent activity.

Requirement for Periodic Vacation

In some industries, especially the financial sector, periodic vacations are required as part of the employment agreement. Periodic, or mandatory, vacations are a security measure. If an individual in a highly sensitive position is doing something dishonest, requiring that person to take 1 or 2 weeks off from work provides time for evidence of dishonesty to surface.

Another benefit of periodic vacations, which isn't often considered, is that they can reduce the success of social engineers. When an individual holds a high-stress position for a long period of time, that stress can create a sense of burnout or constant crisis. Both of these states of mind are easy for a social engineer to exploit, because they prevent the victim from seeing a situation clearly. To combat this, a required vacation period is sometimes necessary.

Separation of Duties

Separation of duties, also seen as segregation of duties, ensures that a single person does not handle all crucial decisions and activities, especially those involving a high level of trust. The goal is to avoid the temptation to commit fraud or other illegal activities. Most people consider themselves reasonably honest and consider stealing wrong or immoral. However, life is messy, and concepts like right and wrong can get blurred when surrounded by the realities of life.

Consider the following scenario: A CFO at a mid-sized financial firm has worked hard to achieve his position. He is well-respected and known for finding diamond-in-the-rough investments that pay off well for his firm. His bonuses are tied to investment decisions that produce profits—if the firm does well, the CFO receives a lucrative bonus. His wife is a database administrator for a large consulting firm. They have three young children, a large home in a desirable neighborhood, and a significant amount of debt.

On Friday evening, the wife comes home from work obviously shaken. Due to an economic downturn, her company has just announced that it will lay off 50% of its consultants. She has been offered a small severance package in return for her voluntary resignation. Faced with their income being cut in half, the CFO starts looking for ways to increase his personal income to make up the difference.

As their financial situation becomes more strained, he begins to take bigger and bigger risks, hoping for a big payoff that will allow them to pay off their debts and get back on their feet until his wife finds another position. Three months after his wife loses her job, the foreclosure notice arrives. Unless they can pay off several months of overdue mortgage payments, they will lose their home.

The CFO knows that the market will eventually go back up and he will find the big payoff, but he can't wait any longer. He issues himself a corporate check for $50,000—enough to bring his mortgage current, pay off overdue bills, and give his family a few months of breathing room. He will pay it all back, he promises himself, as soon as the market rebounds. As the CFO, he has the final authority to issue checks and knows that no one below him will question the expenditure.

The CFO did not set out to embezzle from the firm. He simply found himself in a desperate situation and did what he felt he had to do to in order to buy himself some time to solve the problems he faced. Desperation coupled with opportunity resulted in the theft.

Concept of Two-Person Control

Two-person control is designed to eliminate the opportunity for theft, fraud, or other harmful activity. In this concept, there must be two authorized individuals available to approve any sensitive activity. In the preceding scenario, a two-person control would have prevented the CFO from embezzling because he would have needed a second signatory, such as the CEO, on the check. Requiring two signatures would have removed the opportunity to embezzle.

Collusion

Two-person control is not foolproof. In the above scenario, the CFO may have been able to tell the CEO his story and convince him to co-sign the check as a personal favor. This situation is a form of collusion. However, broaching the subject would have been risky, as simply asking another officer of the company to help him embezzle could have been grounds for his own termination.

Monitoring and Oversight

Although two-person control can be an effective way to remove the opportunity for harmful or dangerous activity, it is only as effective as those who enforce it. If the financial firm required two signatories on all checks, but the CFO knew that the bank did not enforce this rule, the two-person control would have been ineffective.

Similarly, there should always be oversight of any significant activity requiring two-person control to prevent collusion. Whenever two individuals consistently share a significant responsibility, a bond can form between the two individuals. This friendship can become more important to the individuals than the shared task. In the scenario above, if the CEO and CFO were close friends, the CFO would have trusted that his friend would not take action against him and would be likely to help him take out a private loan from the company. In this case, a regular monthly review by the board of directors of all large expenditures would provide some oversight to the two-person control.

Auditing, both internally and by an external firm, is a common way to ensure that all transactions are legitimate and complete. A firm that uses internal auditing must have a team of employees who have the authority to investigate any potential misuse of resources. An internal audit is only useful if the auditors have the freedom to follow up on any information they find, and they are part of an organization that independently reports to the chief executive.

External audits must be performed by an objective outside organization. Unfortunately, when the auditing company is hired by the organization it is supposed to audit, the same weaknesses can surface. A good example of the failure of external auditing is the Enron collapse. Enron was able to hide important financial information from both stakeholders and banks. Their auditing firm, Arthur Andersen, did not discover the hidden information and lost their right to conduct audits. This eventually led to the demise of both Enron and Arthur Andersen in one of the greatest corporate scandals in history.

Responsibilities of Access Owners

Ultimately, it is the responsibility of the owner of sensitive systems, data, and other resources to monitor their use and prevent abuses. A data owner should be responsible for:

- Disclosing to users any relevant legal, regulatory, or ethical issues surrounding the use or disclosure of the information
- Implementing a data classification system and rating the data according to its sensitivity, confidentiality, inherent value, and other factors
- Maintaining a list of authorized users
- Implementing procedures to safeguard information from unauthorized use, disclosure, alteration, or accidental or intentional destruction
- Developing a policy governing data retention and disposition
- Providing users with adequate training in the use and protection of the information

Owners of other sensitive resources should have similar responsibilities to classify their resources and safeguard them from unauthorized use or destruction.

Training Employees

A well-trained workforce is a valuable asset in any access control system, especially when it comes to defeating social engineering tactics. Employees cannot be expected to respond appropriately to security situations if they have not been trained in the proper way to handle them.

Simply handing a new hire the employee handbook and expecting him or her to read the sections on security policy is not enough. A good security awareness program should:

- **Be ongoing**—Telling employees about a security policy once is not enough. Security awareness messages should be repeated and reinforced on a regular basis.
- **Include multiple formats**—Not every individual learns in the same way. Some people are better at processing written information, while others are auditory learners. Some respond better to visual representations or dramatizations. Presenting information in a variety of formats helps to ensure that every employee understands security concepts well.
- **Be interactive**—People remember information more clearly when they are able to interact with it. Role-playing activities are a great way to allow employees to interact with security information and practice recognizing and responding to security events.
- **Include multiple points of contact**—It can take up to a dozen repetitions before a concept becomes internalized. Place security awareness signs around the workplace, schedule workshops and seminars, and conduct security awareness drills. Each time employees encounter security awareness messages, that information will become a little more ingrained.

What should employees learn about security? Two common policies, the acceptable use policy and the security awareness policy, cover the common security information most employees need. Neither of these policies is a one-size-fits-all solution. Each organization will have its own version.

Acceptable Use Policy

An acceptable use policy (AUP) defines how employees may use the IT infrastructure supplied by an organization. In general, an acceptable use policy specifies whether employees may use organization resources such as networks, Internet connections, and email accounts for personal use. It may also define whether employees may download files from the Internet, forward humorous or chain letters via email, or engage in sending spam. An acceptable use policy generally forbids any activity that is prohibited by federal, state, or local laws or that violates regulatory compliance. Common elements in an acceptable use policy are:

- Keep all passwords secure and do not share accounts.
- All workstations and laptops must be secured with a password-protected screensaver.
- Use of organizational communications resources, including email, telephone, Internet, and interoffice mail, shall be limited to business purposes only. Personal use is strictly prohibited.

- Sending unsolicited junk email or advertisements is prohibited.
- Any form of harassment, including email and telephone messages, is prohibited.
- Creating or forwarding chain letters, pyramid schemes, or other similar messages is prohibited.
- Circumventing the security of any network or host owned by the organization is prohibited.

Most acceptable use policies go into more depth; however, these are some common items found in every acceptable use policy.

Security Awareness Policy

A security awareness policy specifies what individual employees are responsible for in terms of information security. It also defines the responsibilities of managers and information owners. Because security is an ever-changing field, many security awareness policies do not lay out specific procedures, but rather, refer employees to another resource for up-to-date information, such as a page on the organization's Intranet.

In general, employees must agree to read and follow security procedures. Managers are responsible for providing training and security resources for those under their supervision, and information owners are responsible for classifying their information and taking appropriate steps to safeguard it. Some common elements in a security awareness policy include:

- The organization will provide ongoing training and resources on information security.
- Information owners will classify the information according to its sensitivity and take reasonable precautions to safeguard the information.
- Employees should understand common security threats and maintain a sense of vigilance, especially with regard to social engineering attacks.
- Employees should immediately report any suspicious activity to their manager.

Many security awareness policies also include references to other documents, both internal policies and external resources, to which employees can refer if they are unsure of whether a given situation constitutes a security threat.

Ethics

As children, most people learn the basic concept "treat others as you would want them to treat you." Of course, life for adults is rarely that simple. Adults tend to complicate things. The study of ethics is essentially the study of those complications and how to navigate them back to the simplicity of "treat others as you would want them to treat you." In this section, you'll examine how ethics affect information security—specifically, the need for access controls.

What Is Right and What Is Wrong

"Right" and "wrong" may seem like basic concepts—most children learn that lying and stealing are wrong—but in the real world of organizational behavior, there is a gray area between the two absolutes. Most decisions people make fall into this gray area.

Ethics Go Beyond "Do Not Steal"

Organizational ethics programs are essential for defining the core values of the organization. However, an organization that forgets or ignores the code of ethics once it has been written does not fully take advantage of this powerful tool. An ethics program is far more than a written document. It involves several stages, which should be reviewed and repeated regularly:

- Define the core values of the organization and ensure that those values are reflected in the stated code of ethics. An organization's core values should be limited to those three to five values that are most critical to that particular organization. An educational institution, for example, may place intellectual development on its list of core values, while a manufacturing company may replace that value with one more suited to its purpose, such as quality assurance. These core values should be reviewed annually to ensure that the stated values still reflect the goals of the organization.
- Solicit input from a wide range of stakeholders across all levels and departments of the organization. Although a code of ethics should have strong backing from the highest levels of management, it is also important for employees at all levels to see that their perspectives are represented in the final document.
- Write or revise the code of ethics, including information on where an employee can go for clarification and how ethical dilemmas should be resolved. Distribute the document to every employee and post copies throughout the organization.
- Create or review structures within the organization that support the code of ethics. For example, many organizations create an ethics committee at the board level, which provides high-level leadership on ethics matters, as well as an ombudsman to assist in clarifying ethical questions by interpreting policies and procedures in the day-to-day operations of the organization. The ombudsman also assists in resolving ethical concerns employees may have about their duties or about the activities of management.
- Conduct training sessions and workshops to further clarify the core values contained within the code of ethics and to allow employees the opportunity to practice analyzing situations and making ethical decisions, in a low-stress environment. This experience will help them when they are faced with an ethical dilemma in higher-stress situations.

This process is critical in times of rapid change and crisis, when there may not be time to deliberate on the ethical implications of behaviors and decisions. By placing a high priority on ethics and ensuring that every employee is well trained in the process of analyzing situations and making ethical decisions, an organization can ensure that its employees will behave ethically when it is most needed. Ongoing attention to the process of ethics management makes the code of ethics a real presence in organizational culture, not just another document in the employee handbook. It should inform every other policy, including those on information security.

Enforcing Policies

Simply writing policies that define the responsibilities of information owners, managers, and employees is not sufficient to actually safeguard sensitive resources. Everyone concerned should understand, accept, and enforce those policies on all levels. For an information security policy to be truly effective, individual employees must accept its importance in meeting their needs and enforce it informally within their working groups.

Employees should understand that safeguarding information is vital to the continued success of the organization, and, therefore, the continuation of their jobs and their personal ability to meet the physical needs of their families. The policy itself should also specify who has the ultimate authority to enforce the policy and specific consequences of noncompliance. Managers should be proactive in providing resources and training for their employees. They are also responsible for formal policy enforcement. Information owners must also take their role seriously and ensure that the information they are responsible for is adequately protected.

Human Resources Involvement

Human resources should be an integral part of enforcing security policy. By providing resources and training opportunities, they can help prevent security policy noncompliance. They are also responsible for implementing the stated consequences for noncompliance, including formal employee censure and termination.

Best Practices for Handling Human Nature and Organizational Behavior

Human nature is a complex thing. It cannot be used to explain every incident of individual or organizational behavior, but it is usually a factor. In this section, you will discover some best practices for working with human nature to achieve positive security behaviors while minimizing negative ones.

Make Security Practices Common Knowledge

Employees cannot follow practices they do not know about or understand. A comprehensive training program is a good way to make sure that everyone in the organization understands which behaviors have an impact on security and how to recognize risky behaviors in themselves and their peers. Offer training workshops and seminars on a regular basis, put up posters reminding employees to create secure passwords or recognize social engineering tactics, and encourage managers to discuss security practices that apply specifically to their area of the organization with their teams.

Foster a Culture of Open Discussion

Many organizations claim to encourage discussion among individual employees and their managers, but few actually do. Encourage managers and team leaders to periodically check in with each of their direct reports and really listen to what they say about the organizational culture. If employees are reluctant to open up to their direct supervisors when asked their opinion on the general culture, they will be far less likely to initiate a conversation about a serious matter such as security.

These "how are things going" discussions should be conducted in a casual way and repeated on a regular basis. This will encourage employees to alert their managers early when they notice a problem rather than waiting until the problem is large enough to warrant requesting a formal meeting with the boss. It will also create a framework for the discussion and can help defuse potential disgruntled employees. Most disgruntled employees feel that they are not valued and that management does not listen to their concerns. Simply asking these employees for their observations and opinions—and sincerely listening and taking their viewpoint into consideration—will go a long way toward making employees feel connected to the organization.

Encourage Creative Risk-Taking

Many negative security behaviors have an element of risk-taking. Channel that urge to take risks into areas where it can benefit the organization rather than hurt it. Encourage employees to take creative risks—both within the organization and in their private lives. Provide a bulletin board where employees with creative outlets such as music, theater, or art can post performance fliers and invite their peers to attend. Within the organization, go beyond the suggestion box. When employees bring up viable ideas for improving processes, let them implement those ideas on a small scale. This will not only give all employees a sense of ownership in the organization but will create a process incubator that could generate innovations that give the organization a real advantage over the competition.

Many organizations now use "innovation days" to spur creativity among their staff. During these days, employees are free to organize themselves into small groups dedicated to creating a new product, solving a nagging problem, or undertaking some other activity that may benefit the organization. They do not necessarily need to work on an issue related to their job responsibilities. These days are often very popular among staff and have led to significant innovations at firms embracing the approach.

Case Studies and Examples

Access control systems that address human nature—and the problems human nature can introduce—focus on social engineering attacks. The case studies in this chapter also focus on social engineering and how to implement access control policies that will prevent those types of attacks.

Private Sector Case Study

Private-sector organizations are often the targets of social engineering attacks. They tend to be less well protected from social engineering attacks than governmental organizations. For this reason, foreign governments as well as competitors often target them.

Consider the case of Acme Software, a large technology firm. They produce software-based firewall and email encryption solutions for home and business use.

Late one Monday afternoon, Janice, an administrative assistant, receives a telephone call from a man who says that his name is "Ed" and that he works in the marketing department. Ed tells Janice that he is working on the marketing collateral for the big trade show next month and needs to know the major features for the new line of encryption software. Being helpful and providing information is a big part of Janice's job, so she knows right where to find the documentation on the new software. She reads off a list of features to Ed, who thanks her profusely for saving him a lot of time on this project.

A few days later, Ed makes another phone call, this time to a programmer on the encryption team. He tells the programmer the same story—that he is from marketing and is working on materials for the trade show—and asks the programmer to explain one of the most technical features from the list he got from Janice. The programmer begins to explain it, and Ed asks questions that clearly demonstrate that he does not understand the technology. As the programmer's frustration grows, Ed suggests that it might be easier if he could just play with a copy of the software. The programmer, at this point eager to get Ed off the phone, agrees. Ed tells the programmer that he's actually working from home and doesn't have his corporate laptop, and asks him to just send the files to his personal email address instead. The programmer agrees and sends an email with a copy of the software to Ed's personal email account.

Unfortunately, Ed is actually a corporate spy working for a foreign government. The U.S. government forbids the export to that country of the kind of encryption technology used in the software in question, but the programmer had no idea he was breaking any laws. He was just trying to get "marketing" off the phone so he could get back to work on his code. The ultimate weakness in this scenario was the employees' tunnel vision. They knew their jobs very well but did not relate their positions to the larger organization. Janice knew that her job was to be helpful, but she did not stop to question whom she was helping. The programmer did not connect the fact that he was working on highly sensitive code to the possibility that he could become the target of a social engineering attack. Better security awareness on all levels of the organization would have prevented this attack.

Public Sector Case Study

University networks are often targets of information theft because they hold valuable information and are accessed by people with minimal—if any—security training. Consider this scenario:

Michelle is a first-year, early childhood education student attending the state university. Monday morning at 7:30 a.m., her phone rings. On the other end of the line is someone claiming to be from Campus Information Security. He tells her they have been monitoring the data usage from her room and have noticed a spike in file transfers over the past week.

Michelle is initially confused, having suddenly been woken up by the phone and unfamiliar with the terms "file transfer" and "data usage." The man on the line asks her how long she has been operating an illegal file-sharing server from her room and informs her that such activity is a violation of university policy. She could be expelled from school and face stiff civil fines, as well as possible jail time.

Fully awake now, Michelle protests. She hasn't been running a file server from her room; there must be some mistake. At first, the man on the phone seems unconvinced, but as Michelle pleads her innocence and ignorance of the issue, he backs down and suggests that she must have a virus that's causing the increased file transfer rate. He'll need to log onto her system to run a diagnostic check and clean out the virus, and to do so he'll need her username and password.

Relieved that he is no longer threatening her with expulsion, fines, and jail time, Michelle agrees and gives him her information. He tells her to give him a couple of hours to work on things, and he'll erase the virus and make a note in his files.

The social engineer who targeted Michelle spends the next couple of hours using her account to explore the university's network and break into more sensitive areas than Michelle has access to.

In this case, the hacker exploited two crucial things: ignorance and fear. First, he targeted a first-year student who was unlikely to have any experience or knowledge of information security. He didn't choose a computer science major, he chose a budding preschool teacher. Second, he bullied her until she was clearly upset then changed tactics and became helpful. He also chose to contact her at a time when she was most likely to be groggy. When people are first awoken, they tend to react to situations more emotionally than they would when fully awake. No one thinks calmly and rationally when woken out of a deep sleep.

The solution to this problem is education. Had the university simply made information security a part of its freshman orientation and emphasized that no one from the university will ever ask for a student's password, Michelle would have had a good chance of recognizing that something about the call wasn't right.

Critical Infrastructure Case Study

Infrastructure facilities usually have strong physical security. They are surrounded by barbed wire and have security guards at every entrance. Those guards are highly trained and aware of the important role they play in keeping things running smoothly, but they are still human and prone to very understandable mistakes.

James was a third-shift guard at a nuclear power plant. He took his job seriously, dividing his time between watching the surveillance monitors in the security office and walking the hallways in his area looking for anything out of the ordinary.

One cold night in January, around 2:00 a.m., he heard voices down the hallway that led to the control room. He hurried to the source of the sound and discovered two young men. He asked to see their ID badges, which they claimed they forgot. They told him they were new employees and gave the name of their manager. James escorted them back to the security office, where he placed a call to the manager, waking her up. The manager confirmed that she does have two new employees and confirmed their names then asked to talk to the two men.

James handed over the phone and listened as one of the young men explained to the manager that he was just in early to finish some paperwork he didn't do the night before and confirmed that he would have a presentation ready for the staff meeting later that day. Then the young man hung up the phone, apologized to James for all the trouble, and explained how he was new and didn't want to get in trouble for not getting this paperwork done. James let the two men go.

James had expected to get the phone back to get a final okay from the manger. He had already woken her up once, so he didn't want to call back and risk getting in trouble. A few minutes after the two men left the security office, the manager called back and informed James that she had no idea who the two men were; they were definitely not her employees. She had tried to ask questions, but the man on the phone simply ignored her and talked about paperwork and staff meetings. Of course, by the time James found this out and began looking for the two young men, they had already found what they were looking for and left the premises.

The weakness in this situation was the security guard's natural fear of angering someone higher up the organizational chart than himself. No one likes being woken up at 2:00 a.m.—especially twice in one night. The solution to this problem is to educate everyone in an organization—managers and employees alike—on the importance of security protocols. If James had felt more certain that as long as he was doing his job he was safe from repercussions, he would not have hesitated to call the manager back and would have caught the two young men in their scam.

CHAPTER SUMMARY

This chapter discussed how human nature both insists upon access control and fights against it. You read about how a skilled social engineer can exploit human nature to obtain unauthorized access to information and systems, and how training, organizational culture, and employee support can mitigate the weaknesses that human nature introduces into any access control system.

KEY CONCEPTS AND TERMS

Disgruntled employee	Pretexting	Target
Hacker	Separation of duties	Two-person control
Human nature	Social engineering	

CHAPTER 3 ASSESSMENT

1. Generally, hackers are motivated by _____ and _____.

2. A target is a system or network that contains valuable data and has attracted the notice of the hacker.

   A. True
   B. False

3. A typical social engineering strategy involves which of the following?

   A. Assumed identity
   B. Believability
   C. Multiple contacts
   D. Requests for information
   E. A and B only
   F. All of the above

4. What element of human nature does a social engineer exploit?

   A. Fear
   B. Ambition
   C. Trust
   D. Desire for status
   E. Greed

5. An employer can obtain an applicant's driving records as part of a pre-employment background check.

   A. True
   B. False

6. An employer can obtain an applicant's medical history and credit reports without special consent of the applicant.

A. True
B. False

7. Passive-aggressive behavior can be an indicator of a _____ employee.

8. Prior to or during an employee termination meeting, which of the following should be locked or changed?

A. The employee's workstation and network accounts
B. The employee's email account(s)
C. Passwords for online accounts accessible to the employee
D. The employee's accounts on databases and file servers
E. All of the above

9. Two-way communication is critical to the organizational structure model of access control.

A. True
B. False

10. Which of the following can help uncover dishonesty, such as fraud or theft, in the workplace? (Select two.)

A. Mandatory vacation
B. Pre-employment checks
C. Job rotation
D. Ethics training

11. _____ is designed to eliminate the opportunity for theft, fraud, or other harmful activity.

12. Access owners are responsible for maintaining a list of authorized users.

A. True
B. False

13. Informing employees of security and acceptable use policies during orientation is sufficient training.

A. True
B. False

14. Human resources should be an integral part of enforcing security policy.

A. True
B. False

Assessing Risk and Its Impact on Access Control

RISK ASSESSMENT IS THE CRITICAL first step in designing an access control system. The risk assessment process allows you to identify potential threats and vulnerabilities within the existing system, prioritize them, and determine ways to minimize or mitigate those risks. A good risk assessment takes into account both the value of the assets to be protected and their impact on the overall organization.

Chapter 4 Topics

This chapter covers the following topics and concepts:

- Terms and concepts involved with risk assessments and access control
- Threats and vulnerabilities
- How value, situation, and liability affect risk assessments
- Case studies and examples

Chapter 4 Goals

When you complete this chapter, you will be able to:

- Define the key terms and concepts relating to risk assessment
- Explain the difference between a threat and a vulnerability
- Understand how value, situation, and liability affect risk assessment
- Use case studies and examples as models of risk assessment

Definitions and Concepts

Risk is a fact of life. There is no such thing as risk-free activity. Even the most common activities, such as walking across your living room, could be risky if, for example, you trip and fall. It isn't possible to completely eliminate risk, as risk-taking is an important part of any organization's business strategy. By taking risks, we introduce the potential to innovate and grow as an organization. However, in IT, we attempt to manage all of the risks we face by making informed decisions to mitigate, avoid, transfer, and accept risks.

Before continuing, let's define some of the key terms you'll see in this chapter:

- **Risk**—Risks occur when there is the potential that a particular threat will exploit a vulnerability, causing harm to an organization; risk is measured in terms of probability and impact.
- **Asset value**—Asset value is the relative value, either in monetary terms or in qualitative value, of the resource being protected by the access control system.
- **Threat**—A **threat** is an adverse event that may jeopardize the security of the organization, its information systems, and/or its data.
- **Vulnerability**—A **vulnerability** is a known or unknown weakness in a system's design. A vulnerability may make it possible for an attacker to take control of a system, access resources to which he or she is not authorized, or damage the system in some way.
- **Probability of occurrence**—The likelihood that a threat will exploit a vulnerability.
- **Impact**—The impact on an organization if a risk materializes.
- **Control**—A technical, physical, or administrative process designed to reduce risk.

Risk assessment is the crucial first step in designing any access control system. In a risk assessment, you determine which risks exist in your environment or may occur in the future. You can measure the level of any risk by calculating the **probability of occurrence** and the potential impact on your environment. The following standard equation determines the level of each risk:

$$\text{Risk} = \text{Probability} \times \text{Impact}$$

NOTE

You'll learn about types of risk assessments later in this chapter.

Knowing the level of risk helps you take appropriate steps to prevent the risk or mitigate it. For example, in most cases, it is probably not necessary to design a highly secure, three-stage access control system to protect a desktop printer. The probability that a desktop printer would be exploited is fairly low, and the overall impact of such an exploitation is similarly low. By the same logic, a simple username and password-based access control system would be inadequate to protect top-secret military documents, as the control is not commensurate with the level of risk.

Risk is not a single problem that can be solved once and then ignored. It is also not just an IT problem. Risk is a multifaceted issue that affects every part of the organization. A user can create a highly secure password, but the system protected by that password is not considered secure if user passwords are not stored in a secure manner, or if numerous operating systems or application-level vulnerabilities allow an attacker to go around the access control system.

FYI

The most effective way to determine which threats are relevant to a given situation is to draw on a combination of research, experience, and brainstorming. Case studies are a good way to understand best practices and missteps to avoid for a given topic. The case studies in this chapter illustrate real-world examples of systems that have been attacked, which could have been avoided with the proper security measures in place.

Threats can take many forms, depending on the nature of the system under attack. Some systems, such as web servers, are most vulnerable to denial of service (DoS) attacks. Servers that contain sensitive data are more susceptible to data theft and user impersonation attacks. Networks and individual workstations are most often threatened by attackers who gain access to them as a stepping stone to other, more valuable resources such as servers and databases.

Vulnerabilities are the weaknesses in a system that allow an attacker to gain access. Vulnerabilities are often obscure bugs in application or operating system code that allow attackers to gain access to low levels of the file system, but they can also take more obvious forms. Weak passwords and lax physical security measures are also vulnerabilities because they allow attackers to gain access to a system.

 TIP

Case studies and background experience can help you identify threats. However, thinking like an attacker is a highly useful way to perceive potential vulnerabilities. If you can look at your infrastructure from the point of view of an attacker, you may be able to see possible weaknesses and strengthen those areas before an attacker finds them.

Probability of occurrence is a crucial aspect of risk assessments. In an ideal world, organizations would mitigate every possible vulnerability, but time and resources can be limited. It does not make sense to devote excessive resources to mitigating a vulnerability that has a very low probability of occurrence, while ignoring a vulnerability with a much higher probability. For example, if a security alert is issued concerning a certain virus that's spreading across the Internet, the probability is high that your systems may be compromised. It makes sense to devote time and resources to scanning your systems for that virus and taking appropriate measures to eliminate it.

Impact describes the potential consequences of an attack. A scenario with a high probability but a low impact is a lower priority risk than one with a high probability and high impact.

For example, a virus that has already infected computers in hundreds of other organizations, costing them millions of dollars in lost productivity and lost data, has a high probability (because it is actively spreading) and a high impact (lost productivity and data). This virus would have a high-risk rating. On the other hand, a badly crafted phishing email that asks the reader to click a link that downloads a 10-year-old virus has a low probability (because most people will recognize it as a fake and delete it) and a low impact (the antivirus software installed on a computer will stop a virus that old). Most risks fall somewhere in between, as shown in **FIGURE 4-1**. Using a visualization, such as the one shown here, is a great way to help management understand risks. This simplifies the risk management process down to, "Start in the upper-right corner and begin addressing each risk, working your way down to the lower-left corner."

IT professionals put controls in place to lower both the probability and impact of a risk. A **control**, as you just read, is a technical, physical, or administrative process designed to reduce risk. The most useful controls strike a balance between the cost of implementing the control—in terms of actual financial cost and in lost productivity— and the value of the asset being protected. A firewall, for example, adds maintenance and configuration costs to your organization. If the assets behind the firewall are valuable, such as a file server or database storing sensitive data, the cost may be justified.

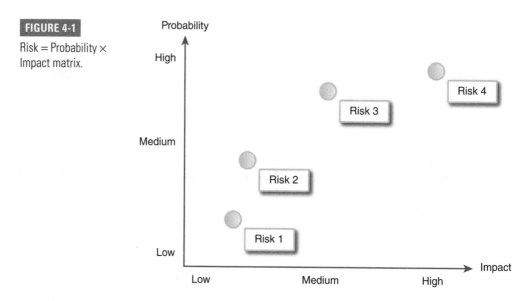

FIGURE 4-1

Risk = Probability ×
Impact matrix.

Controls do not have to be technology-based. Training employees on handling sensitive data is another valuable control because it could lessen the risk of a social engineering ploy. Although employee training is a strategic initiative that takes time and resources to execute, it is an effective method to reduce security breaches and is often well worth the investment.

Threats and Vulnerabilities

In this section, you will learn about access control threats and vulnerabilities and how to assess their impact. Access control threats cannot be 100% eliminated because new ones are constantly being devised. Instead, security professionals try to minimize their probability and impact by eliminating as much vulnerability as possible. In order to correctly prioritize efforts at mitigating threats and vulnerabilities, we perform risk assessments to accurately decide which threats represent the biggest impact to resources and data.

Access Control Threats

There are three primary threats to any access control system:

- **Password cracking**—Guessing or deciphering passwords
- **Heightened access**—The ability of an attacker to log into a system under one level of access and exploit a vulnerability to gain a higher level of access
- **Social engineering**—The use of manipulation or trickery to convince authorized users to perform actions or divulge sensitive information to the attacker

Password Cracking

Password cracking is a constant game of cat and mouse within IT security. Security administrators set password rules to guarantee that users create secure passwords, and attackers use a combination of brute force and sophisticated **algorithms** to break those passwords.

TABLE 4-1 Possible Combinations of Characters

NUMBER OF CHARACTERS IN THE PASSWORD	ALL LOWERCASE CHARACTERS	UPPERCASE AND LOWERCASE CHARACTERS	UPPERCASE, LOWERCASE, AND NUMERIC CHARACTERS
1	26	52	62
2	$26^2 = 676$	$52^2 = 2,704$	$62^2 = 3,844$
3	$26^3 = 17,576$	$52^3 = 140,608$	$62^3 = 238,328$
4	$26^4 = 456,976$	$52^4 = 7,311,616$	$62^4 = 14,776,336$
5	$26^5 = 11,881,376$	$52^5 = 380,204,032$	$62^5 = 916,132,832$
6	$26^6 = 308,915,776$	$52^6 = 19,770,609,664$	$62^6 = 56,800,235,584$
7	$26^7 = 8,031,810,176$	$52^7 = 1,028,071,702,528$	$62^7 = 3,521,614,606,208$
8	$26^8 = 208,827,064,576$	$52^8 = 5.34597285 \times 10^{13}$	$62^8 = 2.18340106 \times 10^{14}$

Security administrators respond by modifying their password policies, and the cycle begins again. Security administrators are hampered by the users' need for convenience, while attackers are limited only by time and computing cycles.

For example, suppose the security administrator at XYZ, Inc., implements a typical password security policy. The policy states that passwords must be a minimum of eight characters long and may contain uppercase letters, lowercase letters, and numeric characters. This policy ensures that there are at least 62^8 or $2.18340106 \times 10^{14}$ possible combinations, as shown in **TABLE 4-1**.

All these permutations are designed to increase the time it takes for an attacker to crack a password. An attacker uses an application designed to generate all possible permutations of case-sensitive alphanumeric characters and a simple script that inputs a known (or guessed) username with these generated passwords to the access control system. If an attacker's password guessing application can try 100,000 passwords per second, it will take a matter of days to break a very simple password, or thousands of years to break a complex one, as shown in **TABLE 4-2**.

Given enough time, the attacker will eventually find a valid username and password combination, thus breaking into the system. The role of a security administrator is to identify this vulnerability and modify the password creation policy to require a longer minimum length and the use of at least one non-alphanumeric character. This does not necessarily make it more difficult for the attacker to break in—the attack is not really difficult to begin with because the cracking software does all the work behind the scenes. However, the longer, more secure password policy simply makes the process take longer. The goal is to push the time frame beyond one of two limits:

- The time it takes for the security administrator to realize the attack is occurring and disable the account under attack
- The expected lifespan—or at least the attention span—of the attacker

TABLE 4-2 Time Required to Break Passwords of Different Lengths

NUMBER OF CHARACTERS IN THE PASSWORD	LOWERCASE CHARACTERS	UPPERCASE AND LOWERCASE CHARACTERS	UPPERCASE, LOWERCASE, AND NUMERIC CHARACTERS
1	< 1 second	< 1 second	< 1 second
2	< 1 second	< 1 second	< 1 second
3	< 1 second	1.4 seconds	2.4 seconds
4	4.6 seconds	1.2 minutes	2.5 minutes
5	2 minutes	1 hour	2.5 hours
6	51 minutes	2.2 days	6.6 days
7	22 hours	4 months	1.1 years
8	24 days	17 years	69.2 years

Even with the most sophisticated computing equipment available, it can take years or decades to crack a strong password. However, computer manufacturers are constantly developing more powerful systems, so a password that takes an average of 10 years to crack today may only take a few months to crack five years from now.

Heightened Access

Continuing with the example in the last section, once the attacker cracks a user's password and can log into the system, the next step is to obtain **heightened access**. Chances are the really valuable assets on a system—sensitive data, for example—are protected by file and group permissions that do not allow every user on a system to read or write to them. However, attackers can exploit vulnerabilities in the operating system as well as within application code to achieve access levels normally denied to the user they are logged in as. You'll learn about these vulnerabilities in more detail later in this chapter.

Social Engineering

Social engineering is the single most common strategy that attackers use to compromise secure systems. Social engineering is any strategy that tricks a user into giving up information that is helpful toward gaining access, or ultimately, the user's credentials.

Not all social engineering tactics are technological. In fact, some of the most effective tactics are the simplest and exploit people's general sense of trust and helpfulness. How many times have you held the door open for someone following you into a building? It is simply the polite, helpful thing to do. In a public place, such as the local mall, there is no security threat from such a simple act. But in a corporate environment where access to buildings or floors is limited to authorized personnel, simply holding the door open for someone could be a serious security breach.

Consider the following scenario: It is 8 a.m. on a typical Tuesday morning. Hundreds of people are filtering into the office to begin their work day. To enter the building, you must swipe your smart card ID badge. The person behind you has his hands full with his briefcase, coffee cup, keys, and a box of doughnuts. He smiles and asks you to hold the door. "Sure, no problem," you answer as you hold open the door for him, assuming he is a fellow employee. He nods his head, smiles again, and thanks you as he heads confidently into another area of the building. This particular threat, where one person uses the successful authentication of another to gain access to a facility, is known as **tailgating** or piggybacking.

As you turn on your computer and check your morning email, the person who followed you into the building roams the hallways looking for unlocked offices and unsecured workstations. Often, employees keep sensitive information on their desks, which could help an attacker obtain access to assets stored on the corporate network.

 NOTE

Phishing is a very common social engineering tactic in which the attacker creates an authentic-looking email or webpage that convinces users to enter their confidential information or install software on their computer that secretly records information and sends it back to the attacker. Phishing attack attempts have become significantly more common and successful since 2019.

Access Control Vulnerabilities

Vulnerabilities are the weaknesses in any security system that make a threat *threatening*. Without a vulnerability, a threat is simply a theoretical danger. For example, you live with the risk of electrocution every time you turn on the lights. The threat in this scenario is the electrical current running through the wires in your home. The vulnerability here is potentially bad wiring. If the wiring is bad, you could get a shock when you turn on the lights. However, if you were to build a home without that vulnerability—without wiring—you would face virtually no chance of electrocution. Yes, in theory, you could still be electrocuted if lightning were to strike you while sitting in your electricity-free home, but the probability of that occurring is low enough to be insignificant.

The primary vulnerabilities you need to mitigate to avoid a password-cracking attack are insecure passwords and insecure storage. Users want passwords that are easy to type and easy to remember. Unfortunately, these parameters do not usually lead to passwords that are difficult to guess or crack.

Even the most secure password is worthless from a security standpoint if it is stored insecurely. Some applications store user passwords as plain text, either in a database or a flat file. This is becoming less common, but you may still run into this situation with legacy code. The more common problem is insecure **password hashes**. Most passwords are stored in an encrypted form. To decide whether the password entered by the user matches what the system has stored, the user-entered password is passed through a hashing algorithm. If this hashing algorithm is weak, an attacker can steal even the most secure password.

 NOTE

Microsoft Windows XP, now no longer supported, used a weak hashing algorithm to store passwords up to 15 characters in length. The algorithm converted the password to all uppercase, then divided it into two fields, which were encoded separately. This allowed attackers to crack each half of the password separately using lookup tables.

4

Assessing Risk and Its Impact on Access Control

The most common vulnerabilities that allow an attacker to obtain heightened access are insecure applications that are run at too high of a privilege level. A common example of this problem is a web server where the web service, or daemon, is run as the administrative or root user. Often, when installing an application, a system administrator may be tempted to run the application under a privileged user account. This prevents problems when the application tries to write to the file system or access the network, but it also makes that privileged user account vulnerable to attack.

Ultimately, the biggest vulnerability in any access control system is its users. As discussed earlier in this chapter, people generally want to be helpful and trusting, which makes them perfect targets for social engineering. Thorough and repeated training is the best defense against social engineering.

Risk Assessment

Once you've identified the threats and vulnerabilities facing an organization, you should turn to a formal risk assessment process that identifies the priority of addressing each risk. You may choose to do this by performing either a quantitative or qualitative risk assessment.

Quantitative Risk Assessment

In a **quantitative risk assessment**, you rely on numeric data and calculations to identify and rank the risks facing an organization. You first need to identify several items:

- You must first determine the **asset value (AV)** for each asset in your scope of work. This is normally done as a dollar value that may be determined based upon:
  - **Replacement cost**—What would it cost the organization to replace the asset if it were damaged or lost?
  - **Purchase cost**—What did it cost the organization to obtain the asset in the first place?
  - **Depreciated cost**—This is the original cost reduced by an aging factor.

> **NOTE**
>
> You calculate ALE by multiplying the SLE by the ARO with the following formula:
>
> $$ALE = SLE \times ARO$$
>
> Using the database with 1,000 records discussed above as an example, the SLE is $50,000. If we expect that the database will be compromised twice per year, the ARO is 2, and the ALE is $100,000:
>
> $$\$50,000 \times 2 = \$100,000$$

- You next determine the **exposure factor (EF)** for each risk/asset pair. This is the expected amount of damage that an asset would incur if a risk materialized. The exposure factor is normally described as a percentage. For example, if you expect that a burglary at your data center would result in 5% of your equipment being stolen, your exposure factor is 5%.
- You then identify the **annualized rate of occurrence (ARO)** by determining the likelihood that a risk will occur in a given year. You write this as the number of times you expect that the risk will materialize in any year. For example, if you expect 2 robberies per year, your ARO is 2. If you expect one robbery every five years, your ARO is 0.2.
- You then calculate the **single loss expectancy (SLE)** by multiplying the asset value by the exposure factor. This gives you the amount of money you expect to lose each time the risk materializes and is represented by the formula:

$$SLE = AV \times EF$$

- Finally, you compute the **annualized loss expectancy (ALE)**, or the amount of money you expect to lose each year to a given risk, by using this formula:

$$ALE = SLE \times ARO$$

Organizations that perform quantitative risk assessments can begin with those risks with the highest ALE. If you can find a way to control the risk where the cost of the control is less than the ALE, it is normally appropriate to implement that control.

Qualitative Risk Assessment

Qualitative risk assessment processes rely on expert opinion rather than cold, hard math. When performing a qualitative assessment, you ask an expert or group of experts to esti- mate the probability and impact of each risk/asset pair. You may then use this information in a manner similar to the way a quantitative risk assessment uses ALE to evaluate the types of controls you should put in place.

Risk Management Strategies

Once you have identified and prioritized your risks, you can move on to managing them with appropriate action. You have four basic options when performing risk management:

- **Risk avoidance**—In this approach, you simply change your business activities so that you no longer incur the risk. For example, if you are concerned about the risk of a fire in your data center, you might choose to shut down your data center! Risk avoidance is not always practical, for obvious reasons.
- **Risk acceptance**—You may choose to acknowledge that a risk exists but deliberately decide to take no action because the costs of other risk management strategies outweigh the benefits.
- **Risk mitigation**—This is the strategy most commonly used by IT professionals. In risk miti- gation, you implement controls designed to lessen the probability and/or impact of a risk.
- **Risk transference**—In the final risk management strategy, you transfer the risk to a third party. The most common example of this is purchasing insurance.

You can take any possible response to a risk and classify it into one or more of these basic strategies.

The Importance of Using a Structured Approach to Risk Assessment

It is important to use a structured approach to any risk assessment. Without an underlying system, it is easy to become too subjective and assign a high risk rating to every scenario. For example, suppose you have been asked to do a risk assessment on the customer orders database for a manufacturing company. The **cost of impact** and the **cost of replacement** for that database are roughly one-third of the annual budget of the organization, so your initial reaction might be to call it a high level of risk. To mitigate this temptation, you should follow predetermined workflows and use risk-assessment models.

Considerations for Designing a Risk Assessment

There are many risk assessment best practices to draw from. The most effective way to perform one depends on the scope of the IT infrastructure and assets, as well as the business needs of the organization. Below are some ideas for you to consider while designing a risk-assessment approach:

- **Create a risk assessment policy**—This policy governs how risk assessments should be performed, both immediately

 NOTE

The four risk management strategies— avoidance, acceptance, transference, and mitigation—are important to keep in mind.

and in the future. It also specifies how frequently to perform risk assessments and the appropriateness of each of the four risk-management strategies—avoidance, acceptance, transference, and mitigation. Many companies create this policy after their first risk assessment.

- **Define goals and objectives**—This allows you to determine the success of the risk assessment. These will vary by organization, but might include things like "reduce the number of significant virus incidents to three per year."

- **Describe a consistent approach or model**—Using the same approach or risk assessment model every time a risk assessment is performed is the only way to accurately define trends within the organization. For example, if the first risk assessment used a quantitative model, and the next used a qualitative model, it would be difficult to decide if the overall risk to the organization had gone up or down.

- **Inventory all IT infrastructure and assets**—If no one remembers that the router sitting behind a stack of boxes in the network closet exists, it is unlikely that the password to administer it will be changed regularly. It seems unlikely that a major component of IT infrastructure, such as a router, could simply be forgotten, but it does happen.

- **Determine the value (either quantitatively or qualitatively) of each asset**—This value helps you prioritize risk mitigation projects.

- **Determine a "yardstick" or consistent measurement to determine the criticality of an asset**—This yardstick can be monetary value, as described above, or it can take into consideration the importance of an asset to the organization, or even whether a particular asset is mandated through industry regulation. The key is consistency. Without a standard way of determining criticality, it is impossible to really know whether the router that one member of the risk assessment team deemed "critical" is really more important than the server that another team member deemed "major."

- **Categorize each asset's place within the infrastructure as "critical," "major," or "minor"**—This exercise is useful if your organization does not have the resources (either time or budget) to thoroughly secure every asset in the infrastructure. This is very common, in fact. Most organizations have budgetary or staff limitations that preclude securing every single asset. In this case, a **multilayered approach** on the most critical or major components offers a reasonable overall level of security by implementing a set of complementary and overlapping security controls.

Do You Have Servers in Your Walls?

A company ran a file server that never went down, and for years, no one needed to work with it directly. It was located in a small wiring closet that was closed up during an office remodel. When an IT technician performed an inventory audit a few years later, he realized the server was missing. He knew it hadn't been stolen, and was still running, because the functionality was available. Eventually, he found the wires and followed them to a blank wall where the wiring closet had been. The company had to cut through the wall to get to the server. This could have been avoided had the company maintained a complete IT inventory and kept it up to date.

Because the risks faced by any given organization are unique to that organization, there is no one right way to conduct a risk assessment. Instead, consider the outcome of the risk assessment: What do you (or your manager) need to know? Often, a risk assessment is done to justify spending on IT security infrastructure. In this case, you would need to concentrate on the quantitative aspect of risk—how much a breach could cost the organization compared with the proposed investment.

Another common driver for risk assessment is an actual security incident. In this situation, your manager wants to know how likely it is that another incident will occur and how your proposed solution will mitigate that risk. Here, a qualitative approach is more appropriate (although a cost analysis would also be an important aspect of the analysis).

Next, consider the assets you are trying to protect. What are they worth, both monetarily and in terms of impact to the organization? Ideally, every asset would be protected, but you should always weigh the cost of protection against the value of the asset. Unless a desktop printer has a deeply strategic importance to the organization, it is unlikely that the asset is worth enough to justify a sophisticated access control system. Such a system is expensive to implement and costs the user time and energy that is probably not justified. A database containing sensitive information that falls under governmental regulation, on the other hand, is important enough to justify significant efforts to protect it.

Value, Situation, and Liability

Once you have assessed the potential risks to a system, the next step is to design an appropriate access control system to mitigate those risks. In the following sections, you will first consider the financial aspect of risk. This is where you get the clearest picture of the worst-case scenario, the crisis you are working to avert. You'll then evaluate where access controls are most needed, and how secure those controls must be in order to protect the assets at risk.

Potential Liability and Nonfinancial Impact

You read about determining the financial impact of a security breach earlier in the chapter. However, security breaches are not only a financial risk. Depending on the information being protected, a security breach could also result in criminal prosecution. Governmental regulations of the healthcare and banking industries, for example, carry heavy criminal penalties as well as fines for companies that fail to prevent a security breach. If you are responsible for securing systems in a regulated industry, the financial impact of a loss is likely less of a concern than the nonfinancial consequences, such as prison time.

Where Are Access Controls Needed Most?

You cannot secure everything, so you must prioritize. At the same time, many resources can be grouped to share a single access control. For example, a single point of access control at the entry point of the network may be sufficient to protect all the assets on the network. Unless there is an asset of special importance stored on the network, it is unnecessary to place separate access controls on each asset.

FIGURE 4-2

Network diagram.

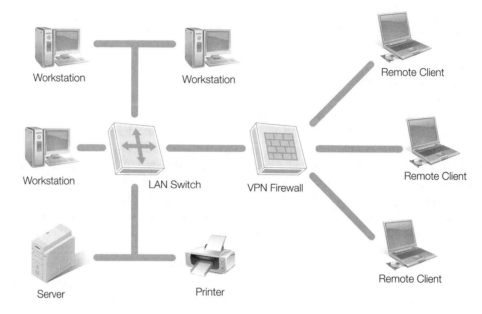

A network diagram, such as the one shown in **FIGURE 4-2**, is a helpful tool in determining where to place access controls on a network. In Figure 4-2, each of the elements shown is an access control point. The workstations and servers all may have access controls limiting who may log on. The firewall has access controls limiting the traffic that may enter and leave the network. The switch may control which ports are able to view traffic. Finally, the printer may be restricted so that only certain users may access it.

How Secure Must the Access Control Be?

Once you know where the access controls should be placed within the system, the next step is to determine how secure they must be. Again, you should weigh the value of the assets and their relative-risk level against the cost and inconvenience of the access control. A high-priority asset with a risk level of "high" justifies a more sophisticated (and probably more expensive and inconvenient) level of access control than a low-priority asset.

In many cases, a simple username and password system is sufficient to protect the assets in question. For more critical assets, two or more layers of access control provide additional protection. For example, the U.S. government uses a multilayered approach to securing classified information. Classified documents may only be opened and discussed within areas defined as Sensitive Compartmented Information Facilities, or SCIFs. These areas have physical and informational security measures around the perimeter, including armed guards and smart card ID scanners. Once inside the SCIF, a user must provide a fingerprint or retinal scan, as well as a username and password to access the computers and files stored within the SCIF.

You may not ever deal with classified documents, but you should be able to design a multilayered access control system for sensitive information such as health records or banking information. In the private sector, the most common multilayered access control systems use a token or challenge-response device coupled with a username and password.

Case Studies and Examples

Case studies are an invaluable tool when performing a risk assessment. Rather than trying to re-invent the wheel, you can use case studies to learn how others assessed risk in similar situations to yours. In this section, you will see how risk assessments are performed in real-world situations.

> **NOTE**
>
> No access control system is 100% secure. A determined attacker, with plenty of resources and time, can break into just about any system. The key is to deter the casual attacker and to make your organization a hard enough target to encourage even dedicated attackers to look elsewhere. This way, only an attacker with a specific interest in your organization will continue the attack.

Private-Sector Case Study

In private industry, risk is understood in terms of profit and loss, and business continuity. How would a security breach affect the ability of the business to continue to run? What would it cost the company in lost revenue?

Let's look at the example of Acme Pharma, a large pharmaceutical company in the United States. Acme Pharma needed to update their network security infrastructure to bring them into compliance with new federal regulations. The first step was to identify what needed updating and the risks they were intending to mitigate. The existing system consisted of a border firewall with a demilitarized zone (DMZ) for web servers. There was email antivirus and antispam software and some access controls implemented on the internal network.

The first step in the update was assessing what the risks to the environment were, and what the highest-risk systems were. Their IT department determined that some of the highest-risk systems did not need to be on the corporate Intranet and were segmented off into their own protected LAN. From there, extra layers of security were implemented in case of border network breaches. Network-based **intrusion detection systems (IDSs)** and **intrusion prevention systems (IPSs)** were implemented to detect and block suspicious network traffic.

On web-facing systems, automated patching was implemented, as well as host-based firewalls and host-based intrusion prevention systems. It was also determined that the servers themselves exposed too much information. Each website hosted on the server was given its own users, with rights limited to the directories that the website needed to have access to.

The risk assessment showed that certain websites were actively targeted for attacks. These systems were segmented away from the rest of the DMZ and further protected with pass-through proxies and application-level firewalls. It was then determined that security needed to be an ongoing priority. To achieve this goal, a new monitoring team was formed. Log shipping (automatic backup of transaction logs) was implemented and automated monitors were created. Procedures for manual monitoring were also created, and there was active human monitoring of the network done to augment the automated monitors.

Finally, they performed a full audit of user rights and file access controls. Any user with enhanced rights was closely examined to determine the need for those rights. New user groups were formed based on the different roles in the company, and document access was

4

Assessing Risk and its
Impact on Access Control

regulated by these groups. Users with a need for heightened rights, such as systems administrators, were not automatically granted rights to all files—they also had to be a member of the appropriate role group.

A new file team was created to handle the roles and access rights. They were tasked with reorganizing electronic document storage. To verify user right levels and create forms to request elevated rights, they established who in each department could authorize access requests and established a policy for adding and revoking rights.

Through honest and accurate risk assessment, Acme Pharma was able to secure their infrastructure and move from a border-only security system to a defense-in-depth environment. The most valuable systems were determined to be too important and removed from the Intranet, removing any possibility of outside intrusion. They also established an access control policy to handle information access inside the organization.

Public Sector Case Study

In the public sector, threats are sometimes literally about life and death. Consider the U.S. Department of Defense. If an unauthorized user accesses sensitive battle plans, soldiers' lives could be at risk. Of course, the public sector encompasses far more than just the military. The U.S. Department of Energy is a very high-profile target—especially the various research labs they maintain around the country.

Consider the Pacific Northwest National Laboratory (PNNL). PNNL is a U.S. Department of Energy Office of Science National Laboratory. It works on solving problems in energy, the environment, and national security. It has over 4,000 employees conducting research that translates into practical solutions to some of the most vital challenges facing the United States. This makes PNNL a very tempting target.

According to Jerry Johnson, CIO of PNNL, 10% of their connection requests are attacks. That translates to around 3 million attacks a day. They also receive over 1 million spam messages a day—around 97% of all email sent to the laboratory.

These intrusion attempts come from a wide range of attackers, including organized crime and foreign governments, as well as skilled individuals. Motives for these attacks include economic, national security, and the challenge of breaking into a government facility. The targets of the attack include intellectual property, other proprietary data, and valuable employee information such as Social Security numbers.

To add further complexity to the problem, the lab needs the ability to share data and computer resources with authorized scientists around the world. Security is important, but collaboration is vital. The attackers are also evolving and becoming more sophisticated. Given time, they could defeat any one security mechanism put in place.

To handle this difficult situation, PNNL has implemented a seven-layer defense-in-depth strategy. Each layer is intended to stop any attacks that defeated the layer above it:

- Layer 1 is the implementation of enclaves. They have Extranet enclaves to host their publicly accessible servers, as most companies do. Unlike most companies, they also utilize Intranet enclaves. There are three internal security enclaves based on the sensitivity of the information and the threat to it. This allows PNNL to further secure its most sensitive information from security breaches.

- Layer 2 consists of border firewalls. They use a traditional network layer firewall both between the Internet and Intranet and between the Intranet enclaves. Application layer firewalls scan and remove known malware before it reaches the Internet. Over 4 million attacks a day are filtered out by the firewalls.
- Layer 3 is strong authentication. PNNL follows the recommendations of the National Institute of Standards and Technology. They require at least eight characters, using mixed case and a numeric or special character. Users are also required to change their password every 6 months. All user-generated passwords are tested to make sure they cannot be guessed easily.
- Layer 4 is configuration and patch management. It is vital to effectively manage your security devices. A border firewall does no good if it has an exploitable bug. PNNL utilizes automated patch and configuration updates to every network device, from firewall to network printer. The organization also utilizes a least-user privilege policy, which mandates that users be given the most restrictive set of privileges possible to perform necessary functions. This reduces the risk of users intentionally or accidentally introducing security flaws.
- Layer 5 is host-based firewalls. Malware can enter your network through numerous channels that circumvent your border protections. websites, thumb drives, and installation disks are some examples. There is also the risk of insider threats. To defend against this, the PNNL utilizes host-based firewalls. These serve two purposes:
  - They protect workstations from attacks that have defeated the border protections.
  - They isolate infected workstations.

  If malware gets onto a workstation through an unknown attack vector, the host-based firewall keeps it from spreading to the Intranet.
- Layer 6 is data encryption. Any mobile device that stores data at the PNNL is required to have full disk encryption. This extends past laptops and includes smart phones and USB thumb drives.
- Layer 7 is one of the most important and least technical: awareness and training. Users are the weakest link in any network security effort. People can make mistakes and can override controls. Effective user training is the only defense against phishing attacks, especially sophisticated **spear phishing** attacks tailored to attack specific users. These can get malware, especially malware that attacks unknown vulnerabilities, into an Intranet. PNNL's aggressive user awareness program has reduced its phishing victimization rate far below that of similar organizations.

No network is 100% secure, but by using a defense-in-depth strategy, PNNL can reliably secure their sensitive infrastructure. This strategy allows them to further secure data and facilities that are at the highest risk.

> **NOTE**
>
> PNNL requires two-factor authentication for any remote access to the PNNL network. PNNL utilizes a token system that requires a user to know a PIN and have the token. This is a little inconvenient to the users but adds very strong protection against session attacks and keystroke loggers.

Critical Infrastructure Case Study

In some cases, the biggest factor in a risk assessment does not directly affect profit and loss or even injury to patrons, but damage to critical infrastructure. That infrastructure can include loss of IT resources such as a network or Intranet site, or it can refer to physical infrastructure like the controllers for a hospital's emergency power generators. In these cases, risk assessment should be focused on the loss of productivity or the ability of an organization to fulfill its core mission, rather than on loss of revenue. Let's look at a case where a failure to assess the risks to the system led to lax access controls with unfortunate consequences.

The incident happened at a local water treatment facility in Maroochy Shire, Queensland, Australia. A large amount of sewage was released into parks, rivers, and the grounds of a hotel by a former contractor who worked for the facility, causing major environmental and economic damage. While he was eventually caught, the damage was already done.

The attacker had several advantages because he was familiar with the system and had a copy of the software needed to communicate with the controllers. However, several vulnerabilities contributed to the incident. The system used inadequately protected wireless communication, giving the attacker an easy vector to compromise the system. The administrators at the treatment facility also failed to have a proper access control policy in place. As it turned out, the contractor still had full security rights to the system even after he was terminated. A proper access control policy would incorporate procedures for quickly removing accounts that should no longer have rights, thereby preventing or complicating an attack.

The administrators of the system also never considered the threat of an inside attack. They assumed that the proprietary nature of the controlling software and complexity of systems would keep the systems secure. An access control policy that included provisions for removing access when necessary would have greatly reduced the possibility for this attack. Had the risks to this system been accurately assessed, the access control policy would have been expanded and an effective wireless security system could have been implemented.

CHAPTER SUMMARY

Risk assessments are used to identify potential threats and vulnerabilities and prioritize steps designed to minimize or mitigate those risks. There are two basic types of risk assessment: qualitative and quantitative. Qualitative risk assessments are the more subjective of the two types. In a qualitative risk assessment, you assign a label of high, medium, or low, based on a number of factors including overall impact of a perceived threat, its probability of occurrence, and the value of the assets being threatened. In a quantitative risk assessment, you would assign a dollar value to each element of risk, making it easy to prioritize mitigation projects.

Case studies are a good place to start when considering a risk assessment project. Rather than reinventing the wheel, you can learn from what others have done and apply those lessons to your own situation. Assessment models are another useful tool. They help ensure that you analyze risks logically and do not overestimate the true risk.

KEY CONCEPTS AND TERMS

Algorithm
Annualized loss expectancy (ALE)
Annualized rate of occurrence (ARO)
Asset value (AV)
Control
Cost of impact
Cost of replacement
Exposure factor (EF)

Heightened access
Intrusion detection system (IDS)
Intrusion prevention system (IPS)
Multilayered approach
Password cracking
Password hash
Phishing
Probability of occurrence

Qualitative risk assessment
Quantitative risk assessment
Risk assessment
Single loss expectancy (SLE)
Spear phishing
Tailgating
Threat
Vulnerability

CHAPTER 4 ASSESSMENT

1. Risk is measured in terms of _____ and impact.

2. Risk assessment is the first step in designing any access control system.

A. True
B. False

3. The two types of risk assessments are qualitative and _____.

4. Vulnerabilities and threats are synonymous.

A. True
B. False

5. A vulnerability is a weakness purposely designed into the system.

A. True
B. False

6. You should consider probability of occurrence in order to prioritize limited time and resources.

A. True
B. False

7. What are the three primary threats to any access control system?

A. Password cracking
B. Heightened access
C. Social engineering
D. Forgotten passwords

8. A strong password that would take an attacker 10 years to crack in 2010 would take 10 years to crack today.

A. True
B. False

9. As long as users choose strong, secure passwords, how those passwords are stored is irrelevant.

A. True
B. False

10. Insecure applications run as the administrative user is the most common heightened access vulnerability.

A. True
B. False

11. You should weigh the value of the assets and their relative risk level against the cost and inconvenience of the access control.

A. True
B. False

12. You calculate ALE by multiplying SLE by 12.

A. True
B. False

13. You should install every patch that is released for the applications running in your environment.

A. True
B. False

14. Calculate the ALE of a threat that can be expected to occur three times per year and will cost the organization $50,000 per incident.

15. You are evaluating the risk of an attack on your data center. You estimate that an attack attempt will succeed three times per year. The value of the data center is $1.5 million and a successful attack will damage 10% of the data center.

    A. What is the asset value?
    B. What is the exposure factor?
    C. What is the SLE?
    D. What is the ARO?
    E. What is the ALE?

PART II

Implementing Access Control Systems

Access Control in the Enterprise

ACCESS CONTROL AND AUTHENTICATION within an enterprise is a large-scale problem with multiple solutions. Each enterprise has its own way of handling it, depending on the risk associated with the information and activities on the network. The higher the risk of an attacker entering an organization and seeing or removing information, the more constraints the enterprise will put on users. An organization that maintains a large amount of credit card information or personally identifiable information (PII) on its customers will sustain a higher impact if that information is removed or accessed illicitly. Corporations are now required to let a third party know when certain information has been compromised within their systems. The reaction to this breach in information may stop people or other enterprises from doing business with them.

Chapter 5 Topics

This chapter covers the following topics and concepts:

- Access control lists (ACLs) and access control entries (ACEs)
- Which access control models are common in enterprise environments
- Authentication factors and the risks associated with them
- What Kerberos is and how it works
- How Layer 2 and Layer 3 access controls protect the network
- Which access controls are associated with wireless local area networks (WLANs)
- What single sign-on is and how to use it
- Which best practices help you implement access controls in an enterprise environment
- Case studies and examples

Chapter 5 Goals

When you complete this chapter, you will be able to:

- Understand how ACLs and ACEs are related and how to use them
- Identify mandatory access control (MAC), discretionary access control (DAC), role-based access control (RBAC), and **attribute-based access control (ABAC)**, and other models
- Understand authentication factors and the strengths and weaknesses of something you know, something you have, and something you are
- Understand Kerberos, the Kerberos-trusted Key Distribution Center (KDC), the Kerberos Ticket-Granting Service (TGS), and the Kerberos Authentication Service
- Identify Layer 2 and Layer 3 techniques for controlling network access
- Implement security for a WLAN infrastructure
- Plan for single sign-on access control
- Apply best practices to access control implementation in an enterprise environment
- Apply lessons learned from case studies to real-world situations

Access Control Lists (ACLs) and Access Control Entries (ACEs)

In this section, you'll review the definitions of access control lists and access control entries, then take a closer look at these important security features. An **access control list (ACL)** is made up of **access control entries (ACEs)**. An ACE contains at least two items, a **security identifier (SID)** and one or more authorization levels for each SID. A SID is created for a user, group, or computer account when a new account is first created on a network. The authorization levels established against a user, group, or system are allowed, denied, or audited.

TABLE 5-1 provides an example of ACL permissions and what they mean. These permissions define the capabilities that are given or denied to the access control subject.

An ACL is bound to any object that has security permissions, such as a file, directory, port, process, or event. An ACL can be used in applications, operating systems, and configuration of network devices such as routers. There are two types of access control lists:

 NOTE

Most ACLs contain access control entries. However, an ACL can contain no entries. This permits either full access or no access to an object, depending on the operating system.

- **Discretionary access control list (DACL)**—Contains ACEs that allow or deny subjects permission to interact with objects
- **System access control list (SACL)**—Contains ACEs that allow system administrators to require auditing of the success and failure of attempted interactions with objects

TABLE 5-1 ACL permissions

PERMISSIONS	DEFINITIONS
Delete	Allows the ability to delete the object
Read	Allows the ability to read the object
Write	Allows the ability to write to the object
Modify	Allows the ability to read, write, execute, and delete (may not include file permissions)
Execute	Allows the ability to execute a program
Full Control	Allows all abilities including permissions
No Access	Denies access to the object

An SACL is usually established by a systems administrator. A DACL is set up by the owner of an object. An object ACL may have multiple ACEs associated with it. Some ACEs create permissions conflicts. In this case, permission resolution takes place based on the operating system such as Windows or UNIX. Most systems use a least-privilege security principle. This principle states that if a user is in multiple groups with multiple permissions, the least permissive permission will be granted. For example, let's say Kevin is an employee who has been granted access rights. He has full control permissions (most permissive) and no access permissions (least permissive) applied to him, which causes a conflict. To resolve the conflict, Kevin will be provided no access.

> **⬛ NOTE**
>
> When people discuss an ACL, they're usually referring to the DACL. If no criteria have been established against an object, the system grants an implicit "deny" to prevent access.

Confidentiality, Integrity, and Availability

Confidentiality, integrity, and availability (C-I-A) are large components of access control. In order to define risk associated with a subject accessing an object, you must understand the object and the system being accessed. The following are brief descriptions of the components of C-I-A:

- **Confidentiality**—Ensuring the right information is seen only by subjects that are authorized to see it
- **Integrity**—Ensuring a system is not changed by a subject that is not authorized to do so
- **Availability**—Ensuring a system is accessible when needed

Some systems' security professionals refer to the C-I-A triad as the "A-I-C" triad (availability, integrity, and confidentiality) to avoid confusion with the U.S. Central Intelligence Agency, which is commonly referred to as the CIA. Either abbreviation is acceptable. However, if you use C-I-A, make sure people understand you're referring to confidentiality, integrity, and availability.

Access Control Models

Access control models are the core that identifies how a user accesses an object. An enterprise determines the best model based on the organization's structure, the policies within the organization, and the benefits and risk associated with implementation. You'll read about several models in the next section.

- **Discretionary access control (DAC)**—Policy defined by the object owner
- **Mandatory access control (MAC)**—Policy defined by the system
- **Role-based access control (RBAC)**—Policy defined by the functions the user performs within the organization—for instance, roles can be Human Resources or Finance
- **Attribute-based access control (ABAC)**—Policy a function of a subject's characteristics
- **Rule-based access control (RuBAC)**—Policy defined by a set of rules determined by the system administrator
- **Risk-adaptive access control (RAdAC)**—Policy changes dynamically based on the risk environment

 TIP

Be careful not to confuse the acronyms for rule-based access control (RuBAC) and **role-based access control (RBAC)**. To make things more confusing, some people use the acronym RBAC for *both* models. For this reason, it is a good idea to simply write out the entire term instead of relying on the acronyms for these two models.

The following sections describe access control models in more detail.

Discretionary Access Control (DAC)

The **discretionary access control (DAC)** model is the most widely used access control method. It is defined by the Trusted Computer System Evaluation Criteria (TCSEC) as "a means of restricting access to objects based on the identity of subjects and/or groups to which they belong. The controls are discretionary in the sense that a subject with certain access permission is capable of passing that permission (perhaps indirectly) on to any other subject (unless restricted by mandatory access control)."

DAC allows the owner of a resource to manage who can or cannot access the item. Owners maintain this access through ACLs, and they can delegate the ability to modify permissions to others. This removes the need for systems administrators to determine the importance of a document and who should have the necessary control. It puts the responsibility in the hands of the owner of the resource. Other than some highly specialized cases in the defense industry, every modern operating system supports DAC.

FYI

The Trusted Computer System Evaluation Criteria (TCSEC) are a set of requirements used to rate the security of a computer system. The U.S. Department of Defense (DoD) National Computer Security Center established the TCSEC. An entity in the "Rainbow Series," it is often referred to as the **Orange Book** because of the color of its cover, but its official listing is DoD 5200.28-STD. The original version was created in 1983 and was updated in 1985. TCSEC was replaced by the **Common Criteria for Information Technology Security Evaluation** (ISO 15408) in 2005. These days, it is referred to as simply Common Criteria or CC.

Mandatory Access Control (MAC)

Mandatory access control (MAC) allows a systems administrator to maintain the security aspect of an object. It was established by TCSEC and is defined as "a means of restricting access to objects based on the sensitivity (as represented by a label) of the information contained in the objects and the formal authorizations (i.e., clearance) of subjects to access information of such sensitivity." MAC systems are sometimes used by government agencies to implement the national security classification system. The use of MAC in these cases ensures that one user cannot grant a second user access to information that would exceed the second user's security clearance. For example, a user with access to a Top Secret document could not delegate that access to a user who possesses only a Confidential security clearance.

The access for an object is based on the sensitivity of the object versus the subject matter. The object's access is related to the user who is attempting to access it. For example, if an object has a classification of Secret, the subject attempting to access the object must have a clearance of Secret or Top Secret. No ACLs are associated with the object, and neither the object nor the system user can change the sensitivity level. Similarly, a subject with a Top Secret clearance has access to an object that is at or below the clearance level.

MAC is considered one of the most secure access methods because it requires both the object and the subject to have security labels assigned to them. It is often used in a **multilevel security (MLS) system**. A MLS system allows the computer system to simultaneously process information of different classification levels and ensures a subject with the correct clearance can access only the information at his or her authorization level. In contrast, a **multiple single level (MSL) environment** does not allow different classification levels to commingle. A separate system would be used for each classification level.

FYI

Most access control systems can also be described as **identity-based access control (IBAC)** systems. This simply means that the access control decisions made by the system are based on the identity of the user.

Role-Based Access Control (RBAC)

Role-based access control (RBAC) is also known as nondiscretionary access control. It grants access to an object based on the subject's role within the system. Three aspects are taken under consideration within an RBAC system:

- **Role assignment**—A subject can execute a transaction only if the subject has selected or been assigned a role. All active users are required to have an active role. For example, if the user Kevin is assigned to the Human Resources role, he is allowed to perform only the actions that this role allows.
- **Role authorization**—A subject's active role must be authorized for the subject. This ensures that users can only take on roles that they are authorized for.
- **Transaction authorization**—A subject can execute a transaction only if the transaction is authorized for the subject's active role.

Bell-LaPadula Model

Confidentiality rules within the U.S. government were established through the **Bell-LaPadula Model** and are described in the Orange Book. A MLS system is a Bell-LaPadula system. Three security principles are used in this model:

- **Simple security rule**—A subject cannot read an object that maintains a higher security level. It is also known as the "no read up" rule. A user with a Secret security clearance cannot read a document with a higher classification such as Top Secret.
- ***- property rule**—A subject cannot write to an object that maintains a lower security level. It is also known as the "no write down" rule, or the "star property" rule. A user with a Top Secret clearance cannot write to a document that has a lower classification such as Secret.
- **Strong *- property rule**—A subject can read and write to an object only if the object classification and the subject's clearance match exactly.

Administering access within an RBAC system is considered easier for the administrator because the access is based on roles within the organization and what each role is allowed to do. For example, an administrator may define a Human Resources role for the entire HR organization. If Kevin moves from the HR department to the finance department, he is simply removed from the Human Resources role and placed in the Finance role.

Separation of duties expands the RBAC controls. For example, although Kevin's role may be Finance, this does not mean that he needs full access to all financial data. Separating each role into the activities users are responsible for provides more granular access control. This ensures that no single user has enough control to compromise the system. This mechanism helps to deter fraud, ensuring that at least two people are required to perform a critical task. Separation of duties is also related to the least-privilege security principle. This principle states that a user should not have any more access than is necessary for the user to do his or her job.

FYI

Some complex access control systems that span multiple organizations may also use **organization-based access control (OrBAC)**, which also applies differing policies based on the user's organizational membership.

Attribute-Based Access Control (ABAC)

Attribute-based access control (ABAC) systems grant access to the subject based on additional attributes that they must verify. For example, when accessing a system that is available only to residents of a particular town, the subject may have to enter an address within that town. This allows the administrator to have a more granular access control capability to the particular objects.

> **FYI**
>
> A MAC or DAC system uses ACLs for managing the access of information within a system. The RBAC method defines the access specifically on the role that the user has within the organization, and the operations in which that role can participate. A MAC or DAC focuses more on the information, whereas a RBAC system focuses more on the people and the actions they can or cannot do.

Attribute-based access control systems are an example of contextual access controls that use information about the current state of the user, connection, and device to make authorization decisions. Another common example of contextual access control is **history-based access control (HBAC)**, which takes the past and present activity of the user into account when making access control decisions. For example, if a user who never logs on from nonoffice locations suddenly logs on from a foreign country, an HBAC system might deny this connection attempt because it differs from past activity.

 TIP

ABAC systems are growing in popularity among security administrators. If you would like to learn more, the definitive reference on this topic is NIST Special Publication 800-162, "Guide to Attribute Based Access Control (ABAC) Definition and Considerations."

Many organizations today are adopting **Bring Your Own Device (BYOD) policies** that allow users to access corporate systems and data using personally owned devices. To protect assets, organizations often limit BYOD device access to data. For example, companies might allow BYOD devices to access email and calendaring systems but deny those same devices access to restricted file servers containing extremely sensitive information. This is another example of an attribute-based access control system, where the attribute used in the access decision is an attribute of the device being used, rather than the user's identity.

Rule-Based Access Control (RuBAC)

Rule-based access control (RuBAC) systems operate in a manner quite similar to MAC systems. The system administrator defines a set of rules for a system, service, or device, and then that set of rules determines future access.

The most common example of rule-based access control is a network firewall. Firewall administrators create a set of rules that describe the types of network traffic that are allowed to pass through the firewall. These rules may be based on source and destination Internet Protocol (IP) address, network protocol, network port, time of day, user identity, and many other attributes of the connection. When the rules used in RuBAC incorporate attributes of the user into those rules, the system may be considered both RuBAC and ABAC.

Risk-Adaptive Access Control (RAdAC)

Risk-adaptive access control (RAdAC) systems take a more sophisticated approach to security decisions by incorporating information about both the security risk of an access control decision and the operational need for action into the risk determination process. Traditional access control systems simply grant or deny access based on the defined access control policies. Risk-adaptive approaches take additional information into account, as shown in **FIGURE 5-1**.

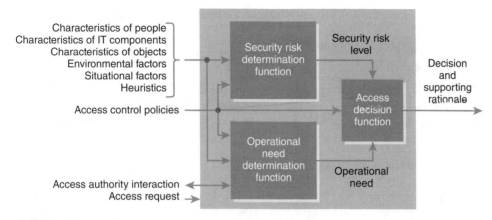

FIGURE 5-1

Risk-adaptive access control.

Data from National Institute for Standards and Technology.

Authentication Factors

Authentication, with regard to a subject, is validating the subject's claim of identity. There are multiple ways in which subjects can prove themselves.

Types of Factors

Ensuring the authenticity of the subject can be determined by three factors. The more factors a subject can provide, the more trust one can put in that subject:

- **Something you know**—An item that the subject is aware of or has knowledge of
- **Something you have**—An item that the subject has possession of
- **Something you are**—A characteristic of the subject

Something You Know

Having specific knowledge that is unique to a subject is one method of authentication. Examples of this factor include a password, a personal identification number (PIN), or a passphrase.

A password is generally combined with a unique identifier such as a username (or user ID), and it provides the additional authentication that the subject is legitimate. A password can have multiple limitations based on length, special characters, complexity, and reuse factor, or it may have no limitations. The more specific or unique a password is, the stronger it is, and; therefore, it has a lower chance of being guessed or cracked.

In the past, security best practice typically stated that users must use highly complex passwords and change those passwords regularly. In 2017, NIST released Special Publication 800-63B, "Digital Identity Guidelines," which turned conventional wisdom about password policies on its head. Under the new guidelines, NIST recommends the following practices:

- Do *not* require password changes unless the account is believed to be compromised. Password expiration policies promote bad habits such as writing down passwords.

- Require the use of multifactor authentication to strengthen access control security.
- Require the use of passwords that are at least eight characters long but do not implement any other complexity requirements, as these make passwords more difficult to remember.
- Implement password filtering that prevents users from adopting a password that:
  - Appears in a password dump list from previous breaches at other organizations
  - Consists only of dictionary words or slight variations of dictionary words
  - Contains repetitive or sequential character sequences, such as 12345678 or abcd1111
  - Contains contextual cues about the user's identity or the organization

With so many applications and tools that you log on to these days, using best practices and keeping passwords safe is becoming more difficult. Tools such as password managers or password vaults are available for storing your passwords, but these also require a form of authentication to retrieve the information. Tools that allow you to answer questions about yourself are a method that tends to remove passwords altogether or, in some instances, may be used to retrieve your password from an application. For example, Kevin may have forgotten the password for his mobile service online account. After Kevin selects "Forgot password," the application asks him security questions that were configured previously in his profile. Such questions may be:

- What is the name of your high school?
- In what city were you born?
- What is the name of your favorite childhood pet?
- What is the title of your favorite book?

Additional tactics could be a passphrase related to the application or the subject. For example, Kevin may be trying to log on to his 401(k) account but cannot remember the password. By creating a passphrase based on the tool he is accessing, Kevin may be able to add complexity and provide something he can easily recall:

Saving money for my future keeps me a happy Kevin = S$4mfkma:)K

Almost everyone is aware of the purpose of passwords, and many people use passwords daily. The problem is that passwords have turned into a risk. Years ago, when passwords were first implemented, they were relatively simple. Knowing how simple they were made it easier for attackers to steal them. Some of the ways that attackers steal passwords are:

- **Dictionary attacks**—Matching common words found in a dictionary to a user's password until a match occurs
- **Brute-force attacks**—Using software code to run through various password schemes with numbers, symbols, capital letters, and characters until a match occurs
- **Eavesdropping**—Listening in on a network to learn usernames and passwords
- **Social engineering**—Convincing users that they are connecting to a secure and well-known website, which is actually a site created by the attacker to obtain usernames and passwords

Weaknesses of knowledge-based methodologies. One of the biggest challenges in using passwords is memorizing them. As previously stated, you should avoid reusing passwords and avoid writing them down. Accessing applications irregularly only adds to the problem with passwords. For example, Kevin accesses his mobile online account once a month to pay the bill. He often forgets the password and the passphrase he created for the account. Today, he makes multiple attempts at logging on, but after his fifth failed password he is locked out. He now needs to call the mobile carrier and speak with a representative, who might ask Kevin for his Social Security number and date of birth. Answering these questions over the phone is a security risk, and one-on-one customer service is an extra expense for the mobile phone carrier. Due to the extra expenses and risk of resetting a password, an organization might not choose the safest mechanism because it may be too expensive to maintain and administer.

Third-party participants and tools also create havoc when only knowledge-based access authentication factors are used. You might have downloaded malware, such as a keystroke logger, to your computer without knowing it. These tools are used to steal your password, and your account can then become compromised. This can lead to the loss of money, personal information such as account numbers and Social Security numbers, and additional PII.

Trojan horse malware, which is also referred to as a Trojan, is another tool often used by attackers to pull password information from a user. When the Trojan is installed on a computer system, the attacker has complete access to the system. The subject may never know that it is there. Some of the malicious activities carried out by Trojans include:

> **NOTE**
>
> **Malware** is malicious software that inadvertently gets downloaded to your computer system without your knowing it. This software can be downloaded when surfing webpages, clicking on webpage items, opening email attachments, or executing an application that has malicious code embedded. Examples of malware are Trojan horses, keystroke logging tools, worms, and viruses.

- Viewing the screen of the computer system
- Keystroke logging
- Stealing passwords and PII
- Changing, deleting, and installing files

In addition to malware used on computer systems to gather information about the user, additional tactics have been implemented with changes and additions to technology:

> **⚠ WARNING**
>
> Removing a Trojan can be difficult because you don't know what damage it has inflicted on your system. Antivirus software can assist in blocking Trojans. It's highly important to keep antivirus software up to date; however, there is no fail-safe method for keeping a computer system secure.

- **Man-in-the-middle attacks**—The entire conversation between two parties is controlled by an attacker. The attacker can read and, at times, change the communication.
- **Phishing**—Used to steal **credentials** of subjects by sending them an email and asking them to log on to a site, answer questions, and provide information that compromises their account. This is a form of social engineering.
- **Spear phishing**—A form of phishing that targets specific individuals. The phishing communication may be sent to a large group of people, hoping that specific information for several of the individuals will be returned. When all the data is consolidated, a broader understanding of the organization and various credentials will allow the attacker access.
- **SMShing**—A form of phishing that is sent directly to the subject's phone. This is done through a Short Message Service (SMS) message.

5

Distribution of Passwords and PINs

So how exactly does a subject get an initial or saved password or PIN? How does authentication ensure that the subject is valid if the initial authentication failed? Should you allow the subject to reset his or her own password, or should you provide a temporary password?

Several options for password and PIN distribution are the postal mail, SMS messages, email, and the phone system. For instance, when Kevin is unable to log on to his online banking portal, the bank may choose to send him a temporary PIN. One option is to send this PIN to the cell phone he has registered with the bank. The bank sends Kevin an SMS message and asks him to enter the PIN into the portal within a preset amount of time, such as 60 seconds. The bank has identified this cell phone as Kevin's because he provided it during his initial enrollment process. The SMS message is the fastest and one of the safest ways to get the temporary PIN to Kevin. The bank may also choose to send a follow-up email to Kevin to inform him that the text was sent with a temporary PIN. If Kevin did not receive the SMS message, he should inform the bank as a precaution.

Another tactic for gaining information is called shoulder surfing. For instance, Kevin likes to work on his computer at his local coffee shop, but people around him may be able to see what he is doing, including entering passwords for his accounts. Although a password may be blocked out on the screen, the username is still available, and people can watch Kevin type his password on the keyboard and memorize the keystrokes.

The passwords used for various systems are also kept internally, on a workstation or server. How do enterprises secure them? How are passwords stored when you check a Remember Me checkbox on a website? The passwords maintained through a third-party application or through another tool should be encrypted so if hackers access them, the passwords cannot be read and used to gain access to your accounts.

Something You Have

In addition to something you know, something you have can help identify you and/or prove your claim of identity. This identifier can be an automated teller machine (ATM) card, a token, a driver's license, or a passport—anything that supports your identity claim simply because you have it. These forms of authentication do not require you to remember a password, but they are something you must have in your possession to authenticate. Consider an example where you visit a bank and request the withdrawal of funds. You can't simply walk up to the teller and say "I'm Bob, please give me $500." (Wouldn't that be nice?) The teller will certainly ask you to prove your claim of identity. You'd most likely satisfy this request by showing her your driver's license. The license contains your name and picture, and the teller uses it to authenticate you before giving you cash.

A token is a physical or software device that can be used instead of a password or in conjunction with a password or PIN. Tokens come in many forms, such as a card with a screen and/or a keypad. There are two varieties of token devices:

- **Synchronous tokens**—Use time or a counter as a means of authentication
- **Asynchronous tokens**—Use a challenge and response as a means of authentication

Smart card. A smart card is a card that is the same size as a credit card and has a computer chip embedded in it. The computer chip holds data pertaining to the owner of the card and is used in various transactions through a smart card reader. Smart cards are also referred to as integrated circuit cards (ICCs). Smart cards are considered reliable because the information stored within the card cannot be easily accessed if the card is lost or stolen, but it can be used by other subjects if additional forms of verification are not required.

There are two primary types of smart cards:

- **Contact smart card**—This type of card must be inserted into a smart card reader to gain authentication or access for the subject.
- **Contactless smart card**—This type of card is often used for access into facilities. Instead of having to insert the card into a reader, the subject waves the card in front of the reader to verify his or her access credentials. The subject receives access or is denied access to the location. Contactless cards are also known as proximity cards or "prox" cards.

Time-variable token. A time-variable token is a synchronous token in the form of a one-time password. It is a dynamic password in that it can be used only once. After a single use, it is no longer valid. A time-variable token is valid for a specific period of time, such as 60 seconds. When authentication is based on time, the token (hardware or software) time must be synchronized with an authentication server. The time and the seed record are the main components. The seed record is the **symmetric encryption** key, which is shared between the token and the authentication server. This seed record encrypts the clock time; the result is a one-time password. The same seed record is used for both the token and the authentication server. Because the authentication server knows that this token is the only other device with that seed record, it knows that the token code entered comes from the person holding this particular token.

FYI

A Common Access Card (CAC) was implemented under Homeland Security Presidential Directive 12 (HSPD-12). It is used by the DoD for authentication and access to federal facilities and computer systems. This card holds information regarding the user such as his or her identity, clearance level, and physical and logical access capabilities. In 1987, the International Organization for Standardization (ISO) and International Electrotechnical Commission (IEC) implemented ISO/IEC 7816 for ICC with contacts, such as smart cards.

Challenge-response device. A challenge-response device is an asynchronous token. Authentication occurs via communication with the token device, the authentication server, and the user. A request is sent to the authentication server and a challenge (a random set of numbers) is returned. The user enters this challenge into the token, the token encrypts it, and another value is returned. The user then uses this end value as the password. Once the authentication server receives this end value, it decrypts it. If the end value matches the challenge, the user is authenticated. This exchange between the user, authentication server, and token device is shown in **FIGURE 5-2**.

The most significant weakness in "something you have" authentication is that a possession-based authentication factor may be lost or stolen.

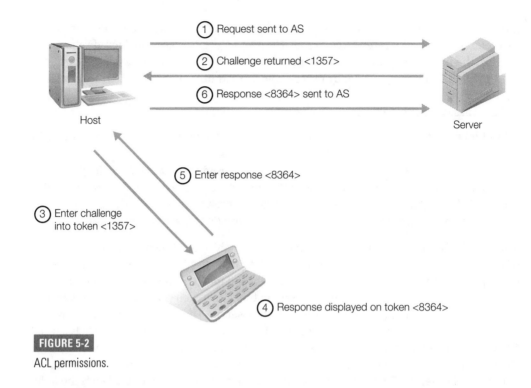

① Request sent to AS

② Challenge returned <1357>

⑥ Response <8364> sent to AS

Host

Server

⑤ Enter response <8364>

③ Enter challenge into token <1357>

④ Response displayed on token <8364>

FIGURE 5-2

ACL permissions.

Something You Are

Something you are authentication is based on characteristics about a specific person. The characteristics can be voice, facial features, retinal patterns, handwriting, and repetitive actions. These characteristics are called biometrics. This section provides only a brief summary of biometrics.

> **■ NOTE**
>
> Enrollment in a biometric system brings an extra level of security to the authentication system because the person must be physically present during the process. It is also an advantage for individuals because they will not need to remember a password to gain access.

The technology behind biometrics involves scanning and analyzing the unique characteristics of a user and matching them against information that was collected during enrollment. The information about individuals can be used for either identification or verification. Biometric access control systems may be physiologically based or behavior-based.

Physiologically based biometrics. Physiologically based biometric authentication uses attributes of the user that are unique. Such attributes include fingerprints, facial features, and retinal patterns. A scanning device scans for biometrics, and the subject must enroll his or her information before access is granted. When a user accesses a scanner, multiple points of reference are scanned, analyzed, and compared with the data stored in the database. If enough points match between the user and the database, access can be granted or denied.

The number of devices that use biometrics for authentication is increasing. Multiple universal serial bus (USB) and laptop manufacturers are incorporating this technology into their systems. Many companies now sell portable external fingerprint biometric scanners.

Behavior-based biometrics. Behavior-based biometric authentication creates a characteristic about users based on their patterns. These patterns can be generated from aspects such as their typing rhythm, which can be unique—different people type at a different pace and rhythm. Organizations can use biometric software to analyze users' typing rhythms. The software records the time that each key is depressed, as well as the length of time between keystrokes. A unique profile is created for each user. If an attacker tries to impersonate a user but types the user's password too slowly or too quickly, the attacker won't be authenticated.

Financial institutions use pattern matching for online web access. They may create a profile of a user based on the times he or she logs onto the system. If a user rarely logs onto the system at 3:00 a.m. on a Saturday, for example, the financial institution's website might prompt the user to enter additional information for verification purposes.

An individual's handwriting can also be used as an authentication method. This requires additional hardware when used with computer systems. Many stores already use handwriting authentication devices when accepting credit card purchases. Your signature is compared with the signature on your credit card.

The major weakness with biometric authentication is that users often find these techniques intrusive and inconvenient.

Factor Usage Criteria

Now that you understand the various methods of authentication, it is important to understand how they can work together to create a more secure environment and thwart identity theft. Understanding what the user is trying to access and the risk associated with a loss of the data determines what methods or combination of methods should be used.

Single-Factor Authentication

A **single-factor authentication** uses only one of the authentication factors (something you have, something you are, or something you know). This type of authentication tends to be associated with a password, and it's the least secure because of the simplistic nature of passwords. Because passwords have been around for a while, attackers have created tools and methods to get past them. Using symbols, special characters, and additional controls when creating passwords can help strengthen them. Some additional examples of a single-factor authentication are a driver's license and a house key.

Multifactor Authentication

Multifactor authentication approaches are the current standard for securing access to sensitive systems. In a multifactor authentication approach, individuals are asked to authenticate using at least two different techniques that fit into different factor categories. For example, a user might be asked to combine something they know (a password) with something they have (a mobile phone). Two of the most common forms of multifactor authentication are two-factor authentication and three-factor authentication.

Two-factor authentication requires a user to provide two independent authentication mechanisms from different categories in order to authenticate. Two-factor authentication is also referred to as strong authentication. It generally combines something you

NOTE

Is a debit or credit card a single-factor or a two-factor authentication method? Recently, some vendors have chosen not to require a PIN or signature when using a debit or credit card if the purchase is below a certain amount. Does this now make the credit card a single-factor authenticator? If the cashier does not compare the signature on the credit card with the signature on the slip, is the credit card a single-factor or two-factor authenticator?

have and something you know or something you have and something you are. For example, Kevin's organization has implemented two-factor authentication, which requires him to enter a PIN (something you know) and a token password (something you have). In order for an attacker to be able to access the same resource, he or she would need to know Kevin's PIN and have the token in hand. Another example of two-factor authentication is an ATM card (something you have) and the PIN (something you know). When Kevin wants to access the money in his banking account through an ATM machine, he needs to provide the debit card and the PIN in order to start the transaction.

Another form of two-factor authentication is something you are and something you have. For example, security managers of a government facility want to implement two-factor authentication for access to a secure area, but they do not want to use smart cards because the cards can be lost or stolen. To ensure that only authorized people can access the secure area, the managers may choose a two-factor authentication that requires a retinal scan followed by a PIN.

Three-factor authentication, also a form of strong authentication, includes all authentication factors of something you know, something you are, and something you have. For example, obtaining access to a highly classified room may require a badge, a PIN, and a retinal scan. Because the room is restricted to only a few people, authentication of those who enter is extremely important to ensure that the classified information inside the room does not get into the wrong hands.

SIDEBAR: Four or Five Factors?

Most security professionals recognize these three factors (something you have, something you know, and something you are) as the three standard authentication categories. You may also see lists of authentication factors that refer to four or five factors.

The first of these, somewhere you are, uses location-based authentication. This approach uses the physical location of the user as an authentication factor, assuming that someone in a restricted area is authenticated to some degree. It is arguable whether this is actually an authentication factor, as the person may have gained access to that facility using some other authentication approach, making location simply a proxy for those other techniques. Location is also not directly tied to an individual, because many people could have authorized access to the same physical location. While location-based controls are commonly used, they are not actually a means of authenticating an individual.

The second commonly cited factor, something you do, is known as behavior-based authentication. These techniques look at characteristic patterns of the user's behavior, such as their rate and patterns of typing, time of access, and similar characteristics. These approaches are not commonly accepted as reliably confirming a user's identity on their own, so they cannot be considered an authentication factor.

Kerberos

Kerberos is a network security protocol that provides authentication and authorization services on a network. Communication on an unsecure network allows attackers to listen in on the network to steal your credentials. Kerberos uses strong **cryptography** in order for the client to prove its identity to the server. Once the identity is proven, the communication is encrypted. Credentials obtained are used to verify the identity of the user and ensure the integrity of messages between the client and the system it's authenticating to. Some of the benefits associated with implementing a Kerberos system are:

- It prevents plaintext passwords from being sent over the network.
- It centralizes username and password credentials, making them easy to maintain and manage within any infrastructure size.
- It removes the vulnerability associated with storing passwords local to the computer system.

Kerberos is based on three systems: the Kerberos-trusted **Key Distribution Center (KDC)**, the Kerberos **Ticket-Granting Service (TGS)**, and the Kerberos **Authentication Service**. Kerberos provides the ability for systems to communicate in a secure manner over an unsecure network. Kerberos is also an example of a single sign-on system, providing enterprises with scalability and flexibility. Kerberos provides:

- **Transparency**—The user does not need to know that the Kerberos system exists. He or she simply knows that his or her credentials work across systems.
- **Security**—An attacker should not be able to obtain users' credentials. It provides confidentiality and authentication.
- **Scalability**—Administrators can use Kerberos to manage authentication in small to large-scale environments.

> **NOTE**
>
> The name "Kerberos" comes from Greek mythology, the three-headed dog that guarded the entrance to Hades. It is an authentication and authorization method that is currently being used in Windows operating systems.

FYI

Kerberos was developed in the late 1980s at the Massachusetts Institute of Technology (MIT) under the Athena program. It is based on Needham and Schroeder's trusted third-party authentication protocol. Kerberos is freely available through MIT but is implemented in many **commercial off-the-shelf (COTS)** products. The mechanisms for Kerberos are validated in Request for Comments (RFC) 4120. You can view RFC 4120 on the Internet Engineering Task Force website at *http://www.ietf.org/rfc/rfc4120.txt*.

How Does Kerberos Authentication Work?

The process for Kerberos authentication involves three primary steps: client authentication, client service authorization, and client service requests. It is important to understand the entire process because Kerberos authentication proves an identity across an unsecure network connection.

The following steps are performed during client authentication:

1. The user enters a user ID and password into the client.
2. The client performs a hash on the password, creating a secret key for itself and for the user.
3. The client sends a message of the user ID to the authentication server (AS) and requests services. This message is sent as **cleartext**—unencrypted. The AS performs a hash on the password of the user ID in its database. This creates a secret key.
4. The AS responds with two messages if the user is successfully authenticated. The two messages are:
   - A Ticket-Granting Ticket (TGT) for the server that has been encrypted using the secret key of the Ticket Granting Service (TGS)
   - A client/TGS session key, which is a temporary key encrypted using the secret key of the client/user
5. The client receives the two messages. After decrypting the client/TGS session key, the client uses the session key when communicating with the TGS in the future.

NOTE

An **authenticator** is a message that consists of the client ID and the timestamp.

The following steps are performed during client service authorization:

1. The client sends two messages to the TGS when requesting services:
   - The TGT and the ID of the requesting service
   - An authenticator encrypted by the client/TGS session key
2. When the two messages are received, the TGS decrypts the TGT with the TGS secret key. This results in the client/TGS session key. The TGS decrypts the authenticator and sends two messages to the client:
   - A client-to-server ticket, which is encrypted with the service's secret key. The client-to-server ticket includes the client ID, client network address, validity period, and client/server session key.
   - A client/server session key, which is encrypted with the client/TGS session key.

When a client requests a service, the following steps are taken:

1. The client connects to the service server and sends the following two messages:
   - A client-to-server ticket encrypted using the service's secret key
   - A new authenticator encrypted using the client/server session key; the new authenticator has the client ID and timestamp
2. The service server decrypts the ticket with its own secret key to retrieve the client/server session key. With the session keys, the service server decrypts the authenticator and sends a message to the client to confirm its identity and willingness to serve the client. The message includes the timestamp from the client's authenticator, which is encrypted using the client/server session key.
3. The client decrypts the confirmation message using the client/server session key and checks to see if the timestamp is updated correctly. If so, the client can trust the server and starts issuing service requests to the server.
4. The service server provides services to the client.

The Kerberos authentication, authorization, and service request processes are shown in **FIGURE 5-3**.

FIGURE 5-3

Kerberos for authentication, authorization, and service request.

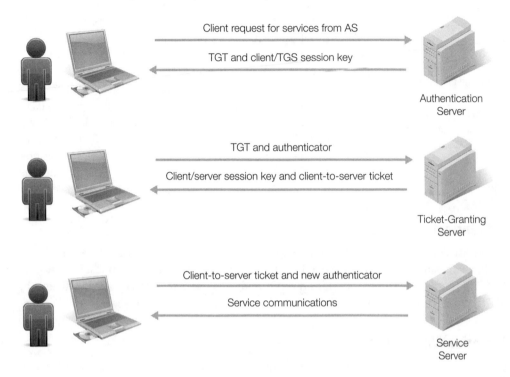

Client request for services from AS

TGT and client/TGS session key

Authentication
Server

TGT and authenticator

Client/server session key and client-to-server ticket

Ticket-Granting
Server

Client-to-server ticket and new authenticator

Service communications

Service
Server

Use of Symmetric Key and Trusted Third Parties for Authentication

Kerberos performs authentication as a trusted third-party authentication service via a shared **secret key** (symmetric key). When a client wants to obtain authentication credentials for a server that it does not have credentials for, the exchange between the authentication server and the client is initiated by the client. The client's secret key is used for encryption and decryption. This exchange obtains credentials for a TGS, which will also be used for obtaining subsequent credentials.

One of the primary reasons for implementing Kerberos is that without it, the principals do not trust one another. Principals can be applications, users, or network services. The principals trust only the Key Distribution Center (KDC), which is why the KDC creates tickets for the communication among the principals. Communication among principals is vouched for by the KDC, and the KDC ensures that it is acceptable for the principals to talk to one another.

Key Distribution Center (KDC)

The KDC acts as a trusted third party. The purpose of a KDC is to provide a secure environment for distributing keys. It provides tickets and temporary session keys for both initial tickets and ticket-granting requests and acts as both an authentication service and a ticket-granting service.

Because Kerberos is formed on symmetric encryption and shared secret keys, the database for all of the secret keys for the principals on the network is maintained by the KDC. As an authentication server, it authenticates a principal via a pre-exchanged secret key. After the authentication occurs, the KDC acts as a TGS. As a TGS, it provides a ticket to a principal establishing a trusted relationship among other principals. The principals trust the integrity of the KDC, which is an essential part of Kerberos security.

Principals are preregistered with a secret key in the KDS through a system registration process. A set of these principals is called a "realm," and the realm is used to administer logical group resources and users. When added to the Kerberos realm, the principal is given a realm key used for initial trusted communications. Once a principal becomes a member of a Kerberos realm, the principal can then be authenticated by the authentication server.

> **⬛ NOTE**
>
> A secret key has a long lifetime and is shared between the KDC and the client or server. It may be used for subsequent needs such as password changes. A session key is destroyed after the session is complete and is generated only when needed. The session key is shared between the client and the server.

Authentication Tickets

Tickets are generated by the KDC and provided to the principal when authentication is needed. For example, when Kevin needs to access a specific file share, a request is made to the KDC. The KDC, in return, provides the TGT and client/TGS session key. Kevin will use the TGT for authorization to the file share.

Potential Weaknesses

As a whole, Kerberos is a very secure protocol. However, all protocols have weaknesses. It is important to note that any weaknesses with Kerberos are based on the concepts within the protocol and not the underlying cryptography.

Like any authentication system, Kerberos can have weaknesses if improperly implemented. Security administrators should be aware of these potential weaknesses, which include:

- **Brute-force attacks**—The system is susceptible to brute-force attacks. Brute-force attackers simply repeatedly guess an account's password until they are successful. They typically start with a list of dictionary words and move on to try combinations and variations of dictionary words. If a user has a weak password, especially one that consists of dictionary words, it may be easily discovered.
- **Key storage**—All keys must be stored securely for the user and server. If this is not done correctly and an attacker gains access to the keys, the entire system could be compromised.
- **Kerberos tickets are cached on a user's computer system**—If an attacker were to obtain access to these tickets, he or she could impersonate that user on the network.
- **Clocks must be synchronized to complete authentication**—There is a time availability period, and if the times are more than 5 minutes apart, authentication will not occur.
- **Central server continuous availability requirement**—Authorization on a network is an occurrence that happens multiple times for principals. Loss of time can be costly to enterprises. Organizations must design networks so that the Kerberos components are always available to users and authentication is never compromised.

- **Requirement for host synchronization**—Ensuring that servers are available at all times requires the servers to have the same information. Synchronizing information between multiple servers and sites will minimize any downtime that occurs when a server or site goes offline.
- **Potential single point of failure**—The KDC is a single point of failure in the communication line. If the KDC were to go down, users would no longer be able to authenticate to any systems on the network. Loss of the KDC has a critical impact to the enterprise, and a business continuity plan needs to be designed around it. Part of this plan should include multiple KDC systems sharing information so that end-user access and productivity is never diminished.

Kerberos in a Business Environment

Many organizations use Kerberos daily for employee authentication and access to resources. Consider this example of appropriate use of Kerberos in the business environment, featuring Kevin.

Kevin logs on daily to the corporate network with his computer system. He provides a username and password. When Kevin logs on, his user ID is sent to the authentication server on the KDC. A TGT is provided to Kevin, and it is encrypted with Kevin's password (secret key). If it is the correct password, the TGT will be decrypted and access is granted to the computer system. The secret key will reside temporarily on the computer system.

Later in the day, Kevin needs to print some documents for his meeting. Kevin's system sends the TGT to the TGS on the KDC. The TGS creates a client/server session key and provides it to Kevin's system, which he uses to authenticate to the print server. This second ticket contains the session key that is encrypted by Kevin's secret key and another session key that is encrypted by the print server's secret key. This second ticket also contains a time-stamp and the computer system's IP address. These components added to the second ticket are the authenticator.

Kevin's system receives the second ticket, decrypts it with his secret key, and removes the session key. Kevin's system also adds a second authenticator and sends the ticket to the print server. The print server receives the second ticket and decrypts it with its secret key and removes the session key and the two authenticators. If the print server is able to decrypt the session key, it knows to trust Kevin's system because it knows the KDC created the ticket.

Remember that only the KDC has the key to encrypt the session key. Also, if the authenticators from the KDC and Kevin's computer system match, it knows the request was sent for the correct principal.

The beauty of Kerberos is that Kevin does not even need to be aware that any of this is taking place. It is the responsibility of Kerberos and the operating system to handle all of these ticket requests. Kevin merely needs to provide the correct username and password for his account.

Network Access Control

Network access control (NAC), sometimes called network admission control, is the use of policies within a network infrastructure to limit access to resources until the system proves that it has complied with the policy. Policies are defined by the network administrator and can apply to antivirus software, software versions, software updates, and other aspects of the computer system that might affect the security of the system and/or the network.

The components involved with NAC include computer systems, routers, switches, servers, and network firewalls. For example, a router might not allow you network access if you do not have the correct IP address associated with your computer system. Additional aspects for NAC are:

- Address tables on network devices such as routers or switches
- Segmenting the network via virtual local area networks (VLANs)
- Blocking or limiting access of certain protocols on the network VLANs
- Network devices similar to intrusion detection systems (IDSs) and intrusion prevention systems (IPSs)

Layer 2 Techniques

Layer 2 of the **Open Systems Interconnection (OSI) Reference Model** is referred to as the Data Link Layer. The Data Link Layer allows communication of systems within a **wide area network (WAN)** and communication of systems on the same **local area network (LAN)**. These networks may use Ethernet and **wireless local area network (WLAN)** protocols. Devices that support these protocols and, therefore, are associated with Layer 2 of the OSI model are bridges and switches. Sublayers to the Data Link Layer are:

- **Logical Link Control (LLC)**—Provides flow control, error notification, and acknowledgment
- **Media Access Control (MAC)**—Provides the determination as to who can talk when on a network connection

FIGURE 5-4 shows the OSI reference model and the location of the LLC and MAC layers.

MAC Address Database for LAN Switches

The MAC address is a unique identifier of a network device. Each MAC address is assigned by the vendor of the device and is associated with the network interface card (NIC). A MAC

FIGURE 5-4

The OSI Reference Model.

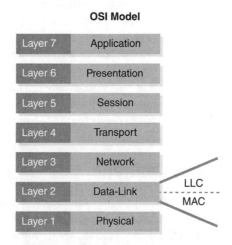

address is 48 bits in length and is identified as 12 hexadecimal digits. The first six hexadecimal digits identify the manufacturer and are provided by the IEEE (formerly known as the Institute of Electrical and Electronics Engineers). The last six hexadecimal digits identify the interface, like a serial number, and are provided by the vendor. A MAC address is burned into read-only memory (ROM) and is, therefore, considered permanent to the device. MAC addresses are written in this format:

MM:MM:MM:SN:SN:SN

When a device is powered up, the MAC address is sent out on the network connection, or the wire. The switch adds the MAC address and the port number on which it received the information to its MAC address table. The switch uses this table when it needs to communicate with a specific device. When the switch receives a communication request, it looks for the MAC address in its table and sends the communication out through the port identified in the table.

> ## IEEE
>
> IEEE is a professional not-for-profit organization designed to foster technical innovation. It was founded in 1884 in New York. The organization develops standards through the IEEE Standards Association (IEEE-SA) for information technology, power, transportation, information assurance, and other technologies and sciences. The IEEE 802 series of standards that specifically address local and metropolitan area networks are:
>
> - **IEEE 802.1**—Bridging and Management
> - **IEEE 802.2**—Logical Link Control
> - **IEEE 802.11**—Wireless
> - **IEEE 802.15**—Wireless Personal Area Networks
> - **IEEE 802.16**—Broadband Wireless Metropolitan Area Networks

MAC spoofing is done to bypass a network access control or to identify a system as one that has already been authorized by the access control. For example, a specific network allows only a certain set of MAC addresses. An attacker can find an approved MAC address and change his or her system to match it. This will allow the attacker to gain access to your network.

Defining Broadcast Domains

Broadcast domains fall within the Data Link Layer and allow network devices to broadcast their MAC addresses to everyone on that LAN. By limiting the number of devices on a domain, you limit the number of network devices that can talk to one another without a switch.

IEEE 802.1q Virtual Local Area Networks (VLANs)

VLANs are defined in the IEEE 802.1q standard. VLANs can be used to segment network traffic and limit communications among multiple networks. A VLAN is a collection of devices in a single broadcast domain. VLANs are used within an organization to separate networks with different resources. For example, a company may create a VLAN specifically for the HR department so that members outside this VLAN cannot access HR resources. It becomes another mechanism for defense in depth.

VLANs may even be used on a temporary basis for projects. If an organization has contractors working on a specific application, an administrator may restrict the contractors to a particular VLAN that allows access only to the specific application. The contractors can communicate with one another and the application within the VLAN, but they cannot generate traffic to the entire network. VLANs also reduce broadcasts, and; therefore, an administrator may design the network to limit such network traffic.

Layer 3 Techniques

Layer 3 of the OSI model is referred to as the Network Layer. It is responsible for transmitting traffic from a source network to its destination on a separate network. Some of the functions provided on the Network Layer are routing, forwarding, and addressing. Routers are the most common Layer 3 devices, although other devices, such as switches and firewalls, often perform Layer 3 functions. Routers maintain routing tables, which provide instructions on how to direct traffic to reach other networks.

Access Control Lists

You can configure access control lists on a router to deny certain access to a network or deny certain traffic from traveling on a network. A router examines each packet and determines whether the packet should be forwarded or dropped based on what is stated in the access control list. For example, an administrator may use an access control list to block File Transfer Protocol (FTP) traffic on part of a network but allow Simple Mail Transfer Protocol (SMTP) traffic for email.

Route Maps

Route maps are a way for an administrator to direct traffic on a network. A route map allows an administrator to define a routing policy before the routing table on the router is referenced. Creating a route map is sometimes called "policy-based routing." An administrator sets a policy that states "if . . . then." A route map can use multiple policies requiring that multiple matches of packets must occur before routing changes occur.

ACLs can be used to match specific policies. Route maps are similar to ACLs in that they are an ordered sequence of events resulting in either a permit or deny permission. A route map and an ACL are scanned in a specific order until a match occurs. A route map may use an ACL in order to match the specific criteria.

When a route map is applied to an interface and tested against specific criteria and the criteria matches, an action is taken. These actions can be used to modify the packet or modify the route. For example, a route map would be used to ensure only traffic with an internal IP address (192.168.1.X) is allowed out of a specific interface. If an IP address that does not match (192.168.5.X) is on the network, the route map's action would be to drop the packet. In this case, you can use a route map to ensure that IP addresses within a certain range do not leave the network.

Disabling IP Routing for Complete IP Traffic Isolation

In certain situations, disabling an entire IP network may be a necessary step. For instance, there may be a virus on the human resources network. Instead of allowing the virus to spread to other networks such as engineering or finance, an administrator may disable the network altogether.

> **NOTE**
>
> In practice, the CSO often delegates this emergency disconnect authority to individual members of the information security team. Providing trusted team members with this authority reduces the time to respond to a security incident in progress.

CEO/CIO/CSO Emergency Disconnect Prime Directive

Executives within an organization may take it upon themselves to remove any connection that their organization has to outside networks. For example, if an organization is being bombarded with **denial of service (DoS) attacks**, instead of trying to address each attack individually, the chief security officer (CSO) may decide to cut the connection so that the organization's network can be restored internally and an assessment of the damage can be made.

Wireless IEEE 802.11 LANs

IEEE has established the standard for WLANs. This particular standard is numbered 802.11 and was established in 1997. Subsequent amendments have been added to the standard to address connections at a higher radio frequency.

Establishing a standard ensures that all WLANs can operate with one another and that the controls for the networks are similar. Enabling WLANs within an organization is an easy way to control access, especially if people are not permanently located at the facility. In addition, an organization may have an area in the building where customers are allowed to gain network access. Instead of having multiple wired network connections, a wireless access point may be added to allow many people access to the network with little effort.

Access Control to IEEE 802.11 WLANs

A **service set identifier (SSID)** identifies a wireless network. It is the friendly name displayed to network users. For example, an organization might have two SSIDs: AcmeWidgets-Employees and AcmeWidgets-Guests, designated for their private and guest networks. All APs within range display their SSIDs, if they aren't configured to hide them.

Some APs may have security enabled, such as **Wi-Fi Protected Access (WPA)**. An attacker can connect directly to an access point if no security or access controls are configured on the AP. This creates an enormous risk to an organization and all of the information maintained on the internal network.

Identification

Enabling the MAC address table on a wireless AP limits the devices that are able to connect directly to it. For example, a building may hold a single company on each floor, and each of these companies may have several access points. Allowing the company on the 7th floor to

> ⚠️ **WARNING**
>
> Wired Equivalent Privacy (WEP) is not secure and should not be used. WPA provides stronger security and should always be used to protect wireless connections.

get on the company's network on the 8th floor is a security risk. Security may be enabled on each of the APs, but directly limiting the devices that are able to connect with the APs provides in-depth defense. In practice, very few companies use MAC address filtering because of the heavy burden of maintaining MAC tables each time the organization purchases a new device.

Confidentiality

WEP was designed to provide encryption between an access point and a client. The WEP algorithm uses a secret key to protect the confidentiality of the information between the two devices attempting to connect. Tools were developed shortly after the release of WEP to break its encryption. If an attacker uses such tools and the encryption fails, the communication between the AP and the client is in cleartext. WEP uses a fixed 40- or 104-bit encryption scheme and a 24-bit initialization vector (IV) as the two components of its secret key. The IV is relatively short, so when an attacker monitors a network, the key shows repetitions and enables the attacker to obtain the base key. Using a short IV causes these encryptions to break. Therefore, it is strongly advised not to use WEP.

WPA provides much greater security than WEP. WPA was developed in 2003 by the Wi-Fi Alliance and is now in its third version. The different WPA standards include:

- WPA, released in 2003, implemented the **Temporal Key Integrity Protocol (TKIP)** with Message Integrity Check (MIC) in order to tackle the inherent security problems with WEP. TKIP replaced the WEP encryption key with a 128-bit-per-packet key. WPA dynamically generates keys and removes the predictability that was inherent to WEP keys. WPA also includes MIC, designed to prevent an attacker from capturing, altering, and resending data packets.
- WPA2, released in 2004, replaced TKIP with the use of the **Advanced Encryption Standard (AES)** through the **Counter Mode Cipher Block Chaining Message Authentication Protocol (CCMP)**.
- WPA3, released in 2018, continues to use CCMP but adds a new approach for initial authentication on nonenterprise networks using the **Simultaneous Authentication of Equals (SAE)** approach for establishing connections.

Authorization

Having access to WLANs may require you to accept certain risks or agreements that the work being done on the network will not **compromise** the network or the organization that the network belongs to. A banner message may appear before the organization allows you access to other resources. This protects the party providing the wireless connection and ensures that whatever activities occur on the network are not something the organization supports.

For example, Alexandra may use the WLAN at her local coffee shop to snoop on other systems using those access points. The coffee shop does not agree with Alexandra doing this, but the shop is not capable of monitoring her work. The coffee shop, or its Internet service provider (ISP), can add a disclaimer letting others know that there are security risks to being on the WLAN. The warning provides **transparency** to customers and removes liability for the coffee shop.

Single Sign-On (SSO)

Single sign-on (SSO) is a method of access control that allows a user to log on to a system and gain access to other resources within the network via the initial logon. If SSO was not implemented, the user would need to log on multiple times and remember multiple passwords for the various systems. For example, when Kevin needs to access the file share, the print server, the customer database, and his email, he does not want to have to remember a different password for each resource. Fortunately, his organization implemented Kerberos, a single sign-on system, and instead his initial logon credentials are used for these resources. Use of SSO:

* Eliminates the need to remember multiple passwords. By reducing the number of passwords, you reduce the amount of time spent by administrators who must reset user passwords.
* Ensures that the same password policy is applied to all resources.
* Reduces the need for an administrator to manage various accounts on individual resources. Having centrally managed access also helps when employees leave the organization. Removing all of their access to multiple accounts at one time is efficient and ensures that employees cannot access the accounts later.

To understand if you should implement SSO, it is also important to understand the risks associated with allowing the same credentials to be used by multiple resources. Some risks of using SSO are:

* If an attacker obtains the initial password, he or she will have access to all resources.
* If an employee leaves his or her system unlocked and steps away, the employee essentially provides full and open access to all resources.

> **NOTE**
>
> Constantly resetting passwords can be demanding on IT resources and increases costs. However, an SSO system might be too expensive for smaller organizations. If the organization is small and resetting passwords is not a costly factor, an SSO solution may be more of a drawback than a benefit.

Defining the Scope for SSO

The scope for SSO is to provide a unified sign-on interface for end users that allows them to authenticate once and access multiple systems and applications. In particular, the interface should be independent of the authentication mechanisms. An SSO interface provides the capability to use credentials for other systems, but it does not specify a mandatory authentication mechanism, leaving that decision to individual access control administrators. The administrator might, for example, require two-factor authentication for sensitive applications while only requiring a username and password for more routine access.

Configuring User and Role-Based User Access Control Profiles

Adding the access controls previously discussed in this chapter provides an extra layer of security for SSO. Using credentials to limit access to resources and documents is essential for an organization attempting to limit the level of risk. Configuring user- and role-based access control profiles in an SSO system is a task that can be simplified with identity and access management software. This software is available through third-party vendors, and it allows you to incorporate SSO capabilities and control user- or role-based access control in a few steps.

These tools allow organizations to manage authentication and authorization for large numbers of users or groups from a single source. The advantages and disadvantages do not change with the implementation of additional capabilities but add to the security needed to ensure the right information gets into the right hands at the right time.

Common Configurations

There are various ways to implement SSO within an infrastructure. Determining which system to deploy within the network must be done by analyzing the benefits and risks of the system as well as the return on investment (ROI). The following are three common SSO configurations implemented within an enterprise:

- **Kerberos**—As previously stated, Kerberos is a form of SSO that employs a trusted third-party infrastructure for authentication.
- **Cookies**—Once a user logs on to a system, a cookie is placed on his or her machine. When the user wants to access this system again, the system checks for the cookie. If the cookie is available and valid, the user will not need to log on again.
- **Smart cards or biometrics**—Authenticating directly to the computer system through either a smart card or using biometrics will subsequently allow access to the other tools available on the system, such as email or enterprise communication tools.

Enterprise SSO

Enterprise SSO allows credentials to be passed outside of the corporate domain or network. Participation in an enterprise SSO system ensures that the logon credentials will work with any resource even if its credentials do not match. For example, suppose Kevin logs on to his computer system with the username of kevin1. The credential for his time card is his employee ID, 13579. Being a part of an enterprise SSO means that his kevin1 username will work as his time card logon.

Best Practices for Handling Access Controls in an Enterprise Organization

Enterprise organizations that implement access controls must understand the risk that is associated with materials being accessed by unauthorized users. How important is it to allow customer support engineers access to financial records? If the company is open to sharing all documents and information with all employees, access controls may not be needed. But no business runs that way. Enterprises always limit access to data on the network. Some of the best practices that are used across enterprises to reduce risk are:

- Discovering and identifying all data on the network.
- Developing policies based on the risk associated with the data. For example, if an organization maintains its customers' credit card and Social Security numbers, the risk is high if

left in cleartext. To reduce this risk, a policy may be put in place to ensure that data such as credit card and Social Security numbers can be stored only on an encrypted file share.

- Placing appropriate access controls on data based on risk level. For example, a software development firm may allow software engineers access to code under development but deny access to customer service representatives.
- Continually monitoring and testing the policies and access controls to ensure that a loop-hole has not opened. Continually testing the system will help determine if changes within the controls are needed.

Case Studies and Examples

It is important to look at examples of how various enterprises use access controls to keep their information and infrastructures safe. The following case studies offer insider views of access controls that solve business challenges.

Private Sector Case Study

The KMU Organization in Connecticut is a small software development company with under 10 employees. KMU employees were all founders in the company, and the majority of company data were viewable by all employees. There were no access controls placed on the network; however, some documents required passwords to open them. These passwords were provided on a need-to-know basis. Once a user no longer needed the document, the password was changed by the document owner. Network authentication required a user ID and password. Constraints were put on network passwords to ensure they were strong and had to be changed every 90 days.

KMU acquired the Acme Software Company in Ohio. The Acme Software Company was much larger than KMU. Acme Software had 75 employees and more access constraints, but the constraints were limited and not very secure. KMU realized it needed to make changes to the IT infrastructure and data access controls now that the two networks would be joined. KMU reviewed all of its options and decided to establish roles within the company that would cover both KMU and Acme Software. The company would still have a Founders' role, but it would also implement roles based on job functions in the two companies.

KMU also determined that its user IDs and passwords were not secure enough for some of its software development tools. The company's software assets were the cornerstone of the company, and losing them would be detrimental to the company. The organization decided to purchase a two-factor authentication solution for access to the software tools. This method of authentication was used to ensure competitors could not access the software being developed.

After implementing a role-based access control system, the network administrators of the two companies were able to know who was responsible for which tasks within each organization and could easily control access based on role. Granting access to documents and systems was no longer done on an individual basis but by a company-wide policy. Two-factor authentication also reduced the risk of the information being accessed by unauthorized users.

Implementation of the two systems was difficult because the administrators had to start from scratch, but they knew that as the company grew, the systems would grow with it.

Public Sector Case Study

The Town of Springfield recently experienced a security lapse in which some important, confidential documents were made available to the public. Although most of the
documents it maintains could be viewed by any resident of the town, some documents
need to remain private until they are deemed public records. The documents that were
made available to the public were bids by various construction companies to build the
new high school. Until the town decided which construction company would win the
bid, the documents should have been kept private and available only to certain town
employees.

To avoid this problem in the future, the town's IT staff decided to implement a mandatory access control system on the network. They felt this was better than a role-based access
control method because classification of the documents would change more often than user
roles. For instance, the mayor's staff would probably not change often, but document classifications might change from confidential to unclassified on a monthly basis. There may
also be times when the governor of the state would need to see information, and that person
would be provided "as needed" clearance.

The Town of Springfield felt these changes would resolve its document access issues and
would further ensure that documents were not seen by people who did not have the appropriate clearance.

Critical Infrastructure Case Study

A large government contractor had the schematics stolen from its network for the aircraft
used to fly the president of a large nation. These documents were critical to national security, and the loss was detrimental to the company's integrity. The schematics were clearly
in an unprotected area, and access to them was not secure. The government contractor was
also not aware the documents were removed from their location until a third party identified them on a server in a separate country.

After further investigation, it was determined that software installed on one of the contractor's computer systems made changes to the network configuration, allowing files to be
shared outside of the contractor's network domain without prior knowledge or approval.
Although the risk was great, the contractor had not employed some of the tactics available to
secure such data:

- Policies were not in place to limit who could install software on the computer systems.
- Access to documents was not limited based on the importance of the document.
- Controls were not put in place to limit connections made to and outside the corporate
  network.

After the network breach was detected, the government contractor limited administrative rights for the computer systems to the Administrator role. This ensured that users on
the systems were not able to download software without going through the appropriate
approvals. The contractor also reevaluated access controls on its documents and tested
them regularly. This helped to ensure the documents did not get into the hands of those who
were not authorized to access them. The last measure the contractor took was to have the

administrator continuously monitor network access and network traffic. This action helped the administrator understand normal traffic on the network and whether changes occurred on systems or the network without the administrator's approval.

CHAPTER SUMMARY

In this chapter, you learned that understanding the significance of information within an enterprise helps an administrator grant proper access to those working within the infrastructure. Limiting access reduces risk for an enterprise and assists in ensuring data does not get into the wrong hands. Limiting access can also be a hindrance to employees; therefore, planning is essential before implementing controls.

Access to systems and data should be granted only after a user is authenticated. Types of authentication, their benefits, and their risks are factors in the planning process to keep employees, customers, and data safe.

KEY CONCEPTS AND TERMS

Access control entry (ACE)
Access control list (ACL)
Advanced Encryption Standard (AES)
Attribute-based access control (ABAC)
Authentication Service
Authenticator
Bell-LaPadula Model
Bring Your Own Device (BYOD) policy
Cleartext
Commercial off-the-shelf (COTS)
Common Criteria for Information Technology Security Evaluation
Compromise
Counter Mode Cipher Block Chaining Message Authentication Protocol (CCMP)
Credentials
Cryptography

Denial of service (DoS) attack
Discretionary access control (DAC)
History-based access control (HBAC)
Identity-based access control (IBAC)
Kerberos
Key Distribution Center (KDC)
Local area network (LAN)
Malware
Mandatory access control (MAC)
Multifactor authentication
Multilevel security (MLS) system
Multiple single level (MSL) environment
Network access control (NAC)
Open Systems Interconnection (OSI) Reference Model
Orange Book
Organization-based access control (OrBAC)

Risk-adaptive access control (RAdAC)
Role-based access control (RBAC)
Rule-based access control (RuBAC)
Secret key
Security identifier (SID)
Service set identifier (SSID)
Simultaneous Authentication of Equals (SAE)
Single sign-on (SSO)
Single-factor authentication
Symmetric encryption
Temporal Key Integrity Protocol (TKIP)
Three-factor authentication
Ticket-Granting Service (TGS)
Transparency
Two-factor authentication
Wide area network (WAN)

5

Access Control in the Enterprise

CHAPTER 5 ASSESSMENT

1. What does ACL stand for?

A. Access control level

B. Access control limit

C. Access control logic

D. Access control list

2. List the four types of access control models.

3. Which of the following are components of a Kerberos system? (Select two.)

A. TKIP

B. AS

C. TGS

D. BGP

4. A switch is a device used on which layer of the OSI model?

A. Layer 1

B. Layer 2

C. Layer 4

D. Layer 5

5. Which of the following are authentication factors? (Select three.)

A. Something you need

B. Something you have

C. Something you are

D. Something you believe

E. Something you know

6. VLANs are used to segment networks.

A. True

B. False

7. Which are types of access control lists? (Select two.)

A. DACL

B. MACL

C. SACL

D. TACL

8. Of the following, what is the most recent wireless security standard?

A. WPA

B. WPA2

C. WPA3

D. WEP

9. Which of the following is the most secure encryption method for WLANs?

A. DAC

B. WEP

C. WPA

D. MAC

10. How many hexadecimal digits are provided by IEEE for vendor identification?

A. 6

B. 12

C. 18

D. 24

11. Which IEEE standard defines WLANs?

A. 802.11

B. 802.10

C. 802.5

D. 802.1q

12. Which of the following is an example of SSO?

A. Keystroke logger

B. Trojan horse

C. Kerberos

D. Broadcast domains

13. Which of the following is an access control system in which rights are assigned by the owner of the resource?

A. Discretionary access control

B. Mandatory access control

C. Role-based access control

D. Media access control

14. Which of the following is an access control system in which rights are assigned based on a user's role rather than his or her identity?

A. Discretionary access control

B. Mandatory access control

C. Role-based access control

D. Media access control

15. Which of the following is an access control system in which rights are assigned by the system itself?

A. Discretionary access control

B. Mandatory access control

C. Role-based access control

D. Media access control

Mapping Business Challenges to Access Control Types

I N THIS CHAPTER, YOU WILL TAKE SOME THEORETICAL concepts about the need for access control systems and apply them to solve real-world business problems.

The first section of this chapter discusses the types of business challenges that can be solved with access control systems. The second section describes the tools and techniques that can help you apply access control solutions. The chapter concludes with case studies of access controls in the real world.

Chapter 6 Topics

This chapter covers the following topics and concepts:

- How access control types apply to business challenges
- How access controls can be used to solve business challenges
- Some access control system design principles
- Case studies and examples

Chapter 6 Goals

When you complete this chapter, you will be able to:

- Explain various access control types and map them to business challenges
- Create a comprehensive access control strategy to solve business challenges

Access Controls to Meet Business Needs

The goal of any access control system is not only to simply keep people out or to organize who has access to a particular resource but to also meet a business need. In this chapter, you will discover how to apply various access control methods to solve a range of business challenges.

Business Continuity and Disaster Recovery

Business continuity and **disaster recovery** both refer to keeping organizations operating efficiently and their essential functions continuing in the event of a natural or manmade disaster. Business continuity plans consist of controls designed to mitigate risks to an extent that they do not disrupt critical business functions. Disaster recovery plans kick in when business continuity plans fail and attempt to get the business up and running again as quickly as possible.

Business Continuity

When creating a business continuity plan, you should start by brainstorming a list of "what-if" scenarios. Some disasters cannot be prevented—earthquakes will happen, regardless of whether you prepare for them or not. Others, especially criminal activities and accidents, can be prevented or minimized through careful planning and strong access controls.

For example, consider a cruise line with corporate headquarters located in Miami, Florida. This region is highly susceptible to natural disasters, such as hurricanes and flooding. Business continuity planners must take the risk of these disasters into account and develop plans to keep the cruise line running even in the face of a major natural disaster. Planners have several potential strategies at their disposal.

First, the cruise line could decide to separate its data center from its corporate headquarters and move it to a location in the central United States, where hurricanes and flooding are less likely. While this will address the hurricane risk, planners must then consider the new risks in the chosen location. For example, tornadoes threaten large parts of the central United States.

Second, the cruise line could choose to keep the primary data center operating and open a second data center in a facility located in a distant state. This data center may run in active-active mode, mirroring all transactions processed at the primary data center in real time. In the event that the primary data center fails, the backup data center would be ready to operate at a moment's notice. This approach provides the greatest degree of confidence in the organization's ability to survive a disaster, but at the highest cost.

Third, the cruise line might choose to leverage cloud computing options to create a virtual remote data center. Using this approach, the business could mirror critical servers and data stores in a cloud provider's environment but activate the servers only when needed. Many cloud providers present the advantages of built-in fault tolerance across multiple data centers and very low costs. The tradeoff with this approach is that the organization no longer maintains full control over its operating infrastructure and must ensure that the cloud environment is configured to meet its security requirements.

Finally, the cruise line could keep its data center in the current location but send backup tapes to an offsite location. This would provide the benefit of having a safe copy of the data at a remote site but would involve significant recovery time if the primary data center were destroyed. IT staff would need to purchase servers, install software, and load backup data from tape.

The primary job of business continuity planners is to weigh these risks and choose an option that is in the best interests of the organization. At the same time, they must consider access control issues surrounding their chosen strategy. For example, how will the organization limit physical and logical access to the primary and/or secondary data centers? What controls will be used to restrict access to data on backup tapes stored at a remote site?

When physical and administrative controls fail. Strong access controls are also important components of a defense-in-depth approach to personnel issues. Consider, for example, the following scenario:

A senior account manager at Acme Public Relations is called to a closed-door meeting with her department head and a representative from human resources. The account manager believes she has been passed over for promotions and bonuses unfairly, and to compensate, has been embezzling funds from the company for the past year. The department head became aware of her activities and has been monitoring her for the past 3 months, gathering evidence. In this meeting, the account manager is given a choice: If she leaves quietly, the company will not pursue a legal case against her.

She agrees and requests an hour to clean out her office. Her department head agrees, and the account executive goes back to her office and closes the door. She spends the next hour deleting important files and data, downloading malware from the Internet, triggering the transmission of spam messages from a corporate account, and sending her clients' contact information to her personal email account. Once she is gone, she contacts her former clients and informs them that she has decided to open her own firm and will offer them a significantly reduced rate if they will leave Acme Public Relations. Many of her clients agree to send their business to her new firm. The malware she downloaded before she left infected a large portion of the Acme network before being detected and eliminated. The spam she sent caused the company to be listed on several spam blacklists, causing their legitimate emails to be classified as spam.

This scenario illustrates a failure in both physical and administrative access controls. While the account manager was meeting with her department head and the representative from human resources, someone in IT should have been disabling her workstation and network accounts. This would have prevented her from deleting data, infecting the network with viruses and spam bots, and sending her clients' contact information to her personal email account. Without that contact information, she would not have been able to poach some of Acme's best clients, causing further damage to Acme. Finally, she should not have been allowed to return to her office unescorted. Once she was terminated, she should not have been considered "authorized personnel" and should have been treated as any other visitor.

Disaster Recovery

Access controls are not only important in preventing disasters; they are also crucial in the aftermath. In a natural disaster, key personnel may not be immediately available. Rather than leaving mission-critical systems unavailable until a system administrator can return to the office, procedures should be in place to allow anyone to perform the basic tasks necessary to bring servers back online and restore essential business functions.

Let's look at a disaster recovery scenario: On Monday at 2 a.m., an electrical fire breaks out in the basement of the Acme Financial Services' office building. Acme is a midsized investment and portfolio management company. As soon as the fire is out, Acme's chief executive officer (CEO) and chief operations officer (COO) make their way downtown to survey the damage. Much of the building has been damaged in the fire, and emergency personnel remain in the area, preventing anyone from entering the building until it can be inspected and deemed structurally sound.

Because the entire building is without power, the COO knows that the company's customer-facing website, which is hosted on servers located onsite, must be down. Employees will not be allowed to enter when they come in to work later that morning. The COO's primary goals in this situation are to reassure customers that Acme is handling the situation and will be available to meet their needs as quickly as possible and to arrange for alternative facilities so that employees can do their jobs in the days or weeks ahead as the damage is repaired.

First, the COO must get the website running on an alternate web server offsite. To do this, he needs the account information for the company's hosted offsite backup account. Because he normally does not deal with backups as part of his job, he does not have access to this account. Instead, he must call the systems administrator to obtain access to the backup account and have those files restored to an offsite web server. He posts a message on the website informing customers of the situation and assuring them that business will resume as quickly as possible.

Next, he must inform employees of the situation and give instructions on where to report to work later that morning. Unfortunately, the company directory is located on the Intranet, which is also hosted onsite and is currently down. He eventually resorts to publishing a brief notice to television and radio news outlets, informing employees of the disaster and advising them to wait to hear from their department head for further instructions.

In this scenario, a difficult situation was made more chaotic because crucial information was not available when and where it was needed. First, the COO did not have access to the offsite backup account. Normally, this makes sense under the need-to-know principle. Because managing backups is not one of the COO's job functions, he doesn't need to know the account number, username, or password to that account. However, in a disaster situation, an organization needs to have a way to quickly authorize first responders to access crucial information. In the scenario described here, all it took was a quick phone call to a systems administrator who recognized the COO's voice. In a larger organization, this would not have been a practical solution.

On the other hand, this scenario could have been nothing more than a social engineering ploy designed to con the systems administrator into giving up sensitive account information. To counteract this possibility, key personnel, such as systems administrators and department heads, should be trained in disaster recovery procedures so they know what to expect and can quickly spot any anomaly in the procedure that might signal a social engineering ploy.

To compound the problem, the COO did not have the company directory at hand to pass along information and instructions to various department heads in a timely manner. Hard copies of a company directory, especially if that directory includes employees' home or cell phone numbers, should not be widely distributed, but that information must be available to first responders in an emergency situation.

A good solution and access control method for this issue would be to program the contact numbers of key personnel, such as the systems administrator, in a company cell phone, which would be kept by a member of senior management such as the COO or an official emergency coordinator. This way, only the cell phone number is made public, and sensitive information—the home phone numbers of key personnel—is kept private.

The existence of an emergency cell phone also helps prevent social engineering attacks. If someone calls a systems administrator's home phone number claiming to be the COO or the official emergency coordinator, the system administrator can verify the caller ID to ensure that the call came from a known number. Better yet, given that the caller ID can be spoofed, the administrator can call the COO back at the known number to verify its authenticity.

Customer Access to Data

The Internet makes it easy for customers to order merchandise online, view their order history, track packages, and update their own customer records. Unfortunately, this freedom brings a host of access control challenges. Customers should be able to view their own information but not that of other customers, for example. To meet this need, an access control system must be able to accommodate three key specifications:

- Allow customers to create and update their own account information
- Allow customers to create orders
- Deny access to any information not directly associated with that customer

The key access control method here is a typical username and password combination. A website visitor who has not logged in should not be allowed to view anything but the public-facing portions of a company's website. A visitor who wants to place an order will need to create an account. This process generates a row in the customer database keyed to the customer's username or customer ID. This unique key will also be used to identify rows in the order database that are affiliated with that customer. Keying rows in the order database on customer ID or username will prevent the system from inadvertently displaying customer B's order history to customer A. This system is only as secure as the passwords customers create.

Consider this scenario: Acme Library Supply, a major supplier of books to school libraries, creates a secure ordering website for its customers. Acme does not sell to the general public because it carries books at a steep discount for library use, and it is not set up to collect sales tax because libraries are exempt. Most of Acme's customers are located in North America, although Acme did supply books to a few South American and European schools.

An operations manager at Acme notices that her department has been fulfilling a large number of orders for a specific South American customer. She contacts a member of the systems team, concerned that the orders are being faked. A check of the log files shows that the orders are coming from a large number of Internet Protocol (IP) addresses across Brazil,

Venezuela, and Peru. The systems administrator does a Google search for the affected customer's username and discovers he has posted his username and password on a web forum, inviting people to use his account to order books. When the books arrived, the customer would forward them to the appropriate parties.

There is nothing wrong with Acme's access control system. It has worked perfectly. The access control weakness is the customer, who shared his authentication information publicly.

The scenario emphasizes the point that it's not enough to create a strong logical or physical access control system and forget about it. Employees must be trained to recognize and report anomalies that may suggest an access control failure.

Maintain Competitive Advantage

In a competitive marketplace, information can be a key advantage. Trade secrets, product specifications, and business methods are all resources to be leveraged. However, if the competition also has access to the same information, the value of the information is considerably lower. Keeping secret information out of the hands of the competition is clearly an access control problem that requires several layers of defense:

- **Need to know and least privilege**—Only those employees with a legitimate need should have access to sensitive information such as trade secrets and product formulations. The more people who know and have access to this information, the higher the likelihood that it will be intentionally or accidentally divulged.
- **Technological access controls**—Strong password policies should be enforced using scripts that reject weak passwords. Intrusion detection systems and firewalls should be in place to protect information stored on network resources.
- **Physical security**—Key facilities such as server rooms and data warehouses should be locked at all times. Visitors should be escorted to and from their destinations.
- **Administrative policies**—Policies should be in place to handle lost or stolen ID badges, acceptable use of computers and other resources, and other potential security risks.
- **Employee training**—Employees should be trained to recognize social engineering tactics and to know how to handle those situations. They should also be periodically retrained in security policies and best practices.

Taking these steps will minimize the risk of corporate espionage or accidental sharing of secret information that could lead to a loss of competitive advantage.

Risk and Risk Mitigation

There are four ways to handle risk:

- Risk avoidance
- Risk acceptance
- Risk transference
- Risk mitigation

Each of these methods has its benefits as well as some drawbacks. Choosing the correct method depends on the specific situation and goals of the organization.

Risk Avoidance

Risk avoidance is choosing to avoid an activity that carries some element of risk. For example, you may choose not to take your vacation in an active war zone, regardless of how much natural beauty may be found in that part of the world. Risk avoidance always carries with it some aspect of loss. In the vacation example, you lose the chance to experience the natural beauty that exists in that area, but you avoid the risk of being harmed. In this case, the risk to be avoided—possible injury or worse—is more pressing than the missed opportunity— seeing the natural beauty in a certain part of the world.

However, risk avoidance is not always the best solution to a problem. Doing business in the healthcare industry carries a certain level of legal risk due to federal regulation. If your business does not comply with regulations, you could face fines or even prison time. However, if you choose not to do business in that industry, you lose out on the potential profits of a multi-billion dollar industry. In this case, avoidance is not the answer.

 NOTE

Businesses must accept any risk they cannot avoid, transfer, or mitigate.

Risk Acceptance

Risk acceptance is simply accepting the risks and doing what you need to do anyway. Firefighters, police officers, military personnel, and other individuals in high-risk occupations do this every day. A firefighter knows that she risks her life every time she responds to an emergency call. She could choose to stay behind at the fire house, but she knows that her skills are needed and that her efforts may save lives. She accepts the risk to her personal safety in order to fulfill a greater good.

Risk Transference

Risk transference shifts the potential negative consequences of a risk from one organization to another. The two most common examples of risk transference are the purchase of insurance policies and the signing of contracts that contain indemnification clauses.

Purchasing health insurance is one way of transferring risk. Consider the following scenario: A woman slips on the ice on her driveway, falls, and loses consciousness. She is rushed to the emergency room, where the doctors perform an MRI exam and diagnose her with a serious concussion. She goes home several hours later with a prescription for painkillers and instructions to rest.

Without health insurance—a method of risk transference—this event would cost the woman several thousand dollars in hospital and physician fees. These fees would cause her serious financial hardship. However, because she has health insurance, she pays only a small co-pay fee. The risk of a major medical expense is transferred to the insurance company. In this situation, risk transference makes sense.

Not all risk transference situations are as effective. Consider the case of a small medical practice. Because it operates in the healthcare industry, it is subject to regulation under the Health Insurance Portability and Accountability Act (HIPAA). In a small business, the medical practice is without the resources to manage compliance itself, so it hires a third-party compliance firm. Unfortunately, the compliance firm cuts corners and the medical practice discovers the problem during an official audit.

The compliance firm is contractually responsible for the medical practice's noncompliance, but the officers of the medical practice are still held personally responsible for bringing the practice back into compliance and paying any fines associated with their noncompliance. The medical practice could sue the compliance firm for financial losses, but the suit would likely drain the practice of funds necessary to continue doing business.

In this case, while the risk of noncompliance is contractually transferred from the medical practice to the compliance firm, in the end, the medical practice is still penalized and held responsible for the actions of its contracted compliance firm.

Risk Mitigation

Risk mitigation is a strategy that combines attempts to minimize the probability and consequences of a risk situation. Access control is an example of risk mitigation. It attempts to minimize the probability of a risk situation by denying unauthorized users access to resources. It also minimizes the consequences of a breach by isolating one user's data from data owned by other users.

For example, suppose the CEO of Acme Devices receives phone calls from several board members who are concerned about an article that was published in the *Wall Street Journal*, giving detailed specifications for the company's newest high-tech product. He believes the information must have come from an internal source, and upon investigation, finds out that the Research and Development folder on the network is accessible to all employees. Any one of the employees could have been the source for the *Wall Street Journal* article.

Had this proprietary information been properly secured with strong access controls, only the engineers within the research and development (R&D) department—those who had a legitimate need for the information—would have had access to the product specification documents. Restricting access to employees within the R&D department would not, by itself, prevent the information leak, but it would minimize the opportunity. The reporter from the *Wall Street Journal* would have had to contact a member of a specific department, reducing the number of leak opportunities from several thousand—the total number of employees of Acme Devices—down to a few dozen—the number of employees in the R&D department.

Access controls are not the only answer to risk and risk mitigation, but they are an important part of the solution.

Differences to Keep in Mind

There are significant differences between threats, risks, and vulnerabilities:

- A vulnerability is any weakness in a system that can be exploited.
- A threat is a potential attack upon a system.
- Risk occurs when a particular threat will exploit a vulnerability. The degree of risk is measured in terms of probability and impact.

Threats and Threat Mitigation

Any organization faces certain types of threats to its IT infrastructure. The goal of access control is to mitigate those threats as much as possible.

There are three main threat categories that you need to be concerned with:

- **Confidentiality** ensures that private or sensitive information is not disclosed to unauthorized individuals.
- **Integrity** ensures that data have not been modified without authorization.
- **Availability** ensures that information is available to authorized users when they need it.

A good access control system will guard against all three primary threat categories. It will restrict access to sensitive information to authorized users and deny access to anyone else. It will provide an audit trail to prove that unauthorized individuals have not altered data. Finally, it will prevent unauthorized users from destroying data or launching denial of service (DoS) attacks, making data unavailable to authorized users.

For example, consider the Acme Aeronautics Company. It designs experimental aircraft, primarily for military use. Its design specifications are considered highly sensitive. If those specifications were to be divulged to the wrong people, at best, Acme could lose its biggest customer to a competitor that could produce the same technology less expensively (having not invested millions in research and development). At worst, enemy nations could use those specifications to design weapons systems to exploit the weaknesses of those aircraft.

Any access control system designed to protect those specifications documents must account for all three threat categories:

- It must preserve confidentiality by ensuring that information is not disclosed, either accidentally or intentionally, to unauthorized individuals. This is the primary purpose of the access control system, and where the majority of resources are devoted. To accomplish this goal, a two-stage authentication system is implemented, which requires individuals to use a challenge-response token to access the login screen for the file server that stores specification documents.
- It must ensure the integrity of the information. If design specification documents are changed even slightly, the planes that are built from those specifications could fail catastrophically. To meet this goal, the documents are placed under version control that notifies the entire project team, as well as departmental management, any time a key document is changed. This ensures that an official document cannot be changed outside of the approved workflow.
- It must ensure that the data are available to authorized users. Physical access controls on the data center are the primary method for meeting this goal. If the data center is compromised, the data stored there could be stolen or destroyed. Security guards, biometric scanners, and smart card ID badges work together to maintain physical security on the data center.

Vulnerabilities and Vulnerability Management

A vulnerability is a weakness in a system that can be exploited. Every system has vulnerabilities, so a good access control system must manage those vulnerabilities to minimize the risk of exploitation. The most common vulnerability categories you will need to manage are:

- **Operating system**—All operating systems are vulnerable to a variety of threats including viruses and other malware, unauthorized access, and overflow attacks. As new attack vectors are discovered, operating system manufacturers release patches to harden their software. Keeping the operating system up to date is the most important thing you can do to manage vulnerabilities in the operating system.

- **Applications**—Applications can introduce vulnerability into a system either through design flaws in the application itself or through bugs in the programming language used to code the application. Thorough testing and patching is the only way to manage this vulnerability, as you will probably not have complete control over the application design process. Even if all of your applications are coded in house, you will not have control over the design of the programming languages you use.

- **Users**—Users are primarily vulnerable to social engineering tactics and insecure password practices. Training and policy mandates are the best way to manage user vulnerabilities.

> ▶ **TIP**
>
> The best way to manage vulnerabilities using access controls is by running applications as their own, unprivileged user. This way, even if an application does have a vulnerability that is exploited, the damage is limited.

Consider a shared web hosting firm. It has dozens of clients, each running various applications on their websites. The websites are hosted on a few shared servers. Unfortunately, one of those clients installs an unsecure message board on one of the shared servers. Through the message board application, attackers are able to gain access to the client's web-hosting account and then to the administrative tools of the shared server. The attackers deface every website hosted by the shared web server. They also install a backdoor and dozens of spam bots on the shared web server. The server administrator learns of this problem when his customers call him, asking why their websites have been taken down and replaced with a defacement page. It takes the administrator several days to completely remove the artifacts left by the attacker and to have his clients' IP addresses removed from the spam blacklists.

If this shared web server had better access controls, the attack still might have happened, but the effects would have been limited to a single client instead of the entire server. The message board application should have been run as an unprivileged user instead of under the client's user account, and each client should have been strictly segregated from the others.

Solving Business Challenges with Access Control Strategies

> ⬛ **NOTE**
>
> Remember, a subject is anything that acts upon another entity. An object is anything that is passively acted upon by a subject.

The key to applying access controls to solving business challenges is in taking a systematic approach to designing a comprehensive strategy. As you consider each element of access control, you will begin to see how various strategies interrelate to form a multilayered security system.

The first step in creating a comprehensive access control strategy is to define your subjects and objects.

The most common subjects are:

- **Users**—They are generally the individuals who need access to resources. In some cases, applications can also have user accounts. The most common example of this scenario is a web-server application that is typically run under the "nobody" user account.

- **Applications**—Applications often access the file system directly by reading or writing files, make database connections, and utilize the mail system on a server. These are all access control requests to be managed securely.
- **Network devices**—A proxy on one network will often request access to resources on another network on behalf of a user or application on its own network. The proxy is, in effect, making an access control request, and is, therefore, acting as a subject.

Your infrastructure may have other subjects. These are simply the most common types of subjects. Once you have defined all the subjects in your infrastructure, you can begin to categorize them into groups and roles.

Groups are useful because they allow you to generalize the access privileges needed by several subjects. They also allow you to create specialized combinations of privileges by adding a subject to two or more groups. To remove certain access privileges, you would simply remove the subject from one or more groups.

Roles also allow you to generalize and separate a subject's function from its identity. For example, Bob Smith may hold the role of user on his workstation most of the time and the role of administrator only when he needs to install a new application. Rather than assigning administrative rights to Bob's user account when he only needs those rights occasionally, he will have access to two separate role-based accounts.

Once you have defined your subjects, you will need to similarly define your objects, or the data and resources in your infrastructure. This list of objects should contain every significant asset as well as notes about the asset's worth and value to the organization.

Employees with Access to Systems and Data

Even nonsensitive data should be stored under some level of access control. For example, the company newsletter is available to every employee but should not be available to the general public. As soon as you limit access to data or resources, you have an access control scenario. Some employees will have no need to access IT systems and data. The custodians and groundskeepers, for example, will probably not need access to the network or the data stored there. They may, however, need access to the automated time clock system or the maintenance schedules stored on the company Intranet. Whether certain employees require access to IT resources depends upon the individual organization and its business processes.

Who Needs Access to Which Resources?

When creating an access control strategy, the main question to ask is, "Who needs access to what?" If a user does not have a legitimate need to access data or resources, that user should not be granted access. If the user does need access at some point in the future, that user's access privileges can be modified then. Do not be tempted to assign high levels of access to a user simply based upon his or her status within the organization. Chances are the executive vice president of accounting does not actually need administrative rights to the web server. Assigning those rights to that user would represent a significant vulnerability in the access control system because it is unlikely that the executive vice president of accounting has the technical knowledge and background to safely administer the web server.

Creating Groups and Roles

When deciding which users need access to resources, try to think in terms of roles or job functions rather than individuals. Individuals may leave the company at any time, and some other individuals will be found to take over their roles. As discussed above, an individual may hold several roles depending on the task at hand.

Groups and roles also simplify the task of administering permissions. Take the scenario of an employee who transfers from one department to another. Rather than auditing the employee's permissions individually, the systems administrator simply needs to remove the employee from the old department's group and add the employee to the new department's group.

External Access to Systems and Data

Finally, determine whether any external subjects will have access to internal systems and data. An external subject is anyone who is outside the organization's physical and network boundaries. Why would someone outside the organization need access to internal systems and data? The following is a list of common external subjects who have a legitimate need to access internal resources:

- Third-party vendors and application service providers (ASPs)
- External contractors
- Employees with remote access

Each of these subjects needs some of the same rights and access to resources as an internal employee, and like internals, each should be restricted to the lowest level of privilege needed to perform necessary tasks. Employees who work remotely are a special case here, because they are both internal and external. They are employees but access resources from outside the organization's network and physical boundaries. The primary access control challenge with remote workers is that of creating a **virtual private network (VPN)** and ensuring that sensitive data are not compromised due to a lack of infrastructure security at the employee's location, which could be the employee's home, a coffee shop, or some other public place.

Once you have determined who should have access to resources in general, you can go further and consider which employees should have access to sensitive systems and data.

Employees with Access to Sensitive Systems and Data

At this point, you already have a comprehensive list of objects. Now you should go back over that list and note which of those objects should be considered sensitive. Consider that a variety of factors may make a given system or data set sensitive:

- Regulatory compliance
- Privacy, either for customers or employees
- Business continuity
- Competitive advantage

Any system or data resource that, if it were lost, stolen, damaged, altered, or publicly divulged, would cause a significant negative impact to the organization should be considered sensitive.

Administrative Strategies

Once you know what subjects to account for and which objects to protect with access controls, you can devise administrative strategies to support access controls. There are two issues to consider when defining administrative access control strategies around new and expiring accounts:

- How will new accounts be created and new access levels be granted?
- How will accounts be removed and access levels be lowered?

New employees and employees who take on additional job functions may need new accounts. Employees who are given temporary responsibilities may need higher access levels for the duration of their increased responsibility.

Normally, a manager fills out an account request form, which explains what access is needed and what business need this access will fill. The form should also specify whether the new account or heightened access is temporary (and when it will expire) or permanent. The manager submits the form to the security team, which reviews the request and either approves or denies it. Once the request is approved, it is forwarded to a member of the accounts team to actually create the account or modify the user's access level.

Access levels that were granted temporarily should be lowered as soon as the need for heightened access is no longer present, and accounts for employees who leave the company should be removed immediately.

The workflow to remove or downgrade accounts is similar to that described for creating accounts. A manager fills out an account request form and submits it to the security team, who forwards it to the accounts team. When an employee is terminated or leaves the company, his or her accounts should be locked immediately.

Keep in mind that the goal of these administrative strategies is to minimize the human error inherent in any access control strategy.

Technical Strategies

The technical aspect of an access control strategy may include some or all of the following techniques:

- **Discretionary access control (DAC)**—DAC is an access control system where rights are assigned by the owner of the resource in question.
- **Mandatory access control (MAC)**—MAC is an access control system where rights are assigned by a central authority.
- **Role-based access control (RBAC)**—In an RBAC system, rights are assigned based on a user's role rather than his or her identity.
- **Automated account review**—All accounts should be reviewed periodically to ensure that they still need the access to resources and privileges they currently hold. As job functions change and evolve, so do their access needs. An automated system cannot replace human knowledge of business processes and the resources those processes require, but it can determine which access rights have not been used recently. Unused rights are a vulnerability in any system.

- **Automated expiration of temporary access**—When accounts are created for temporary employees or access levels are temporarily raised, those accounts should be downgraded or removed promptly. Automated expirations are an easy way to ensure that a temporary account is not forgotten and left sitting around on the system, just waiting to be exploited.

NOTE

The terms "separation of duties" and "seg-regation of duties" are synonymous with "separation of privileges."

Every organization has unique business challenges, so there is no one-size-fits-all technical access control strategy. Use the methods and techniques that make sense for your situation.

Separation of Privileges

The principle of **separation of privileges** is designed to ensure that if an attacker compromises one account, he or she will be denied access to highly sensitive information because it is protected by two separate conditions. Both conditions must be met for access to be granted. If one condition is met but not the other, access is denied. Separation of privileges is a strategy that is used extensively in many areas:

- Accounting department employees usually do not have the ability to create new vendors and cut checks. This policy exists to prevent a single employee from creating a fake vendor, then creating checks made out to the fake vendor. It will take at least two employees working in tandem to embezzle this way. The two conditions that must be met to pay a new vendor are executed by two separate employees: one to create a vendor and one to cut checks.
- Safe deposit boxes usually have two keys that are kept physically separate. Both keys must be present to open the box.
- Missile launch procedures require two military officers of sufficient rank to give the correct command and turn launch keys in order to arm a missile launch system. A single officer is not sufficient, as this would place too much power in the hands of a single individual.

In access control systems, separation of privileges has two aspects: compartmentalization and dual conditions. **Compartmentalization** is the practice of keeping sensitive functions separate from nonsensitive ones. In practice, this is implemented by isolating programs running under one user account from other users. **Dual conditions** are most often implemented through two-stage authentication methods, which require both a biometric scan or token device and a password to grant access.

Least Privilege

The principle of **least privilege** is based on the idea that a subject—whether a user, application, or other entity—should be given the minimum level of rights necessary to perform its legitimate functions. The purpose of this principle is that if an account is compromised, an attacker will have a minimal set of privileges and will not be able to use the compromised account to do real damage to the entire system.

NOTE

On Windows servers, the administrator account is called Administrator. On UNIX and Linux servers, the administrator account is called root.

In practice, the principle of least privilege is usually implemented as **least user access (LUA)**, which requires that users commonly log onto workstations under limited user accounts.

Administrative accounts should be reserved for administrators and then used only when performing administrative tasks.

Risks Associated with Users Having Administrative Rights

On a server, having an administrator logged into a privileged account can create an opportunity for an attacker to hijack the administrative session.

If an administrator regularly logs into the server using the administrative account to perform routine tasks, the window of opportunity is larger than if that account is activated only for specific tasks and promptly logged off.

Workstations are not usually connected directly to the Internet the way a server is, so the risk is much lower that an attacker will attempt to hijack the administrator account. On a workstation, the major risks to allowing users to log onto the administrator account for routine tasks are malware and misconfigurations.

Malware, such as viruses, Trojan horses, and spyware, usually require administrative privileges to install them, just as any other application does. If a user is logged in as administrator on his or her workstation, the chances of infection by any given piece of malware are greater.

The risk of misconfigurations is based on the fact that many users are not experts in computer maintenance and configuration. If users without sufficient knowledge attempt to change their firewall settings because they read a blog post or heard someone talking about the latest virus, they are likely to do more harm than good.

Common Roles

There are three common roles on any system, either workstation or server: administrator, user, and guest. Many systems have other customized roles as well, but the ones discussed here are the ones you will find on any system.

Administrator. The administrator, or root user, has the ability to perform most tasks on a system. At a minimum, the administrator can:

- Create user accounts and assign privileges
- Install software and devices
- Perform low-level system maintenance tasks, such as registry maintenance, start and stop services, installation of drivers, and management of log files

> **NOTE**
>
> Some user accounts are limited to a subset of the applications installed on a computer. It does not make sense to enable a user account to run the user-creation application because that is an administrative task.

This is by no means an exhaustive list of the tasks an administrator can perform. These are simply the primary categories of tasks for an administrator.

User. There will usually be more than one user account on any given system. Some user accounts are tied to individuals, while others are used by applications. In general, a user account can:

- View the status of services, drivers, processes, and so on
- Run programs
- View log files

- Make limited changes to registry entries
- Add, modify, and delete data and files owned by that user

This is the most common type of account and may be further defined into specific types of users with more granular privileges.

WARNING

In practice, it is rare—and a bad idea—for an authentication system to query a database with a plaintext password. More likely, the system will query the database with the results of a password hash equation.

Guest. Some systems will have a guest or anonymous account. Others will have this account disabled or removed. The guest account is a severely limited version of a user account that is enabled to run only specified programs and view specific data. On a system without a clear need for a guest account, it should be disabled or removed. An attacker could potentially use the guest account to attack the more privileged accounts on the system.

Need to Know

Users should be given access to the minimum amount and sensitivity levels of data and resources necessary to perform essential functions. If a user does not need to know the Social Security number of a client in order to do his or her job, he or she should not be given access to that information.

> **FYI**
>
> When users enter their usernames in an authentication system, the system sends a request to the database: "Does a record with the supplied username exist?" If the record exists, the database returns the Boolean result TRUE. If the record does not exist, the database returns FALSE. Likewise, when users enter their passwords, the system sends another request to the database: "Does the password in the database record keyed on the supplied username match the user-supplied password?" Again, the database will return a Boolean result, either TRUE or FALSE. The authentication system uses secure hashing technology to avoid sending the password across the network in cleartext. This prevents an eavesdropper from observing the password. Additionally, the authentication database contains only hashed passwords, not the corresponding plaintext passwords that would be needed to access the user's account. A hash of the password is not the password, and it is not the password encrypted. It allows the verification of a password without possession of the password itself.

There are three basic levels of need for information:

- **Existence of information**—At this level, the subject only needs to know whether or not a certain piece of information exists or if it matches a predefined pattern. Username and password authentication systems are a good example of this level of need.
- **View partial information**—This is the most common level of need. Most users will need to know some sensitive information, but not all. For example, an office manager preparing a letter to be sent to a firm's entire client list will need to know the clients' directory information—names and addresses—but will not need those clients' Social Security or account numbers. Another employee in the accounting department may need clients' account numbers but not their directory information.

- **View full record**—The need for this level of access is rare and should be granted only to those who cannot perform their job functions with partial access to information.

In all cases, the need to know principle dictates that users be granted access only to the information they actually need, and no more.

Input/Output Controls

Input and output controls dictate a user's ability to interact with devices and data. The guiding principle for input and output controls is the same as for everything else: Users should have the least access possible to perform their job functions.

Input Controls

Input controls dictate how users can interact with data and devices that introduce new data into a system. For example, input controls might dictate whether a user is entitled to write new data files or modify existing rows in a database. Input controls are also concerned with physical security such as automatically locking server rooms and securing unused network jacks on servers. Left unsecured, an unused network jack could be used to attach an unauthorized device to the network via a server.

Output Controls

Output controls are similar to input controls, except that they are primarily concerned with the output of data, either to a screen, printer, or another device. A user's ability to read a data file would be the focus of an output control rule, as would a system that requires a personal identification number (PIN) to retrieve print jobs. This type of system is usually put in place to prevent unattended output on a shared printer.

Access Control System Design Principles

As designers create access control systems, they should keep in mind a set of commonly accepted design principles. These principles are intended to create access control systems that meet business requirements in a manner that is acceptable to users and provides adequate security while balancing complexity and cost. These principles include:

- **Least privilege** and **separation of privileges**, which were discussed earlier in this chapter.
- **Economy of mechanism**, also known as **simplicity of design**, which says that access control mechanisms should be as simple as possible, using as few components and procedures as necessary to meet the requirements. Increasing the complexity of a mechanism increases the likelihood that it will fail.
- **Least common mechanism**, also known as **minimization of implementation**, suggests that the mechanisms used by different classes of users should be separated to the extent possible. This reduces the likelihood of privilege escalation attacks.
- **Least astonishment**, also known as **psychological acceptability**, relates to usability. It says that security mechanisms should be as nonintrusive as possible, providing security while minimizing disruption to user activity.

- **Open design** is the opposite of **security through obscurity**. It says that the security of an access control mechanism should not depend upon the secrecy of its design or the secrecy of details of its implementation.
- **Complete mediation** says that access control decisions should not be cached for later use. Each attempt to access an object should be verified. This allows the immediate revocation of credentials.
- **Default deny** says that the base assumption of any access control mechanism should be that the access is denied unless it was explicitly authorized. This principle is closely related to the idea of minimizing the trust surface or implementing a reluctance to trust.

Case Studies and Examples

Now that you understand the theory behind designing a comprehensive access control system, let's examine how these systems are implemented in real-world situations.

Private Sector Case Study

Cloud Collaboration recently launched a **Software as a Service (SaaS)** office suite. This suite includes a word processor, as well as presentation, email, calendar, and spreadsheet applications. Also included are collaboration and web-authoring tools.

SaaS is a model of software distribution that hosts software in a cloud-based environment on a subscription basis. Instead of simply selling an application, a SaaS vendor offers access to the applications for a small subscription fee. The application and data are stored on the vendor's servers and the customer accesses them remotely. This benefits the customer by lowering operating costs and adding security and portability. SaaS sometimes costs less, both in upfront and ongoing costs, than buying software in a traditional manner. This is especially true for a small-business environment that may not have the capital necessary for the hardware associated with large centralized applications.

> **NOTE**
>
> Cloud Collaboration's office suite provides services for many organizations from a single server, just as many families might live in a single apartment building. Each organization's data are segregated from the others, but it all resides on the same server.

SaaS also adds a new layer of document security; even if a workstation is physically stolen, the information is safe because all of the documents are stored on the vendor's servers instead of the customer's workstation. Storing the information remotely also gives the customer an amazing amount of portability. Any system with appropriate access software can access the data. In Cloud Collaboration's case, the office suite is web-based, so any system with a web browser can be used to access the applications, including smartphones. The portability of SaaS can be seen in **FIGURE 6-1**.

SaaS has its challenges as well. Privacy is a major concern because multiple organizations will have access to Cloud Collaboration's systems. Cloud Collaboration's customers do not want other groups or even Cloud Collaboration employees to have the ability to access their data. These are concerns above the normal data security issues internal to an organization. There is also the issue of ease of use. For example, end users at the organizations using Cloud Collaboration's SaaS do not expect to have to log into their word processor. For Cloud Collaboration's SaaS offering to be widely adopted, its security features must be seamless to

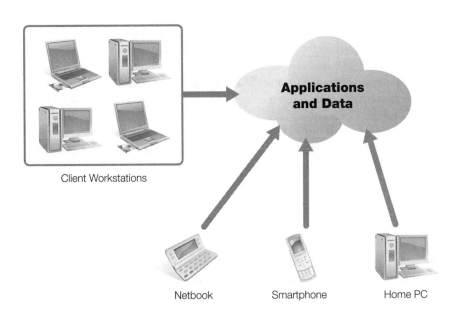

Client Workstations

Netbook   Smartphone   Home PC

Applications and Data

FIGURE 6-1

Portability of SaaS.

end users. While these problems are daunting, they can be addressed with a well-designed access control system.

The first obstacle that Cloud Collaboration needs to address is cording off users and organizations to make sure information is not unintentionally shared between unrelated groups. This is handled with a RBAC system. Each organization is a "role" in Cloud Collaboration's design; data are restricted then by role. Only the organization that created the information has access to it initially, but access can be explicitly granted to other roles by sharing the data. Cloud Collaboration's own employees are included in this layer of control, guaranteeing that even internal Cloud Collaboration users can see only the data that they have rights to see.

Cloud Collaboration customers also have the ability to set up a mandatory access control schema. They can set up an administrator or group of administrators for their SaaS applications. These administrators control organization-wide rights to accessing the data. Administrators can explicitly add or deny access to users and groups of users in a similar manner to data that are stored locally. This allows organizations to have strict access controls based on their own access-control policies.

There is also the ability to have DAC on user-created data. If an organization does not have the infrastructure for a centralized administrator, each document owner can set the access controls for his or her documents by explicitly allowing or denying access to other users in the organization and even to other organizations.

Cloud Collaboration also wanted to allow customers the ability to verify document integrity, as required by various regulations. To achieve this, it implemented a granular, robust document logging and auditing system. Managers and end users can see what changes were made to a document, who made them, and when they were made. Users can also revert to a previous version of a document. This robust logging allows users to verify the integrity of the information stored in the system.

Cloud Collaboration also wanted to make all of this security seamless and invisible to the end user. Users are not used to logging in to a word processor or calendar application, and it would be difficult to convince new customers to adopt Cloud Collaboration's SaaS offering if it added a layer of unfamiliarity or complexity to applications that are constantly used and needed in an organization. To avoid this, Cloud Collaboration created an authentication API utilizing **Security Assertion Markup Language (SAML)** 2.0. SAML is an XML-like markup language that allows web applications to pass a security token for user identification. This allows for organizations using Cloud Collaboration's SaaS to utilize a single sign-on (SSO) system. The end user logs onto his or her workstation, and that username and password acts as the login for Cloud Collaboration's SaaS business suite as well. This also allows organizations to take advantage of existing password complexity and expiration rules.

Utilizing a deep and robust access control system, Cloud Collaboration was able to provide information privacy and integrity for its SaaS customers.

Public Sector Case Study

The U.S. military needed a way to communicate information quickly and securely in the rapidly changing environment of a battlefield. Wired communications, while secure and robust, had significant drawbacks. Communication lines could easily be severed, and military personnel were limited to communicating only at fixed locations. Radio and wireless communications removed the threat of cut lines and extended the range of communications, allowing military personnel to communicate with mobile units, but only to a fixed range. Stationary installations were still needed as base stations, and throughput degraded the farther the units were from the base station. That led the military to turn to a new type of wireless networking called wireless mesh networking.

Wireless mesh networks are based on a distributed network mesh topology. Each node in the network connects with multiple nodes. Each node also acts as a router for the nodes it connects with, allowing traffic to hop along multiple paths to a destination. This allows for a very robust and flexible network. The loss of one node will not hurt the network, and nodes can be added at will. Range of the total network is also massive because nodes don't need to be close to a central point. They need just one other node to function. An example of a mesh network can be seen in **FIGURE 6-2**.

While a wireless mesh network solved part of the military's requirements, security remained a major concern. To make sure the communications were secure, the military implemented both physical and logical access controls on the network.

For the physical security of the communications, the military use frequency hopping on the radios connected to the network. The radios are constantly changing frequencies. This allows them to prevent jamming and eavesdropping.

For logical security, the mesh network relies on MAC addressing to identify all of the devices in the network. A list of all allowed Media Access Control (MAC) addresses is generated and each device knows whom it talks to. A MAC address can be faked, so they also utilize a shared secret style encryption key to handle security. When devices in the network first link together, they will authenticate each other utilizing public key infrastructure (PKI) and then develop a shared key, which will get renewed periodically to handle encryption. Now any communications between nodes can be validated with that key. These two network access control methods give the military the ability to secure its wireless communications.

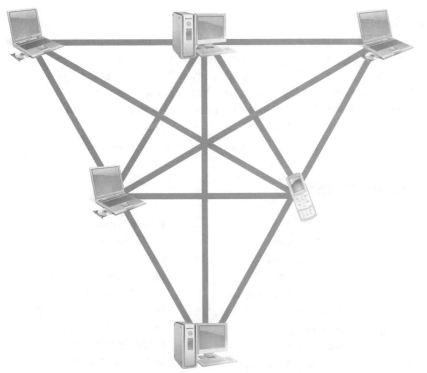

FIGURE 6-2

Mesh network topology.

Critical Infrastructure Case Study

Power plants are an important part of critical infrastructure and local, state, and national economies. Therefore, power plants need deep and multilayered access controls due to concerns over physical security. There are a number of sensitive areas that must be secured, and various employees need different levels of access to these locations. At a plant in the upper Midwest, this access is handled with identity badges that include images of the user and a RFID with the user's access rights.

The RFID handles access through multiple levels. There is a security checkpoint at the entrance to the parking lot and at the entrance to the building. Both points require a badge to enter. From there, the badge allows personnel to enter the facilities they are authorized to enter. It also acts as "something you have" for multipoint authentication onto secure systems. These are all standard functions for a RFID badge system.

The badges also have an automatic deactivation feature, which is useful for certain personnel. Maintenance personnel, for example, do not have enhanced access and do not require access to secured areas of the site. However, the maintenance team may need access to any area of the facility regardless of its sensitivity in the case of a breakdown or special project. To allow for this, the badges can be granted access rights that decay over time. This allows for temporary access to secure areas that is then automatically revoked over a number of hours or days. This lowers administrative time and reduces the risk of human error in rights assignment.

CHAPTER SUMMARY

All access control systems are about solving problems and meeting business needs. In order to do this effectively, you should be familiar with a variety of access control types and understand how to map those types to various business challenges. Understanding how access control systems are used in the real world is a good way to integrate what works into your own access control systems.

KEY CONCEPTS AND TERMS

Availability	Integrity	Risk mitigation
Business continuity	Least astonishment	Risk transference
Compartmentalization	Least common mechanism	Role
Complete mediation	Least privilege	Security Assertion Markup
Confidentiality	Least user access (LUA)	Language (SAML)
Default deny	Minimization of implementation	Security through obscurity
Disaster recovery	Open design	Separation of privileges
Dual conditions	Output control	Simplicity of design
Economy of mechanism	Psychological acceptability	Software as a Service (SaaS)
Group	Risk acceptance	Virtual private network (VPN)
Input control	Risk avoidance	Wireless mesh network

CHAPTER 6 ASSESSMENT

1. In terms of business continuity, a hostage situation could be considered a disaster.

   A. True

   B. False

2. _____ is choosing not to engage in an activity that carries some element of risk.

3. _____ is carrying on despite the risks involved in a given activity.

4. _____ is the process of assigning risk to someone else.

5. _____ combines attempts to minimize the probability and impact of risk.

6. The three main threat categories are information confidentiality, _____, and availability.

7. Even nonsensitive data should be kept under some level of access control.

   A. True

   B. False

8. Any system or data resource that, if it were lost, stolen, damaged, altered, or publicly divulged, would cause a significant negative impact to the organization should be considered _____.

9. A user account with "root" privileges best fits into which one of the following access roles?

   A. User

   B. Service

   C. Daemon

   D. Administrator

10. A school district was hit with a ransomware attack that prevented teachers from accessing their computer systems. Which term best describes the effect of the attack?

   A. Disclosure
   B. Confidentiality
   C. Integrity
   D. Availability

11. The principle of separation of privilege requires a minimum of how many conditions to be met before access can be granted?

   A. 1
   B. 2
   C. 3
   D. 4
   E. 5

12. Least user access impl ___ requirement?

   A. The group with the lea ___ access control granted the highest leve ___ ld be
   B. Users should commonly l ___ under limited user accounts ___ kstations performing administrative fu ___ ey are
   C. No user should have administr ___ workstation. ___ ts to a
   D. All users should have administrati ___ a workstation. ___ s to

13. The three basic levels of need for informa ___ existence of information, view partial infor ___ re tion, and _____.

Access Control System Implementations

ACCESS CONTROL SYSTEMS ARE AN ESSENTIAL PART of any organization's information security infrastructure. An access control system protects both the organization and its users. Limiting who can have access to certain documents, computer systems, or applications—but ensuring that those who need access have it—is a security measure that needs to be developed and continuously tested.

Identifying and implementing an access control system can be challenging. This chapter addresses how policies, standards, guidelines, and procedures help you implement and maintain an access control system. The procedures you create should be easily understood by those implementing them and by the users who must abide by them.

Chapter 7 Topics

This chapter covers the following topics and concepts:

- How to transform access control policies and standards into procedures and guidelines
- What identity management is in terms of access control
- Which issues affect the size and distribution of staff and assets
- How to implement multilayer access controls
- Which access controls are geared toward employees, remote employees, customers, and business partners
- Which best practices you should follow when implementing access controls
- Case studies and examples of access control implementations that solve business challenges

---

Chapter 7 Goals

When you complete this chapter, you will be able to:

- Create guidelines and procedures based on standards and policies
- Identify various standard bodies
- Compare various multilayer access controls
- Set up access controls for internal and external employees
- Tighten security for access to web portals, such as for e-commerce and banking
- Use best practices when implementing an access control system
- Use examples and case studies to design your own access control implementations

---

Transforming Access Control Policies and Standards into Procedures and Guidelines

Access controls limit who can be in a specific area and what they can do once they get into an area. This area can be physical, such as a building, or logical, like a file structure. Limiting access on a personal or enterprise network will assist in securing what "lives" on that network, such as documents and personal information. Access controls are a cornerstone to a secure and vital network.

An important part of any access control system is creating clear guidelines and instructions for using it. In this section, you will learn how to use policies and standards as the foundation for creating access control system guidelines and procedures. The following are items to help you get started:

- Begin the formal process with a plan. State your goals, what you need to reach them, and how you'll achieve them.
- Determine which policies and standards you will reference. You don't have to reinvent the wheel when other documents and resources already exist that can help you create your own guidelines and procedures.
- Determine how you can make the documentation process and system implementation easy for everyone. Once a task and process becomes difficult, people may reject the entire concept.
- Come up with effective ways to spread the message and ensure that everyone understands the policies, standards, guidelines, and procedures.

Transform Policy Definitions into Implementation Tasks

Everything starts with a policy. A policy specifies the requirements or rules that need to be followed. It sets the direction for the organization. An example of a policy is an acceptable use policy stating how employees may use employer-owned computer resources, including the network and systems. A **standard** specifies how to support the policy. The standards can be industry standards or organization-specific, or a combination of both. **Guidelines** provide recommendations on how the requirements are to be met. Procedures define how the policies, standards, and guidelines will be implemented. An example of this process is:

- **Policy**—The organization must ensure that all employer-owned computer systems are secure.
- **Standard**—The organization may implement ISO 27002.
- **Guideline**—The organization recommends that passwords should be a minimum of eight characters and a maximum of 16.
- **Procedure**—The organization should follow the steps in the Password Creation procedure to support the policy and standard.

Approaches

There are various approaches an organization can take when implementing access controls. You should consider each approach when creating procedures. Two of these approaches are the phased approach and prioritization.

> **NOTE**
>
> A phased approach may be used when an organization has specific controls in place that ensure all steps that are related to each other are resolved together. In other words, changing one control does not affect another control. If an organization has the time to address all problems, a phased approach may be used.

A phased approach starts at the beginning and works through to the end, but only on one section of a project at a time. For example, a systems administrator performs an **assessment** of the infrastructure, determines the goals, and sets the procedures based on the goals. He or she must then implement the procedure. After all systems have been configured, they must be tested and the results evaluated. Let's say a user named Kevin breached the security of a network folder. A systems administrator may review all the steps that led up to the breach. Was Kevin correctly granted access to the network? Was Kevin correctly allowed access to a particular folder? Did the access controls on the folder function properly or was there a failure? If there was a failure, why did it occur? Are changes to the access control system required?

> **NOTE**
>
> A prioritization approach is used when an organization has limited resources and wants to resolve the important processes first.

A prioritization approach means the administrator deals with procedures and network changes on a case-by-case basis. If an attack has occurred on the network, the administrator may make appropriate changes to adjust for that immediate weakness in the system. For example, if a user breaches network security and accesses a folder without authorization, a prioritization approach would require a systems administrator to resolve the access control failure. Very little testing may be done after the remediation occurs. Prioritization may be used when an organization feels that ranking the tasks from most important to least important will provide an efficient system for resolving the tasks.

Implementation

Once you decide which approach to take, you can begin turning policy statements into implementation tasks and procedures. Various questions that need to be addressed are:

- What is the mission of the implementation? What is the organization trying to achieve? In this case, you are taking a plan of action and putting the controls around it to ensure the policy is implemented.
- What are the factors needed to ensure the policy is met? An organization must consider multiple factors when implementing a policy. Some examples of factors are access controls, secure communications to networks outside of the corporate network, and authentication measures.
- Which tools will you need to address the access controls, secure communications, and authentication? What standards will be followed? Which access control models, such as discretionary access control (DAC), mandatory access control (MAC), and role-based access control (RBAC), will be used? What secure protocols, such as Secure Shell (SSH) or Transport Layer Security (TLS), will be implemented? What authentication methods, such as user ID and password or multifactor authentication, will be implemented?
- How will the methods be implemented? Will they be put in place all at once or in a phased approach? Which risks are associated with the timing of the implementation?
- How will these access, secure communications, and authentication measures be tested? How often will they be tested? What will the organization do with the results?
- How often will the policies be reviewed? How will you document the policies and implementation tasks?

Transforming policies into implementation procedures ensures that all business units are aware of the policies and security needs of the organization. The implementation procedures formalize the structure and policies of the corporation and allow the organizations within the company to be measured against them. These implementation tasks help ensure a safer organization by having a common mission and implementation method that all employees will follow.

Follow Standards Where Applicable

Standards are an important baseline for incorporating security and specifically access controls within an organization. This section examines some of the organizations that set security and technology standards and which standards are important for creating access control implementation procedures.

FYI

The NIST National Vulnerability Database (NVD) is a United States repository maintained by the government providing information on standard-based vulnerability management data. The NVD uses the Security Content Automation Protocol (SCAP). Organizations that use the NVD are provided with vulnerability management, security management, and compliance information on software and hardware products and their implementations.

IEEE

IEEE was created in 1963. This not-for-profit professional organization has created over 1,100 information technology standards. Some of these standards include IEEE 802.1X, which addresses authentication for Layer 2 (bridges and switches) devices when communicating on a network. The standard 802.1AC defines Media Access Control (MAC), and 802.1AE discusses MAC security. The IEEE Standards Association (IEEE-SA) is the standards contributor to IEEE. The IEEE-SA promotes "the engineering process by creating, developing, integrating, sharing, and applying knowledge about electro- and information technologies and sciences."

National Institute of Standards and Technology (NIST)

NIST was founded in 1901 as a nonregulatory federal agency under the U.S. Department of Commerce. NIST's mission is "to promote U.S. innovation and industrial competitiveness by advancing measurement science, standards, and technology in ways that enhance economic security and improve quality of life." When it comes to information technology, NIST was given direction by the Computer Security Act of 1987, the Cyber Security Research and Development Act of 2002, and the Federal Information Security Management Act (FISMA) of 2002. Under these three acts is the development of cryptographic standards and procedures, guidelines, and best practices for federal IT security. This IT security includes Federal Information Processing Standards (FIPS) and NIST Special Publications.

 NOTE

NIST Special Publication 800-53 Revision 3 provides guidelines for selecting and specifying security controls for information systems.

Federal Information Security Management Act (FISMA)

The **Federal Information Security Modernization Act (FISMA)** sets forth security requirements for all federal government agencies. It requires each federal agency to "develop, document, and implement an agency-wide program to provide information security for the information and information systems that support the operations and assets of the agency, including those provided and managed by another agency, contractor, or another source." NIST sets the FISMA standards for federal IT systems.

According to FISMA, an information security policy should consist of:

 NOTE

You might see the "M" in FISMA used to mean "Management" or "Modernization." The original Federal Information Security Management Act was passed in 2002 to set federal cybersecurity requirements. Congress later updated the law in 2014 and kept the acronym the same when they passed the Federal Information Security Modernization Act.

- Periodic risk assessments
- Policies and procedures based on the risk assessments
- Subordinate plans for providing adequate information security
- Security awareness training
- Periodic testing and evaluation of the effectiveness of information security policies
- Process for planning, implementing, evaluating, and documenting remedial actions
- Procedure for detecting, reporting, and responding to security incidents
- Plans and procedures to ensure continuity of operations

As previously discussed, you must understand risk to appropriately identify or create security policies for your organization. You should use your knowledge of that risk to implement a framework of controls. FISMA has built a risk management framework that you can apply to new and current systems to manage your risk:

- Step 1: Categorize the information system.
- Step 2: Select a baseline of security controls.
- Step 3: Implement the security controls and document how the controls are deployed.
- Step 4: Assess the security controls.
- Step 5: Authorize information system operations based on a determination of risk.
- Step 6: Monitor and assess selected security controls.

ISO

ISO is the largest developer and publisher of international standards. ISO is not associated with any government entity but works with the public and private sectors. Approximately 18,000 standards have been established through ISO, including:

- ISO 9001, "Quality Management Systems"
- ISO 31000, "Risk Management—Principles and Guidelines"
- ISO/IEC 27001, "Information Technology—Security Techniques—Information Security Management System Implementation Guidance"
- ISO/IEC 27006, "Information Technology—Security Techniques—Requirements for Bodies Providing Auditing and Certification of Information Security Management Systems"

ISO develops standards based on recommendations from industries and those that may be affected by the standard. The recommendation is passed on to an ISO member and the technical committee that would create the standard. If the technical committee feels that the standard is needed and is a global requirement, the committee discusses the relevance and will work together to develop the standard.

In 2008, IEEE and ISO joined forces to create the Partner Standards Development Organization (PSDO). This organization combines the resources from both governing bodies to "focus on the subjects of information technology, intelligent transport systems, and health informatics."

> **NOTE**
>
> An ISO/IEC prefix indicates joint work between ISO and the International Electrotechnical Committee (IEC). Its mission is to provide information about standards and standardization.

Internet Engineering Task Force (IETF)

The Internet Engineering Task Force (IETF) was formed in 1986. IETF is an international organization that focuses on the Internet and Internet protocols. This includes the Transmission Control Protocol/Internet Protocol (TCP/IP) suite, which includes the **Application Layer**, **Transport Layer**, **Internet Layer**, and **Data Link Layer** (described in RFC 1122). The IETF develops Requests for Comments (RFCs). An RFC addresses the methods and behaviors of Internet systems including routers, switches, and computer systems. Each RFC has its own set of numbers assigned to it. These numbers are never changed. If an RFC needs to be rewritten or have additions, a revised document is written and released. RFCs can be superseded by other RFCs, making the original or previous RFC obsolete. Examples of some RFCs are:

- RFC 1457, which addresses the security-level framework for the Internet
- RFC 1938, which addresses one-time password messages

- RFC 2716, which touches on Transport Layer (Layer 3) security
- RFC 4301, which focuses on the security architecture for Internet Protocol (IP)

PCI Security Standards Council

The PCI Security Standards Council (PCI SSC) was developed in 2006 for developing, managing, educating, and providing awareness for the payment card industry (PCI) security standards. These standards include the Data Security Standard (DSS), payment application data security standard, and PIN-entry device requirements. The companies that founded the PCI Security Standards Council are American Express, MasterCard, Visa, Discover, and JCB International.

Payment Card Industry Data Security Standard (PCI DSS) is a security standard for security management, policies and procedures, network architecture, software design, and other protective measures. This standard helps organizations protect customer payment card account data. PCI DSS specifies six primary requirements that merchants need to meet to process credit and debit card transactions:

- Building and maintaining a secure network
- Protecting cardholder data
- Maintaining a vulnerability management program
- Implementing strong access control measures
- Regularly monitoring and testing networks
- Maintaining an information security policy

The PCI DSS is updated every 3 years, using a defined life cycle approach that seeks input from merchants, service providers, banks, and other industry stakeholders. The current version of PCI DSS at the time this book went to press was version 3.2.1, published in May 2018. The PCI SSC frequently publishes updates to the standard, so be sure to check their website at *http://pcisecuritystandards.org* for the most recent version.

Center for Internet Security

The Center for Internet Security (CIS) in a nonprofit independent community of professionals that provides best practice standards for the secure configuration of network devices such as Apple iPhone, Check Point Firewall software, and Cisco devices, just to name a few. The professionals associated with CIS establish:

- Benchmarks detailing best practice security configurations for IT systems
- Benchmark audit tools that enable IT and security professionals to assess their IT systems for compliance with benchmark and security best practices
- Metrics that can be used across organizations to collect and analyze data on security processes and performance outcomes

CIS promotes consensus-based standards that organizations can use and implement to increase the security, privacy, and integrity of the business and other functions and transactions that occur on the Internet.

Create Simple and Easy-to-Follow Procedures

Although standards have been established by credible organizations in the United States and internationally, you need to incorporate them into your procedures in a way that's easy for users to follow. Policies, too, need to be incorporated and expanded upon with details that specify how to perform tasks and when.

Converting a policy into an implementation task requires multiple steps. You must first identify a policy that addresses your needs. Some examples of policies are a password policy and a system configuration policy. You then compare your current system with the system described in the policy. You must perform a gap analysis to understand which steps will need to be implemented.

7

Access Control System
Implementations

FYI

When managing procedures, establish who may change procedures and under what conditions. Is the person who created procedures the person who needs to change them? Will the person who needs to change them understand how and why the original policies and procedures were put in place? The developers of an organization's security policies often move on to other programs or other companies. If their thoughts and beliefs behind the design, implementation, and testing of policies and procedures are not well noted or are incomprehensible to new administrators, the policies and procedures become a security risk themselves.

Let's walk through a policy–standard–procedures–guidelines example for an organization. This example will show you how theory is put into practice:

1. **Policy**—The organization wants to implement a more defined password policy for its access control policies. Not only does this include individual computer systems, such as desktops and laptops, but servers that are maintained throughout the organization as well.

2. **Standard**—The organization has determined that it wants to implement the standards and recommendations that NIST has established—for example, NIST Special Publication (SP) 800-53. This document provides the recommended security controls for federal information systems. Although this organization is not a federal entity, it feels that the standards and recommendations that NIST has established meet its stringent needs. The organization will also use the standards and recommendations established by NIST in NIST SP 800-118, "Guide to Enterprise Password Management." This document recommends the following constraints for password usage and creation:
   - Storage:
     - Encrypt files that maintain passwords.
     - Use operating system access control features to restrict access to files that contain passwords.
     - Store the cryptographic hashes of the passwords instead of storing the actual password.
   - Transmission:
     - Encrypt communications when transmitting passwords.
     - Transmit cryptographic password hashes versus a plaintext password.

- Use secure protocols when transmitting passwords (Secure Shell or HTTPS).
- Use network segregation and switched networks for internal networks in order to reduce the possibility of an attacker identifying the password.
- Use a secure password-based authentication protocol (Kerberos).
- User knowledge and behavior:
  - Be aware of nontechnical tactics for password capturing such as shoulder surfing. Although a password may be hidden by asterisks, an attacker may still be able to gain certain characters in the password that can be used to determine the full password.
  - Be aware of technical tactics for password capturing such as keystroke logging. Protect the systems to ensure malware is not loaded onto the computer systems. Users should also not enter their password into public computer systems, such as those at airports or hotels, which are high risk, or the password may be compromised.
  - Be aware of social engineering. An attacker might ask a user specific questions to gather additional data that will be used to determine the password or to reset a password. Phishing e-mails are an example of social engineering that is used to gather password data.
  - Be aware of malicious insiders who may use the passwords or provide passwords to others to gather data or files for the organization, even though they or others are not allowed access to them.

3. **Procedures**—These are the steps that an administrator takes to implement controls. In this example, part of the procedure for implementing passwords is to identify all the systems that require passwords. Once they are identified, it is necessary to apply the procedures to make sure the passwords meet the password policy and standards. Documenting the specific procedures based on protection of passwords, strength of passwords, and reuse of passwords will help ensure the goals are met.

4. **Guidelines**—These are suggestions and best practices based on standards. Regarding a password policy, for example, suppose the organization has decided to base its guidelines on the best practices established by NIST. If employees follow the guidelines, the organization will be in compliance with the standards.

These steps are put in place to ensure a secure organization and computer systems.

Define Guidelines That Departments and Business Units Can Follow

Guidelines are optional actions or controls that are based on policies, standards, and procedures. Guidelines are also recommendations and best practices that are provided by standard bodies such as NIST, ISO, and CIS. Creating guidelines that employees follow can be difficult or easy. How this is determined is based on the steps that were taken beforehand. Previously, you learned about procedures and that they need to be simple and easy to follow. If this philosophy is not adopted, the subsequent steps for implementing security will be much more challenging. When the security teams within an organization focus on security, they must realize that this needs to be accepted by both technical and nontechnical parties. This is where broad-based security training can benefit everyone. Administrators and employees need to understand the value and importance of what they are being asked to do.

Guidelines that may be established based on the password policy example, NIST standards, and password procedures are:

- Encrypt all passwords.
- Ensure secure communications are used for each entry.
- Educate employees on shoulder surfing, malware, and social engineering, and how these tactics are used to retrieve passwords.
- Lock out users after five failed logon attempts.
- Require all passwords to be a minimum of 8 characters and a maximum of 16 characters.
- Require all passwords to include a minimum of one capital letter, one number, and two special characters.
- Ensure that passwords are changed every 90 days.
- Configure the system to store up to five previous passwords so that they cannot be reused.
- Use an enterprise-wide password database system.

Guidelines within the organization assist in educating administrators. Guidelines identify what is expected of various groups to ensure compliance with policies and standards. Security is a day-to-day mandate and requires everyone to participate in the actions, policies, and guidelines. All employees should receive training to fully understand the value of security to the organization.

> **NOTE**
>
> An enterprise-wide password database system, also called a single sign-on system, allows individual users to encrypt their user ID and password. These tools allow users to store their user IDs and passwords for multiple systems and applications. The data is encrypted and can be unlocked only by a user's password. Instead of having to remember several passwords, the user will need to remember only one.

Identity Management and Access Control

Identity management is an important concept for information security professionals. It involves creating accounts for users across all of the systems they interact with and coordinating those accounts so that changes are reflected across all systems. Identity management programs often implement a single sign-on (SSO) system that facilitates the management of user accounts.

One of the main benefits of a well-coordinated identity management program is clean integration with an organization's access control system. Consider an organization that adopts a role-based access control (RBAC) system. With this approach, individuals are assigned to roles based on their job responsibilities. If a user changes jobs, the identity management staff only needs to change the user's role in the centralized access control system, and that change will then be reflected in permission settings across all of the organization's information systems. Similarly, if a user leaves the organization, his or her account needs to be disabled in only one place—the SSO system. This change will then ripple through all of the information systems that rely on SSO for authentication.

User Behavior, Application, and Network Analysis

Identifying how users, applications, and networks behave helps create a **baseline** for the infrastructure. By understanding normal behavior, you are able to detect activities that are unusual. For example, suppose an accounting employee named Scott ordinarily accesses financial servers; this is considered normal behavior. If Scott begins accessing engineering servers, you know that the access control is not working correctly and you may need to question Scott's actions. Is there a virus on his system, or is he trying to obtain intellectual property? Tracking the behavior of all systems on a network will help you understand normal activities and identify breaches as well.

Examining user behavior reveals the times a user may log on to a system, the applications he or she uses and how often, the websites a user frequents, and servers that are accessed. In general, user behavior is any type of activity that defines a user's actions.

Application analysis has similar characteristics. By analyzing applications, you may learn:

- How often applications are accessed
- Who accesses them
- What actions are performed once an application is accessed

You must understand these aspects of an application for security and management purposes. If an administrator is aware that an application is not accessed from 2:00 a.m. to 5:00 a.m., he or she may decide to schedule system upgrades during that time. This ensures that resources are available when needed and that adjustments won't affect the majority of employees. Availability is an essential part of network security, and user behavior analysis and application analysis provide the data needed to ensure systems are available.

Network analysis provides details on both users and applications as well as network traffic. Understanding the behavior of the network verifies the access and security controls that are in place. It provides guidelines for normal and abnormal activity. For example, if Scott's system is sending out abnormal traffic, there could be a virus on the network. Analyzing all inbound and outbound traffic may pinpoint attackers coming in as well as internal employees creating havoc within the network. Network analysis ensures that security controls are in place and indicates whether they are effective.

Monitoring Library Access

Digital libraries have a large array of data covering all types of topics. If an administrator keeps track of who is downloading what, he or she can build a profile on each user. Reviewing composite data of all users over time reveals trends in users' interests. For example, if a user downloads a large number of files unrelated to his or her work duties, it could signal the user has dangerous motives.

Monitoring your system is a way to track employees and possibly determine ulterior motives. For example, you may find that a particular user is downloading a large number of documents. Is this normal behavior for her? If not, you should question why she needs the documents.

Understanding the behavior of users, applications, and network activities assists in identity and access management. It identifies access controls that are not functioning correctly and lets an administrator know if changes are needed. Behavior analysis can prove that access is set up correctly because network patterns and access are working as planned. Combining behavior analysis and identity and access management provides a blueprint for the network regarding normal behaviors and the expectations of the systems.

Size and Distribution of Staff and Assets

Creating a complete inventory of IT assets is one of the first steps in implementing access controls. Which servers, routers, firewalls, workstations, databases, and so on are on the network, and where are they located? What are the software, folders, and files that are on the servers and workstations? What data is in the database? Once you determine the asset inventory, it is important to determine the risk associated with the assets and data. You can determine risk by evaluating the value of the data and the cost to the organization if the data were exposed or had to be replaced.

The access control system you implement should be based on the risk against the data and network access. Understanding how the staff and assets are distributed within the organization will help determine the controls needed for accessing high-, medium-, and low-risk assets. For example, if there is high risk associated with specific data, additional access controls may need to be placed on the data. If you have a large staff, it may be beneficial to implement a single sign-on tool. This enables you to centralize management of assets and the access granted to them.

Network administrators must always be aware of which assets are available to be accessed and where these assets are. For example, if human resources (HR) information is available on a network that has been segmented for finance, a security breach may occur. Administrators must ensure that the network and computer resources support the staff and staffing requirements. Administrators must ensure the tools that employees use are available when employees need them.

You cannot secure users, objects, and tools if you don't know they exist. Unencrypted files on a server, applications on computer resources that open ports on the network, and servers that maintain intellectual property are targets for attack. Large infrastructures can be difficult for an administrator to manage. In addition, if a server that holds quarterly confidential financials is available only during normal business hours, an employee might copy or e-mail these files to work on them during off hours. This poses a security risk. E-mailing the document via an unencrypted connection provides an opportunity for an attacker to see these data. Leaving confidential data on a laptop poses a risk if the laptop is stolen.

It is important to have the tools available that allow an administrator to manage any size staff and assets. Large organizations tend to experience a flux of employees due to hiring, terminations, and resignations. Administrators need to be able to add and remove employees and groups in a matter of hours. Ensuring that authentication and authorizations systems are able to handle a large-scale employee base is important when designing and implementing an organization's infrastructure.

Multilayered Access Control Implementations

Implementing multiple layers in security is providing a **defense-in-depth** mechanism and, therefore, stronger protection for the network and users. Multiple layers provide multiple road blocks for a user and attacker. Having multiple controls in place before something can be accessed may be tiresome for a user; however, the goal is to have the same effect on an attacker. If an attacker is able to find a hole and access a company's network, additional layers of security might stop the attacker from reaching other systems, applications, or sensitive data.

Creating layers within the network can be done physically by segmenting users and servers onto separate networks. This can also be done logically through virtual local area networks (VLANs). Implementing security measures at each logical level of access such as application access or file access puts up additional road blocks for attackers. Making security a hierarchical structure with layers versus implementing just a few controls provides the strong defense needed to protect the overall infrastructure.

User Access Control Profiles

User access control profiles identify authorizations allowable for each user, such as what access is allowed and what is denied. You can implement user access control profiles with role-based access controls. Implementing a role-based access control allows you to manage the infrastructure with greater control. Role-based access is implemented for a large group of people who perform similar tasks and helps prevent a single user within a role from having more rights than others. Role-based security saves you time by ensuring all controls are applied to a particular role. For example, suppose you've already defined the access controls for the Sales Representative role. When a new sales rep is hired, you simply assign that person to the Sales Rep role instead of assigning access controls separately.

This technique benefits a multilayered access control implementation because the role may have additional access controls added or removed, depending on the risk associated with a user's job functions. If the risk associated with a role increases, the access controls placed on the roles can change with it. For example, sales reps may be given less access to their territories' sales figures at the end of the quarter because the finance department is compiling the financials for all regions. Allowing the sales representatives to change data while the finance department is using the data would create a problem for the entire organization.

System Access Control Lists

System access control lists (SACLs) identify which users have access to systems and what rights they have once each system is accessed. Is the system a read-only database or can users write to the database? Providing accessibility metrics and monitoring user actions help ensure the system is secure. They can also indicate that access changes need to occur.

Designing a system that meets the needs of the users but does not provide more access than is needed should be at the core of system security. Restricting access at the system level limits what changes can occur on the system. One example is restricting the installation of software, which makes the system more secure and limits the chances of Trojan horses and malware being installed. **FIGURE 7-1** identifies categories of software restriction policies in the Microsoft Windows operating system.

The three policies that can be implemented for software download restrictions are:

- **Enforcement**—Enforces additional policies automatically (see **FIGURE 7-2**)
- **Designated File Types**—Determines what types of files can be downloaded to the system, such as EXE files, scripts, or ActiveX controls (see **FIGURE 7-3**)

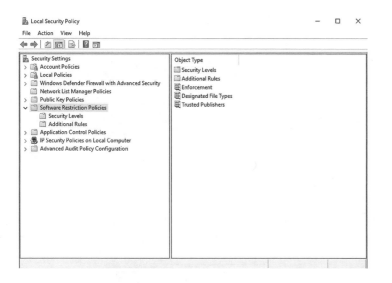

FIGURE 7-2

Enforcement properties.

Used with permission from Microsoft.

- **Trusted Publishers**—Provides the ability to allow or not allow code that was provided from a trusted source (see **FIGURE 7-4**)

Implementing security at the system level is important when implementing a multilayer access control system. It limits access to the greater system. This ensures that employees who should not be installing software or making changes to the system are not given access. As you learned earlier in this chapter, best practices for computer systems have been established by standard bodies. If an organization bases its computer system configuration on these best practices, an administrator should ensure that there are no computer system configuration changes that will result in an unsecure system.

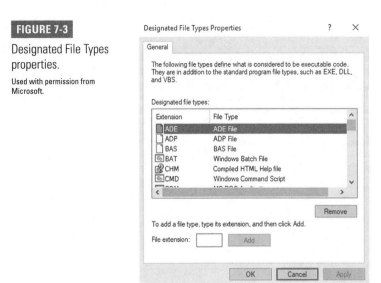

FIGURE 7-3

Designated File Types properties.

Used with permission from Microsoft.

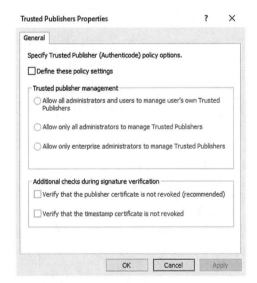

FIGURE 7-4

Trusted Publishers properties.

Used with permission from Microsoft.

Applications Access

Employees may be given full or limited amounts of access to the systems and applications that access data. Applications may have direct controls placed on them, such as limiting execution. Once launched, an application may have access controls that allow only specific users to view certain fields or that allow certain features to be used within the application.

In addition, applications may be read-only for some users but not others. Changes or additions may be restricted to only the owner or administrator of an application. Policies are established for each application, ensuring the accessible information is not compromised by a user or an attacker. These controls can also identify the types of data each user can view in the application and how the data should be displayed.

For example, an administrator can place specific controls on Microsoft SQL Server to ensure users cannot access data, create new databases, or change the application without appropriate permission. A SQL server has various roles that provide specific access. Several of these roles and the access granted are:

- **dbcreator**—Can create databases and alter and restore its own databases
- **serveradmin**—Can change server-wide configuration options and shut down servers
- **sysadmin**—Can perform any activity in the server

These access controls provide yet another layer of security on top of controls at the system level. If a failure occurs at the system level, the application access controls provide security. These layers ensure that the system and data are not completely vulnerable to attacks.

File and Folder Access

If users are not given access to certain applications, access to the location of the data may be limited as well. Assigning controls to files and folders adds yet another layer to a multilayer structure. Limiting read and write access to files and folders ensures the data cannot be compromised. Privileges need to be limited by whom and what can access specific files and folders. Administrators should assign privileges based on need.

Scott, for example, has documents that are customer-specific, such as organizational charts and contact information, on his corporate computer system. Scott's customer wants assurance that this information is not available to its competitors. Scott needs to block access to his coworkers who support his customer's competitors. **FIGURE 7-5** shows how these controls could be put in place against a file or folder.

Employing this access control provides yet another layer of protection in a multilayer access control implementation.

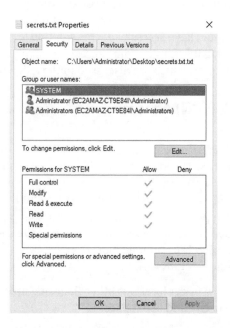

FIGURE 7-5

File system access control.

Used with permission from Microsoft.

Data Access

After passing through most of the layers of access control, limiting access to the data itself is your last method of protecting it. A privilege such as read or write is an example of a security measure placed against data. As mentioned previously, many database applications, such as Microsoft SQL Server, provide controls to limit access to data.

Results or statistics are only as reliable as the data that they are based on. If the data are changed or augmented, the work that is being done on the data will be unreliable. Limiting access to data protects all who rely on the data, including individuals and systems. Allowing full access leaves data vulnerable to attack and human error. It may not be the intent of an individual to erase or destroy data, but accidents happen.

Access Controls for Employees, Remote Employees, Customers, and Business Partners

Companies have many types of identity groups that need access to the network. The identity groups include employees, remote employees, customers, and business partners. Managing the access controls of various identity groups can be cumbersome. An administrator must understand how they will access the network, when they will access the network, and the amount of access that is required by role.

For example, a business partner of a software development company may need full access to documentation and software but not to the source code. The business partner may be treated like an employee, but the partner cannot receive access to everything an employee in a similar role would have. For example, a business partner should not have access to internal distribution lists, the HR site, or IT sites that are provided specifically for employees. Business partners are important to an organization, but they still work for another company, and data need to remain separate. Careful consideration must be given to every role as well as every group they are a part of. Customers may have access to product A documentation, but this does not mean that the customer should have access to documentation for products B and C as well. There are multiple tools available for providing access to employees, remote employees, customers, and business partners, which are discussed in the following sections.

Remote Virtual Private Network (VPN) Access— Remote Employees and Workers

Remote access **virtual private networks (VPNs)** are established to allow remote employees access to an organization's internal network. The idea is to provide the same capabilities off site that you have on site. A remote VPN provides a secure connection by creating an encrypted tunnel from point A to point B, usually across the Internet. If point B is an organization's internal network, point A is a computer system or mobile device that can be located anywhere, such as a coffee shop, a house, an airport, or any place that provides Internet access. **FIGURE 7-6** provides an overview of VPN communications.

The benefits associated with remote access VPNs are:

- It reduces costs by allowing the user to work at locations other than an employer site. This may reduce facility costs for electricity and floor space.

FIGURE 7-6

VPN communications.

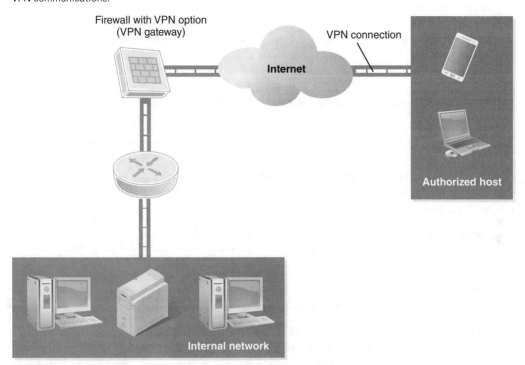

- It improves flexibility by giving users the ability to work whenever and wherever. For example, an employee may be given access to employer resources after hours. The employee may also work at a coffee shop before a customer meeting.
- It provides secure communications through encryption and access rights based on the user.

Before remote access VPNs were available, many organizations used expensive leased lines. This technology was not considered a secure option because these lines can easily be tapped and the communications monitored. With the advent of VPNs with encryption and access controls, security was enabled by protecting the data and controlling who has access to which resources within an organization's domain. Remote access VPNs provide secure communications for laptops, mobile devices such as smartphones and tablets, and even external servers.

Remote access VPN access controls are managed through authentication of the user, VPN firewalls, VPN routers, and applications. Access controls can be based on user IDs or mandatory access control limitations. The ability for remote access VPNs to provide security and access controls establishes an optimal solution for remote employees as well as customers and business partners. This solution gives the administrator a more granulated access control by limiting or allowing access based on:

- **Authentication methods**—Incorporating a multifactor authentication method adds the extra level of security for gaining access to the corporate network. For example, when

Scott goes into the office, he may use a user ID and password. If Scott is at home and accessing the corporate network remotely, he will still use his user ID and password, but another layer of authentication will be required with the VPN server.

- **Membership in groups**—Creating groups based on a user's role within the organization ensures that customers and business partners have access only to specific files and applications and limited access to others.

Intranets—Internal Business Operations and Communications

An intranet is an internal private network. Intranets generally consist of web applications or portals and provide a system for internal employees to collaborate securely. Intranets limit outside communications by allowing only systems and users that have been authenticated on the corporate network. Intranets may be set up to allow a group of people such as a software development team to collaborate, or it can be a tool available to all employees. Some common items stored on an intranet are:

- Company directory
- Company locations and directions to them
- Organizational charts
- Corporate announcements
- Search capabilities for additional corporate resources

Intranets have been set up as a single repository for all employer-focused information. An intranet can update employees regarding holiday dates, building closures due to inclement weather, and changes to 401(k) or benefits information. It can also be a tool for employees to provide thoughts or opinions about the organization. Portals can also be developed for products. These portals can have software updates, roadmaps, documentation, and a section where questions can be asked and answered about a particular product.

Securing the intranet can be done using the same tools that are used for protecting any web application that is maintained by the employer. Authentication, access controls, and tools such as single sign-on or identity and access management, will ensure the information is accessed only by people with the proper credentials.

Extranets—External Supply Chains, Business Partners, Distributors, and Resellers

Extranets extend an intranet in a limited fashion, providing access to business partners, distributors, and resellers. For example, an organization might have a product site for its partners and distributors that contains software downloads and updates, documentation, and questions and answers regarding a specific product.

Extranets expand the usage and availability of intranets. Extending access to your external supply chain, business partners, distributors, and resellers lets these parties know that your relationship with them is important. Giving them the same access to materials and accessibility to resources that customer service and engineering have helps build the relationship and the trust between your organizations.

Security for extranets is provided via isolation, access controls, authentication, and encryption, if communication between the user and web portal is needed. Isolation of the network into a private and public network ensures that only certain users have access to certain networks. Extranets provide remote access to only the limited portions of a company's infrastructure that are approved for third-party use. Extranets also limit access to specific resources on the extranet. Limiting access to specific applications, services, files and folders, and data ensures that confidential information does not get into the wrong hands. As previously discussed, authentication factors verify that users are who they say they are. Employing a stronger authentication method ensures this. Encryption secures the communication paths between the systems so that no one can access the data while on the network.

Secure E-Commerce Sites with Encryption

Many businesses sell goods and services online using e-commerce websites in a **business to business (B2B)** and/or **business to consumer (B2C)** fashion. Customers often provide sensitive information, such as passwords and credit card numbers, on these websites. This sensitive information must be protected against eavesdropping through the use of encryption technology, such as that provided by Transport Layer Security (TLS). This protocol supports a number of different cryptographic algorithms, relying on digital certificates (such as the one shown in **FIGURE 7-7**) and public key encryption, and works as follows:

1. The web server sends its **digital certificate** to the web browser. The web browser extracts the web server's **public key** from the digital certificate.
2. The web browser verifies the web server's certificate by comparing the certificate authority with the trusted authority list that the web browser was shipped with. The web browser computes a hash of the certificate and compares it with the hash in the

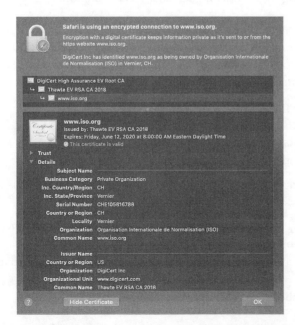

FIGURE 7-7

Example of a certificate.

Screen shot(s) reprinted with
permission from Apple Inc.

certificate. The hash is decrypted using the trusted authority's public key. If the hash matches, the certificate has not been tampered with. The web browser checks the validity date to ensure the certificate has not expired. The browser also checks to verify that the system that sent the certificate has the same uniform resource locator (URL) that was encoded into the identification information. After these checks match, the public key of the server is extracted from the server's certificate.

3. The web browser generates a random symmetric encryption key. This key will be used to encrypt the conversation between the web browser and the web server. The symmetric encryption key is encrypted with the web server's public key—in other words, the symmetric encryption key has been "wrapped." Remember that the web server's public key was extracted from the web server's digital certificate.

> ▶ **TIP**
>
> How do you know if a website is encrypted? If the web address starts with "https" and displays an icon that looks like a padlock, the website is secure.

4. The web browser sends the wrapped key to the web server. The web server decrypts the wrapped key with its **private key**. At this time, the web browser and the web server have the same symmetric encryption key. This encryption key will be used to start an encrypted conversation. The symmetric key will be used to encrypt and decrypt the messages.

Secure Online Banking Access Control Implementations

Online banking is another web portal access that implements encryption capabilities. The user and the bank want to ensure that the credentials entered are not retrieved through a separate entity such as an attacker. Banks that provide online access will also limit the amount of access available. If one user is able to see the accounts of a separate user, a security risk has occurred. Limiting the access for each user ID is a component on online banking.

Online banking sites require specific controls not only to protect the user's access but to protect the bank's as well. The Federal Financial Institutions Examination Council (FFIEC) is a body of the U.S. government that provides standards for financial institutions. The FFIEC has stated that an information security strategy should be based on the following:

- Consideration for prevention, detection, and response mechanisms
- Implementation of least privilege and the least permissive controls
- Layered controls between threats and organization assets
- Policies that guide employees and officers in implementing a security program

The FFIEC has established best practices for administering access rights. These access controls are:

- Assigning users and devices only the required access to perform their necessary functions
- Updating access controls based on personnel or system changes
- Periodically reviewing users' access rights based on the risk associated with the application or system
- Designing the acceptable use policies and having the users agree to them

Formal access control administration consists of the following processes:

- An enrollment for all new users.
- An authentication process to identify the specific users. The appropriate authentication process should match the risk associated with the user. These authentication methods can include multifactor authentication as well as challenge and response mechanisms.
- An authorization process for authorized users. This process will employ controls around a user's ability to add, delete, or modify applications, files, and specific information pertaining to that user.
- Monitoring and managing the access rights of specific users.
- Encrypting the transmission of user IDs and passwords.

The FFIEC has also established best practices for financial institutions to ensure secure access over multiple layers to protect against unauthorized access. These actions are:

- Grouping network servers, applications, data, and users into security domains
- Establishing the appropriate access requirements within and between the security domains
- Implementing the appropriate technical controls to ensure the access requirements
- Monitoring cross-domain access for security policy violations and anomalous activity

Implementing access controls for applications used by financial institutions is done via:

- Using authentication and authorization controls based on the risk of the application
- Monitoring the access rights to ensure that only the minimum access controls are granted to the users
- Using time-of-day access controls
- Logging of access and security events
- Using software that enables analysis of users' activities

Best practices for remote access to financial institutions are identified by the FFIEC as:

- Disabling remote access if no business exists
- Controlling access through approval by management and audits
- Implementing controls on both ends of the communication in order to avoid malicious activities
- Logging and monitoring all remote access communications
- Securing remote access devices
- Using strong authentication and encryption to secure communications

Logon/Password Access

Online banking sites require multiple modes of authentication. Users should be comfortable sending this information if the site uses secure communications. Online banking portals may require users to follow strict password polices, ensuring they have a strong password. This authentication information will identify a user's separate accounts and ensure that he or she is the only person who can access them. Users want to ensure that others cannot see their accounts and account number, and they do not want access to accounts they should not have access to. Using access controls reduces the security risks for both users and their banks.

As identified by the FFIEC, accessing an Internet banking environment with only single-factor authentication is not adequate for high-risk transactions that include access to customer information and movement of funds. The FFIEC recommends that if a financial institution provides an Internet-based service to customers, the appropriate multifactor authentication should be used. Providing the appropriate authentication method for users is necessary for protecting customer information. Not employing these mechanisms can result in credentials being compromised; therefore, identity theft, money laundering, and fraud can occur. The level of authentication should match the level of risk that a financial institution is willing to undertake.

Identification Imaging and Authorization

Online banking portals may provide secondary tactics for users to verify that their communications have not been hijacked. If a session were to be hijacked, a user would be providing his or her credentials to an attacker, and the account would most likely be compromised. Using a second authorization and identification provides a second layer of security. Identification that the website is a valid website protects the user.

Some online banking portals enable you to choose a custom image when you first set up your account. This image often appears before you enter your password. If the image you see is not the same image you originally selected, you know you should not continue logging on. Some banking portals even allow customers to create custom phrases, further enhancing the security of the financial information. You are likely required to enter a PIN as well to gain access to your accounts. Online banking portals aim to provide multiple layers of security to ensure that both the user's information and the banking information is secure.

Federated Identities and Third Party Identity Services

In many cases, organizations wish to share identity information with other organizations. For example, many websites rely on credentials provided by major technology companies for their authentication, allowing users the convenience of logging in "with Google" or connecting with "your Facebook account." This approach, where one organization depends on the identity information provided by another organization is known as **federation**. In a federated identity system, the organization that provides the accounts is known as the **identity provider**, while the organization that depends on those identities is known as the **service provider**.

There are several major approaches to federated identity, using different technologies:

- The **Security Assertion Markup Language (SAML)** is an approach used by websites where the user attempts to access a website and is redirected to their identity provider for authentication. SAML is widely used by websites.
- **OpenID Connect** is an alternative to SAML that works in a similar manner from the end user's perspective. The major difference between OpenID Connect and SAML is that OpenID Connect includes a process where the user is asked to consent to the sharing of

specific attributes before they are provided to the service provider. SAML does not have a similar consent process.

- **Shibboleth** is an implementation of SAML that is widely used among educational institutions. Academic resources often integrate with Shibboleth to allow faculty and students to log onto those resources using the identities provided by their home institutions.

Federation is a powerful concept that facilitates the interoperability of access control systems, the use of single sign-on, and cooperation between different organizations.

Today, many organizations also choose to adopt third-party identity and access control services that outsource some or all of the access control implementation to cloud service providers. This approach reduces the need of the organization to hire identity management specialists and transfers responsibility for maintaining complex technical infrastructures to specialist providers. These providers are known as **Identity as a Service (IDaaS)** providers.

Best Practices for Access Control Implementations

Ensuring an organization has the highest level of security is a daily exercise for security professionals. Some best practices for access controls and their implementation are:

- **Understand the roles within the organizations**—Identify users and their roles to determine which access controls to put in place. Segregating access by role ensures that someone in the customer service department, for example, does not have access to the company's financial records.
- **Understand the data that resides on the network**—An administrator cannot protect what he or she does not know about this includes data and software. If a certain application needs access to specific ports, the administrator needs to ensure these ports are open but that other tools or attackers do not have access as well. Knowing where all the data resides, on which servers, and on which network is necessary to configure proper access controls. Knowledge of this data is also necessary for designing policies and limiting where the data can be stored.
- **Establish a baseline**—Understanding normal behavior on a network helps you understand which access controls are necessary and pinpoint when unusual activities occur.
- **Monitor activities on a continuous basis**—After establishing a baseline, it is important to monitor it on a regular basis. Monitoring can identify new activities that are allowed, such as use of new software, or malicious activity, such as a virus on the network.
- **Create guidelines and policies that are easy to understand and implement**—No one wants to follow rules that are not understandable. Security is a role that everyone within an organization must know, advocate, and adhere to daily. If employees feel that rules hinder their job performance, they look for ways around the system and cause a larger security risk.
- **Manage user accounts appropriately**—Removing access for a user who has left the company and not reusing user IDs once deactivated reduces security risks.
- **Manage remote access capabilities**—Access for business partners, customers, and remote users must be managed effectively and securely. Ensure that communications are secure and protect organization resources from those who should not have access.

- **Provide strong security**—Protecting assets, files, people, and applications is a best practice for any organization. The risk associated with data getting into the wrong hands is not something an organization can afford. Ensure that proper access controls are in place, make sure authentication is efficient and effective, and communicate the security message to employees.

Case Studies and Examples

In order to understand some of the concepts discussed with access control implementations, it is beneficial to see how they are used in the real world. This section provides three case studies from real-world situations that cover some of the topics previously discussed.

Private Sector Case Study

A small tax filing company employs contractors for the tax season. Three contractors handle state taxes, and two of those contractors file federal taxes. The administrator needs to ensure that the two contractors have access to the state and federal forms for a select number of clients, and that the other contractor has access only to the state returns. The administrator has access to all client information.

The administrator applies access controls to the folders to limit the amount of access to what each of the contractors needs. It is also determined that each of these contractors will need his own account on the network. Limiting the amount of access for the three contractors ensures that the client information is kept secure and seen only by the appropriate user. Providing full access to everyone within the company would create risk that the administrator is not willing to accept.

Ensuring that each contractor has his own user ID allows for tracking in case a client is audited and the tax returns need to be reviewed. If additional access needs to be added for emergency purposes, the administrator grants the access on a temporary basis. The administrator also audits all of the activities to ensure correct access is provided.

These policies are shared with the clients, who feel secure knowing that the data will not get into the wrong hands. Implementing access controls proves successful for the company, and because the policy was documented and followed, updates can be done easily for each new batch of contractors.

This case study is an example of implementing a multilayer access control approach. The tax filing company defined the roles that each of the employees and contractors had within the organization and defined the access based on those roles. Each contractor was provided his or her own user ID for auditing as well, complementing the multilayer approach. The user role allowed contractors to see federal and state forms as appropriate, but they could not see every client's forms.

Public Sector Example

The U.S. government manages millions of employees, consultants, and contractors. These entities are assigned identity credentials to access various agencies' networks and systems. In many cases, individuals must remember a user ID and password for network access, and another user ID/password combination for each application they access. Although security personnel in each agency manage credentials for their users, the effort is still time-consuming and expensive. Overall security is also a concern. The current decentralized management of identities allows attackers to move from one system to another without their patterns being noticed right away.

For budgetary and strategic reasons, U.S. government security leaders have been collaborating on a project to create a centralized identity management system. The CIO Council lent a hand to the effort in 2009 by creating an implementation roadmap. The U.S. Department of Agriculture has already started a project to centralize 70 identity databases. Employees will receive a smart card and a PIN to access multiple databases rather than using unique credentials for each database as they do now. The Department of Homeland Security has started a similar initiative as well.

Some of the expected benefits of a centralized identity management system include:

- A more consistent approach to security
- A reduction of risk in inconsistent policy enforcement and mishandled passwords
- Reduced administrative expenses, including help desk calls to reset passwords
- Better cross-agency communications

Security leaders admit that the cost of implementation will be high, but they believe the cost of doing nothing may be even higher.

Critical Infrastructure Case Study

Reliant, a large healthcare facility, needed to upgrade its paper recordkeeping system to an electronic version. Knowing that the upgrade was needed, Reliant decided to implement a more secure infrastructure by using access controls to protect confidential information and upgrading its network configuration.

Access to the Reliant database is available through the corporate network. Employees use computers and handheld devices to access the data. Every patient at Reliant has personal data pertaining to him or her such as medical history, allergies, and blood type. Data such as patients' likes and dislikes and emergency contact information is also available. Doctors and nurses are able to review all the medical information on every patient in the database. Some healthcare providers are only able to see patients' history from the present date to 1 year back. Hospital volunteers are not able to see any patient medical histories but are able to see the emergency contacts as well as each patient's likes and dislikes.

Reliant established an intranet for schedules, planned activities, food menus, and any updates pertinent to all. Access points were established for visitors and the handheld devices used by the doctors and nurses. The handheld devices were required to have an SSL VPN connection to ensure the communication was encrypted. The devices also required user IDs and passwords as a form of authentication. Biometrics were not considered because the staff often wore gloves, preventing the scanners from reading the fingerprints.

The information that is stored in Reliant's system is confidential and must be kept secure. Access to the documents must be limited and constrained to only those individuals who have the rights to see it. Each user has a specific user ID that limits his or her access. Authentication and access are audited daily to ensure the constraints are in place and the patient data are not accessed. The access controls were carefully implemented and tested after every step to ensure they worked properly. Having volunteers see patients' medical histories would have violated Reliant's policy, and the healthcare facility could not risk access controls being set up incorrectly. Implementing the access control on the access points was essential as well. Ensuring that visitors were not able to access the intranet or any of the corporate resources was important. Providing encryption on the handheld devices protected the data from getting into the wrong hands.

All of these implementations for access control and encryption ensured the electronic version was safer than the paper records. It protected the patients, all healthcare providers, and the volunteers.

CHAPTER SUMMARY

Understanding the importance of access controls and security policies is vital for every organization. Security is only as strong as the weakest link, and if employees feel that security measures negatively affect their job performance, they may find ways around it.

You have read about best practices for access controls and how they benefit everyone in an organization. Whether it is implementing system access controls, application access, file and folder access controls, or data access controls, or combining them in a multilayer implementation, access control systems are essential for protecting all data, systems, and applications. This chapter also examined ways to secure remote connections and extranets. Data can be secured through VPNs and TLS encryption to protect it while in transit over the Internet.

KEY CONCEPTS AND TERMS

Application Layer
Assessment
Baseline
Business to business (B2B)
Business to consumer (B2C)
Data Link Layer
Defense-in-depth
Digital certificate
Federation

Federal Information Security
    Management Act (FISMA)
Guideline
Identity as a Service (IDaaS)
Identity management
Identity provider
Internet Layer
OpenID Connect
Private key

Public key
Security Assertion Markup
    Language (SAML)
Service provider
Standard
Transport Layer
Virtual private network
    (VPN)

CHAPTER 7 ASSESSMENT

1. E-commerce and banking sites should have no encryption enabled because the communication between the two points is already protected via the user ID.
   A. True
   B. False

2. _____ is the largest developer and publisher of international standards.

3. Intranets are extensions of the corporate network for business partners and customers.
   A. True
   B. False

4. Which of the following indicates you are using a secure website? (select two.)
   A. Web address starts with "shttp"
   B. Web address starts with "https"
   C. Padlock icon
   D. Key icon

5. Which organization develops RFCs?
   A. NIST
   B. FISMA
   C. ISO
   D. IETF

6. _____ is a body of the U.S. government that provides standards for financial institutions.

7. You are creating a SQL Server database account for a user who must be able to create databases on the server. What is the minimum level of access that will allow this activity?
   A. dbcreator
   B. sysadmin
   C. serveradmin
   D. rootadmin

8. What is a trusted source for a digital certificate called?
   A. Trusted certificate
   B. Trusted authority
   C. Certificate authority
   D. Certificate trusted

9. _____ sets the FISMA standards for the federal IT systems.

Access Control for Information Systems

THIS CHAPTER FOCUSES ON THE SERVERS and networks that store sensitive information and how to use the built-in access controls provided by various operating systems to control access to files and data. In the case studies at the end of the chapter, you'll read about how access controls are built into server and network infrastructures.

Chapter 8 Topics

This chapter covers the following topics and concepts:

- How access controls protect data
- How access controls protect file systems
- How access controls protect executables
- How access controls are implemented on Microsoft Windows workstations and servers
- How access controls are implemented on Linux systems
- How access controls are implemented in supervisory control and data acquisition (SCADA) systems
- Best practices for information systems access controls
- Case studies and examples of access control solutions

Chapter 8 Goals

When you complete this chapter, you will be able to:

- Explain how access controls protect data
- Explain how access controls protect file systems
- Describe how access controls protect executables
- Implement access controls on Microsoft Windows workstations and servers
- Implement access controls on Linux systems
- Implement access controls in SCADA and other industrial control systems
- Describe best practices for access controls for information systems

Access Control for Data

A major concern for any IT department is the security and integrity of data, or information. The major method of securing that information is through access controls. Let's take a look at some methods for securing information in its various forms.

Information can exist in one of two states: at rest or in motion. Data at rest is data that is in a storage system. Data in motion is data that is in transit, such as on a network. To truly protect data, you need to consider both of these states.

Data at Rest

Data at rest (DAR) is simply stored data. The data may be in archival form on tape or optical disc, on a hard disk, or even in memory. Depending on where the data are resting, they can be at very high risk. Some devices such as web servers are accessible from outside an organization's network and are open to attack. Portable devices like smartphones, tablets, flash memory devices, and laptops are prone to physical theft and inadvertent loss. Unless properly secured, data at rest are vulnerable to theft. For this reason, it is critical to use appropriate access controls on this information.

Securing DAR

Administrators designing access controls for data at rest have a variety of models at their disposal. In high-security environments, they may choose to use a mandatory access control (MAC) model, where only the administrator grants access. Those seeking more flexibility will likely adopt the more common discretionary access control (DAC) model that allows users to delegate permissions. Users of both MAC and DAC models may also choose to implement role-based access control (RBAC) to simplify administration through the use of permissions based on individuals' role(s) within the organization.

Let's look at an example of file server access and DAR. A large corporation is establishing network storage for archival purposes for all of its employees. Each user's local Documents directory is mapped to a folder on a network file server. The users are told that any document that needs to be backed up should be stored in the Documents folder. For ease of management and organization, each user's folder on the file server is named with his or her logon. These folders are then organized by department, so each user folder is within his or her departmental folder.

Although documents are more easily backed up, end users raised concerns, especially users in the human resources (HR) and accounting departments. Some documents contain sensitive information that should not be accessible to all employees. This is where access controls come in. Each user is granted full rights to his or her network folder and limited rights to the departmental folder. For document-sharing purposes, users have rights to read and modify files in other user folders in their department; however, those rights may be altered by the owner of the document. Users do not have any access rights to any other department's folders. Using access controls, the company is able to guarantee the privacy of sensitive data on the file share.

Access controls alone are not enough to secure DAR. Portable devices can be stolen and access controls can be circumvented. When a malicious user has access to the medium on which information is at rest, the user can circumvent standard access controls. A malicious user could mount a stolen laptop hard drive, for example, on another system on which he or she has administrative rights. The user could then take ownership of files and folders, modifying the access rights at will. This is where disk encryption becomes vital.

Disk encryption, especially whole disk encryption, is essential to securing data at rest, especially on a portable device. It's difficult for an unauthorized user to extract data from an encrypted disk. Although a malicious user could attempt to decrypt the disk, it would take months or even years.

You must also consider physical security when dealing with DAR. If an organization uses backup tapes or optical media for archival purposes, how and where are those tapes stored and transported? How does the organization decommission and dispose of obsolete systems? Some organizations have discovered that improper data and device disposal can lead to information leaks. Here are some examples of data leaks due to poor data disposal practices:

- In 2018, SSM Health St. Mary's Hospital in Jefferson City, Missouri, reported that improper storage of paper records led to a data breach affecting 301,000 individuals.
- In 2017, ShopRite Supermarkets reported that they improperly disposed of a pharmacy signature capture device that had stored the health records of as many as 12,172 individuals.
- At the end of the 2008 U.S. Presidential campaign, the McCain campaign sold off smartphones that were no longer needed. They neglected, however, to clear the devices' memory before the sale and exposed the personal phone numbers of high-end donors and campaign officials.
- In 2006, a U.S. defense contractor sold obsolete hard drives on eBay. Information found on these drives included Top Secret documents on a new U.S. missile defense program.
- In 2005, a German police department sold a hard drive containing detailed plans on the department's alarm systems as well as sensitive police procedural documentation.

There are countless other examples. A study by British Telecom found that 34% of the hard drives the company bought on eBay contained sensitive information. This included personal data, financial information, and even classified documents belonging to various nations.

Data in Motion

Data in motion (DIM) is the term used to describe data any time they travel from one place to another. For example, webpage files are considered in motion while they are sent from a web server through the Internet to a web browser (see **FIGURE 8-1**). DIM is vulnerable to improper disclosure and theft. DIM is vulnerable as it travels over the network, whether the network is wired or wireless. During transit, standard access controls applied by the operating system are irrelevant. Data packets on a network do not carry ownership information and are not modified by access controls that protect data at rest. Therefore, anyone with access to the network could access the data. The data are vulnerable at any point in transit.

DIM can also be at less risk than DAR, which seems counterintuitive. In a modern switched network, data travels from point to point. For an attacker to gain access to the DIM, she would have to know the path the data take while in transit. She also needs access to the physical wires or routers to insert her packet-sniffing equipment inside that path. This also

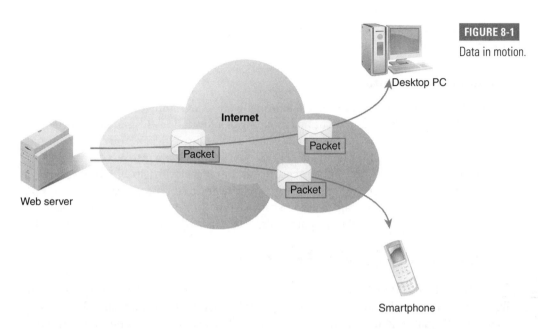

FIGURE 8-1

Data in motion.

Desktop PC

Internet

Packet

Packet

Packet

Web server

Smartphone

applies to sending data over the Internet. The data travel a distinct path and are not shared with systems that are not on that path. An attacker could use various techniques to trick the switch or router into acting like a hub, which would broadcast the packets to multiple points, including her packet sniffer. However, the attacker would still need undetected access to that device for a significant period of time. At that point, an attacker would have access to an organization's network and be able to compromise routers and switches. This represents a significant security breach, meaning that DAR will be at risk as well. If a switch can be compromised, any system on the network can be compromised.

Standard network security includes **intrusion detection systems (IDSs), intrusion prevention systems (IPSs)**, and border protections like firewalls. These systems can effectively secure most DIM that doesn't leave the local area network (LAN). An organization should further secure high impact data. There are two methods for securing DIM, encrypting data, and securing the communications channel.

Securing DIM

One way to secure DIM is to encrypt data. This is especially common with email. The information sender and receiver agree on an encryption technique and then share the appropriate keys. The sender then encrypts the information and the receiver decrypts it. Anyone who intercepts the data packets in transit is left with meaningless bits of data.

Another method is to secure the communications channel. You can use protocols such as **Transport Layer Security (TLS)** to accomplish this. TLS creates encrypted two-way communications at the Application Layer of networking. You'll see this most commonly with **Hypertext Transfer Protocol Secure (HTTPS)**

 NOTE

You may see references to HTTPS using an older protocol, the Secure Sockets Layer (SSL), to encrypt data. SSL is outdated and insecure and is no longer appropriate for use. There are several known attacks that make it possible for a malicious individual to defeat the encryption used by SSL and gain unauthorized access to communications.

communications. You can also secure the path with a virtual private network (VPN) to provide a secure encrypted tunnel through a public network such as the Internet.

Object-Level Security

An object is an item or a distinct group of information in a data storage system, usually a **relational database (RDB)**, but it can be any grouping of information. By grouping information as an object, applying access controls can be significantly more efficient. You can set controls at the object level. This allows you to manage groups of related data instead of managing individual items. Not only does applying security at the object level help with DAR security, it can also help with DIM security. If the network security device is object-aware, you can apply security rules to objects. This can be used to control how and where data can get transmitted. Application Layer firewalls and web content filters use object-level security to protect DIM.

Access Control for File Systems

When securing DAR, applying an access control policy to an organization's file system is the first step. This is done by creating an access control list (ACL) to handle both rights management of the data and to audit data access. File system access controls deal directly with accessing data stored on a system or a group of systems sharing a common file system. You can manage ACLs in a Microsoft Windows environment using **Active Directory**, or in a Linux environment using built-in ACL capabilities.

Access Control List

An ACL is a list of security policies associated with an object. An ACL is commonly composed of a collection of access control entities (ACEs). These are security objects that define access for one distinct user, group, or system. An ACE has four properties:

- A security identifier (SID) that identifies what the ACE applies to—the specific user, group, or system
- An **access mask** that lists the specific rights granted or denied
- Flags to indicate the type of ACE and whether **child objects** can inherit the rights from the object to which the ACE is attached

There are three primary types of ACEs you can apply to any security entity: access-denied, access-allowed, and system-audit. Each ACE allows, denies, or audits a specific right, such as read or modify for the SID to which it is attached. **TABLE 8-1** lists types of ACEs.

An ACL is applied directly on the file system of one system and affects only users and data on that system. There are two types of ACLs: discretionary and system ACLs. Each list uses ACEs and handles a different aspect of access control.

Discretionary Access Control List

A **discretionary access control list (DACL)** controls access to an object. It handles what access is allowed or denied. When an object is accessed, all of the ACEs contained in the DACL are checked to see what access, if any, should be granted. Although the DACL can be directly accessed, it generally is not. The ACEs contained in it are the combined result of access

TABLE 8-1 Types of ACEs	
TYPE	**DESCRIPTION**
Access-denied	Denies SID-specific access to an object
Access-allowed	Allows specific rights to a SID
System-audit	Causes the creation of an audit record when the SID performs a specific action

controls set by an object's owner on an object, by rights set by administrators on the object and its container, and by system rules.

When applying the rights from a DACL, the system begins by denying all rights and then processing the ACEs in the DACL until one granting access is reached. This means if a DACL is empty and contains no ACEs, access will not be granted to any user. This also means that it is important to create a DACL for every object that needs security. In the absence of a DACL, the permissions assigned to an object are inherited from objects at upper levels of the object hierarchy.

System Access Control List

A **system access control list (SACL)** is a system-created access control list that handles the information assurance aspect of access controls. Although a user can modify an SACL, this is generally not done. The SACL is a system-generated list based on the auditing rules set by the systems administrators. It contains the ACEs that handle what access needs to be audited and where to store the audit information. SACLs may be configured to record all attempts to access an object in the audit trail. Alternatively, administrators may decide to log only successful or unsuccessful access attempts. It is important to note that the SACL doesn't actually allow or deny access; it only records the access attempt and the success or failure of that attempt.

The information gathered in audit logs by SACL rules can be invaluable to security investigators. When stored elsewhere, this information provides an unalterable log that contains crucial evidence for evaluating the scope and impact of a security breach and reconstructing the events that took place on a system.

Access Control for Executables

In addition to applying access controls to end users and objects, you can apply them to applications as well. This takes two forms—internal to the application and through the operating system.

You can assign an application its own user ID and directories. From there, you can grant the application rights only to the files and directories it needs to run and explicitly deny access to the rest of the system. This gives the application a **sandbox** to work in. If the application is compromised through an exploit in its code, the malicious user will only have access to the information that the application had access to. This type of access control is common on web servers and application servers, which are highly accessible to the general public. Database servers typically operate behind a firewall and have little direct exposure to the public, but web servers are public by design. This accessibility requires additional security measures that are not necessary on more protected servers, such as a database server.

Certain executables have their own internal access controls as well. Internal access controls are necessary where the application holds sensitive information in a format that is not accessible to the general file system. This situation is common in database management systems, where data are stored in raw form in tables or in **binary large objects (BLOBs)**. In these cases, information must still be secured but is inaccessible to the file system ACLs.

Let's take a look at an example of internal access controls. Suppose a homeowners' insurance company needs a way of controlling access to claims data—not only information on individual customer claims but also sensitive pricing information. The pricing information is especially critical. The price lists give the company a competitive advantage because its estimates are more accurate than its competitors'. The accuracy is due to the extensive real-time pricing data in the price lists. The information is also legally protected. Due to recent lawsuits in the industry, the insurance company has to show that the price lists cannot be modified at will.

The claims files and the pricing information are stored in a **relational database management system (RDBMS)** as binary large object (BLOB) data and inaccessible to the file system. The only way to access the data is with an estimating tool, but that doesn't guarantee data privacy or integrity as most of the company has the tool. In fact, it is an off-the-shelf application that other insurance companies and independent contractors have access to as well.

To secure the information, the insurance company works with the application vendor to develop an RBAC system built into the application. This involves roles like claim representative, who has the rights to create and modify estimates; pricing specialist, who can create and modify price lists; and super user, to handle administrative and support aspects of the application.

Adding the roles takes care of data privacy but not necessarily data integrity. To handle that, an auditing log and rollback functionality is added to the application. A user can see who has made changes to a file, when, and what changes were made. This includes claims files and price lists. If a file is changed incorrectly, a user with super rights can restore the file to a previous version.

All of this is done inside the application. The file system is unaware of any of the roles or protected data that resides inside the RDBMS.

Delegated Access Rights

In a discretionary access-control environment, users have the ability to delegate access rights to the objects under their ownership. **Delegated access rights** are granted from something that owns an object to another user or system. Delegated rights come in two forms—explicit and implicit.

Explicitly delegated rights are access rights that are actively given to a user by an object owner. This occurs when the object owner identifies a user, group, or system and then grants a level of access to it. In most access control systems, the owner of an object may grant any rights on that object to any other user, including delegating to another user the right to assign access permissions.

CHAPTER 8 | Access Control for Information Systems **167**

Implicitly delegated rights happen automatically due to previously delegated rights from the object owner. This happens when an object owner delegates rights to a folder or other container object. Unless otherwise specified, all child objects of the container will inherit the delegated rights of the **parent object**. Similarly, when a user creates a new file within a folder, that file automatically inherits the permissions of the folder and users with access to the folder will have the same access to that new file.

Microsoft Windows Workstations and Servers

Microsoft Windows-based systems have highly granular file-based access controls. On a local level, an administrator works with users, groups, and objects. The administrator may group users together to grant rights. The administrator may control objects with both basic and advanced rights. **TABLE 8-2** lists the basic access rights available in Windows and what they affect.

TABLE 8-2 Basic Access Rights in Windows

NAME	DESCRIPTION	FILE OR FOLDER
Full Control	Change permissions, take ownership, and delete subfolders and files. Perform actions permitted by all other NT File System (NTFS) file or folder permissions.	Both
Modify	Delete a file or folder. Perform actions permitted by the Write permission and the Read & Execute permission.	Both
Read & Execute	Navigate folders to reach other files and folders, even if the users do not have permission for those folders. Perform actions permitted by the Read permission and the List Folder Contents permission. Run the application.	Both
List Folder Contents	View the names of files and subfolders in the folder.	Folder
Read	See files and subfolders in the folder. View folder ownership, permissions, and attributes, such as Read-only, Hidden, Archive, and System. Read the file. View file attributes, ownership, and permissions.	Both
Write	Create new files and subfolders within the folder. Change folder attributes. View folder ownership and permissions. Overwrite the file, change file attributes, and view file ownership and permissions.	Both

The Windows operating system can get far more granular with the utilization of advanced rights. The basic rights are just preset groupings of the more granular levels. These groupings cover most roles that an organization would want to give a user or group. The advanced rights for files are listed in **TABLE 8-3**.

This gives you a partial picture of the level of granularity. Groups of objects or users—called **organizational units (OUs)**—provide advanced rights that allow thousands of different options. General administrators use basic rights for ease of management.

An organizational unit is a logical structure that allows you to organize users, computers, and other objects into separate units for administrative purposes. The main difference between an organizational unit and a group is that groups apply only to users while an OU can include any type of object.

Rights in Windows can be either explicit or inherited from parent folders. A user's rights on any given object is based on all of the inherited and explicit rights granted or denied by every OU of which the user is a member. It is important to note that Deny rights always takes precedence over Allow rights. For example, suppose Julie is a member of both the Accounting and IT OUs. She needs to access the accounts payable spreadsheet. Although the Accounting OU has been granted Read permission to this document, the IT OU is explicitly denied Read rights. Regardless of rights granted to Julie, the explicit denial will block her access.

TABLE 8-3 Windows Advanced File Permissions

NAME	DESCRIPTION
Full Control	The sum of all other rights
Traverse Folder/Execute File	The ability to navigate the file system and execute files
List Folder/Read Data	The ability to list the contents of a folder
Read Attributes	The ability to view ownership and access control attributes on a file or folder
Read Extended Attributes	The ability to view all file or folder attributes
Create Files/Write Data	The ability to create new files and write to existing files
Create Folders/Append Data	The ability to create new folders
Write Attributes	The ability to change file and folder ownership and access control attributes
Write Extended Attributes	The ability to change extended attributes such as the ones in this list
Delete	The ability to delete files and folders
Read Permissions	The ability to view access control permissions on a file or folder
Change Permissions	The ability to change access control permissions on a file or folder
Take Ownership	The ability to change the ownership attribute on a file or folder

Granting Windows Folder Permissions

On a Windows system, you may change the permissions settings for a folder by accessing the folder properties. Open File Explorer and right-click on the folder that you wish to modify, choosing Properties from the pop-up menu. When the Properties dialog box opens, select the Security tab. An example from a Windows Server 2019 system is shown in **FIGURE 8-2**.

You may then edit the permissions assigned to users by clicking the Edit button. Windows will then present a Permissions dialog box, such as the one shown in **FIGURE 8-3**. You may add or remove users or groups from the listing by clicking the Add or Remove button. To modify the permissions assigned to a specific user or group, highlight the user or group

FIGURE 8-2

Folder security properties in Windows Server 2019.

Used with permission from Microsoft.

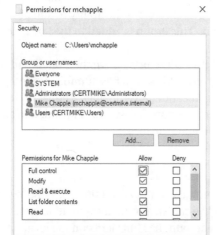

FIGURE 8-3

Editing folder permissions in Windows Server 2019.

Used with permission from Microsoft.

Windows Server
2019 advanced folder
permissions.

Used with permission from
Microsoft.

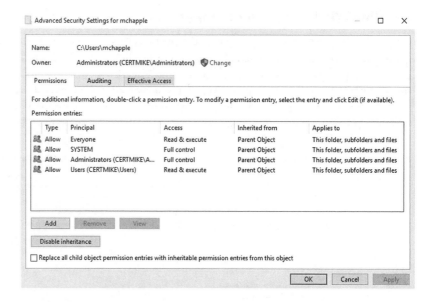

in the top pane and then modify the checkboxes in the bottom pane to reflect the desired settings. Note that the checkboxes correspond with the settings that appear in Table 8-2.

If you wish to modify the permission settings found in Table 8-3, you may do so by clicking the Advanced button. This will open the dialog box shown in **FIGURE 8-4**, where you may edit advanced permission settings.

Domain Administrator Rights

A **domain administrator** in Windows is a member of the special Domain Administrators group in Active Directory. Members of this group have full control over all computers in the domain, including any file or folder that they haven't explicitly been denied access to. Members of this group have the ability to assign and modify the ACL of users, files, and folders on all systems in the domain. This group also has the ability to add or remove computers and OUs from the Windows domain. This group is added to the Local Administrators group on any computer joined to the domain.

This is not the top-level authority in Active Directory. Above the Domain Administrators group is the Enterprise Administrators group. This group has administrative rights to the entire Active Directory **forest** in an organization. It is the only group with the ability to add or remove domains from the Active Directory forest and is included in all Domain Administrator groups when a new domain joins the forest.

Super Administrator Rights

The **Super Administrator** is a built-in "secret" account in all versions of Windows, including Windows 10. This account is the local administrator on a standalone installation of Windows and is disabled by default. This account has full rights on the local system and can take ownership of all objects. It is generally not needed in a standalone installation, but users with a lot of legacy applications may find a need to activate this account.

To activate the Super Administrator account, a user must first launch a command window with administrative rights using the runas command. In the command window, enter the following commands:

```
Net user Administrator /active:yes
```

To deactivate the account, run the following command:

```
Net user Administrator /active:no
```

The Super Administrator account has no password by default. If it is activated, the first thing you should do is give the account a password.

Pass-the-Hash Attacks

Some operating systems, including versions of Windows, cache password hashes locally in order to facilitate authentication. This leads to the potential for a **pass-the-hash attack**, where an attacker gains access to those hashed passwords and uses them to move laterally across the network.

For example, when a user logs onto a Windows system, the system retains the NTLM password hash for that user's account in memory. If an attacker is able to log onto that same system with local administrator privileges, the attacker can then harvest those NTLM passwords. If the cache includes password hashes for any administrative accounts, the attacker can use that hash to connect to other networked systems that the attacker might not already be able to access. Using the hash harvested from one system to log onto another is known as "passing" the hash.

> **NOTE**
> While the techniques required to conduct a pass-the-hash attack require knowledge of Windows' internal functions, there are tools available that automate these techniques, making them simple for an attacker to use. For example, the Mimikatz tool automates pass-the-hash attacks, allowing them to occur with just a few keystrokes.

8

Access Control for Information Systems

Linux

Linux is a popular open-source operating system that is widely used in server environments. By default, Linux systems have simplified ACL-based file permission systems. Unlike a standard ACL-based system, rights are not inherited in Linux and must be applied to all files and folders explicitly. There are three rights and three classes to which those rights can be assigned.

The rights in a Linux environment are:

- **Read**—Grants a user or group the ability to read a file. If the right is set on a directory, the requestor may read the list of files in that directory.
- **Write**—Grants the requestor the ability to modify a file. If the right is set on a directory, the requestor may create, rename, or remove files in the directory.
- **Execute**—Grants the right to execute a file. This allows the requestor to run a binary or script file. If the right is set on a directory, the user may access files in the directory and access subdirectories but not view the list of files in the directory.

There are three classes of users as well: owner, group, and world. The group class refers to the group that the file or directory is a member of. Each one of these classes can have any, all, or none of the permissions applied to them. If no permission is set, the system denies access to the file.

Linux File Permissions

There are two standard ways Linux-based file permissions are written: symbolic notation or octal notation. Symbolic notation is simply listing the permissions by the first letter of the right. For example, the read right is listed as "r." This is done in a nine-character string with dashes in place of unassigned rights. The order in which the classes are listed is always the same, with user coming first, followed by group, and then world. The order in each three-character set is also standard, with read coming first, then write, and followed by execute.

Octal notation is based on assigning each triplicate in symbolic notation a numerical value between 0 and 7. These values are then expressed as a three-digit number. No permissions has a value of zero, read adds 4, write adds 2, and execute adds 1. Adding the rights together gives a value for each class.

TABLE 8-4 lists some examples of Linux-based rights in both notations.

To calculate the octal notation for full rights to the user and for read and execute for the group and world:

- For the user: r + w + x or 4 + 2 + 1 = 7
- For the group: r + x or 4 + 1 = 5
- For the world: r + w or 4 + 2 = 6
- Combine the results of the addition: 756

To change the permissions on a file or folder, use the chmod command, as shown here. Replace *myfile* with the name of the file or folder to be changed:

```
chmod 756 myfile
```

You can also use the letter notation or add or subtract rights from the user, group, or world. The command:

```
chmod g+rwx myfile
```

adds read, write, and execute permissions for the group on the file *myfile*. The command:

```
chmod w–x myfile
```

removes the execute permission from the world on the file *myfile*.

An example of modifying Linux file permissions with these commands appears in **FIGURE 8-5**. Take a few minutes to follow the sequence of steps that uses different

TABLE 8-4 Examples of Linux-Based Rights

RIGHTS	SYMBOLIC NOTATION	OCTAL NOTATION
Full rights for all classes on a file	Rwxrwxrwx	777
Full rights for user, read execute for group, read for world	rwxr – xr – –	754
Read write for user, read for group, none for world	rw – r – – – – –	640
Full rights for user, write, execute for group, read for world	rwx – wx – – x	731

```
○ ○ ○ ▣ Filters — ubuntu@ip-10-39-115-108: /opt/nessus/bin — ssh — 80×24 ⤢
bash-3.2$ ls -al myfile
-rwxr-xr-x 1 mchapple campus 0 Mar 30 16:34 myfile
bash-3.2$ chmod 700 myfile
bash-3.2$ ls -al myfile
-rwx------ 1 mchapple campus 0 Mar 30 16:34 myfile
bash-3.2$ chmod a+rwx myfile
bash-3.2$ ls -al myfile
-rwxrwxrwx 1 mchapple campus 0 Mar 30 16:34 myfile
bash-3.2$ chmod 777 myfile
bash-3.2$ ls -al myfile
-rwxrwxrwx 1 mchapple campus 0 Mar 30 16:34 myfile
bash-3.2$ chmod o-rwx myfile
bash-3.2$ ls -al myfile
-rwxrwx--- 1 mchapple campus 0 Mar 30 16:34 myfile
bash-3.2$ chmod g-rwx myfile
bash-3.2$ ls -al myfile
-rwx------ 1 mchapple campus 0 Mar 30 16:34 myfile
bash-3.2$ []
```

FIGURE 8-5

Changing Linux
file permissions.

Apple Inc.

variations of the chmod command to alter file permissions and the ls –al command to
display the new permission settings on that file. You should be able to explain each of the
changes that result from permission modifications.

Although this simplified ACL is useful on a standalone server or workstation, it has a lack
of granular control and does not allow for multiple groups with different permissions. This
causes difficulties and confusion in a network environment. In most organizations, the basic
Linux-based permissions have been extended with more full-featured ACL-based systems.

The Root Superuser

Root is a special class of user in a Linux environment, also known as the superuser. It is similar to the administrator user in Windows. Root has full access to the system. It has the ability
to override file system permissions and run any process. Therefore, it is not a good idea to
run a system when performing ordinary tasks as root. Not only is it a security concern but a
user can also accidentally damage the system. Linux assumes you know what you are doing
and that you intend to run all the commands you enter. If root is logged in, it is possible to
accidentally delete major parts of the operating system.

However, some administrative tasks must be run with root access. Linux offers a solution:
the sudo command. **Substitute user do (sudo)** allows you to run any process as if another user
were running it. This allows an administrator to be logged into the system with a standard
user account and still perform tasks that require enhanced rights on the system by using
sudo to run the command with root permissions.

Supervisory Control and Data Acquisition (SCADA) and Industrial Control Systems

An **industrial control system (ICS)** is a mechanism used to control the output of a specific
industrial process. For example, heating a room is a specific process with the desired outcome of maintaining a defined temperature over time. An ICS would receive information
from a device, in this case, the thermostat, and decide to heat or not to heat based on the

desired temperature. **Supervisory control and data acquisition (SCADA)** systems are basically large, complex ICSs.

Information systems access controls are generally not built into SCADA or ICS systems. Systems located on the perimeter of a network must rely on physical access control. The programs controlling these systems can use the access controls built into the environment. Linux and Windows environments can control which users have rights to execute programs; those controls can be utilized to limit access to the SCADA back end to only users who need to access them. The best method would be to create a group that has access to the systems and remove rights from all other users. Only authorized users, or members of that group, would be able to access the application.

Securing industrial control systems requires specialized knowledge of the protocols and standards used in ICS environments. These include a wide range of wired and wireless communications technologies, ICS communications protocols, and ICS approaches. It is quite common to implement ICS-specific security controls, such as segmenting ICS systems onto isolated networks and deploying SCADA firewalls that focus on securing these highly specialized networks.

Best Practices for Access Controls for Information Systems

Access controls for information systems are only as good as the policies and procedures that dictate their use. There are a few general best practices that you should follow to ensure reasonably secure access controls on information systems:

- **Create a baseline for access**—Build a baseline for the current access levels in the environment. This will help identify holes in access and identify which users have rights beyond their needs.
- **Segregate users' rights by their role**—Developers do not need access to production databases; sales executives do not need access to the accounts receivable system.
- **Automate user creation**—Have prebuilt groups for the major roles in the organization so that when an employee joins or switches roles, you can modify his or her rights quickly and correctly.
- **Tie access controls to the environment**—Some situations, such as accessing a VPN, call for two-factor authentication. In other instances, such as accessing an intranet site, you can put lighter controls in place.
- **Have a clear standard for decommissioning data storage devices**—When decommissioning a storage device, which may include a hard drive, thumb drive, or digital camera, have a standard method to guarantee that data is removed from the device before disposal.

Case Studies and Examples

Every organization implements some type of access control on its information systems. In this section, you'll read about three real-world examples of how access controls are implemented on information systems. In one case study, you'll learn how an organization converted from a paper-based to a digital records system with granular access controls. In another, controlling file access locally and remotely is a key factor.

Private Sector Case Study

Access controls are not just important for large enterprises. Small- and medium-size businesses also benefit from the security and organization that implementing access controls can provide.

Diva Construction is a small Midwestern construction company specializing in urban condos and building rehabilitations. In the late 1990s, the company needed to upgrade its infrastructure. It consisted of a Windows desktop acting as a file server, a few Windows workstations for the office staff, and a dozen laptops for the sales and field staff. The entire network was set up as a Windows workgroup, with the possibility of discretionary access controls, but only the accountant was implementing them.

There were a number of issues with Diva's original network environment. Its sales staff was commission-based, and there was some concern about customer poaching because a former employee had contacted customers belonging to other sales staff before he left. Diva management wanted to be able to access files from the field securely, and as the company grew, management wanted to move to a computer-based HR system.

The initial plan for securing sensitive information in Diva's infrastructure was based on enforcing the current DAC system in place, with each user responsible for securing and granting access to his or her documents. This was quickly dismissed as too intrusive because not all employees are computer-savvy. Expecting them to handle all access control issues was not feasible. The other issue with the current environment was remote access. As it was currently set up, remote access was not possible.

Diva decided to add a Windows server to the environment and migrate from a Windows workgroup to an Active Directory domain. The company also upgraded the workstation acting as a file server to a Windows server. The new environment allowed for MAC to be set up, centralizing access controls. Groups based on user roles were created, including Accounting, HR, Support Staff, Sales, Management, and Construction. These groups were given space on the file server that only they and managers could access. Network shares were turned off on the workstations, and each user's Documents directory was mapped to the file server with access limited to the owner and management. The Windows domain controller was also configured as a **Remote Authentication Dial In User Service (RADIUS)** server and had an ISDN modem, allowing users to connect from the field over cellular modems.

By implementing a **Lightweight Directory Access Protocol (LDAP)** environment using Windows Active Directory, Diva Construction was able to better secure its information, manage that information more efficiently, and enable remote access for its field employees.

Public Sector Case Study

Implementing information systems access controls is critical for public sector entities, large and small. Anglican Care is a small aged-care facility in New South Wales, Australia. The facility handles 80 patients utilizing paper records. To stay in compliance with healthcare regulations, the facility needs to convert to an electronic documentation system. Anglican Care could build the system from the ground up with information security in mind. The Australian government worked with Anglican Care to design and implement the system as a demonstration of the use of clinical IT in aged-care facilities.

Anglican Care's paper records stored personal, financial, and medical information on patients. Contact information for staff and visiting professionals, staff salaries, and other financial information were kept in paper records as well.

The electronic version of the system will replace the use of paper and provide remote access to the health information system (HIS) stored on the server. One PC will be used by the manager, with a number of PCs available for the staff. Doctors and physical therapists can make use of mobile devices that connect with the network.

The access controls must be created for the various system users. The controls need to maintain at least the strictness of the current paper-based system, ideally by implementing a least-privileged scheme. To do this, it is necessary to first understand the sensitive data that are to be stored.

There are two basic kinds of data stored for each resident. The first is static data that are entered into the system when the resident is admitted. This includes personal information such as name, gender, religion, as well as medical insurance information and medical history. Emergency information is also included in this information such as allergies, blood group, primary doctor, and a contact person in case of emergencies. Currently, this information is stored on a card-based system that makes the information available rapidly.

The second kind of information is used and updated in the day-to-day running of the facility. This includes the patient care plan and progress notes. Progress notes are used to update the care plan and medical records. In the current paper-based system, medical entries older than 1 year are archived and filed in a locked room. Recent medical entries are stored in locked filing cabinets in an accessible location controlled by the facilities manager.

To mimic the access levels in the paper system, an LDAP-based data store was created with the following groups:

- **Manager**—This group has the broadest range of access, with the ability to view most information on the system. This is also the only group with the rights to create entries for new staff and residents, and the only group with rights to remove information. For most information, they have full control. The one exception is doctors' private notes, to which they are denied access. Any user accessing care plans is also logged, and these logs are reported to the manager group.
- **Healthcare workers**—Members of the healthcare workers group can view care plans, add progress notes, and access all emergency information. This is achieved by giving them read rights to the care plans and append rights to the notes.
- **Doctors**—Members of the doctors' group have access to the medical information of the residents who are their patients. They can modify the medical information and care plans for their patients. Doctors have read, write, and modify privileges for their patients' medical information. Doctors can also create private notes on each of their patients. This information is not accessible to anyone but the doctor and the patient.
- **Patients**—Patients have rights to read all of their medical records, including doctors' notes, but they cannot modify or remove the information.

Implementing these rights allows the facility to move to a paperless environment while maintaining strict access control to sensitive HIS.

Critical Infrastructure Case Study

One of the major bottlenecks with any access control system is the provisioning and deprovisioning of users. This is especially daunting in large organizations. In the following case study, you'll learn how the Alabama Medicaid agency handled this issue.

User management at the agency was a manual decentralized process. The creation of a new user required manual entry into the help desk, HR, email, mainframe, resource store, and data store. This was an intensive process that left a lot of room for manual error. User rights had to be audited and crosschecked on all of these various systems. Sometimes, rights and roles were assigned incorrectly. Deprovisioning of users was an even larger problem. With all of the different user areas, sometimes usernames and rights were missed in the manual removal process. There were times when former employees still had email access months or even years after leaving the agency.

User management was obviously a major problem for the agency. The process was very labor- and cost-intensive, and security was a major problem. Although no incidents had occurred yet from a user with incorrectly enhanced rights or a former user that had yet to be removed from the agency systems, it was only a matter of time.

To solve this issue, the agency moved to centralized access controls and centralized user life-cycle management. Now, user information can be entered in one location and propagated out to all of the various systems. This also simplifies the user's life, as he or she now has a single sign-on. Once users log on to their workstations, they can automatically log on to any other system that they have rights to. By centralizing, rights can be modified easily and quickly. Rights audits only need to look at one location to make sure everyone has the privileges they need and no more.

Decommissioning of users is now a much quicker process. Users are disabled at a central location, and within a half hour, their accounts are suspended on all of the systems. This is a much more secure way of decommissioning users, as there is no longer a worry of missing an account on one of the multitude of systems that the agency has users logging into.

By utilizing single sign-on, the agency was able to reduce workload of the IT department by removing the need to create separate user accounts on every system. This reduced the time it takes to manage users and closed major holes in access controls.

CHAPTER SUMMARY

In this chapter, you read about how access controls are implemented in various operating systems and how those security features are used to solve real-world challenges. The goal of any access control system in a server or network environment is to decide whether any given user can access data and what they can do with it. To achieve this goal, operating systems implement a system of granular user rights. Users are bundled into groups to simplify rights management.

KEY CONCEPTS AND TERMS

Access mask
Active Directory
Binary large object (BLOB)
Child object
Data at rest (DAR)
Data in motion (DIM)
Delegated access rights
Discretionary access control
   list (DACL)
Domain administrator
Explicitly delegated
   rights
Forest

Hypertext Transfer Protocol
   Secure (HTTPS)
Implicitly delegated rights
Industrial control system (ICS)
Intrusion detection systems (IDSs)
Intrusion prevention systems
   (IPSs)
Lightweight Directory Access
   Protocol (LDAP)
Linux
Organizational unit (OU)
Parent object
Pass-the-hash attack

Relational database (RDB)
Relational database management
   system (RDBMS)
Remote Authentication Dial In
   User Service (RADIUS)
Root
Sandbox
Substitute user do (sudo)
Super Administrator
Supervisory control and data
   acquisition (SCADA)
System access control list (SACL)
Transport Layer Security (TLS)

CHAPTER 8 ASSESSMENT

1. A(n) _____ is a mechanism used to control the output of a specific industrial process.

2. In a Linux file system, what value corresponds to read, write, and execute access?

   A. 9
   B. 7
   C. 5
   D. 3

3. A(n) _____ is a list or collection of access control entities.

4. The three primary ACEs are access-denied, access-allowed, and _____.

5. _____ in a database are an example of an application with internal access controls.

6. Compared with Windows, the Linux operating system implements more granular access controls.

   A. True
   B. False

7. In a Windows environment, what is an organizational unit?

   A. A logical structure for organizing users, groups, and computers
   B. A business unit
   C. A group of related data
   D. A logical structure for organizing firewall rules

8. A Windows domain administrator has full control over all the computers in the domain.

   A. True
   B. False

9. A Windows domain administrator is the top-level authority in a Windows environment.

   A. True
   B. False

10. In which operating systems is rwxr – xr – x an example of rights notation? _____

11. What does the sudo command in Linux allow systems administrators to do?

   A. Log in as root.
   B. Run any process as if they were logged in as another user.
   C. Disable the root user.
   D. Disable a user account.

12. Why should an organization automate user creation? (Select two.)

   A. To save time and effort for the IT staff
   B. To allow individuals to manage their own user accounts
   C. To accurately add, modify, or remove access rights
   D. To minimize the need for a full IT staff

Physical Security and Access Control

P HYSICAL SECURITY IS OFTEN the branch of security most overlooked by cybersecurity professionals. Organizations that are diligent about creating strong passwords and monitoring their firewall and intrusion detection systems aren't always as thorough with physical facility security. In this chapter, you will discover ways to secure the facilities that house sensitive resources and how to use biometric technology to verify an individual's identity.

Chapter 9 Topics

This chapter covers the following topics and concepts:

- What physical security comprises
- How to design a comprehensive physical security plan
- Physiological and behavioral biometric access controls
- How to use technology for access control
- Pros and cons of outsourcing physical security
- Best practices for physical security
- Case studies and examples

Chapter 9 Goals

When you complete this chapter, you will be able to:

- Design a holistic physical security plan
- Choose a biometric identity verification system that meets the unique requirements of your organization
- Choose an appropriate technological access control solution

Physical Security

Physical security is humanity's oldest form of access control. Chances are good that you encounter many types of physical security every day, without really thinking about what they are and why they are there. As a security practitioner, it is important that you understand the purpose behind physical security measures and how they contribute to an overall access control strategy.

A good physical security strategy is designed in layers. This ensures that if an intruder bypasses or breaks through one layer, another layer will delay or stop him or her. In this section, you will read about the various layers that comprise a physical security strategy.

Designing a Comprehensive Plan

Perimeter security is any method that restricts access to a defined area, such as a military base, corporate campus, infrastructure facility, or office building. It is the first layer of defense in a physical security strategy. A backyard fence is a common example of perimeter security. It surrounds an area—a parcel of land that is designated for use by a homeowner—and restricts access to that area. Not only does it keep others out of a homeowner's yard but it also keeps the homeowner's pets inside the perimeter. In this way, a fence serves two purposes. It restricts access both to the yard and to the outside world.

Landscape design is an important aspect of perimeter security. From a purely aesthetic point of view, it may seem natural to improve the look of a fence by planting trees or bushes around it. Unfortunately, these natural elements can also provide a way for an intruder to climb over the fence. They can also provide cover for an intruder. This is not to say that every fence must be surrounded by 50 feet of bare ground. Landscape elements can also double as perimeter security devices. Thorny or spiky bushes can be planted below windows and other potential vulnerable spots in the perimeter of a facility. A well-placed bush will not stop a determined intruder, but it will encourage the intruder to look for another entry point.

Lighting is another key point in both landscape design and perimeter security. You should design lighting to illuminate official entry points and those areas that an intruder may use to break in. However, landscape lighting design should also avoid creating large areas of shadow that could provide cover for an intruder.

Security guards and closed-captioned video play an important role in perimeter security as well. Prior to the development of closed-captioned video systems, security guards could only patrol the area they could physically see from any given location. Therefore, to provide full perimeter coverage, a facility needed enough guards that each one could maintain line of sight with the guards on either side. Video cameras placed in such a way that their fields of vision overlap slightly, as shown in **FIGURE 9-1**, provide the same level of coverage with fewer guards. If they view suspicious activity on the monitors, one can investigate while the other continues to monitor the video system for additional activity in other areas of the facility.

Although fences, landscaping, and guards are all designed to keep people out of a facility, there also needs to be a way to let authorized individuals into the facility. Gates of various types allow for monitored, controlled access to a secured facility. Not only do they allow for

FIGURE 9-1

Video cameras provide perimeter coverage.

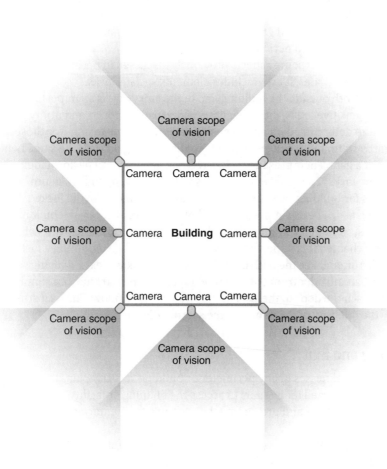

identification and authentication of individuals wishing to gain entry but they also restrict the flow of traffic into and out of a facility.

Gates are also a weak point in the perimeter, so their security should be heightened to compensate. The mere presence of a security guard at the gate is a deterrent, because it sends the message to intruders that the area is actively monitored and their presence may be detected. The same guard can perform identification and authentication tasks by checking ID badges of those wishing to enter through the gate and cross referencing with a list of authorized individuals. A guard can also strengthen the use of ID cards as an access control by physically inspecting the card to ensure that the picture on the ID matches the face of the individual attempting to use the card.

Building Security and Access

In some cases, building security and perimeter security are the same. This is most often the case with organizations located in urban office buildings. The organization's perimeter is the outer wall of the building itself. In other cases, the building will be located at the center of a large, open expanse of landscaped ground. Under those circumstances, building security is a second layer of defense behind perimeter controls.

Building security involves some aspects previously discussed in perimeter security: lighting, security guards, and gates. It also includes elements such as locks.

Lighting design, both outside the building and in the entryway, is an important part of building security. Sensitive areas, including entryways, loading docks, and utility boxes, should be well lit to deter intruders and to enable security guards to monitor those areas.

Security guards stationed at the entry points to the building provide the same benefits as those stationed at a gate. Their presence is a deterrent, and they can perform identification and authentication tasks. The next section covers securing entry points in depth.

Access controls for building security revolve around the concept of the locked door. A locking mechanism can be as simple as a deadbolt with a key held by the building owner, or it can involve a system that combines ID badges and biometrics, which you will learn about later in this chapter. It is important to remember that when designing a locking mechanism, an intruder often takes the path of least resistance. A complex and highly secure lock might not prevent an intruder from entering the building if the intruder can simply remove the hinges that attach the door to the wall or break a nearby window. The lock strength must be matched by the integrity of the door and the surrounding area.

Points of Entry and Exit

Points of entry are weaknesses in any perimeter or building security plan. They must be designed to allow authorized individuals to access the building or facility, while identifying unauthorized individuals and preventing those people from entering (or exiting, in some cases).

Ensure your entry points are designed so that it is difficult or impossible to approach them undetected. They should be well lit and free from heavy landscaping that might provide cover to an intruder. Security guards posted nearby provide another layer of security at entry and exit points.

Cameras filming these areas not only allow security guards to monitor for suspicious activity but they also provide a record of who comes and goes. Although this may not prevent an intruder from entering the facility, it will provide evidence of his or her activity later.

It is important to note that when designing a physical security system, you should not only be concerned with who enters a facility but also with who leaves. This is especially important in specialized facilities such as daycare facilities, hospitals, and prisons, which are designed to keep people in as much as to keep people out. In a daycare center, it would be a catastrophic failure of physical security if a child were to wander away from the facility. Potential exit points must be monitored as closely as the official entry points to prevent this type of situation. Similarly, in healthcare facilities, especially those that serve mental health patients, exit points must be secured to prevent patients from leaving and becoming lost or harmed.

Physical Obstacles and Barriers

Physical barriers play an important role in perimeter and building security. **Bollards** are short vertical posts designed to control traffic and prevent vehicular attacks on a building. Bollards are designed to allow easy pedestrian access to an area while preventing vehicular access. They are often installed in areas where terrorist attacks are a concern. Some bollards, such as those shown in **FIGURE 9-2**, are retractable.

Moveable concrete barriers are used in places where access and traffic patterns must be changed to suit differing circumstances. They are often used in large public areas during special events such as festivals and concerts, where crowd control and security are a major concern.

Granting Access to Physical Areas Within a Building

Once inside the building, different areas require different security measures. Generic work areas, for example, may not require any additional security systems beyond perimeter and building security. Simply monitoring those areas for suspicious behavior is usually sufficient. Sensitive areas such as data centers, however, require additional layers of security.

Non-Sensitive Work Areas

The primary physical security concern in nonsensitive work areas is suspicious behavior. These areas are often lightly monitored for the health and safety of employees and to ensure that employees are engaged in work activities.

These areas can also be targets for social engineers. Appropriate lighting, visible security personnel, and surveillance cameras are common ways to secure nonsensitive work areas.

FIGURE 9-2

Bollards are permanent or retractable barriers designed to block vehicular access to an area.

Courtesy of KVDP.

Sensitive Work Areas

Sensitive work areas are those areas where the general public is not allowed and are places the average employee may not have access to. Consider a bank branch. The general public is restricted to the lobby area, while employees have access to the area behind the teller windows where cash is counted and stored.

In a bank branch, physical barriers are used to separate the public area—the lobby—from the sensitive work area. A reinforced counter topped with bulletproof glass generally acts as a barrier between the two areas. Security cameras, both hidden and overt, are placed to provide complete coverage of the entire area. Most bank branches have at least one uniformed security guard in attendance at all times.

As another example, consider a technology company engaged in software development work. They might have some nonsensitive areas, such as the reception area, vendor conference rooms, and a common dining area, but then, treat the majority of their work area as sensitive due to the nature of the software development that takes place there. An unauthorized individual accessing the area might be able to discern sensitive product development plans or even tamper with the software.

This company might choose to use a simple badge-based access control system to enter the nonsensitive areas of the facility but require biometric authentication, such as a hand geometry scan, before granting access to the sensitive areas of the building.

Government Facilities

Government facilities often have more stringent security requirements than private-sector facilities. Federal facilities, and the security measures they require, are divided into five levels by the Federal Protective Service (FPS):

- **Level I**—This facility has 10 or fewer employees, 2,500 or fewer square feet of office space, and little public contact.
- **Level II**—This facility has 11 to 150 employees, 2,500 to 80,000 square feet of office space, and a moderate volume of public contact. Level II facilities are often located in shared office buildings with private sector businesses.
- **Level III**—This facility has 151 to 450 employees, 80,000 to 150,000 square feet of office space, and a moderate to high level of public contact. These facilities are usually multistory buildings and often contain several agencies or offices.
- **Level IV**—This facility has more than 450 employees, 80,000 to 250,000 square feet of office space, and a high volume of public contact.
- **Level V**—This facility is occupied by one or more agencies with critical national security missions. Level V facilities require tenant agencies to secure the site according to their own needs, insofar as those needs exceed the security levels dictated by a Level IV facility. Examples of Level V facilities include the headquarters buildings of the National Security Agency (NSA), Central Intelligence Agency (CIA), and the military facilities at the Pentagon.

These facilities have strict access control and physical security standards that include control of parking facilities, receiving and shipping procedures, employee and visitor identification, and training requirements.

Regulations at government facilities require that parking facilities be restricted to government vehicles and personnel and that authorized parking spaces be assigned. Systems to tow unauthorized vehicles must be in place. Adequate lighting and closed-circuit television monitoring are also required to ensure the safety of employees and to deter illegal and threatening activities.

Shipping and receiving at government facilities is another area where physical security measures differ from most private-sector facilities. All packages arriving at a classified government facility must be x-rayed and visually inspected to prevent attacks on government employees and facilities through the mail.

As with many secure private sector facilities, all employees at governmental facilities must display an agency-issued photo ID at all times. Visitors must wear a visitor identification badge, sign in with a receptionist or security guard, and be escorted at all times while within the facility.

Computer Rooms and Data Centers

Computer rooms and data centers are specialized forms of sensitive work areas. Access to these areas should be restricted to a few select individuals, and some data centers go one step further by going "dark." A dark data center is one that is monitored and managed remotely. Robotic devices in dark data centers perform tasks that normally require human intervention, such as cycling the power on a server or changing tapes in a backup system. Because human beings don't ordinarily work in a dark data center, the lights are usually off. This provides another layer of security. If the lights are on, or light from a flashlight shines through a window or across a video monitor, security personnel will most likely notice this suspicious activity.

Any data center, whether staffed or dark, should have access locks on all server racks and individual systems, as well as restrictions on electronic devices that can be brought into the data center. This prevents unauthorized data removal. Modern electronic devices, such as smartphones and flash storage devices, can hold a significant amount of data and are so small and ubiquitous that they often escape notice.

Port locks on servers and racks prevent intruders from downloading data to a portable device by restricting access to USB ports. Without access to these ports, it is impossible to physically connect a portable device to the server, although wireless access may still be possible.

Computer rooms and data centers usually have strict policies against bringing in food or drink. Although these policies do prevent accidental spills that could damage sensitive equipment, they also minimize the need for custodial maintenance. If the server room rarely needs to be cleaned, custodial staff do not need regular access to that room. The fewer people who have access to a data center, the more secure it is.

Biometric Access Control Systems

Biometric access controls are those based on physical or behavioral traits. Traditional access controls are based on three concepts:

- **What you know**—A password or pass phrase
- **What you have**—A smart card or token
- **What you are**—Biometric traits

This section focuses on the last item and breaks it down further into "what you are" and "what you do." The first concept deals with physical traits such as fingerprints and retinal patterns. The second covers behavioral traits such as typing speed and voice modulation.

Principles of Operation

Biometric systems are essentially sophisticated pattern recognition systems. They require a two-stage process:

- **Enrollment**—The process of taking one or more sample readings from an individual in order to form an accurate image of that individual's traits. These data are stored in a database for later retrieval. Systems based on physical attributes may only require a single sample reading, whereas those based on behavioral traits often require a more significant enrollment period during which many readings are taken. This is done to ensure that the data stored on an individual are truly typical of that individual and not an anomaly.
- **Verification**—The process of taking a reading on an individual and comparing it with the previously stored data on that individual to verify their identity. Verification may be either an identification process, where the individual is being checked against a large database of known individuals, or an authentication process, where the individual makes a claim of identity and the biometric security system verifies that claim.

During the verification process, an algorithm examines key match points in the live reading and compares them with the same match points on the stored sample.

Types of Biometric Systems

There are many traits that a biometric system can analyze. They fall into two distinct categories, as mentioned above: physical characteristics and behavioral characteristics. In this section, you will learn more about the specific attributes that fall into each of these two broad categories.

Physiological Types

Physiological biometric types are physical attributes that are unique to an individual. The accuracy of these traits can vary widely for identification and verification purposes. Some traits, such as fingerprints, are set at birth and do not change over an individual's lifetime. Others, such as facial recognition and hand geometry, can change significantly during childhood but are relatively constant during adulthood.

Fingerprint. Fingerprints are composed of two of characteristics:

- **Ridges**—The raised layers of skin that form loops, whorls, and arches
- **Valleys**—The depressed layers of skin between ridges

They are measured in two ways:

- **Minutiae matching**—Matches specific points within the fingerprint ridge pattern. Minutiae that are considered for match points include ridge endings, spurs, and crossovers.

- **Pattern matching**—Matches the overall characteristics of the fingerprints, rather than specific points. Pattern matching takes into account variations of characteristics such as ridge thickness, curvature, and density.

There are a variety of technologies used in fingerprint matching. The most common are optical, silicone, and ultrasound readers. They each capture data about the ridge characteristics of the fingerprint and recognize specific data points.

Retina. The retina is a membrane on the back of the eyeball that is sensitive to light. It contains a pattern of blood vessels that are unique to an individual, making it ideal for biometric identification and verification. During a retinal scan, users must remove their glasses, place their eyes close to the scanner, and stare at a specific point for 10 to 15 seconds. During this time, a low-intensity light is shone into the eye to illuminate the blood vessels on the retina. The retina is photographed and the pattern of blood vessels is compared with a known sample and analyzed.

 NOTE

Retinal scans are extremely accurate and difficult to fake. They are also fairly slow and some users consider them invasive because of the required proximity to the scanner.

Iris. The iris is the colored part of the eyeball. It has subtle patterns of rings, coronas, and furrows, and does not change throughout life. Iris scanning is often considered preferable to retinal scanning because glasses, contact lenses, and even eye surgery do not affect its accuracy. Users find these scans more acceptable than retinal scans because they are performed relatively quickly and do not require close physical proximity to the scanner. In fact, in 2015, researchers at Carnegie Mellon University demonstrated the ability to scan irises at a distance of 40 feet.

Hand geometry. Hand geometry is not as accurate as retinal or iris scanning, but many users consider it less intrusive. In this type of biometric scan, the user places his or her hand on a reader, which takes a series of measurements. It examines the length and width of the fingers, joints, and palm. Hand scanners may also examine the ridge patterns on the palm.

Facial recognition. Facial recognition involves measuring and analyzing key facial structures, including the distances between features such as the eyes, nose, cheekbones, jaw line, and mouth. A facial recognition system analyzes the size and proportion of these features and compares them with photographs taken at enrollment.

Behavioral Types

Behavioral biometrics take advantage of many characteristic behaviors that individuals exhibit consistently. Although you may not be aware of it, you follow certain rhythms when you type or write your signature. When you speak, you modulate your voice in specific ways that are unique to you. Behavioral biometrics analyze these behaviors to identify an individual.

Behavioral biometrics focus on actions that most people do automatically. You probably are not aware of your tempo when you type or the pressure you put on the pen when you write your signature. These are subconscious actions that are difficult to change consciously. Behavioral biometrics can be tricked by someone who takes the time to study a subject's behaviors and who learns to imitate them. They are best when used for lower security targets or when used in combination with another biometric or traditional access control method.

Typing tempo. When individuals type, especially when they type words they are accustomed to typing frequently such as their username and password, they tend to develop rhythms that are idiosyncratic. Biometric software can be used to analyze the time each key is depressed, as well as the length of time between keystrokes. Although this type of biometric access control is easy to implement and most users do not consider it intrusive, it also has a high false negative rate. A false negative can be triggered if a user types standing up, for example, or has an injury that impacts his or her ability to type.

Signature analysis. Signature analysis works in a similar way to typing tempo, by measuring the speed and pressure an individual uses to write the letters in his or her signature. It is generally well accepted by users, who are already accustomed to signing their name on documents, contracts, and visitor logs.

It is difficult for an imposter to accurately mimic the way that a given individual writes. The end result—the actual written signature—can be easily faked, but the rhythms used to sign are much more difficult. This method suffers from the same issues as typing tempo: false negatives. If a user injures his dominant hand, he will not sign his name in his normal way until the injury has healed.

Voice recognition. The human voice has two components: the vocal tract and the individual's accent. Accents are learned behaviors and are relatively easy to duplicate. The vocal tract is a physical attribute and is almost impossible to duplicate exactly. Even identical twins have slightly different vocal tracts. Voice recognition systems can recognize and differentiate between small variations in the spoken word by two individuals.

Typically, a voice recognition system uses an audio capture device, such as a microphone or telephone, to record an individual as she repeats random phrases. The system compares the recording to one made during the enrollment process.

Implementation Issues

Implementing a biometric access control system is more difficult than implementing a traditional access control system. User acceptance is one common barrier to biometric analysis. Many users who are unfamiliar with the technology find it intrusive or even frightening to undergo a retinal scan or facial recognition. Many users have privacy concerns over the idea of their biometric data being stored.

User acceptance problems are not the only issue with implementing a biometric access control system. When choosing a biometric access control system, weigh the potential for false acceptances and rejections, crossover errors, and failures in the enrollment and capturing processes.

False Acceptance Rate

The **false acceptance rate** of any access control technology is the percentage of imposters that will be recognized as authorized users. A system with a high false acceptance rate may simply be calibrated with too low a sensitivity. In this instance, if the system has a record of a user with a blue iris, for example, any individual with blue eyes is recognized as the authorized user. In most cases, false acceptances are the result of a deliberate attempt to fool the system. False acceptances are often called **Type II errors**.

False Rejection Rate

The **false rejection rate** is the percentage of attempts by legitimate users that are rejected by the system. This can happen when a user's behavior does not match the known sample. It can also happen when the sampling equipment is not calibrated properly or if the user's physical features are obscured. For example, a fingerprint reader would produce a false rejection if the user's fingers were covered in dirt or grease, obscuring the characteristics of the fingerprint. False rejections are referred to as **Type I errors**.

Crossover Error Rate

The **crossover error rate (CER)** is the point at which Type I errors and Type II errors are equal, as shown in **FIGURE 9-3**. All biometric systems can be calibrated to reduce either the false acceptance or false rejection rates to near zero. Unfortunately, calibrating the system to reduce or eliminate Type I errors generally raises the rate of Type II errors. A biometric system could be calibrated such that the sensitivity is turned all the way down, so that it accepts everyone. Of course, this would produce a large number of false positives but zero false negatives. Likewise, the sensitivity could be turned all the way up so that the system doesn't accept anyone, eliminating the false positives but producing a large number of false negatives. The CER is an accurate way to compare the real accuracy of various biometric systems. The smaller the CER, the more accurate it is. In other words, a system with a CER of 3% is more accurate than one with a CER of 5%.

Failure to Enroll Rate

All biometric systems require subjects to enroll, or present sample data, before they can use the system. As with any system, things do not always work the way they should and the sample data can be lost. The percentage of failed attempts to create a sample data set for an individual, divided by the total number of attempts to enroll users is called the **failure to enroll rate**.

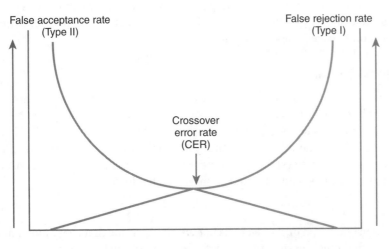

FIGURE 9-3
Crossover error rate.

Failure to Capture Rate

The **failure to capture rate** (or failure to acquire rate) is the percentage of an individual's authentication attempts that fail because the system is unable to obtain the information necessary to make an authentication decision. This is most often caused by a dirty or smudged scanning device or user error.

Modes of Operation

Biometric systems are used for two primary purposes: verifying an individual's stated identity and ascertaining the identity of an unknown user.

Verification

In **verification mode**, a biometric system makes a simple one-to-one comparison and returns a binary result. The individual presents a claim of identity—a token or user name, for example—and a biometric sample such as a fingerprint or retinal scan. The access control system simply retrieves the known user record for the claimed identity from a database and then compares that to the sample data provided by the individual. If the two data sets match, the user is authenticated and the system returns a positive result. If the two data sets do not match, the system returns a negative result.

 NOTE

Most biometric access control systems are used in verification mode.

Identification

In **identification mode**, the individual presents a sample data set such as a fingerprint, which the system analyzes. The system then searches the database of known users in an attempt to find a matching profile. Biometric systems are less effective in this mode because of the large number of matching user profiles that can be returned from a large database. For example, in a database of 750,000 records, a match rate of just 0.01 will return 7,500 records, which must be sorted through manually. Some systems can reduce the number of matches by cross referencing with other user data such as age, gender, and other characteristics, but it is very difficult to obtain an exact identity confirmation in this mode. Biometric systems in identification mode are most often used in law enforcement.

Biometric System Parameters

All biometric systems operate under some basic parameters, which you should be aware of when choosing and implementing a biometric access control system. Some types of biometric systems have advantages under one parameter but fall short under others. The right system to use depends on the goals and users of the system. In a controlled environment in which user education is possible, a system with some user acceptance issues can be considered because users can be trained and educated about the technology.

Universality

A biometric system must be based on a universal characteristic, or one that every individual will possess. A system that relies on signature analysis, for example, will not be effective in identifying very young children who cannot write.

Uniqueness

The system must measure a characteristic that is not duplicated among users, such as a fingerprint or iris pattern. You are not likely to find a biometric access control system on the market that does not meet this requirement.

Permanence

The characteristic measured by the system must be relatively permanent across the user base. Hand geometry and facial structure, for example, change significantly throughout childhood but in adulthood are fairly permanent. Fingerprints, retinal patterns, and iris patterns are determined before birth and do not change throughout an individual's lifetime, barring a disfiguring injury.

Collectability

A biometric system must be able to collect sample data from an individual in an easy and reliable way. There are many unique, universal, and permanent characteristics that could be used for biometric access control that you will not find in use because data collection is too difficult or intrusive. DNA is a good example of this. It can be used to identify individuals very accurately, but collecting a DNA sample is impractical for the purposes of access control.

Performance

A biometric access control system must be able to return a positive or negative result quickly. Usually, 5 to 10 seconds is the most an individual is willing to wait for access to needed resources. The system must be able to analyze the sample data and perform a database lookup extremely efficiently to avoid performance issues that will produce a bottleneck effect on an organization's operations. Think of the delays and long lines at airport security checkpoints. Most travelers accept these delays as unavoidable hassles inherent in the system, and because most do not have to deal with them every day, they do not object too strenuously. However, if those users faced a similar line just to get into work every morning, they would be less likely to accept the system.

Acceptability

User acceptance is a big hurdle to some biometric access control systems. This is often due to a lack of understanding of the technology by users and a concern over privacy. Users are more likely to accept a biometric system based on a technology they understand, such as fingerprinting or signature recognition, than one that is based on unfamiliar technology, such as iris or retinal scanning.

Privacy concerns are usually based on worries over biometric data that are collected and stored during the enrollment process. Before implementing a biometric access control system, users must be assured that their biometric data will be used only for authentication purposes and will be stored securely.

Anti-Circumvention

Biometric systems should also be designed with anti-circumvention controls to prevent an individual from presenting a biometric sample belonging to another person. For example, voice recognition systems will require the individual to repeat a random phrase to avoid the possibility of authenticating using a recording of another individual.

Legal and Business Issues

As with any access control system, there are legal and business issues to consider before implementation. Users' concerns over privacy and personal safety should be given sufficient consideration, as well as the overall cost of a biometric solution and its efficiency and effectiveness compared with a traditional access control system.

Privacy Concerns

Privacy is a significant concern in any biometric access control solution because it involves deeply personal characteristics such as physical traits and subconscious behaviors. There are two types of biometric samples: those that are consciously given and those that can be captured without the subject's knowledge.

Iris and retinal scans, for example, are nearly impossible to perform without the subject's knowledge and consent. Facial recognition, however, can be performed at a distance with a camera and a good telephoto lens. This presents a significant privacy concern because there is the potential for individuals to be enrolled and monitored without their knowledge or consent.

Cost-Effectiveness of Biometric Solutions

Biometric access controls tend to be significantly more expensive than traditional methods of access control such as a username and password. The technology involved is fairly new and is more sophisticated than other methods. However, this cost is justified in some cases where accurate identity verification is crucial. Trigger locks on firearms are a good example. Biometric trigger locks that use a fingerprint scan are designed to ensure that only the owner of the gun is able to fire it. Biometric trigger locks are more expensive than typical combination-style locks, but the risk that the gun will be stolen and used in a crime is significant enough to justify the additional expense.

The same argument holds up in other situations as well. Biometric access controls are frequently used in highly sensitive areas, such as classified military facilities. Adoption of biometric technology has been slower in less-sensitive areas including banking, where traditional access controls combined with emergency plans are sufficient to provide an acceptable level of access control.

For example, it makes sense to use biometrics to authorize credit card purchases. Only the owner of the credit card should be using it, and use by an unauthorized individual is a significant threat. Signature analysis would be a natural choice to implement a biometric component to existing access controls on the credit card, but that would require that every merchant who accepts credit cards purchase a special biometric signature pad, which would be costly. It would also be ineffective in preventing online credit card fraud, as no signature is required (or possible) for online purchases.

Cost of Deployment and Maintenance

As noted in the credit card example above, cost of deployment is a significant inhibitor to widespread adoption of biometric access controls. In that example, every merchant who wanted to accept credit cards would have to obtain a signature capture device. The initial cost of the devices, as well as the cost of maintaining such a large number of devices at various locations, is significant.

Database Storage and Transmission

Storage of biometric data is a significant part of any deployment project. The data, like any personally identifying information, must be stored as securely as possible to avoid potential identity theft or invasion of privacy. This is especially true where users have a strong concern over the privacy and safety of biometrics.

Database transmission and lookup must be optimized to avoid bottlenecks at the access control site. In most cases, the database lookup takes more time than the analysis algorithm. For very large databases, lookup of an individual record can take a significant amount of time. Given that most users are unwilling to spend more than a few seconds on any access control, the database must be optimized to minimize lookup time.

Database transmissions must be secured to avoid data theft while in transit, and they must be optimized for speed and reliability. If the connection to the database goes down, the entire biometric system will not function. For this reason, the database server as well as the server that hosts the matching and analysis software should both be configured for high availability.

Law Enforcement Databases

Law enforcement pioneered the use of biometrics with fingerprint identification. They maintain large databases of biometric information, including fingerprints and, in some cases, DNA, on individuals processed through the criminal justice system. Although most organizations use biometrics for authentication purposes, law enforcement agencies use biometric data primarily for identification. DNA matching has been used in many cases to prove conclusively that an individual was present at the crime scene. In other cases, DNA evidence has been used to prove that an individual—sometimes years after a conviction—could not have been the perpetrator of the crime.

The cost of DNA analysis has prevented it from being used as routinely as fingerprinting, but it has been proven extremely effective for identification purposes.

Personal Danger Issues

Users often cite theft of biometric components as a concern over the adoption of biometric access controls. In reality, most biometric systems are designed to prevent the use of stolen or fake biometric components. Hand geometry systems require the subject to move his or her fingers and test for hand temperature to avoid authenticating an artificial hand. Iris and retinal scanning devices also test for body temperature and movement. Voice recognition systems require users to repeat random phrases to prevent the use of prerecorded voice samples.

However, the fact that biometric technologies are designed to prevent the use of stolen biometric components does not mean that this concern can be ignored. Users must be convinced that the biometric system is not dangerous before they willingly adopt it.

Hygiene is a far more realistic concern. There is the potential for spreading disease through fingerprint pads or other scanning devices that are touched by large numbers of individuals. However, this is no more risky than handling cash or touching a door handle—actions that most of us take many times a day without a second thought. Again, user training and education, coupled with the availability of hand sanitizer, will help assuage user concerns over hygiene.

Technology-Related Access Control Solutions

There are many ways of identifying and authenticating users on a system. In this chapter, you have read about perimeter security and physical barriers to buildings and facilities. You have explored the realm of biometric access controls. In this section, you will read about other technologies that are designed to grant or prevent access to key areas or data.

Physical Locks

The most common and widely used physical access control technology is the lock. There are a wide variety of locks, each with their own level of sophistication:

- **Warded locks**—A typical padlock is a warded lock. It is the simplest of all mechanical locks. It consists of metal projections, or **wards**, in the locking chamber that match up to the grooves on the key. Once the key is inserted, it uses leverage to turn the bolt to the unlocked position. These locks are inexpensive and are the easiest to pick. They are secure enough to deter the curious but not the determined thief.
- **Tumbler locks**—These are more sophisticated than warded locks. They have a series of spring-loaded tumblers that are moved into alignment by the grooves on the key. Once all the tumblers are in position, the bolt can be slid into the unlocked position.
- **Combination locks**—Combination locks, such as those used on high school lockers, provide a higher level of security than warded or tumbler locks. They work by aligning a series of wheels. When the dial is spun to the right and left in a specific sequence, the wheels are aligned and the lock will release. Electronic versions do not align a series of wheels but rather act as a simple password system. When the user enters the combination on a keypad, it is checked against the stored password. If the two match, the lock is released.
- **Cipher locks**—These locks are programmable and are the most sophisticated type of lock. Unlike previous styles, cipher locks can be programmed with many combinations and can be combined with a swipe card or biometric identity verification system. This type of lock can also have added security features built in, such as a door delay alarm that triggers if the door is held open for another individual, or hostage alarms. To trigger a silent alarm, an individual under duress would enter a panic code instead of his or her normal combination. When a user enters a duress code, the cipher lock opens to make the hostage-taker think that everything is operating normally. However, the lock also triggers a silent alarm to notify security responders that a hostage situation exists.

Mechanical locks are most commonly used to secure equipment such as laptops that are easy to steal. Combination and cipher locks are often used to secure sensitive areas within a facility, such as data centers.

Electronic Key Management System (EKMS)

In facilities with a large number of physical keys, keeping those keys secure can be a challenge. Electronic key management systems are locked boxes designed to control who has access to the keys and to keep a record of which keys are checked out and by whom. Typically, an EKMS has a keypad or smart card reader mounted near the lockbox. When an individual needs to check out a set of keys, he or she scans the smart card or enters a combination on the keypad. If the credentials are acceptable, the lockbox opens and the user can remove a set of keys from a chamber. The EKMS logs the user ID, a timestamp, and which keys are removed from the lockbox. The system also logs when the keys are returned.

Fobs and Tokens

In situations in which more sophisticated access controls are needed, challenge-response tokens on key fobs are useful. These are small devices that display a new code every minute, which are based on public key encryption. The key fob tokens are convenient for the user because of their small size. They are often designed to attach to a key ring, making them more difficult to lose than a loose device.

To access a secured facility, VPN, or other resource, the user is given a challenge. Typically, this is simply a request for a code. The user then uses the key fob device to generate a code, which the user enters into the access control system. If the code is accepted, the user has the opportunity to enter a username and password or some other authentication factor. Challenge-response tokens are generally used in two-stage authentication schemes.

Common Access Cards

The **Common Access Card (CAC)** is a smart card issued by the U.S. Department of Defense to military and civilian personnel and contractors. It is used as a single sign-on for secured resources and as an identification card for access to facilities. The CAC includes a magnetic stripe used in card readers for access to facilities. It also includes a digital photograph for visual identification purposes and a microchip that stores a **card holder unique identification (CHUID)**, personally identifying information and privilege data on the cardholder. CACs store basic identity verification data such as name and Social Security number, as well as two fingerprint biometrics.

Outsourcing Physical Security—Pros and Cons

Strong physical security requires that many disparate factors all work together—from landscape design to security guard training to programming and maintenance of biometric access controls. Rather than overseeing all of these details in-house, many organizations choose to outsource. In this section, you will examine the benefits and potential risks of outsourcing physical security.

Benefits of Outsourcing Physical Security

Outsourcing physical security can be beneficial, especially to small and mid-sized organizations that do not have the personnel or expertise to handle physical security in-house. A dedicated security firm will have the experience and expertise to prevent many types of security breaches and may be able to point out areas in your organization that are not as well protected as you thought.

A third-party security firm will also be able to be more impartial about security than an in-house team might. For example, security guards from a dedicated security firm are more likely to question every individual who enters a secured area, while a guard employed by the organization may be tempted to make exceptions for friends, coworkers, or upper executives. An external security auditor will also be able to see the organization's security situation with fresh eyes, while an internal security audit may overlook some areas simply because "that's the way we've always done it."

Risks Associated with Outsourcing Physical Security

The major risk associated with outsourcing physical security is lack of control. Your organization has final responsibility for the security of facilities and resources, but the implementation details are handed off to a third party. If the outsourced security firm cuts corners or does not perform adequate background checks, your organization could be held liable for any damages caused by a security breach. To mitigate these risks, any organization considering outsourcing physical security should perform due diligence:

- Conduct a thorough audit of your organization's security needs. Vendors are likely to conduct their own audits as well, but you will be better able to choose vendors who can meet your organization's needs if you already have a good idea of what those needs are.
- Conduct onsite audits of each vendor on your list of potential security partners. The best way to see how they will handle your security needs is to see how they are already securing their other clients.
- Negotiate the details of staffing, background checks, equipment, and **service level agreements (SLAs)** to protect your organization. Be sure to include language describing the penalties for failure to prevent a security breach and procedures for handling a breach after the fact.
- Remember, a third-party security firm can only implement your organization's policies. Outsourcing does not absolve your organization from its ultimate responsibility for securing facilities, resources, and data.

Outsourcing physical security can be beneficial, especially for small and mid-sized businesses, but there are risks associated with outsourcing. Conducting due diligence can mitigate many of those risks.

Best Practices for Physical Access Controls

There are many best practices, depending on your organization's security needs. If your organization owns its own facility, landscaping and perimeter security will be a concern you will need to address. If your facility contains a data center or other highly sensitive areas, you will need to consider additional access control methods such as biometric identity verification and mechanical or programmatic locks.

The first step in ensuring physical security is to conduct a security audit. A security audit allows you to identify potential targets within your organization as well as any existing physical security risks. Some things to include in a physical security audit are:

- Documentation of existing physical security measures, including perimeter security and access control systems.

- Nonstandard entry points to the facility as a whole and to sensitive areas within the facility.
- Standard access levels. For example, certain employees may have access to the data center, while other employees and external contractors do not.
- Differences in security at various times, especially after hours.

Once existing physical security has been audited, any deficiencies or weaknesses can be dealt with. If outsourcing is an option, the organization can begin to evaluate vendors.

Case Studies and Examples

The best way to learn the real effects of physical security is to see it in action—both in their failures and successes. In this section, you will read about physical security measures that prevent both internal and external attacks.

Private Sector Case Study and Example

Physical controls are important aspects of protecting data from both internal and external malicious users. Although attacks are a major reason that strong physical access controls are needed, there are plenty of completely mundane actions that can disrupt an operation and endanger data integrity. Listed below are two incidents in the private sector in which physical access controls solved major IT issues.

A new Midwestern biotechnology company, Acme Medical Technologies, had just expanded its offices, adding a server room to the main IT floor. This new server room was designed to handle a high-availability, Windows-based web server that contained customer-facing websites. The server room was in a part of the office in which access was limited. Only the networking and web server teams in the IT department had access to the area. Because of the security in that section of the office, further physical access controls were not implemented on the server room.

An unusual issue started almost immediately. Every night around midnight, the web servers went offline. The server configurations were verified and when the logs were checked, they showed that the servers had ungraceful shutdowns every night around the same time. To determine the root cause, the web server administrator stayed late to see if anything physical was causing the outage.

That evening, the server administrator watched as a janitor walked into the server room and proceeded to unplug the web server from the **uninterruptable power supply (UPS)**. He then proceeded to plug in his vacuum cleaner to vacuum the server room. The simple solution to this issue was to utilize the electronic keypad lock that had been installed on the server room and explain to facilities management that their services were not needed in the server room.

Another example shows the need for physical security within the private sector. Agents for a major Midwestern insurance company had direct connections to the corporate mainframe systems via microcomputers at each agent's office. One office was having an intermittent connection issue. Approximately once a week, usually on Fridays, the system would crash. Due to the nature of the jobs that the system ran, it wasn't worth restarting the system until the next morning, so the agent was losing a few hours of productivity every week.

A technician was sent from IT to inspect the system. It was quickly determined that there were no hardware faults or heat issues that could be causing the problem. Oddly, the system refused to crash while the technician was onsite—the first week in months that it didn't fail at least once. After hearing this, the technician suggested installing a lock on the closet that the microcomputer was housed in. After the door was locked, the server stopped crashing. It seems the staff enjoyed getting out early on the days that the server crashed and had been occasionally manually rebooting the system.

Public Sector Case Study

Primary schools and school districts face a number of issues when it comes to physical access control of their facilities. School districts must protect their students, staff, and school property. This must all be done while maintaining a friendly learning environment. Most districts have neither the ability nor the desire to hire full-time gate guards, but they must monitor the entry points to the schools to make sure no unauthorized adults enter, and that no unauthorized individuals leave with a child. A school must also be vigilant of student activities and be prepared to respond quickly to altercations among students. The school districts also have a secondary goal of preventing theft, vandalism, and graffiti.

Consider how Moss Point School District in Mossville, Mississippi, handles these challenges. The district serves 3,100 students spread out among a high school, a junior high school, and six elementary schools. A few of the schools had VCR-based security cameras, but that solution had too many drawbacks. The images were grainy, making it hard to identify people. The systems could only be viewed onsite, and only after an incident occurred, which didn't allow the schools to identify and react to incidents as they happened.

This gave the school district two main requirements for a new system. It had to be centralized, and it had to integrate with existing access controls, such as alarm systems. The solution was to implement an IP-based video surveillance network.

This network utilized over 200 digital video cameras, all connected to a digital video recording (DVR) server connected to a central management system at the district office. Now, by looking at a single screen, school officials can see the feed from all of their schools' cameras, and district security officials can monitor all of the schools from one location in real time. Before the fall semester of 2000, the school district first installed cameras in the 10 facilities, most in hallways and on campus perimeters. Each camera is housed in a protective enclosure to prevent tampering. Eventually, the school district plans to have cameras in all of the classrooms as well.

The cameras allow officials to see what is happening in the schools when it is happening. This allows for a more proactive approach to safety and security. For example, the officials can detect signs that a fight may occur and defuse the situation before it starts. The cameras also act as a significant deterrent. Cases of vandalism and unsafe driving at the high school dropped dramatically after the system was installed.

By adding digital video cameras to their physical access controls, the Moss Point schools were able to greatly enhance the safety and security of the learning environment that they provide to students.

Critical Infrastructure Case Study

Physical access controls in the case of critical infrastructure have a number of obstacles to overcome. There are a lot of organizations that intermingle. If they do not share a common authentication method, controlling access becomes unwieldy. There is also a large volume of requestors needing access at any given time. A universal, secure, and quick method of identifying requestors and granting access is required. This is further complicated by various rules and regulations that critical facilities must adhere to. In this section, you will learn how U.S. port facilities handle these issues for maritime workers.

The Transportation Worker Identification Credential (TWIC) program is a joint program involving the Transportation Security Administration (TSA) and the U.S. Coast Guard (USCG) within the Department of Homeland Security (DHS). TWIC is intended to strengthen the security of U.S. maritime infrastructure through the vetting of civilian maritime workers and through the issuance of tamper-resistant, biometrically-enable identification credentials to workers. TWIC was developed in response to the regulations found in two legislative acts: the Maritime Transportation Security Act (MTSA) of 2002 and the Security and Accountability for Every Port (SAFE Port) Act of 2006. TWIC is a massive program, with over 1 million workers issued a TWIC card. Possession of a TWIC card is required for unescorted access at over 3,000 land- and ocean-based facilities and over 10,000 vessels that are subject to MTSA regulations.

In the early stages of developing the TWIC card, the maritime industry expressed concerns about the proposed approach, which called for the TWIC card to be fully compliant with the Federal Information Processing Standards (FIPS) 201 standard. FIPS 201 allows access to biometric data on a smart card only through a contact interface, requiring insertion of the card into a contact interface slot on the card reader. The concern was that this standard was not appropriate for the high volume of physical access and rapid access operational requirement of the industry. There was also a concern that the extreme conditions at the port facilities would allow airborne contaminants into the readers, causing delays and maintenance problems. FIPS 201 also required a personal identification number (PIN) to be entered to access the card, further slowing down the access process.

These concerns resulted in the TWIC Reader Hardware and Card Application Specification, published by the TSA. This specification implements an alternative authentication mechanism allowing for contactless reading of the biometric information stored on the card without requiring PIN entry. To protect personal privacy, the biometric data stored on the card is encrypted. Decryption is accomplished through the use of a symmetric key called the TWIC Privacy Key (TPK), which is generated during card personalization by the TSA and is unique to each TWIC card. The TPK can only be accessed through the contact interface or through a swipe read of the magnetic stripe.

This approach to contactless biometric reading presented a unique challenge for the implementers. To decrypt the contactless biometric information, the reader must first have a way to obtain the TPK. This can be achieved by having a one-time registration process that requires card contact, and then the TPK can be stored in a local server. An alternative method is to have a reader with both magnetic stripe and contactless smart card capabilities. In this scenario, the cardholder would swipe the TWIC card before presenting the card to the contactless interface. It should also be noted that the TWIC card includes separate FIPS 201–compliant information, so the card may be used in conjunction with a traditional PIN and a biometric reader can be utilized with the card. Utilizing biometrics and IT to secure and simplify maritime and port access allowed TWIC to provide a faster and more secure and reliable way to allow authorized access to our nation's critical infrastructures.

CHAPTER SUMMARY

No one physical security method is the answer to an organization's access control needs. Many methods must work together to create a strong net of security. Perimeter security must be in place to deny an intruder access to the building, but if the intruder does get past the perimeter, there should be some other method of access control to protect the most sensitive areas of a facility.

The goal of any physical security plan, whether implemented in-house or outsourced, is to make access convenient for authorized users and as difficult as possible for intruders.

KEY CONCEPTS AND TERMS

Bollard	Failure to enroll rate	Type I error
Card holder unique identification (CHUID)	False acceptance rate	Type II error
	False rejection rate	Uninterruptable power supply (UPS)
Common Access Card (CAC)	Identification mode	
Crossover error rate (CER)	Perimeter security	Verification mode
Failure to capture rate	Service level agreement (SLA)	Ward

CHAPTER 9 ASSESSMENT

1. A good physical security strategy relies on a single strong point of access control.

   A. True   B. False

2. Fencing, lighting, and security guards are all important parts of what aspect of physical security?

   A. Outsourced security

   B. Biometrics

   C. Perimeter security

   D. Access control

3. What is a weak point in perimeter security?

   A. Road

   B. Gate

   C. Pathway

   D. Window

4. Cameras trained on entry and exit points provide which security benefits? (Select two.)
   A. Theft of resources prevention
   B. A record of who enters and leaves the facility
   C. Vandalism prevention
   D. The ability of guards to monitor activity in real time

5. What is a short vertical post designed to control traffic and prevent vehicular attacks on a building?
   A. Balustrade
   B. Barrier
   C. Barm
   D. Bollard
   E. None of the above

6. Every package that arrives or leaves a classified government facility is x-rayed.
   A. True
   B. False

7. A(n) _____ data center has robotic devices that are controlled remotely to change backup tapes and cycle the power on servers.

8. What is the name of the process through which several biometric readings are taken on an individual in order to create an accurate record of the individual's characteristics?
   A. Scanning
   B. Identification
   C. Verification
   D. Enrollment
   E. Creation

9. The two primary types of biometric access controls are _____ and _____.

10. Anyone who can forge another person's signature can defeat a biometric access control based on signature analysis.
    A. True   B. False

11. The crossover error rate of a biometric system is _____.

12. Most biometric access control systems are used in which mode?
    A. Identification
    B. Production
    C. Elimination
    D. Verification
    E. Restrictive

13. Typical padlocks are an example of which type of locks?
    A. Warded
    B. Tumbler
    C. Combination
    D. Cipher

14. What type of lock is often equipped with silent alarms that notify security or police that an employee is in trouble?
    A. Warded
    B. Tumbler
    C. Combination
    D. Cipher

15. What is the first step in designing a physical security system?
    A. Hire a security outsourcing firm.
    B. Conduct a security audit.
    C. Purchase a biometric access control system.
    D. Install a video surveillance system.
    E. Replace traditional locks with programmable cipher locks.

Access Control Solutions for Remote Workers

ALLOWING EMPLOYEES TO WORK REMOTELY is a benefit that many organizations offer. If your organization provides remote access for employees, that means aspects of your network are remote as well. The corporate network now extends to employees' homes, coffee shops, hotels, airports, and other remote locations. Extending the network introduces new security concerns. With the evolution of virtual private networks and wireless network capabilities, network security and solutions have changed to meet demand. This chapter will discuss many of these solutions.

Chapter 10 Topics

This chapter covers the following topics and concepts:

- How the mobile work force has grown in recent years
- Which remote access methods and techniques are commonly used
- Which remote access protocols offer strong protection and which do not
- Remote authentication protocols
- Network authentication protocols
- How virtual private networks (VPNs) protect data in transit
- How web authentication plays an important role in remote communications
- Best practices that support remote access
- Case studies and examples of remote access control solutions

Chapter 10 Goals

When you complete this chapter, you will be able to:

- Identify the difference between the RADIUS and TACACS+ protocols
- Understand how virtual private networks benefit both the organization and the remote worker
- Understand how the remote access protocols address authentication, authorization, and accounting (AAA)

- Discuss the benefits and drawbacks of various remote and network authentication protocols
- Understand the components of Internet Security Protocol (IPSec)
- Understand how knowledge-based authentication is used for web authentication
- Know how to apply remote access best practices

Growth in Mobile Work Force

The rapid growth of consumer and business technologies has forever changed the traditional workplace. The introduction of computers and the Internet increased employee efficiency and productivity. Desktop computers were an important part of this new productivity, but they were expensive and were used only at the corporate office. When prices came down and people were able to purchase them for home use, more people began bringing work home. They used media such as floppy diskettes to transfer data between computers. Over time, computers got smaller and more portable. Laptops quickly became available to the majority of corporate employees. Dial-up access allowed employees to connect to the corporate network remotely. Eventually, new connectivity options such as virtual private networking, high-speed Wi-Fi, and mobile broadband replaced dial-up as the primary means of accessing networks remotely.

Today, armed with a laptop and anytime, anywhere access, many people no longer have to face a long commute to work. You can work from home, in an airport, in a coffee shop, or from your car between appointments. This capability has been highly beneficial to sales representatives, field engineers, consultants, and installation and repair engineers. For example, a sales representative no longer needs to return to the office to update the sales manager on a sales deal. Instead, the sales rep can handle status updates remotely and move on to the next customer. More and more, sales representatives can be based anywhere the customer is located, even working within a customer site, and feel confident that confidential data are not being shared with or seen by the customer. Organizations foster this confidence by deploying secure remote access technologies. You will read about a variety of these technologies in this chapter.

Implementing a system that provides anytime, anywhere access is critical for a growing mobile work force. Organizations must consider the following factors when planning a remote access environment:

- Do remote workers need access from various locations, such as hotels, airports, customer sites, coffee shops, and so on?
- Will network access be granted only to employer-owned computer resources or will employees be allowed access when using personal, customer-owned, or publicly available resources as well?
- Will every employee be allowed to have a laptop for remote access? How will the data on the laptop be protected if it's lost or stolen?

- Do employees need to use mobile phones, smartphones, and tablets? Do they need to access the organization's network with these devices?
- How will remote employees access organizational resources? Will virtual private network (VPN) access be required, or will web access to the organization's resources be sufficient?
- What level of authentication will be required for remote access?

Remote Access Methods and Techniques

Having the correct systems in place to ensure that remote employees are able to work as if they were in a corporate office is called "remote access." Whenever transactions occur between a remote worker and the corporate environment, both entities want to ensure that security is implemented. Remote workers need to know their data are not shared with outside entities. IT security personnel need to know the correct person is gaining access to the internal network, and that the correct access is being provided once those users are on the network. Implementing identification, authentication, and authorization for remote access assists in this protection.

Implementing various technologies and addressing remote access concerns ensures your systems and data are protected. You will learn about a variety of remote access technologies and their benefits throughout this chapter. First, it's important to understand the concerns associated with remote access:

- Remote access connections usually remain open for an extended period of time. This may cause a security problem. Leaving connections open allows attackers to gain easy access. It is a common practice to close connections automatically after some time, such as 24 hours.
- Remote access solutions, such as VPNs, do not protect the computer system. An employee may use a business laptop to do personal activities such as surfing the web and shopping online while he or she is on a public, unsecured network, such as a hotel's wireless network. While the employee is using the unsecured connection, malware may infect the system. The next time the employee connects to the corporate network via a VPN connection, the malware can spread to the corporate network. It is essential that mobile computer systems are protected with antivirus software and appropriate controls. The software and controls help protect the system when it is both on and off the corporate network.

Whenever transactions or communications occur on a network, it is important for users to provide identification and for organizations to ensure users are authenticated and authorized to perform actions, such as downloading data from the organization's intranet. This occurs in three steps: identification, authentication, and authorization.

Identification

Identification is the process of uniquely distinguishing an individual. In most cases, identification needs to be provided prior to authenticating the user. Common forms of identification are a name or an account number. Identification can refer to a person, computer system, or program. Identification is important because if, for example, everyone had the same bank account number, it would be almost impossible for a bank to know how much money you have in your account. In a network environment, a username is your unique identification. Some organizations also provide employees with a corporate identification number or a badge number as a separate identification mechanism.

Authentication

Authentication is the process of verifying that users are who they say they are. Access and privileges should not be provided to a user unless verification has occurred. Authentication can take many forms when it is based on identity. Every form of authentication is based on something you have, something you are, or something you know.

You can set up a remote access authentication using authentication methods such as multifactor authentication. Most enterprises implement two-factor authentication, such as requiring a personal identification number (PIN) and token when connecting to the internal network via a VPN. This is necessary because the security concerns specifically associated with remote access are greater. Allowing a remote computer to directly access an organization's network poses a high risk. It is necessary to use stronger authentication methods so that identity verification is correct and is not being mimicked by an attacker. Remote access authentication can also be achieved through protocols that you will learn about later in this chapter.

Authorization

Once authentication is completed, authorization can occur. Authorization is determining which actions are allowed or not allowed by a user or system. Although a user may have provided identification and been authenticated, this does not mean the user is authorized to access all systems or run all commands. Once the user performs an action, mechanisms such as an access control list are used to authorize or not authorize user actions. Although authorization is not necessarily tied to remote access, it is important to understand how access control systems work together and complement one another. Remote access is an important part of the infrastructure, and authorization provides a secondary layer to securing the network and data that reside on the network.

Access Protocols to Minimize Risk

There are multiple ways an organization can provide remote access identification, authentication, and authorization through protocols. Some of these protocols add an additional component such as accounting. These protocols provide additional security for remote access connections and decrease the risk associated with them.

Authentication, Authorization, and Accounting (AAA)

Authentication, authorization, and accounting (AAA) are network services that provide security through a framework of access controls and policies, enforcement of policies, and information needed for billing purposes. The benefits associated with AAA are increased security, increased control over the network, and the capability of auditing your network. Employing an AAA framework within an organization enables communication between IT systems over multiple networks. Specific protocols can address the AAA framework as a combined AAA protocol or as separate entities. The framework provides the flexibility and control for AAA configuration, using standardized protocols, and allows for scalability. Many of these capabilities will be addressed through the specific protocols described in the following sections.

Authentication provides a way of proving a user's claimed identity. The use of multifactor authentication offers a variety of authentication technologies. As the method increases to two-factor and three-factor authentication, the options increase. Some examples of authentication are a user ID and a password, a PIN and a token, and biometrics. Once a user enters his or her credentials, the authentication server compares them with the user's credentials stored in a database. Authentication is the first of the services provided in the AAA framework because you cannot limit or deny access without knowing who the user is.

Authorization is determining whether a user has the right to do certain actions. These actions may include issuing commands or accessing internal resources. Authorization cannot occur unless the user has been authenticated. Policies define authorization capabilities. Policies based on services or user access requests determine whether the resulting actions are denied or allowed.

Accounting enables the system to collect statistics on networks or users for auditing and billing purposes. Accounting enables tracking of system usage, of start and stop times of resources, of the number of data packets, as well as of other metrics that identify what was used and for how long.

The AAA is a framework on which multiple protocols are based. Protocols may ensure that all or some components of the AAA framework are available in the construct of the protocol. The entities of the framework may work together or separately or may not be included at all. For example, the RADIUS protocol uses the AAA framework to provide the three AAA components but supports authentication and authorization separately from accounting. If a network administrator does not want to employ accounting, he or she has this flexibility. Next you will review several of these protocols whose foundation is focused on this AAA framework.

Remote Authentication Dial in User Service (RADIUS)

Remote Authentication Dial in User Service (RADIUS) is a client/server protocol that provides authentication and authorization for remote users. RADIUS also provides accounting capabilities. Livingston Enterprises developed RADIUS for its network access server product. The standards related to RADIUS are:

- **RADIUS**—RFC 2865
- **RADIUS accounting**—RFC 2866

RADIUS is a network protocol that provides communications between a **network access server (NAS)** and an authentication server. Enterprises use the protocol to provide network authentication for their remote users. Internet service providers (ISPs) use the protocol to authenticate users and to grant access to the Internet. ISPs and internal corporate departments also use RADIUS for billing purposes by tracking the start and stop times of sessions. For example, an internal corporate department may charge other departments for use of its infrastructure. RADIUS can be used to provide the chargeback to the departments. RADIUS provides configuration information, authentication, and authorization between the NAS and RADIUS server. The communications information provided identifies the type of service delivered to the client. A simplified RADIUS infrastructure is shown in **FIGURE 10-1**.

RADIUS can manage a large number of users through a single source. The users' configuration information and user IDs and passwords are stored in a database, text file, or **Lightweight Directory Access Protocol (LDAP)** server. Verification of the user ID and password are a part of the RADIUS protocol. RADIUS also supports Extensible Authentication Protocol (EAP). EAP is an authentication framework that supports multiple authentication mechanisms. EAP will be discussed later in this chapter.

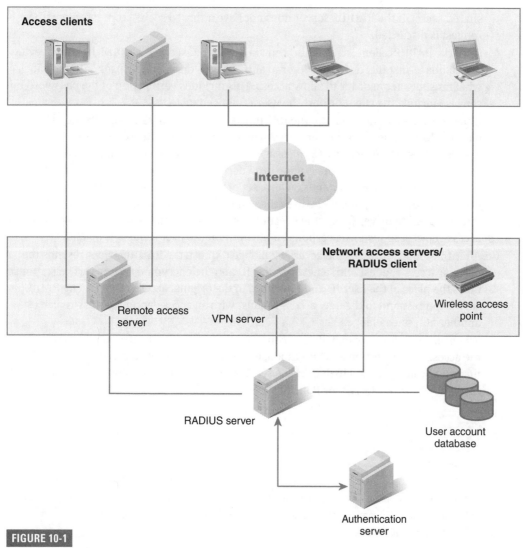

FIGURE 10-1

RADIUS infrastructure.

The RADIUS protocol works as follows:

1. A user provides authentication credentials such as a user ID and password to a RADIUS client such as a remote access server, NAS, or VPN server. The RADIUS client creates an access request containing the user ID and password. Optional information that can be provided in the access request are the ID of the client and port ID that the user is accessing. Passwords are protected from disclosure by using a cryptographic hash instead of a plaintext value.

2. The access request is sent to the RADIUS server. If no response is returned, the request will be sent again. If the primary server is down, the request can be sent to back up RADIUS servers.

3. When the RADIUS server receives the access request, it validates the client through a shared secret. If the RADIUS server does not have a shared secret from the client, the request is discarded.

4. Once the RADIUS client is authenticated via the shared secret, the RADIUS server reviews the database, text file, or LDAP server to authenticate the user. The user entry specifies what must be met in order to allow access. This includes verification of the password but can also include the client or port the user is allowed to access.

5. If the specifications are met and the RADIUS server wants to issue a challenge to the user, the RADIUS server sends an access-challenge response. An example of a challenge is a Short Message Service (SMS) message that the user must enter into the client. For example, a third-party SMS messaging provider can be incorporated into the process. The SMS message provider sends a word, set of numbers, or phrase to the user's previously identified phone. The user then enters this word, set of numbers, or phrase into the client to be verified. If the specifications are not met, the RADIUS server sends an access-reject response. The response indicates that the user request is invalid.

6. After the client addresses the access-challenge request, the RADIUS client resends the original access request with a new request ID and the encrypted response. The response takes the place of the user ID and password in the original access request. The RADIUS server can respond to the new access request with an access-accept, access-reject, or another access-challenge.

7. When all conditions are met, lists of configuration values for the user are placed in the access-accept response. This response includes the type of connection that can be made and values needed to deliver the services, such as Transmission Control Protocol/Internet Protocol (TCP/IP) or Point-to-Point Protocol.

FYI

A shared secret is a case-sensitive text string used to validate communications between a RADIUS client and a RADIUS server. Shared secrets should be long and randomly generated to avoid being cracked by an attacker. Each connection should have a unique shared secret. For example, if a shared secret is used for communications between RADIUS client A and RADIUS server C, the same shared secret should not be used for communications between RADIUS client B and RADIUS server C.

Authentication and authorization are combined in RADIUS. When the user ID and password are found in the database, text file, or LDAP server, the RADIUS server returns the access-accept response. This response acknowledges the user is authenticated. Authentication usually includes only verification of the password, but it can also include a list of requirements that must be met including the port number of the RADIUS client. The RADIUS server also provides authorization to the RADIUS client via an access list. Independent of authentication and authorization, RADIUS accounting provides the start and end time of individual sessions. As stated, this data can be used by an organization to determine the amount of time and data that was used during a session.

In the preceding example, SMS messaging was discussed as a challenge-response authentication method. It is important to know that two-factor authentication is often used for challenge-response authentication. An example of this is the PIN and token combination. If the client receives a request for this information, the user enters the appropriate PIN and token, resulting in a passcode. The second access request sends the passcode and additional data to the RADIUS server. The RADIUS server verifies the passcode against the authentication server. If a match occurs, the RADIUS server sends an access-accept response to the client.

Client/Server Model

A client/server model enables application services to be spread across multiple systems. The client sends a service request to the server. Clients include the user interface and the communication mechanisms to request the service. The server handles the data processing service requested by the client.

For example, a client may request purchase orders for XYZ Corporation from the past 6 months. The client makes the purchase order service request to the server, and the server processes the request and returns the data to the client.

The server may also request information from another server. For example, when Jackie wants to access her online banking records, her web browser makes a request to the bank's web server. The web server forwards that information to the bank's database and returns the results to the web server. The web server then forwards this information to the web browser.

In the case of the RADIUS client/server model, the RADIUS client sends user information to the RADIUS server in an access-request message. After receiving a response from the RADIUS server, the client acts according to the returned information.

Although RADIUS was originally developed for dial-in access, the protocol is currently used for supporting VPNs, wireless, and other access management needs. For example, RADIUS provides authentication capabilities for wireless access points. Using the previous RADIUS communications example, the wireless access point is the RADIUS client, which sends the request with the credentials to the RADIUS server. The RADIUS server also determines the level of access a user has on a network by comparing the authenticated user against the ACLs.

Remote Access Server (RAS)

A **remote access server (RAS)** provides authentication for remote access in an Internet and dial-up scenario. A user connects to the RAS, and his or her credentials are compared with those stored in the database. If the credentials match, authentication has occurred, and the user is granted access to the network. Users and systems use remote access for gaining access to a specific network. It is necessary to implement strong security when using a RAS. Often, organizations forget that modems are connected to servers or assume that other safeguards such as firewalls will protect access. This is not always the case. Therefore, you should implement the following rules for remote access servers:

- No inappropriate or unknown access should be provided through the remote access server.
- Authentication must occur for all users before access to the network or computer system is provided.
- Authorization of the user must occur, which ensures the user or computer system is not performing tasks on the network it is not authorized to do.

TACACS, XTACACS, and TACACS+

Terminal Access Controller Access Control System (TACACS) is a client/server protocol that was developed to control who could use dial-up lines. While we no longer use dial-up lines in any widespread fashion, TACACS technology and its successors live on in many networking applications such as performing authentication for routers, switches, and other network devices.

In the TACACS protocol, the TACACS-enabled device accepts a username and password from a user and sends a query to the TACACS authentication server. The authentication server either accepts or denies the request and sends the response back. The device then allows or denies access based on the response from the TACACS server. Who is allowed or denied access is determined by the administrator of the TACACS authentication server. For example, an administrator may allow access to users only between 8:00 a.m. and 5:00 p.m., Monday through Friday. The administrator who manages the TACACS daemon defines this access control in the system.

> **NOTE**
>
> A daemon is a program that runs in the background.

TACACS combines authentication and authorization over a TCP/IP network. A user may enter a user ID and password to achieve authentication. Authorization determines what the user may access and when. TACACS is not a secure protocol because user IDs and passwords are transmitted in cleartext through a User Datagram Protocol (UDP) packet or a Transmission Control Protocol (TCP) data stream.

> **NOTE**
>
> TACACS was developed in the 1980s by the U.S. Department of Defense and BBN Planet Corporation for the U.S. military portion of the Internet (MILNET). TACACS is described in RFC 1492 but only for informational purposes. It is not an Internet standard.

Extended TACACS (XTACACS) is a client/server protocol developed in 1990 by Cisco. XTACACS is an extension of TACACS. XTACACS separates authentication, authorization, and accounting.

Separating the AAA methods means that they can be achieved individually; one method does not rely on another. For example, suppose a user named Jackie normally authenticates with her user ID and password before authorization to a system is determined. If there is separation between authentication and authorization, authorization can occur without Jackie having to authenticate first.

Terminal Access Controller Access Control System Plus (TACACS+) is a Cisco-proprietary protocol developed to provide access control for routers, network access servers, and other network devices via one or more centralized servers. TACACS+ utilizes TCP, ensuring the delivery of the message. TACACS+ is an extension of TACACS but differs by separating the authentication, authorization, and accounting architecture and allowing for additional methods of authentication. TACACS+ also encrypts the communication, unlike TACACS. TACACS+ uses a client/server model. The following information defines how AAA is achieved with TACACS+:

- **Authentication**—A means of identifying that users are who they say they are. TACACS+ supports a variety of authentication methods such as a user ID and password, PIN and token, and challenge-response devices.
- **Authorization**—Identifies what a user is allowed to do. Authentication provides stronger system security but is not required. Therefore, the authorization controls determine if a particular user is authorized to run specific commands or perform specific actions on a network.
- **Accounting**—Logs what a user has and is doing at a particular time. A TACACS+ accounting record includes accounting-specific information and resource usage data, and information used in the authorization record. With the information that the record contains, TACACS+ uses accounting for billing of services or for auditing for security purposes. The three accounting records supported by TACACS+ are:
  - A start record, which indicates that a service is beginning
  - A stop record, which indicates that a service has ended
  - An update record, which indicates that a service is still being performed

TACACS+ authentication has three packet types: start, continue, and reply. The TACACS+ daemon always sends reply packets, and the client always sends start and continue packets. When an authentication request is made, the client sends a start packet to the TACACS+ daemon. This packet contains the type of authentication to be performed (such as PAP or CHAP) and authentication data. In response, the daemon responds with a reply packet, indicating when it is finished or if additional information is needed. If additional information is required, the client obtains this data and responds with it in a continue packet. TACACS+ is the only one of the three protocols—TACACS, XTACACS, and TACACS+—currently being used because it is the only one that's secure.

 NOTE

Although TACACS+ is based on TACACS, the two are not compatible.

The TACACS+ protocol is responsible for communications between the NAS and the TACACS+ daemon. The protocol also provides confidentiality by encrypting communications between the NAS and the TACACS+ daemon.

TABLE 10-1 TACACS+ and RADIUS Differences

CRITERIA	TACACS+	RADIUS
Transport	TCP	UDP
Encryption	Entire body of packet	Password only
Authentication and authorization	Separated	Combined

Differences Between RADIUS and TACACS+

RADIUS and TACACS+ are both client/server protocols providing AAA capabilities. It is important to understand how the two approaches differ, ensuring the best protocol is provided for a particular system.

RADIUS and TACACS+ both use TCP/IP. RADIUS uses UDP as its transport protocol and TACACS+ uses TCP. UDP is a connectionless protocol and; therefore, packet drops are not detected by the network. TCP is a connection-oriented protocol and; therefore, an acknowledgement is sent after a request has been received. To make up for the deficiency with UDP, RADIUS must use supplemental code to provide lost packet detection.

RADIUS and TACACS+ both use encryption. RADIUS encrypts the password only. Therefore, additional information such as the user ID, authorized services, and accounting are available in cleartext and can be viewed by an attacker. TACACS+ encrypts the entire body of the packet. When implementing RADIUS, you need to use additional security measures to prevent data from being read by an attacker.

RADIUS and TACACS+ both provide authentication, authorization, and accounting. RADIUS is sometimes not considered a pure AAA architecture because authentication and authorization were standardized in one RFC and accounting was standardized in a separate RFC. RADIUS combines the authentication and authorization capabilities, and separation of the two cannot occur. TACACS+ separates authentication, authorization, and accounting. The advantage is that TACACS+ provides flexibility for network administrators by implementing AAA components in stages as opposed to all at once.

TABLE 10-1 summarizes differences between TACACS+ and RADIUS.

Remote Authentication Protocols

When implementing RADIUS and TACACS+, authentication protocols may be used in conjunction with the system. You have learned about a few of the remote authentication protocols available. Let's talk about three more that are used in remote authentication: PAP, CHAP, and MS-CHAP.

Password Authentication Protocol (PAP) is a data-link protocol that provides authentication over PPP. **Point-to-Point Protocol (PPP)** allows an Internet connection to occur over a phone line. Transmission of TCP/IP traffic over telephone lines is available through PPP. PAP provides identification and authentication of users when using a remote server to access a network. PAP establishes identification with a peer, using a two-way handshake. The authentication server receives a user ID and password from the client after the establishment of

TABLE 10-2 PAP, CHAP, and MS-CHAPv2 Comparison

CRITERIA	PAP	CHAP	MS-CHAPv2
Handshake method	Two-way handshake	Three-way handshake	Three-way handshake
Password transmission	Cleartext	Hash value	DES encryption
Security status	Insecure	Secure	Insecure

a link. These credentials are sent in cleartext, creating a security risk. The authentication server database compares credentials with those that are already in the system.

Standardization of **Challenge Handshake Authentication Protocol (CHAP)** occurred in 1996 and is defined in RFC 1994. CHAP provides authentication over PPP. A three-way handshake is used to verify the identity of the client. Description of the handshake is as follows:

> **⚠ WARNING**
>
> Sending cleartext passwords is a fatal flaw from a security perspective. You should avoid using PAP authentication unless you have clear, strong, compensating controls in place, such as tunneling PAP over an otherwise encrypted connection.

1. The authenticator sends a challenge message to the client when the link is established. This challenge is unique to the session.
2. The client responds with a value. This value was created using a one-way hash function on combined fields of the challenge.
3. The authenticator compares the response with the value of its own calculation of the hash. If the values match, authentication occurs. If the values do not match, the connection is terminated.

Microsoft created its own version of the CHAP protocol, known as Microsoft CHAP or **MS-CHAP**. MS-CHAP is used only in Microsoft-centric applications and comes in two different versions: MS-CHAPv1 and MS-CHAPv2. However, both of these protocols rely on the now insecure Data Encryption Standard (DES) and should no longer be used unless the communications are otherwise encrypted.

TABLE 10-2 compares PAP, CHAP, and MS-CHAPv2.

Network Authentication Protocols

Modern networks typically require that users authenticate before gaining access via both wired and wireless connections. The **802.1x** protocol provides a framework for implementing authentication on a network. In 802.1x networks, there are three different roles held by components:

- The **supplicant** is the software running on the client that wishes to connect to the network.
- The **authenticator** is the network device that the client wishes to connect to, typically an Ethernet switch or a wireless access point.
- The **authentication server** is the server that validates requests for network access, using the RADIUS or EAP protocols.

We've already discussed RADIUS in this chapter, so let's move on and discuss EAP.

Extensible Authentication Protocol (EAP) is a framework that enables multiple authentication mechanisms over a wireless network or PPP connection. Standardization of EAP occurred in 1998 and is defined in RFC 2284. EAP sits inside a PPP authentication protocol such as RADIUS and provides the framework for the authentication method. Unlike PAP and CHAP, EAP specifies the authentication mechanism at the authentication phase. The authenticator can specify the use of additional authentication methods such as Kerberos, one-time passwords, biometrics, and other authentication tools.

In an EAP over the RADIUS environment, the RADIUS client communicates with the system requesting authentication using EAP and with the RADIUS server using RADIUS. This communication is shown in **FIGURE 10-2** and works as follows:

1. The client computer initiates a connection to the RADIUS client, and the two systems agree on the use of EAP.
2. The RADIUS client asks the client computer to identify itself by sending an EAP-Request/ Identity message, and the client computer responds with an EAP-Response/Identity message.
3. The RADIUS client creates an Access-Request message containing the client computer's identity and sends it to the RADIUS server.
4. The RADIUS server responds with an Access-Challenge message that contains an EAP-Message requesting the client computer to authenticate.
5. The RADIUS client removes the RADIUS details from the Access-Challenge message and passes the EAP-Message to the client computer.
6. The client computer responds to the authentication request by passing an EAP-Message through the RADIUS client to the RADIUS server in a similar fashion.
7. The RADIUS server replies with either an Access-Accept or an Access-Reject message, allowing or denying the connection.

EAP over LAN (EAPOL) is the encapsulation of EAP over wired and wireless LANs and is defined in IEEE 802.1X. EAPOL as a delivery mechanism for authentication types. Therefore, when used for authentication, EAP works in conjunction with a specific authentication technology. There are many EAP types, including:

- **EAP with Message Digest 5 (EAP-MD5)** uses the outdated MD5 hash protocol and is no longer recommended for use. EAP-MD5 uses one-way authentication, meaning that the client authenticates to the network but the network does not authenticate to the client.
- **EAP with Transport Layer Security (EAP-TLS)** uses certificate-based authentication in conjunction with the standard TLS protocol and is a strong, secure authentication choice. EAP-TLS provides mutual authentication, meaning that the client authenticates to the

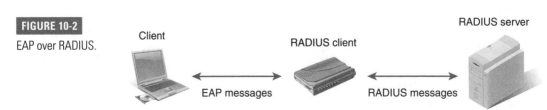

FIGURE 10-2

EAP over RADIUS.

Client

RADIUS client

RADIUS server

EAP messages

RADIUS messages

TABLE 10-3 EAP Authentication Type Comparison

	EAP-MD5	EAP-TLS	EAP-TTLS	PEAP	EAP-FAST	LEAP
Authentication	One-way	Mutual	Mutual	Mutual	Mutual	Mutual
Server Certificate	No	Yes	Yes	Yes	No	No
Client Certificate	No	Yes	No	No	No	No
Security Status	Insecure	Secure	Secure	Secure	Secure	Secure

server and the server also authenticates to the client. In EAP-TLS, both the client and the server require certificates.

- **EAP with Tunneled Transport Layer Security (EAP-TTLS)** also uses TLS to provide network authentication. EAP-TTLS also provides mutual authentication but only requires that the server have a certificate.
- **Protected EAP (PEAP)** is quite similar to EAP-TTLS, differing only in technical implementation details.
- **EAP with Flexible Authentication via Secure Tunneling (EAP-FAST)** is a proprietary Cisco implementation of EAP authentication that provides mutual authentication but does not use certificates.
- **Lightweight EAP (LEAP)** is a Cisco proprietary protocol used primarily on wireless networks. It does not require the use of certificates.

TABLE 10-3 compares the EAP authentication types.

The encapsulation of EAP messages is often used in a wireless LAN. The following are the steps used during this process and shown in **FIGURE 10-3**:

1. A new wireless client attempts to associate with a wireless access point (AP). Another option is when a wireless client associates with a new wireless AP and an EAP-Start message is transmitted.
2. If the wireless AP detects a new client associating with it, the wireless AP transmits an EAP-Request/Identity message to the wireless client.
3. The client replies to this identity request with an EAP-Response/Identity message containing the wireless client's username.
4. The wireless AP sends the authentication request to the RADIUS server in the form of a RADIUS Access-Request message.
5. The RADIUS server sends the AP a RADIUS Access-Challenge message containing a request that the user authenticate.
6. The wireless AP then sends the client an EAP-Challenge Request requesting authentication.
7. The wireless client replies to the challenge with an EAP-Challenge Response containing the requested authentication details.
8. The wireless AP sends a RADIUS Access-Request message to the RADIUS server containing the user's authentication information.

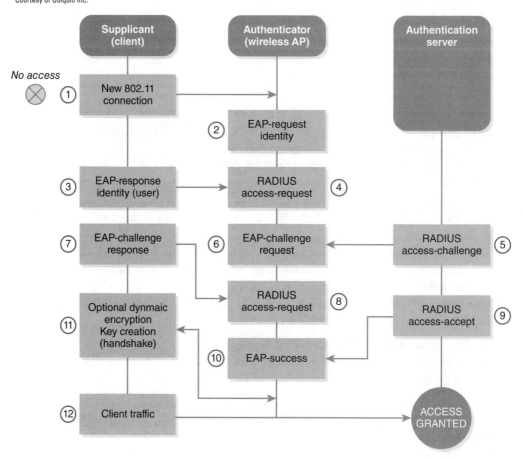

FIGURE 10-3

Process of EAP message encapsulation in a wireless LAN.

Courtesy of Ubiquiti Inc.

9. The RADIUS server verifies the user's identity and sends a RADIUS Access-Accept message if the user is authenticated or an Access-Reject message otherwise.

10. The AP passes an EAP-Success message to the user and the connection is authorized.

11. The AP and client may then agree to a set of encryption tools to use to protect the remainder of the session.

12. Communication continues until the client or AP chooses to close the session.

During the handshake process over PPP, both systems determine the authentication protocol to use. Other factors are also determined, such as connection parameters and the speed of data. Authentication occurs using the most secure protocol. If one of the systems does not have EAP capabilities, CHAP is attempted. If one of the systems does not have CHAP capabilities, PAP is used unless otherwise specified by the administrator. The administrator may choose to use PAP but because of the security risk, it is not advisable to use PAP.

Virtual Private Networks (VPNs)

VPNs are a way for remote access employees to gain secure access to corporate networks. A VPN is a secure connection over an unsecure network—the Internet. Communication security over the VPN is provided through encryption. VPNs can also be used for secure communications between two network devices or two users. A connection, VPN software, appropriate protocols, and the same encryption methods are required for a VPN connection.

A VPN establishes a private network over a public network such as the Internet. Instead of dialing in over a telephone line, a VPN uses an Internet connection that the systems have already established. As previously discussed, remote users may benefit from Internet connections provided in public locations such as hotels, coffee shops, and airports. This connection is beneficial when you want to do personal work such as checking personal email or browsing social networking sites. Organizations, however, are not inclined to leave their infrastructure open. Organizations want to ensure that their intranet is available only to employees and that corporate resources are protected. Implementing a VPN environment provides many of the same benefits an employee experiences when connected directly to the corporate network within a corporate infrastructure.

Organizations can also employ VPN capabilities for internal wireless networks. Although you may be able to connect directly to a corporate access point, a VPN connection may be required for you to access internal corporate resources. This implementation ensures security for you and the organization, even when you are still in the organization's building.

Virtual private networking requires a tunnel. Some of the tunneling protocols that are used for VPN connections are as follows:

- **Transport Layer Security (TLS)** is the modern standard for VPNs. This protocol has the advantage of working on almost every network and being allowed to pass through almost any firewall. TLS VPNs simply tunnel a VPN connection over a standard TLS connection.
- **Point-to-Point Tunneling Protocol (PPTP)** was developed by a group of vendors and standardized in 1999 under RFC 2637. PPTP allows PPP to be tunneled over an IP network. PPTP does this by encapsulating PPP packets. PPTP does not change PPP but defines a way to carry it. PPTP relies on **Generic Routing Encapsulation (GRE)** to build the tunnel between the communicating entities. PPTP allows remote users to set up the PPP connection and then secure a VPN connection. PPTP can only work over IP networks.
- **Layer 2 Tunneling Protocol (L2TP)** provides the same functionality as PPTP but on networks other than IP networks. When combined with IPSec, L2TP provides encryption and authentication. L2TP sets up a connection between two communication entities over PPP.
- The **Internet Protocol Security (IPSec)** protocol provides the method for establishing a secure channel. In a VPN, IPSec secures communications between the computer system and the corporate network. It is often used in the VPN configuration because it provides flexibility to the organization. Because it is an open framework, an organization can use different configurations to achieve the appropriate level of security.

IPSec provides authentication and encryption through two security protocols. **Authentication Header (AH)** is the authentication protocol. **Encapsulating Security Payload (ESP)** provides authentication and encryption. AH is used to prove the identity of the sender and ensure the data is not tampered with. ESP encrypts the IP packets and ensures their integrity. IPSec can work in two modes, transport mode or tunnel mode. In transport mode, the message payload is protected. This ensures that the messages cannot be read if the traffic is collected. In tunnel mode, the payload, routing, and header information are protected. ESP provides greater security than AH because it protects the routing and header information.

A **security association (SA)** is used for each device during each VPN connection. The SA is the record of the configuration that the device needs to support an IPSec connection. When the two systems agree on the parameters used for communication, the data are stored in the SA. The SA may contain the authentication and encryption keys, algorithms, key lifetime, and source IP address. When the system receives the packet over the IPSec protocol, the SA will determine how to decrypt the packet, how to authenticate the source packet, the encryption key to use, and if necessary, how to replay the message. A different SA is used for inbound and outbound traffic.

Internet Key Exchange (IKE), as defined in RFC 2409, provides identification to communication partners via a secure connection. IKE is the de facto standard for IPSec. It is a combination of **Internet Security Association and Key Management Protocol (ISAKMP)** and **OAKLEY**. The OAKLEY protocol carries out the negotiation process, and ISAKMP provides the framework for the negotiation. This includes the negotiation for the algorithm, protocol, modes, and keys. The partners can authenticate through a shared secret or public key encryption. Once this is determined, the SAs are established.

Web Authentication

Web authentication is ensuring users are who they say they are through a web application. Web authentication is needed in situations where virtual private networking is not available. This may occur if a user has to use a secondary system such as a customer's computer or a computer kiosk provided at a hotel. Implementation of the web authentication mechanism is determined by the risk associated with what is being accessed.

A user ID and password is the basic form of authentication that you have seen multiple times in this chapter. High-risk applications should not use a user ID and password combination because it is not a strong form of authentication. For example, an online banking tool should provide stronger authentication for access into a user's account because a password can easily be compromised. This authentication can include multifactor authentication as well as knowledge-based authentication.

One-time password authentication is a form of two-factor authentication. It is based on something you know such as a PIN and something you have such as an authenticator. Combining the PIN and information that is displayed on the authenticator provides a one-time password. This one-time password is unique to the user, and it is difficult for an attacker to compromise this information.

Digital certificates are electronic documents assigned to a user or system. A digital certificate contains information about the user or system. A third party, known as a certificate authority, creates the digital certificate. A digital certificate is unique to the user or system. When a user makes a request to the web application and verification of his or her identity is required, the user's application sends a digital certificate to the web application. The web application verifies the digital certificate with the certificate authority. The user accessing the website can also verify the identity of the site via the web server's digital certificate.

Knowledge-Based Authentication (KBA)

KBA is an identification or web authentication mechanism used in real time as a question-and-answer process. These questions and answers are obtained from public records or private data warehousing firms such as credit bureaus. The questions consist of information such as "What is the license plate number of your 1998 green Toyota Camry?" or "What is the house number where you lived in 1979?" These questions are used to prove that you are who you say you are. They can also be used as an authentication tool before a user establishes his or her challenge-response questions.

These types of questions are set up by the user. Examples of questions are, "What is your favorite book?" and "What is the name of your second grade teacher?" KBA is beneficial for web authentication because it does not require an additional item such as an authenticator or certificate. It is commonly used in situations where the user does not have access to other credentials, such as establishing an account for the first time or gaining access to an account after having forgotten the password.

Best Practices for Remote Access Controls to Support Remote Workers

Remote access controls for remote workers is not a new concept; they have been used by many organizations for years. Some best practices regarding remote access controls are as follows:

* **Determine the security risk associated with remote access**—Understanding who will be working remotely and what tasks will occur assists in determining the security risk. Will the employees be accessing highly confidential material? Will the employees need access 24 hours a day, every day? Will data need to be downloaded to the remote computer systems? Will employees be executing programs remotely? Do the employees need read access or read and write access? These questions and other questions pertaining to the access will define whether this implementation is low, medium, or high risk.
* **Select a remote access option that addresses security needs**—Once you have determined the risk associated with a remote access implementation, you must decide which remote access options will address the level of risk. Is encryption required for the full communication or only certain parts of the communication? Is encryption required at all? Does the remote access need to be available 24/7, or is some downtime acceptable when associated with a system failure or maintenance?
* **Determine the appropriate level of authentication based on the security risk**—The level of risk associated with the system will determine the level of authentication required to keep the systems safe. Can a user ID/password combination be used for authentication

or is multifactor authentication needed? Will the required type of authentication result in additional hardware for the remote employees? For example, if you want to employ a biometrics solution, how will remote access users get a biometrics reader? Will the biometrics reader be built into the computer system or external to the system?

- **Ensure that the systems that are accessing the network meet the security policies of the organization**—How will the remote workers access the network? Will employees use employer-provided systems or will they use their own computers? If employees use their own systems to access the corporate network, will the personal computer systems have the appropriate software and patches installed? Will employees use hotel or airport kiosks to access the network? If so, which safeguards are in place?
- **Ensure protection of the systems that remote workers access**—After determining the level of risk associated with remote access and choosing the solutions, you must protect the systems that will be accessed. Giving employees remote access means possibly allowing attackers access as well. Know what resources will be accessed, who will access them, how they will be accessed, and at what times they will help you set up appropriate access controls. You also need to test the access controls that are already implemented and ensure they are functioning correctly.

Case Studies and Examples

There are various methods for proving the identity of, authenticating, authorizing, and auditing remote access users. The following case studies help you learn how some of these tactics are used in the real world to ensure the communications are secure and the access granted does not compromise the organization.

Private Sector Case Study

Many companies are contemplating the use of VPN versus authentication to applications via the web. The Miller Corporation is no different. Miller Corporation is a small organization with five sales representatives located throughout the United States. There are no remote offices available for the sales reps. Four of the five sales reps work exclusively from home or on the road. One of the sales reps has a work area in the corporate office but the majority of her time is spent on the road.

Jeff, the network administrator, configured remote access so that each user had a unique user ID/password combination for dial-in access to the network and unique user IDs and passwords for each application on the network. Passwords expired every 90 days. The sales representatives began reporting that this method was cumbersome and wanted to know if another solution was available.

Jeff decided to look into VPN access for the sales representatives. Jeff found that a VPN was the best option compared with web authentication and dial-in access because of the security that remote access virtual private networking provided. A remote access VPN would provide a secure connection between the sales reps' computers and the corporate network. A remote access VPN would allow this secure communication over a wireless connection. The other solutions were not effective with this type of connection.

Jeff could manage remote access VPN configurations at a centralized location, rather than managing web authentication for each application. Implementing the remote access VPN would also increase the productivity of the sales reps because they would no longer need to log on to multiple resources, nor keep track of several passwords.

If Miller Corporation hired additional sales representatives, the VPN would scale better than any of the other options. Jeff could also seamlessly add a second level of authentication with the use of VPN, if needed. Jeff felt that a VPN solution was best for the sales representatives, and it would allow other employees to work remotely.

Public Sector Case Study

A major city government needed to ensure its departments were complying with appropriate remote access security policies and regulatory requirements. It also needed to better account for remote access usage of the citywide network by each department for budgeting purposes. The city's chief information security officer (CISO) requested security metrics and usage data from each department. This data indicated system-wide remote access security lapses and weaknesses, and it was apparent that the departments were unable to provide accurate usage figures without going to great effort.

The CISO decided to employ security and auditing through the AAA framework. AAA provides the flexibility and scalability that is needed for the city to meet policy and regulatory requirements. While implementing the framework, access controls were added to every component of the city's network infrastructure to meet authorization requirements. With the accounting component, administrators could more accurately report the resources each user consumed while using the network, and they could use the data for trend analysis and capacity planning. Implementing the authentication, authorization, and accounting components addressed current needs and future concerns.

An AAA framework is important for any organization that needs to standardize its practices based on security. It gives an organization a starting point and assists in future growth. It helps administrators understand what needs to be accomplished and why.

Critical Infrastructure Case Study

Kelly, a network administrator for a gas distribution company, needs to implement a secure dial-in infrastructure for a group of financial employees. She wants to ensure authentication, authorization, and accounting capabilities are provided. Kelly has winnowed her options down to two, TACACS+ and RADIUS, but is not sure which is better for her needs.

Kelly is concerned that TACACS+ is not an IETF standard. She feels comfortable with the notion that RADIUS has been standardized and; therefore, all vendors who support RADIUS will support this standardization. Kelly appreciates the scalability of the centralized authentication service that is offered with both systems. If the implementation proves successful, the technology may be rolled out to additional employees. However, she is concerned about using RADIUS in a large infrastructure because it uses UDP. Implementing TACACS+ will resolve this issue because TCP is used, but there is a lot of network overhead associated with TCP. If each request results in an acknowledgment, network traffic will increase.

Kelly's main concern is encryption, however. Encrypting only the user's password is a risk that Kelly does not want to take. The users employing this service are in the finance department, and Kelly feels that every data packet should be encrypted in its entirety for security reasons. Weighing all of the pros and cons of each solution, Kelly feels that the security of the company's data is the most important concern. Therefore, Kelly decides to move forward with implementing TACACS+.

CHAPTER SUMMARY

This chapter focused on the technologies and security considerations of remote access solutions. There are many security risks associated with these implementations, which can be addressed with the right protocols and access controls. Employing the AAA framework can help ensure a network is configured to support the chosen protocols appropriately. Using these capabilities will create access control solutions to make an organization more secure and productive for all remote workers.

The appropriate solution, such as RADIUS or TACACS+, depends on the risk associated within the environment. You must identify the needs and requirements of your organization and compare them against available protocols to choose the best solution for your environment.

KEY CONCEPTS AND TERMS

802.1x

Accounting

Authentication, Authorization, and Accounting (AAA)

Authentication Header (AH)

Authentication server

Authenticator

Challenge Handshake Authentication Protocol (CHAP)

EAP with Flexible Authentication via Secure Tunneling (EAP-FAST)

EAP with Message Digest 5 (EAP-MD5)

EAP with Transport Layer Security (EAP-TLS)

EAP with Tunneled Transport Layer Security (EAP-TTLS)

Encapsulating Security Payload (ESP)

Extended TACACS (XTACACS)

Extensible Authentication Protocol (EAP)

Generic Routing Encapsulation (GRE)

Internet Key Exchange (IKE)

Internet Protocol Security (IPSec)

Internet Security Association and Key Management Protocol (ISAKMP)

Layer 2 Tunneling Protocol (L2TP)

Lightweight Directory Access Protocol (LDAP)

Lightweight EAP (LEAP)

MS-CHAP

Network access server (NAS)

OAKLEY

Password Authentication Protocol (PAP)

Point-to-Point Protocol (PPP)

Point-to-Point Tunneling Protocol (PPTP)

Protected EAP (PEAP)

Remote access server (RAS)

Remote Authentication Dial In User Service (RADIUS)

Security association (SA)

Supplicant

Terminal Access Controller Access Control System (TACACS)

Terminal Access Controller Access Control System Plus (TACACS+)

Transport Layer Security (TLS)

CHAPTER 10 ASSESSMENT

1. RADIUS uses TCP.

   A. True

   B. False

2. AAA stands for _____.

3. Which of the following best describes the act of verifying that users are who they say they are?

   A. Identification

   B. Authentication

   C. Authorization

   D. Auditing

4. Which of the following are authentication protocols used with PPP? (Select three.)

   A. CHES

   B. CHAP

   C. EAP

   D. MAP

   E. PAP

5. TACACS+ encrypts the entire data packet.

   A. True

   B. False

6. What portion of TACACS+ provides AAA capabilities?

   A. NAS

   B. Client

   C. TACACS+ daemon

   D. XTACACS

7. What are examples of web authentication? (Select three.)

   A. Knowledge-based authentication

   B. Identification

   C. Certificates

   D. User ID/password

   E. Remote access server

8. Which one of the following authentication types requires the use of client-side certificates?

   A. EAP-MD5

   B. EAP-TLS

   C. PEAP

   D. EAP-FAST

9. Cisco developed the TACACS+ and XTACACS protocols.

   A. True

   B. False

10. Which of the following is used to validate the communications between a RADIUS server and a RADIUS client?

   A. NAS

   B. TACACS daemon

   C. RAS

   D. Shared secret

11. PAP is a _____ handshake.

12. CHAP is a _____ handshake.

13. What is a program that runs in the background?

   A. RAS

   B. Encryption

   C. Daemon

   D. PAP

14. What is the de facto standard for IPSec key exchange?

   A. OAKLEY

   B. IKE

   C. ISAKMP

   D. RADIUS

PART III

Managing and Testing Access Control Systems

Public Key Infrastructure and Encryption

E NCRYPTION IS A PART of your everyday life. Each time you access a secure website, conduct a transaction at an ATM, or check your email, encryption lurks behind the scenes, providing the secure transmission of information. Encryption relies on the use of encryption keys to ensure that information is only readable by the intended recipient. Distributing and managing these keys is one of the trickiest parts of implementing an encryption system and, in many encryption approaches, the public key infrastructure (PKI) fills that role.

This chapter covers the essentials of PKI: what it is, how it works, implementation security levels, and how it is supported.

Chapter 11 Topics

This chapter covers the following topics and concepts:

- Public key infrastructure (PKI)
- How integrity, confidentiality, authentication, and nonrepudiation are ensured within a PKI
- What PKI is not
- How businesses use cryptography
- How certificate authorities (CAs) issue, manage, and revoke digital certificates
- Which risks are associated with a PKI
- Best practices for PKI use within large enterprises
- Case studies and examples of PKI use within large organizations

Chapter 11 Goals

When you complete this chapter, you will be able to:

- Understand what a PKI is and what it is not
- Identify the multiple functions within a PKI
- Identify the multiple functions of a certificate authority (CA)
- Understand how digital signatures provide nonrepudiation
- Apply best practices for a PKI within an organization

Public Key Infrastructure (PKI)

A public key infrastructure is important because it provides secure mechanisms for business and eCommerce transactions. It provides a community of trust. Through this community of trust, people are able to browse the web more securely, send secure emails, and download safe software. PKI does not solve all security issues, and it does not make all software safe or ensure that websites do not have malware embedded in them. However, it does provide an infrastructure to make the Internet safer, and it provides a level of security that is needed for a multilayer security system within an organization.

 NOTE

Public key cryptography and PKI are different. Public key cryptography is also referred to as **asymmetric cryptography**. PKI is an infrastructure for the secure distribution of public keys that are used in public key cryptography.

What Is PKI?

A **public key infrastructure (PKI)** is a framework that consists of programs, procedures, and security policies and employs public key cryptography and the X.509 standard (digital certificates) for secure communications. PKI is a hybrid system of symmetric and asymmetric key algorithms. It is also an infrastructure that identifies users, creates and distributes certificates, maintains and revokes certificates, distributes and maintains encryption keys, and enables technologies to communicate via encrypted communications. PKI relies on a level of trust within this framework for it to be successful and secure.

Components of a PKI are:

- **Certificate authority**—An entity, normally a trusted third party, that issues digital certificates for identities. A certificate associates the identity of a person or server with the corresponding public key.
- **Registration authority**—An entity that is responsible for the registration and initial authentication of users who are issued certificates after a registration request is approved. These users are also called subscribers.

- **Certificate server**—The machine or service responsible for issuing digital certificates based on the information provided at the registration process. The certificate server is a component of the certificate authority.
- **Certificate repository**—A database that stores the digital certificates belonging to users of the PKI.
- **Certificate validation**—The process of determining that a certificate is valid and can be used by the user for his or her specific needs.
- **Key Recovery Service**—The service that archives and recovers encryption keys.
- **Time server**—A server that provides a digital timestamp for use by the services and applications.
- **Signing server**—A server that provides central digital signing and verification services.

Essentially, a PKI provides services that protect confidentiality, integrity, authentication, and nonrepudiation of information exchanged between parties. You'll learn about these important concepts throughout this chapter.

Encryption and Cryptography

A PKI provides the capability to distribute public encryption keys while keeping the decryption keys private. In order to understand PKI, it is important to understand the background of encryption and, therefore, how PKI came to be.

Encryption is the process of applying an algorithm to cleartext (or plaintext) data, resulting in ciphertext. To a user attempting to read the ciphertext without the decryption key, it appears random and unreadable. In order for any system or user to read the ciphertext, the data need to be decrypted, resulting in the original cleartext. **FIGURE 11-1** shows this process.

You can use access controls to allow or deny access to data on systems and networks. But how do you protect those data while they are being transferred from one system to another

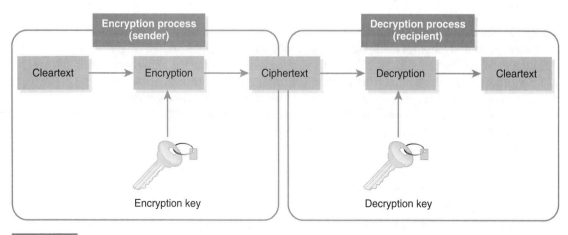

FIGURE 11-1

Encryption process.

or while they are at rest? Encryption ensures that only those with the appropriate decryption key can view the data.

A **cryptosystem** is a hardware or software system that provides encryption and decryption. The cryptosystem is made up of the encryption algorithm, the keys, and the software and protocols. The algorithm determines how the encryption and decryption will take place. Examples of symmetric encryption algorithms are Triple Data Encryption Standard (3DES), and Advanced Encryption Standard (AES). Examples of asymmetric algorithms are Rivest, Shamir, and Adleman (RSA); Diffie-Hellman; and Elliptic Curve Cryptosystem (ECC)

The details of these algorithms are publicly available. Therefore, in order for them to allow the secure exchange of information, some other component of the cryptosystem must be unknown or secret. The secret piece of the cryptosystem is the key. The algorithm can be known to everyone and can be posted anywhere, but it is the key that unlocks all of the information. The ciphertext is secure only if the key is kept secret. In encryption, the key is a value that consists of a large sequence of random bits. The **keyspace** is the range of values that constructs the key. When the algorithm creates a new key, it uses the values that have been identified through the keyspace. A large keyspace means that more keys are possible. The more keys that are possible, the harder it becomes for an attacker to figure them out.

The strength of the encryption comes from the secrecy of the key, although key length, the algorithm, and all of the components working together make the encryption even stronger. In order to break a cryptosystem, an enormous amount of processing power must be used to determine the one key that can decrypt the system. The strength of the encryption is proportional to the amount of processing it takes to determine the value of the key.

Brute-force attacks can be used to break a cryptosystem. This means that every key will be tested in order to find the correct one. The length of the key and the algorithm will determine the number of keys that will need to be tested to break the system. In order to create a strong encryption implementation, one must use a long key drawn from the full pool of all keyspace values, as well as ensure that the key is secure. The specific key length considered secure will vary depending upon the algorithm being used. For example, a 256-bit key used with one algorithm may actually be *more* secure than a 1024-bit key used with a different algorithm. However, longer keys are always more secure when used with the same algorithm.

Symmetric encryption. Symmetric algorithms use shared secret keys for encrypting and decrypting data. Both the sender and receiver use the same secret key. If an attacker were to obtain the secret key, he or she would be able to read the data and the information would no longer be considered secure. Protecting the secret key is essential to the strength of the system. If the key is compromised, the messages sent with that key are compromised. Symmetric cryptosystems provide confidentiality in that they allow only the users who have the secret key to read the data. The strengths and weaknesses associated with symmetric key systems are:

- A symmetric key system encrypts and decrypts information more quickly than an asymmetric system.
- A symmetric key system requires a secure method to create and exchange the secret key.
- Each pair of users requires a unique key, and; therefore, key management becomes difficult as the number of pairs of users increases. For instance, if John wants to communicate with Kelly, they both need to obtain a copy of the same key. If John, Jack, and Kelly all want to be able to

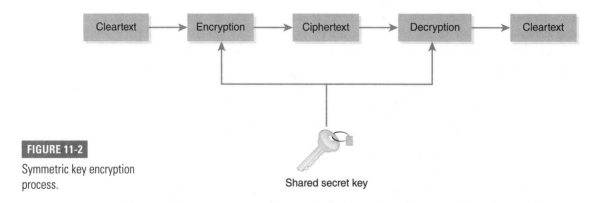

FIGURE 11-2

Symmetric key encryption process.

Shared secret key

communicate privately with each other, three keys are needed—one for John and Jack, one for John and Kelly, and one for Jack and Kelly. If John wants to communicate with 50 people, 1,225 keys are needed. The determination of the number of keys needed is provided by the following equation, where n is the number of people participating in the cryptosystem:

$$\frac{n(n-1)}{2} = \text{number of symmetric keys}$$

FIGURE 11-2 shows how a shared secret key is used in symmetric encryption. Compare this with Figure 11-1 and notice that the same key is used as the encryption key and the decryption key in this case.

Asymmetric encryption. Asymmetric algorithms use pairs of related keys, a public and private key for the encryption and decryption process. A public key can be known by everyone, but the private key can be known or used only by the owner. Public keys can be distributed to anyone in any mechanism. There is no need to protect the secrecy of the public key. Often, a public key is available through directories or databases of email addresses. The public and private keys are mathematically related so that anything encrypted with one can only be decrypted with the other. In a strong cryptosystem, someone who has the public key cannot use it to determine the private key. Asymmetric cryptography can provide confidentiality by having the sender encrypt the data with the receiver's public key. This ensures that only the receiver can decrypt it because the receiver is the only one who knows the receiver's private key.

> ⚠️ **WARNING**
>
> Although you can encrypt data with either key, remember that you can obtain confidentiality only by encrypting data so that a private key is required to decrypt it. Therefore, any time you want to send a secret message, you must encrypt it with the recipient's public key. Encryption with private keys is done only for purposes of authentication or nonrepudiation, such as in digital signatures.

Asymmetric cryptography can also provide authentication when the sender encrypts data with his or her own private key. After the receiver decrypts the message with the sender's public key, the receiver knows that it could only have come from the sender's private key. Note from **FIGURES 11-3** and **11-4** that a public key can be used for both encryption and decryption. If data are encrypted with a public key, they can only be decrypted with the private key. If data are encrypted with the private key, they can be decrypted only with the public key. Asymmetric encryption uses public/private key pairs, with each user having his or her individual pair. Therefore, you need two keys for every user in the cryptosystem.

FIGURE 11-3

Example of asymmetric key encryption process: encrypting with public key for confidentiality.

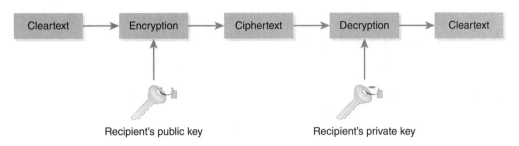

Recipient's public key   Recipient's private key

FIGURE 11-4

Example of asymmetric key encryption process: encrypting with private key for authentication.

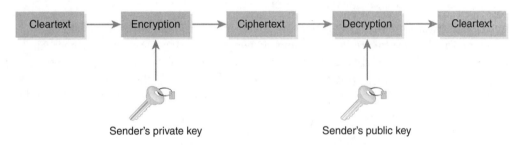

Sender's private key   Sender's public key

The strengths and weaknesses associated with asymmetric key algorithms are:

- The fact that asymmetric systems require only two keys per user makes them much more scalable than symmetric approaches. **TABLE 11-1** shows the number of keys needed for each type of algorithm with different group sizes.
- Asymmetric key algorithms provide confidentiality, integrity, authentication, and nonrepudiation.

TABLE 11-1 The Number of Keys Needed for Different Group Sizes

GROUP SIZE (n)	SYMMETRIC KEYS NEEDED	ASYMMETRIC KEYS NEEDED
2	2	4
3	3	6
5	10	10
10	45	20
100	4,950	200
1,000	499,950	2,000
10,000	49,995,000	20,000
100,000	4,999,950,000	200,000

- Asymmetric key systems are slower than symmetric key systems because they use more complex mathematics during key creation and when encrypting and decrypting data with those keys.

Business Requirements for Cryptography

Businesses require cryptography for multiple uses within an organization. Common examples of the use of cryptography include protecting internal data from external parties, preventing insiders from seeing information that they shouldn't have access to, and ensuring that customer transactions are authenticated.

Some of these requirements for cryptography within businesses are:

- Ensuring software and data integrity
- Ensuring secure collaboration between entities inside and outside an organization
- Ensuring secure cloud computing
- Providing secure transactions with consumers

Ensuring software and data integrity means that software remains secure as it is being developed, and that software that consumers download is secure. Organizations have various developers sign the software as it is being created to ensure its security. Keeping track of these signatures helps organizations know what code was added, when, and by whom. This provides for secure software development and ensures that malicious code was not included in the software without the developer's knowledge.

Secure collaboration within and outside an organization protects communications between multiple entities. It also protects the communications against attackers. Ensuring trusted communications between entities is vital for organizations to ensure their data are secure and seen or received only from trusted users.

With the implementation of **cloud services**, businesses want to ensure that data kept in the cloud are secure and not able to be retrieved or seen by unauthorized users. For example, an organization may choose to store specific data on a cloud provider's server, but the organization needs to be sure that its data will be just as secure in the cloud as they would on-site. Using cryptography will ensure that users or the provider cannot view the data without the appropriate keys. Cryptography is just one step used in addressing the overall concern with cloud providers and the implementation of cloud services.

Many organizations conduct transactions with their customers as a part of doing business. An organization must ensure that security is associated with these transactions. Cryptography provides this business requirement by protecting transaction communications and ensures both the organization and the customer are secure. Not employing this security measure may result in customer dissatisfaction and low confidence. This risk of losing customers is not something an organization wants to take on.

Government agencies must also ensure that the cryptographic algorithms they choose are supported by the federal government and endorsed for the types of information they need to protect. Agencies should consult "Security Requirements for Cryptographic Modules," published as Federal Information Processing Standard (FIPS) 140. The current version of FIPS 140, FIPS 140-3, went into effect in September of 2019.

Digital Certificates and Key Management

Digital certificates are used by individual users, servers, and devices to provide unknown third parties with a known secure copy of their public encryption key. This is especially true with the rise of the Internet of Things (IoT). Digital certificates may be used for a variety of purposes, including email, web servers, and other forms of encrypted communication. Certificate Authorities (CAs) issue digital certificates after verifying the identity of the end user and the end user can then use that certificate to share its public key with others. CAs use the X.509 digital certificate standard to create certificates that contain the following fields:

- Version of the certificate
- Unique serial number associated with the certificate
- Algorithm ID used to sign the certificate
- Name of the certificate issuer
- Validity dates of the certificate
- Name of the subject of the certificate, which could be an individual or device
- Public key of the subject
- ID of the issuing certificate authority
- ID of the owner
- Optional extensions

FIGURE 11-5 shows an example of a digital certificate.

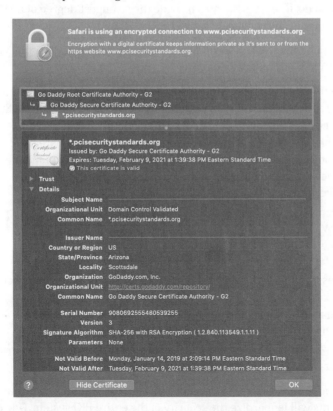

FIGURE 11-5

Digital certificate details.

Screen shot(s) reprinted with permission from Apple Inc.

When digital certificates are stored on a system, they come in the form of files. These files have a variety of different formats, and many systems support some, but not all, of these formats. Make sure that your file format is acceptable for the specific applications you have in mind. Common digital certificate file formats include:

- .PEM format
- .PFX format
- .CER format
- .P12 format
- .P7B format

A **registration authority (RA)** verifies the identity of an individual, initiates the certification process with a **certificate authority (CA)** on behalf of the user, and performs certificate life-cycle management. When a user requires a new certificate, the request is made to the RA, and the RA verifies all necessary information before the request is made to the CA.

Depending on the degree of verification performed by the RA, the CA may issue certificates with different validation levels. The three certificate validation levels are:

- **Domain Validated (DV)**—Certificates simply confirm that the certificate was issued to someone controlling the DNS domain included in the certificate.
- **Organization Validated (OV)**—Certificates go deeper and verify the identity of the business named on the certificate.
- **Extended Validation (EV)**—Certificates provide the strongest degree of trust, verifying the physical presence of the certificate subject.

Key management ensures the security of the cryptographic keys through each key's life cycle. Components of key management are:

- **Key generation**—The initial creation of keys. The technical accuracy behind the creation of symmetric and asymmetric keys is fundamental to key management. Ensuring the randomness of the keys increases the strength of the cryptographic system of the entire PKI.
- **Key distribution**—Moving keys from one point to another. There are two stages for key distribution: initial and subsequent. Establishing a key in a secure manner is essential to the overall security of the PKI system. The initial key is used to distribute other keys. The subsequent keys are securely exchanged using the initial key.
- **Key storage**—Storing the keys after they are distributed.
- **Key usage**—When keys are in a production environment and being used for email, file transfers, secure connections, and so on.
- **Key recovery**—Restoring a key after a failure has occurred to key storage. If the hardware or software associated with key storage fails and a new system is acquired, the keys will need to be recovered.
- **Key termination**—The destruction of keys because they have reached the end of their life cycle or because a key has been compromised in some fashion.
- **Key archival**—Retaining a key that has been terminated. A copy is kept in a key storage for validating data that was protected by the original key.

Each of these components of key management is vital to a PKI system. Failure of one of these components will jeopardize the security of the entire PKI system. One of these may be considered more important than another depending on what is being protected, but the lack of execution for any of them will result in an unsecure system.

Some additional considerations with regard to key management that help to provide a secure PKI system are:

- The key should be long enough to provide the necessary level of protection.
- Keys should be random and the algorithm should use the full keyspace.
- A key's lifetime should correspond with the sensitivity of the data; for example, a highly secure piece of data should have a short key lifetime.
- The more a key is used, the shorter its lifetime should be.

Symmetric Versus Asymmetric Algorithms

Symmetric and asymmetric encryption algorithms are varied in many ways. You just learned about a few ways they can be implemented. A major differentiation outside of the ones discussed is the key length. Asymmetric cryptography requires a longer key length in order to achieve the same level of security that is achieved through symmetric cryptography.

Whitfield Diffie and Martin Hellman introduced the first asymmetric cryptography algorithm in 1976. It was developed for the distribution of symmetric keys and is based on the mathematics of discrete logarithms in a finite field. The **Diffie-Hellman key exchange** enables two systems to receive symmetric keys without a previous communication. It provides key distribution but does not provide encryption or digital capabilities. The following example will help you further grasp the Diffie-Hellman algorithm.

FYI

The Diffie-Hellman algorithm is more susceptible to man-in-the-middle attacks because no authentication occurs when the public keys are sent. In other words, how does Bob know that he is actually communicating with Alice and not someone else who initiated the Diffie-Hellman process on her behalf? If an attacker intercepted the public keys and instead sent his own, the symmetric key would be created using the attacker's public key. The attacker would be the only one who could read the messages.

Mathematically, Diffie-Hellman looks like this:

1. Alice and Bob agree to create a key using a randomly generated prime number (p) and a common integer base (g).
2. Alice selects a private key (a) and uses it to compute her public key (A) with the formula $g^a \bmod p$. Alice makes g, p, and A public—these three numbers make up the public key— keeping a private.
3. When Bob wants to communicate with Alice, he finds her public key and computes some values. He generates a random exponent (b) to build a public key (B) by computing $g^b \bmod p$. He uses the same g and p from Alice's public key.
4. Once Bob creates b and B, he builds the secret value (s) by computing $A^b \bmod p$. Alice can compute the same secret value using the information she has and the formula $B^a \bmod p$.

 NOTE

The names Alice and Bob are commonly used in encryption examples. Alice is normally the sender of a message and Bob is normally the recipient.

TABLE 11-2 Symmetric Versus Asymmetric Attributes		
ATTRIBUTE	**ASYMMETRIC ALGORITHMS**	**SYMMETRIC ALGORITHMS**
Keys	Public key is available to all; private key is kept secret to the owner and never shared	Sender and recipient share a secret key.
Key length required	Longer	Shorter
Example algorithms	RSA, Diffie-Hellman, ECC	DES, 3DES, AES
Key exchange	Easy-to-deliver public key	Requires sharing keys in advance through another secure mechanism.
Encryption speeds	Slower	Faster
Security services provided	Confidentiality, integrity, authentication, and nonrepudiation	Confidentiality, integrity, and authentication

5. Alice and Bob can now communicate using any symmetric algorithm of their choice and the shared secret key *s*.

The **RSA asymmetric encryption algorithm** was developed to prevent man-in-the-middle attacks. The RSA algorithm is named after its inventors Ron Rivest, Adi Shamir, and Len Adleman. It is the most popular public key algorithm available and can be used for digital signatures, key exchange, encryption, and decryption. The algorithm is based on factoring large numbers that are a product of two prime numbers. When used in a PKI system, the cryptosystem generates a symmetric key using a symmetric algorithm such as AES. The cryptosystem encrypts the symmetric key with the receiver's public key. Only the receiver will be able to decrypt the message via the use of his or her private key and retrieve the symmetric key.

Elliptic curve cryptosystem (ECC) provides much of the same functionality as the RSA algorithm, such as digital signatures, secure key distribution, encryption, and decryption, but it is more efficient than RSA. The algorithm computes discrete logarithms of elliptic curves. ECC provides the same level of security as the RSA algorithm but with a shorter key. When a shorter key is used, less processing is required when implementing the ECC algorithm. Providing the security level with less processing means the algorithm can be used by devices with limited power, bandwidth, storage, and capacity, such as mobile phones.

A synopsis of these attributes is provided in **TABLE 11-2**.

Certificate Authority (CA)

A CA is a trusted organization that maintains, issues, and distributes digital certificates. When a user requests a digital certificate, the RA verifies the user's identity and sends the request to the CA. The CA creates the certificate, signs it, sends it to the user, and maintains it over the life of the certificate. When a new user wants to communicate with the subject of the certificate, the new user can verify that the certificate bears the valid signature of a trusted CA.

CAs can be internal to an organization, which allows the organization to have complete control over the distribution and life of the certificate. In this case, the organization is issuing **self-signed certificates**. The CA can also be provided by a third party such as VeriSign. An example of a listing of trusted certificate authorities is shown in **FIGURE 11-6**.

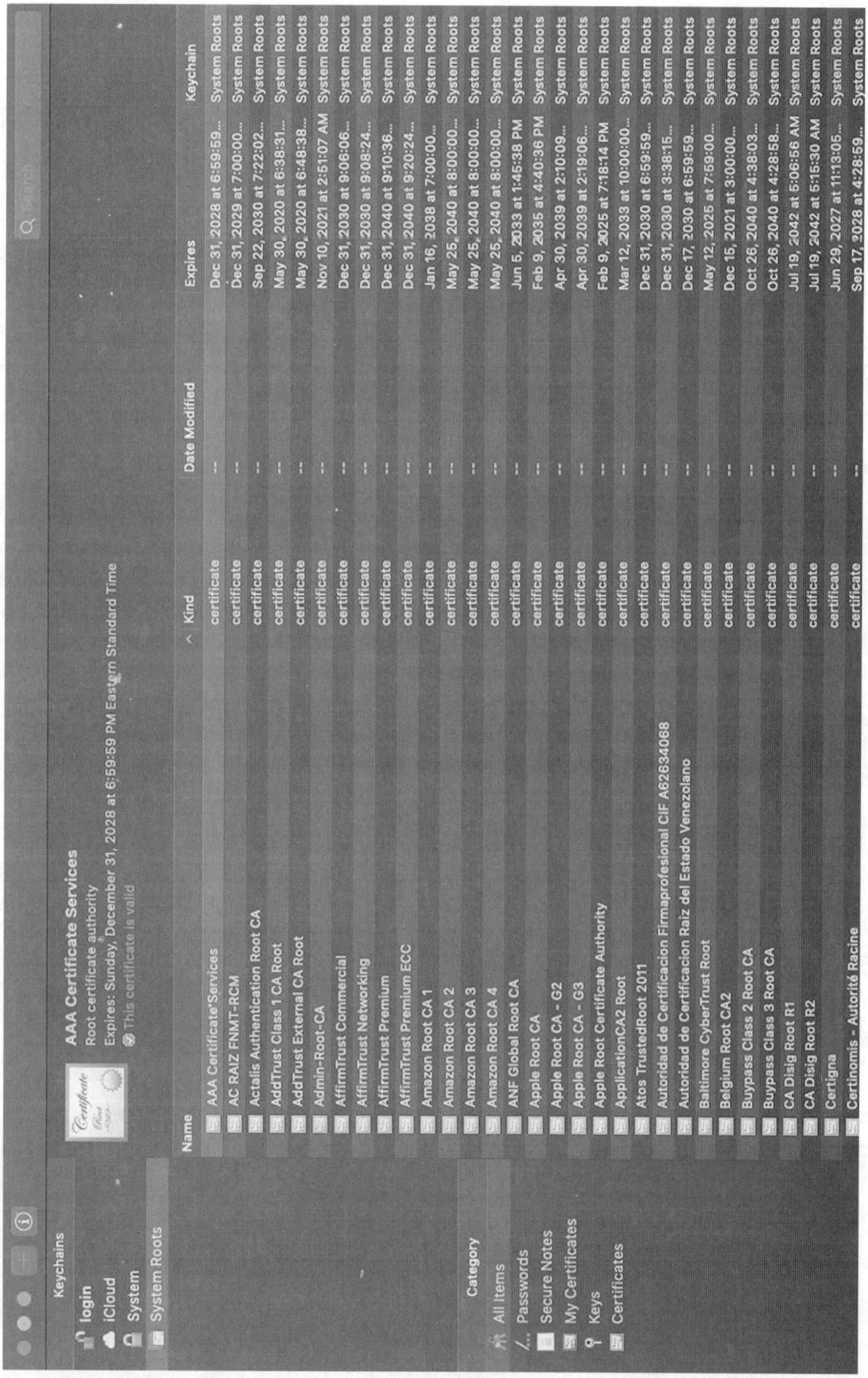

FIGURE 11-6

Trusted certificate authorities.

Screen shot(s) reprinted with permission from Apple Inc.

NOTE

You'll learn more about CAs later in this chapter.

The following example illustrates a CA used in a PKI system:

1. Alice makes a request to the RA.
2. The RA requests certain information from Alice such as her phone number, address, and other identifying information.
3. The RA verifies the information and sends the digital certificate request to the CA.
4. The CA creates a certificate with Alice's public key and information embedded. The public/private key pair can be generated by the CA or on Alice's machine. If the CA creates it, it must be transferred securely. The CA signs the certificate with the CA's private key. Alice can now participate in a PKI.
5. Bob wants to send a message to Alice, so he requests her certificate.
6. Bob receives the digital certificate from Alice.
7. Bob uses the CA's public key to verify the digital signature. If the signature authenticates, he extracts Alice's public key from the certificate and uses it to communicate with her.

This process is shown in **FIGURE 11-7**.

Certificate authorities may revoke digital certificates that have been compromised or are otherwise no longer valid. To do this, they may include the certificate on the CA's **Certificate Revocation List (CRL)**. The CRL is simply a listing of invalid certificates that software is expected to consult before accepting a digital certificate. Due to some limitations in the CRL approach, it is being replaced with the **Online Certificate Status Protocol (OCSP)**, which is a method for live, interactive verification of a certificate's status.

Certificate authorities document their practices for issuing and maintaining digital certificates in a formal statement known as the **Certificate Practice Statement (CPS)**. This statement provides details on the business processes used by the CA to verify the identity of certificate owners prior to issuing the certificate, revoking digital certificates, renewing expired certificates, and other certificate practices.

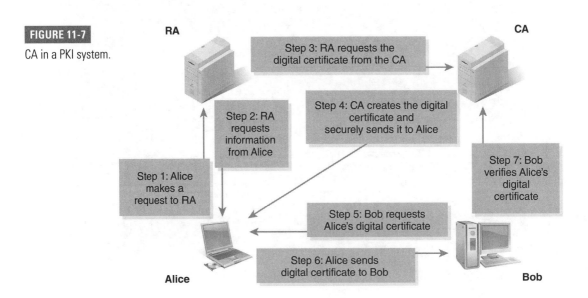

FIGURE 11-7

CA in a PKI system.

Ensuring Integrity, Confidentiality, Authentication, and Nonrepudiation

A PKI system uses symmetric and asymmetric encryption algorithms and digital certificates to provide security for multiple applications and uses. It provides a more secure environment for both organizations and end users. The security that is provided through PKI relies on processes and services that are fundamental. These security services allow for a secure solution to be developed for delivery of information across the Internet. The security services are:

- **Confidentiality**—Confidentiality ensures that only the intended recipient can read a message. Confidentiality is provided in both symmetric and asymmetric cryptosystems through the use of encryption.
- **Integrity**—Integrity ensures that the recipient of a message can be certain that the message received was the message sent. Integrity is provided in asymmetric cryptosystems through the use of digital signatures (discussed later in this chapter). If a message is digitally signed and the recipient verifies the digital signature, he or she can be certain that the message received is identical to the message sent. In symmetric cryptosystems, integrity is provided by virtue of the fact that a message decrypts properly.
- **Authentication**—Authentication allows someone to prove his or her identity to another. In asymmetric cryptography, digital certificates may be used for authentication. In symmetric cryptography, limited authentication is possible when a shared secret key is known only to two people. If one receives a valid message from the other that is encrypted with the shared secret, the recipient knows that the message must have come from the sender.
- **Nonrepudiation**—Nonrepudiation ensures that any objective third party can verify that a message came from the purported sender and was not forged by the recipient or anyone else. Only asymmetric cryptosystems provide nonrepudiation, and they do so through the use of digital signatures.

Use of Digital Signatures

Digitally signing an email allows the receiver to verify the contents were not modified after the data were sent. Digital signatures also provide nonrepudiation. That is, they allow the recipient to conclusively prove to a third party that the sender actually sent the message. Digital signatures can also be used to identify if a user has signed off or approved a particular document.

Creating a digital signature requires that a cryptographic hash function be applied to the message, resulting in a message digest or hash value. The original hash value is encrypted using the signer's private key and decrypted using the signer's public key. If the two hash values match, the signature is verified. When the sender's email client appends the digital signature to the original message, the sender is digitally signing the document. **FIGURE 11-8** walks you through the signing process.

Verifying the digitally signed document requires the receiver to apply the same cryptographic hash function to the document in order to produce the message digest or hash value. The hash value in the digital signature is decrypted with the signer's public key. If the two hash values match, the digital signature is verified. This process is illustrated in **FIGURE 11-9**.

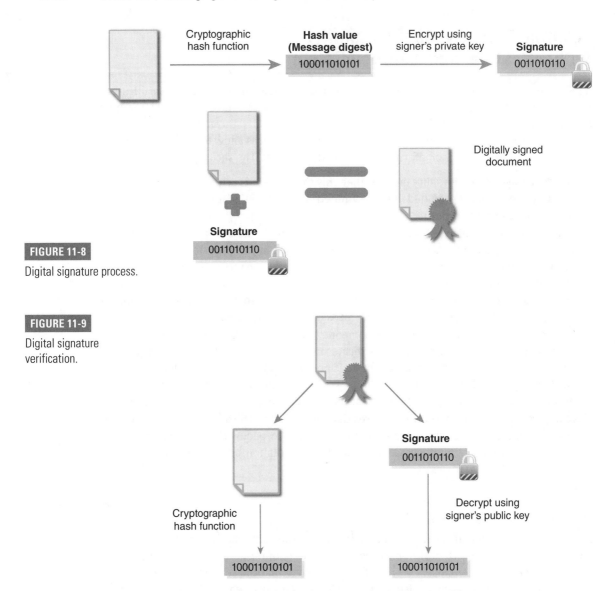

FIGURE 11-8

Digital signature process.

FIGURE 11-9

Digital signature
verification.

What PKI Is and What It Is Not

PKI is a framework used to build a secure infrastructure. It employs many capabilities but can be mistakenly considered the answer for all security within an organization. There are many truths and misunderstandings associated with PKI, which are covered in this section.

PKI is a strong authentication mechanism. The binding of a user to a key pair means that the key pair can be used for digital signing. This task would be difficult in symmetric encryption, for example, because of the need for a new key for each message authentication code.

Employing PKI for digital signatures means that a single signing key can be used for multiple documents over a relatively long time period.

PKI provides a mechanism for ensuring that what is being downloaded or read has not been altered. For example, PKI helps protect data from attackers and ensures that attackers are not able to break the communications link and alter the data as they are transmitted over a network. This is beneficial for organizations, particularly if end users are able to download their own software. Ensuring that software has not been altered during the download process assures the end user and the organization that malware was not injected into the software after the download process began.

PKI provides integrity, confidentiality, authentication, and nonrepudiation in a single framework. PKI is a necessary entity in a defense-in-depth security structure. Using the appropriate software, hardware, policies, and community of trust to protect communications between entities within or outside of the organization is paramount to protecting the organization itself. It not only protects the users of an organization but it also protects the consumers who use the organization's products and services. For example, when a user downloads software, PKI protects the software vendor as much as it protects the user. The user wants to ensure he or she is downloading the correct software from the vendor, but the vendor wants to ensure this too. If there was not a capability provided to ensure integrity of the data, a user could accuse the vendor of injecting malware into the software. The vendor would not be able to prove if this was or was not the case. By comparing the hash values of the correct software and the downloaded software, the vendor can verify what software it developed and intended to be downloaded.

PKI is not an answer to all security questions or concerns. You cannot encrypt all data and communications and assume that everything is fine. Security within an organization requires multiple layers, and PKI is just one layer within the security platform. PKI will not stop attacks on an organization, it will not prevent the downloading of malicious code, and it is not a firewall. PKI does not stop users from making security mistakes. Users will still download software that leaves network ports open, write down passwords, or mistakenly download viruses or Trojan horses to their computer systems. The mere use of a PKI does not ensure an organization is implementing the necessary access controls, training, and standard configurations that help secure an organization.

PKI does not provide authorization. It may authenticate a particular user, but it does not distinguish what that user can or cannot do within the system. Additional tools and capabilities are needed to address this need within an organization.

PKI does not guarantee that the end user can be trusted. PKI employs a community of trust, but it should not be mistaken for trusting the user. For example, Alice trusts that the data she received were sent from Bob, but this does not mean that Bob should be trusted or that the specific information he provided is accurate. This understanding is important when downloading software. You may trust a software vendor and; therefore, you feel comfortable downloading its software. This trust you established was built over time. This may not be the case with other unknown software manufacturers. Just because the data were digitally signed does not mean the original software is secure and that malware has not been incorporated from the start.

> **■ NOTE**
>
> Trusting that software came from a specific manufacturer and trusting that it has not been altered in transit is not the same as trusting the company that manufactured the software.

What Are the Potential Risks Associated with PKI?

There are multiple risks associated with PKI, but many entities feel that the largest risk is with key management. If PKI key management is mishandled, the entire PKI system could fail. For example, allowing attackers access to private keys is literally like giving away the keys to the server room. All of the implemented security measures would be for nothing.

WARNING

Many organizations have not implemented appropriate access controls for their key management system. Lack of controls may allow an internal employee to access the PKI keys as well as decrypt highly sensitive data.

Managing a secure environment with multiple keys and multiple entities can be overwhelming, and it's a challenge some organizations are not willing to undertake. Finding the appropriate resources to understand and execute a PKI within an organization is not an easy task. Some organizations find themselves unable or unwilling to take on the financial burden of properly maintaining a PKI. For example, an organization may hire an employee who is not well versed on PKI in order to save on salary expenses. This may mean that the infrastructure will be implemented incorrectly and, therefore, lack appropriate security. An organization may also choose hardware or software that is inexpensive in order to save on costs, even if the tools do not comply with the organization's standards. Again, this can mean the system will be implemented incorrectly and lack security.

These risks need to be weighed against the potential risk associated with not implementing PKI. How does an organization comply with the standards and regulations of protecting sensitive data if it does not implement PKI? What is the risk associated with customers whose data are stolen from the organization and used to ruin their credit rating or negatively affect other aspects of their life? How do you continue to do business securely if you do not employ the tools to do it correctly?

Risks associated with PKI can come in many forms but, in all cases, the risks must be weighed against the sensitivity of the data. Some organizations must implement PKI because the data they maintain are highly sensitive. Allowing highly sensitive data to get into the wrong hands can be detrimental to an organization and to the people, companies, and nations the users of PKI are trying to protect.

Implementations of Business Cryptography

Transport Layer Security (TLS) encryption uses cryptographic techniques to ensure that communications between two points or two parties are authenticated and secure. Many organizations use TLS for secure communications, including Internet applications and virtual private networks (VPNs). When remote access employees need to access specific tools over the Internet, TLS may be used to secure the transmission of data both through Internet applications and VPNs.

Cryptography can be used for encrypting data at rest and data in motion for various business requirements. Examples of cryptography for business purposes are:

- Encrypting hard drives as a preventive measure in case a laptop or other mobile device is stolen. An organization may choose to encrypt the hard drive to ensure that if the hard drive is removed, the data cannot be read. The organization may choose to require a password during bootup as well. This ensures that the data cannot be read without authenticating the user of the device.
- Encrypting removable devices such as universal serial bus (USB) drives. To remove data or read data that are located on a removable drive requires authentication from the owner of the USB drive.
- Encrypting instant messaging communication that occurs with users inside or outside of the network. This ensures that any information that is shared via this mode of communication cannot be read by an attacker.
- Encrypting file transfers within and outside of the network. This protection secures the data when transmitting outside of the network. It will also provide an extra layer of security even if the network is considered secure.
- Encrypting highly sensitive data such as customer data, credit card information, Social Security numbers, or any data that can cause harm when in the wrong hands.
- Encrypting information on mobile devices, such as smartphones and tablets, which are highly susceptible to loss or theft.

There are many different standards that businesses can follow. The Payment Card Industry Data Security Standard (PCI DSS), for example, requires the protection of consumers' credit card data. One of the PCI DSS requirements is to encrypt the data or file share on which the information resides.

Cryptography is used in businesses for securing email, TLS, and Internet Protocol Security (IPSec). One example of securing email is Secure/Multipurpose Internet Mail Extensions (S/MIME), a standard for encrypting and digitally signing email. S/MIME also provides secure data transmissions by encrypting emails and their attachments. MIME is the official standard used to define how the body of an email is structured. The MIME format allows email to contain attachments via MIME-compliant mail systems. These attachments can be audio or video clips, enhanced texts, graphics, and so on. MIME provides no security; therefore, S/MIME was proposed.

 NOTE

Encrypting an email protects data as they travel between the sender and the receiver.

The use of S/MIME is illustrated in the following example, in which Alice is preparing an email for Bob. Alice wants to encrypt and digitally sign the email, so she performs the following steps:

1. Alice generates a secret key for one-time use. This key can also be referred to as a "session key."
2. Alice uses the session key to encrypt the email that she intends to send to Bob.
3. Alice encrypts the session key with Bob's public key.
4. Alice digitally signs the email and sends the email package to Bob.
5. Bob receives Alice's email and decrypts the encrypted session key with his private key. He uses the session key to decrypt Alice's encrypted email.

In order to send digitally signed and/or encrypted email, valid, appropriate certificates must be loaded into the email client.

Distribution

Distribution of keys within an organization is a vital part of key management. You need to ensure the keys are safe and distributed securely. Some organizations choose to out-source these services. The risk associated with not using the correct resources or not implementing the correct system controls is sometimes left to providers who specialize in the technology. However, outsourcing is not always a good option because of the expense involved, especially if there are many systems, communication paths, or files that need to be encrypted within an organization.

In-House Key Management Versus Outsourced Key Management

Determining whether key management should be done in-house or outsourced requires much consideration. There is a large amount of risk associated with key management in terms of security, quality, and availability of resources; cost; and other factors. Some con-siderations regarding in-house versus outsourced key management are:

- Total cost associated with IT resources and knowledge. Can an organization afford to manage the infrastructure by itself? Will there be appropriate resources available locally to hire, and can the organization afford this resource? Is an organization willing to take on this risk and able to afford to keep training personnel and managing development as the organization grows?
- Managing the keys in-house requires an organization to manage the service level agree-ments with various business units. Can in-house management ensure the system will be running and functioning correctly 24/7? If disaster occurs, does an organization have the appropriate means to recover in-house?
- Can an organization trust an outsourced key management provider? Does this provider have the appropriate resources on-site? Has the provider done necessary background checks on its employees? How can an organization be sure the provider's employees will not provide unauthorized access to resources at the provider's facility?
- What level of support can the outsourced entity provide? Can it grow with the organiza-tion? Can the outsourcer provide appropriate help desk support? Is the outsourcer willing to work with the organization in all situations?

 NOTE

Organzations may choose to outsource key management or manage keys internally. While internal key management provides a greater degree of control over key distri-bution, outsourcing may have significant financial benefits.

Choosing the appropriate resources from in-house or out-sourced key management services is a risky process. Some organizations are uncomfortable with managing such a vital part of security in their own infrastructure. Some feel that leaving this responsibility to providers who know the technology and specialize in its capabilities is more beneficial to them no matter what the cost. Others may feel the opposite and decide that leav-ing such an important security measure in someone else's hands is not worth the risk. Both options are correct for various types of businesses. The process should be carefully planned because changing direction after initial implementation can cause problems.

Certificate Authorities (CAs) and Digital Certificate Management

Certificate authorities were briefly discussed earlier in the chapter. This section provides more details about CAs and helps you decide whether to manage certificates in-house or outsource the task to a third party.

Every digital certification implementation is done through a root CA. Each root CA has a digital certificate that is issued by a root CA and to a root CA. A root CA becomes both an issuer and a receiver. This process is called a self-signed digital certificate, which is the root certificate to all certificate implementations. The certificate PKI software or hardware looks for the self-signed certificate and extracts the public key. It is assumed that the certificate and the public key can be trusted. A root CA distributes its public key in a self-signed certificate to Internet browsers or public Internet sites. In theory, all Internet browsers are shipped with a self-signed certificate. A self-signed certificate provides data integrity.

A root CA signs every certificate. In the case of Alice and Bob, Alice can verify Bob's certificate only with the root CA's public key. Once Alice has verified Bob's certificate, she can trust it. Public keys can be trusted only if they were obtained from a certificate that was granted and issued by a trusted root CA.

Subordinate CAs can be established for more specific needs. For example, a subordinate CA may be implemented specifically for visitors, which would require a separate authentication and registration process. Using this process builds a trusted CA network. If a root CA's private key was compromised, all certificates issued by the root CA and subsequent CAs would need to be revoked and reissued.

A CA in a PKI system has many functions. These individual functions are:

- **Policy authority**—Responsible for establishing, distributing, maintaining, promoting, and enforcing all of the policies of the individual functions. The policy authority is responsible for the policies associated with the content and usage of the certificates, the registration process for certificates, certification revocation, and managing the root and subsequent CAs.
- **Certificate manufacturer**—Generates and manages the digital certificate asymmetric key pairs. The certificate manufacturer may distribute the root public key and sign the certificates. Notification of certificate generation is provided by the certificate manufacturer.
- **Certificate issuer**—Distributes the certificates that are generated by the certificate manufacturer. The certificate issuer provides a way for subscribers to grant and revoke certificates and manage the certificate revocation list.
- **Revocation manufacturer**—Generates and maintains the revocation of the asymmetric key pairs. Notification of the certificate revocation is provided by the revocation manufacturer.

- **Registration authority**—Provides a mechanism for requesting a digital certificate.
- **Authentication service**—Validates the subscriber's credentials for the registration authority prior to the request for the digital certificate.
- **Repository**—Stores and distributes all public key certificates.

All of these functions work as individual and necessary components of a PKI system.

Why Outsourcing a CA May Be Advantageous

Outsourcing a CA may be advantageous to an organization for various reasons. The organization might choose a provider that creates a dedicated CA for the organization's use or might choose to use a shared service from a major CA. Some considerations include:

- Communication with suppliers, customers, and business partners should be seamless. Companies may not want to worry about the security implications of having multiple entities accessing the CA. Which controls are needed, which configurations need to occur, and how do the systems stay updated without affecting the suppliers, customers, business partners, and their own internal users?
- Organizations may be geographically dispersed, and it would be more advantageous to have multiple CAs available at these various locations. Organizations may not have the capabilities or resources to staff at the various sites and; therefore, outsourcing this capability would be highly advantageous.
- Organizations do not want to take on the costs associated with managing a CA on-site. This includes the personnel needed to manage the infrastructure as well as the hardware, software, and data center costs.

Risks and Issues with Outsourcing a CA

Much like the risks associated with outsourcing key management, outsourcing a certificate authority is something that should be carefully considered. There are many concerns associated with implementing a security element at a site that you do not own and having it managed by people that do not report to you.

Risks associated with outsourcing CA capabilities are:

- The security placed around individual CAs. Is access granted to any employee or are there strict constraints around it? How does an organization know that it can trust a person it does not employ? Are appropriate controls in place at the provider's site, and how does an organization ensure the provider always complies with these controls?
- An organization may want to control its own CA because of the higher security requirements. This is not possible when outsourcing a CA. Many organizations with high security requirements are more apt to manage the CA locally where they have more control versus risking a security breach if the CA is managed through a vendor off-site. An organization may need specific certificates with unique fields; therefore, keeping the CA in-house may be more beneficial. Allowing another company to manage these highly specific certificates may not be advantageous.

There are multiple risks and issues associated with outsourcing a CA for a PKI system, and all aspects should be considered to ensure an organization is making the right decisions around this infrastructure.

Best Practices for PKI Use Within Large Enterprises and Organizations

Implementing PKI for use within an organization requires much thought and planning. To determine how the capabilities will be used, it is important to understand why you need PKI in the first place and the impact it will have on the organization. The best practices associated with using PKI within a large organization can be determined by answering the following questions:

- What are the business drivers for using PKI within the organization? Are you implementing it for eBusiness? Are you requiring it for integrity, confidentiality, authentication, or nonrepudiation? What is the problem that the enterprise or organization is trying to solve?
- What applications will be using PKI? Is it being used for secure email, communications, or transactions?
- What does the PKI architecture look like and how will it be used? Do all users require the same values and policies or will they need to be managed separately? What encryption algorithms and key lengths will be used in the certificates? Will certificates be used for digital signing and encryption?
- What impact will this implementation have on the users, customers, and business partners? How will the users be educated on the technology, and how and when should it be used? Who will develop the necessary policies that affect the users, and how will they be trained?
- Where will the infrastructure reside? Will various components be outsourced, or will they all be located in-house? Who will support the infrastructure, and what are expectations around support and disaster recovery?
- Can the current organizational infrastructure support the technology? Is the network bandwidth acceptable?
- Which databases will be used for PKI? Will existing databases be used to streamline enrollment? Will revoked and expired certificates be left in the database? Will a certificate repository be integrated with user account management?
- What are the legal and policy considerations for the CA? How will certificates be renewed? What are the procedures associated with requesting and revoking certificates? Are the policies documented?
- What are the trust relationships and how are they established? What trust model will the PKI use? Do the products support this model? How will you distribute the trusted root's signed certificates to the PKI users?
- How will PKI be deployed? Who are the vendors and how will they support you? How will you install the systems? Who will be trained on the systems? How will you test the system? How will you put the system into production?

- Who will have access to the systems and how will this access be monitored? How will the organization grow with the systems and the resources that are provided?

Understanding the components associated with the entire implementation, infrastructure, and deployment will provide a successful PKI within a large enterprise or organization.

Case Studies and Examples

Understanding the benefits and mistakes made by large organizations that have used PKI will be beneficial to you when implementing a successful PKI. These examples show a few ways PKI is currently used, as well as how it can fail.

Private Sector Case Study

Perot Systems implemented PKI for enhancing authentication for remote access. Perot Systems soon found that PKI could be used to extend authentication to applications in order to enable email encryption for confidentiality, digital certificates for nonrepudiation, and eForms to eliminate paperwork and expedite processing.

Perot Systems used PKI to authenticate users and devices as part of the VPN network for server-to-server virtual private networking, Intranet, and Extranet, and client-to-server virtual private networking for remote access employees. Perot Systems' PKI was also used with other directories and network resources to enable a greater level of identification for users and network devices.

Perot Systems learned many lessons from its PKI rollout. The company found that it was wise to:

- Choose recognized industry leaders as vendors.
- Set clear expectations for management and end users.
- Make sure PKI can be maintained.
- Ensure ease of rollout and use, supportability, and leveragability of resources.

Public Sector Case Study

The United States Patent and Trademark Office (USPTO) manages thousands of patent and trademark requests annually. The USPTO wanted to know with whom it is dealing online and wanted to provide secure communications. To provide this capability, USPTO chose to implement PKI. USPTO needed to:

- Implement confidentiality for information exchange.
- Ensure the integrity of the patent application.
- Authenticate with whom USPTO is dealing electronically.

USPTO implemented PKI to address all internal and external requirements for security, and nonrepudiation, authentication, and integrity for its eCommerce and electronic workplace initiatives. Implementing the PKI system helped build a trusted environment to successfully implement eCommerce. USPTO considered but rejected a password and PIN-based system due to the vulnerabilities of the system. The resources and cost-of-user support to reset forgotten passwords was not a cost that they could afford.

PKI provided the basis for implementing secure eCommerce patent applications and allowed USPTO to move from a paper-based system to an electronic one. The PKI system supported secure and authenticated communications and commerce with USPTO communities, attorneys, agents, international business partners, employees, contractors, and others with whom the USPTO does business. All of these entities require a guarantee of authenticity and confidentiality, and PKI provided that.

USPTO also implemented PKI for integration with its public key technology. This provided a single, scalable security infrastructure to support internal and external applications regardless of the risk level. The implementation provided security and authentication for a range of business applications as opposed to the separate security solutions that were previously used.

Achieving a single solution to meet the USPTO's various needs was the benefit that USPTO saw in PKI. The agency realized that the capabilities achieved with PKI provided a solution that would reduce costs and provide the necessary security its customers and employees expected.

Critical Infrastructure Example

As much as it is important to understand how large organizations solve business challenges, it is also important to understand how protection can be put in place but not secured. The following is an example of a security breach associated with PKI and encryption.

In 2001, two digital certificates were issued to a virus writer who was posing as a Microsoft employee. VeriSign issued these certificates in Microsoft's name. These certificates were necessary for consumers who downloaded software that they thought was created by Microsoft. Instead, the software was designed to deploy a virus onto systems on which it was installed. According to Microsoft, the certificates could have been used to sign programs, Microsoft Office macros, and other executable content.

VeriSign did not provide information as to how it validated the virus writer after receiving the request for the certificates. The company did state that human error was the cause of issuing the certificates incorrectly. Once VeriSign realized that the certificates should not have been issued, the company revoked the certificates. However, VeriSign did not have a way to determine who had downloaded the fraudulent software.

Microsoft released a bulletin to its users informing them that when the "security warning" screen appears regarding details of the signed software, they needed to click the Microsoft Corporation hyperlink to see if the certificate's validity date is January 29, 2001, or January 30, 2001. If one of these dates matched, the software should be considered fraudulent and the software should not be downloaded.

This example shows how the PKI process failed because the CA issued a certificate without the appropriate verification. Although this is not a normal process and was caught immediately, it shows that any weakness in the system can provide disastrous consequences.

CHAPTER SUMMARY

This chapter discussed symmetric and asymmetric encryption algorithms and how they are used with a public key infrastructure. You read about the risks associated with maintaining key management and certificate authorities in-house and outsourcing them. You reviewed the security services that are provided through the various PKI functions and how each of them functions individually. Understanding these concepts will assist you in understanding why this technology is needed and how its use has expanded over time.

KEY CONCEPTS AND TERMS

Asymmetric cryptography
Asymmetric encryption
Authentication
Certificate authority (CA)
Certificate practice statement (CPS)
Certificate revocation list (CRL)
Cloud services
Confidentiality
Cryptosystem
Diffie-Hellman key exchange
Domain Validated (DV)

Elliptic curve cryptosystem (ECC)
Encryption
Extended Validation (EV)
Integrity
Key archival
Key distribution
Key generation
Key recovery
Keyspace
Key storage
Key termination

Key usage
Nonrepudiation
Online Certificate Status Protocol (OCSP)
Organization Validated (OV)
Public key infrastructure (PKI)
Registration authority (RA)
RSA asymmetric encryption algorithm
Self-signed certificate
Symmetric encryption

CHAPTER 11 ASSESSMENT

1. PKI is also known as symmetric encryption.

   A. True
   B. False

2. An encryption algorithm using 2,048-bit keys is always more secure than an algorithm using 128-bit keys.

   A. True
   B. False

3. Which of the following are examples of symmetric algorithms? (Select two.)

   A. RSA
   B. 3DES
   C. AES
   D. Diffie-Hellman

4. Which of the following is an example of an asymmetric algorithm?

   A. RSA
   B. 3DES
   C. AES
   D. Diffie-Hellman

5. Asymmetric encryption is faster than symmetric encryption.

   A. True
   B. False

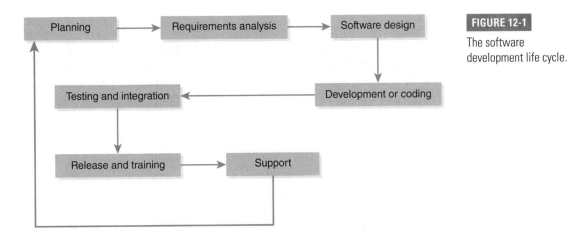

FIGURE 12-1

The software development life cycle.

Security features should be an integral part of each phase in the cycle, as you will see in the following sections.

Planning

The planning stage is where the stakeholders in any given software project meet to brainstorm what the software should do. It is important that the stakeholders have an awareness of security issues and access controls so that the project does not begin with an inherently insecure concept.

During the planning stage, high-level requirements are defined, and an initial project plan is worked out. At this stage, the project plan will not be very fleshed out, except for plans for the requirements analysis stage.

Requirements Analysis

Once the high-level goals for a software project are defined, those goals need to be translated into formal requirements. Formal requirements list each of the major functions of the software product as well as its inputs and outputs.

The deliverables for this stage will be a formal requirement document and an updated project plan. At this stage, areas that should be considered from a security point of view, such as user authentication and authorization, should be noted.

Software Design

Once formal requirements have been laid out, system architects and software engineers can begin to design the low-level functions that will make up the final product. At this stage, specific access control measures should be designed into the software.

At the end of the software design phase, all the major questions surrounding the implementation of the product should be answered.

Development

During the development phase, programmers write and test the actual code that makes up a piece of software. This is the stage where security features are implemented and sometimes flaws or weaknesses make their way into the final product. To prevent unintended security flaws, **unit testing** should be done continuously throughout the development stage.

Testing and Integration

In the testing and integration phase, the finished software should undergo full system **integration testing** to ensure that all of the pieces of the software work together properly. The software must also be tested to ensure that it works well with the rest of the system—the operating system, other applications, and back-end database. The primary goal during this phase is to make sure the new software doesn't break any existing system.

During this phase, the system should also undergo **load testing**, which measures how the software will perform with an average number of users, as well as how it will perform under extreme load conditions. For example, if the organization estimates that 50 users will use the access control system concurrently, it should be load tested with 50 users, 100 users, or even 190 users. This proves that the system can handle both an average load and double or triple that load. Load testing is normally performed using specialized load testing packages that simulate the activity of normal users. If an organization does not use load testing often enough to justify purchasing and configuring a load testing system, it is possible to obtain load testing services from consulting firms as needed.

Release and Training

During the release and training phase, the software is deployed to production servers, and employees are trained on how to use it. This is an important opportunity to educate them on the importance of security and access controls in their workday.

Support

The support phase of any software project is where most security flaws come out. When the software is in production and being used every day, weaknesses and flaws will begin to surface. During the support phase, you will begin the cycle again as you plan for upgrades and security patches. Although upgrades and patches will not have the same scope as the initial development, they still follow the same basic software life cycle.

Security Development Life Cycle and the Need for Testing Security Systems

Testing is not limited to software-based access controls. Every security system should be rigorously tested at each point in the development life cycle. Testing security systems requires an organization's management and security team to anticipate possible scenarios that could

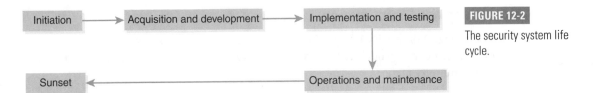

FIGURE 12-2

The security system life cycle.

circumvent the new security system, and to build features into the system to respond to those scenarios. For example, suppose an organization is planning to install a new closed-circuit video surveillance system. During the planning phase, members of the security team should walk through the facility, imagining how an intruder might try to sneak in. During this walkthrough, they should note where the cameras could be placed to catch this imaginary intruder.

The life cycle of security systems is similar to that of software, as shown in **FIGURE 12-2**. The security system life cycle includes five phases:

- Initiation
- Acquisition and development
- Implementation and testing
- Operations and maintenance
- Sunset or disposal

The security system life cycle is simpler than the software development life cycle, but just as important.

Initiation

During the initiation phase, the existing architecture and security systems are documented, and a preliminary risk assessment is conducted. Applicable laws and regulations are identified. The documentation and analysis done during this phase are crucial to identifying what type of security system is needed and how it will work with existing systems.

Acquisition and Development

During the acquisition and development phase, a more complete risk assessment is completed, and a baseline security level is established. Once this is done, the security team establishes security goals and meets with vendors to choose specific solutions to meet those goals.

Implementation and Testing

Once a new system has been purchased, it must be installed. This occurs during the implementation and testing phase. Unit and integration tests ensure that the product performs as expected and works with existing systems. User training is a significant part of this phase.

Operations and Maintenance

This is the longest of the five phases. During this phase, the system is continuously monitored, incidents are dealt with, and the security team creates or modifies an existing business continuity plan.

Sunset or Disposal

Eventually, every security system becomes either unnecessary or obsolete and can no longer be upgraded. At that point, a new security system must be purchased and the old one removed. This happens during the sunset phase. The key to this phase is that the old system must be removed without exposing the organization to additional risk during the migration to a new system.

After a new security system has been installed, the old one must be disposed of securely because it could retain information that an attacker could use to gain entry into the organization's facilities. Physical components must be disposed of or destroyed, electronic media wiped clean, and paper documentation shredded or securely archived.

Security Monitoring, Incident Handling, and Testing

All information security teams regularly perform monitoring, incident handling, and testing. Monitoring and incident handling are the day-to-day activities every team performs. They run automated scanners, review audit logs, and generally keep an eye on the security status of the IT infrastructure. When an anomalous situation is found, the security team responds by investigating the situation and shutting down the avenue of attack. After a security incident, the security team will investigate the affected systems and perform a damage assessment. They will meet with management to discuss how and why the attack occurred, and formulate plans to repair the damage and fortify the infrastructure against future attacks.

Testing and upgrading the system usually occurs annually, depending on the organization and its security goals. The rest of this chapter outlines how most organizations handle testing and upgrades of their security systems. This process varies by organization but most follow this basic procedure.

Requirement Definition—Testing the Functionality of the Original Design

Before an information security team can purchase and implement a new security system, they perform a basic risk assessment to test the functionality of the old system. This tells the team what major weaknesses exist and need to be strengthened in the new system. It also informs the requirement gathering process. The result of this phase is a requirement document that must be approved by senior management.

Development of Test Plan and Scope

Once a requirement document has been written and approved, the next step is to develop a plan for testing including the scope of the test phase. There are several factors to consider when developing a test plan:

- **Impact**—What impact will the testing have on operations? Is some disruption acceptable? If not, testing will need to occur during off hours or be restricted to nonintrusive methods.
- **Vulnerability**—Are there known vulnerabilities to consider during testing? The test plan should exercise known vulnerabilities but should not be limited to them.
- **Breach planning**—What should happen as the result of a security breach? The test plan should include scenarios that test reactions to a breach.
- **Gap analysis**—Security is a concern across the entire infrastructure. The scope of the test plan should reflect this.

The next sections examine each of these factors in depth.

Intrusive Versus Nonintrusive Testing

If it is important for operations to continue without interruption by the security testing team, the test plan must focus on **nonintrusive testing methods** such as **host discovery** or **port scanning**. Host discovery is the process of scanning the network to find out which Internet Protocol (IP) addresses are attached to potentially vulnerable resources such as web servers or database servers. Depending on the purpose of the scan, an interesting discovery may be defined as anything with open ports, anything running a certain service, or even any box with a connection to the outside world.

Port scanning is a technique designed to probe a network's open ports and look for weaknesses. Ports that are not being used should be closed, but often, they will be unintentionally left open by systems administrators who do not think to change default settings. For example, if a machine is intended to be a file server, there is no reason for port 80—the port most web servers use—to be open.

Nonintrusive testing methods can uncover valuable information about potential vulnerabilities, and, in most cases, this information is enough for an organization to justify modifying, upgrading, or replacing its existing security systems. Sometimes, positive proof of a given vulnerability's existence and potential damage is necessary. In those cases, intrusive testing is justified.

Some security vulnerabilities cannot be reliably tested in a nonintrusive way. Weaknesses to social engineering attacks are a good example of this because it is impossible to predict how employees will behave in a social engineering situation until they are actually confronted with it. Other vulnerabilities, such as weaknesses to insecure code, are sometimes easy to test in a nonintrusive way. If a security scanner detects that insecure libraries or applications are installed in the environment, one can infer that the environment is vulnerable to buffer overflows, code injection, and the like.

One distinct advantage to nonintrusive testing is the fact that it is often automated. This allows a reliable scan to be performed by IT staff who may not have extensive security training or experience. However, just as you'd secure an IT infrastructure with more than just a firewall, testing the security of an IT infrastructure should not rely on a single method. If possible, nonintrusive and intrusive testing methods should be used in cooperation to produce a comprehensive view of the status of IT security.

Vulnerability Assessment Scanning

IT crimes are generally crimes of opportunity. Attackers look for weak networks and bypass strong ones unless the resources on the strengthened network are highly tempting. Most of the time, if a network has been hardened, attackers will quickly move on to softer targets. Vulnerability assessment is the first step in **hardening** a network, and is generally performed using an automated scanning tool.

There are three basic types of vulnerability assessment scanners:

- **Network scanners**—A general-purpose scanner that probes a network for a variety of widely known vulnerabilities.
- **Port scanners**—A specialized tool that probes open ports on a system. An attacker could use these open ports to gain entry to a network.
- **Web application scanners**—Scans hosted web applications for known vulnerabilities. Because web applications are public-facing, they cannot be locked down as easily as an internal network.

All of these scanners are automated software packages that run periodically and produce a report of their findings. When choosing a vulnerability assessment scanner, look for one that updates frequently. Like a virus scanner, it is only as good as its vulnerability definitions. It cannot find vulnerabilities that have been discovered only recently and for which new tests have not been written.

Because of this limitation, it is important to use these automated tools as part of an overall security assessment. IT security teams should keep up to date on new vulnerabilities as they are discovered and reported, and manually check the network for them rather than wait for the vulnerability scanner to update its tests.

You have many options when choosing a vulnerability assessment scanner. The best choice depends on your organization's needs.

Nmap. Nmap, or Network Mapper, was originally intended as a network mapping utility. Its port scanning and host detection features can be useful in identifying access points to your network and holes in access controls. The basic version of Nmap is a command-line utility, whereas the Zenmap graphical user interface (GUI) front end adds ease of use, as shown in **FIGURE 12-3**. Nmap is an open source utility and is highly configurable.

After Nmap runs, it outputs a report for the user. This report contains a rundown of which hosts are on a network and which ports are open on those hosts. It also contains the common usage of those ports. A sample Nmap report is shown in **FIGURE 12-4** in the Zenmap GUI.

Nmap is available at *https://nmap.org/*.

Nessus. Nessus is a proprietary security scanner developed by Tenable Network Security. It is network-centric with webzx-based consoles and a central server. It is a useful tool for larger security teams handling larger networks. The configuration screen for Nessus is shown in **FIGURE 12-5**.

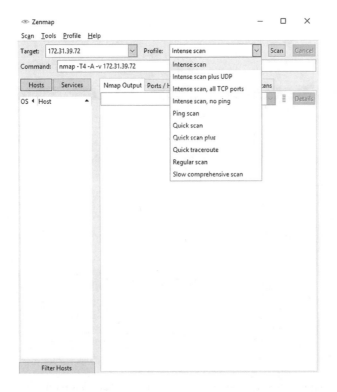

FIGURE 12-3

The Zenmap configuration screen.

Courtesy of Zenmap.

FIGURE 12-4

A sample Nmap report in the Zenmap GUI.

Courtesy of Zenmap.

The Nessus configuration screen.

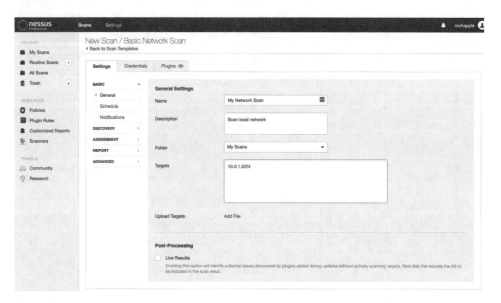

Nessus reports give a good breakdown of which ports are open on which hosts, and any security threats to those ports. A sample Nessus report is shown in **FIGURE 12-6**.

A sample Nessus report.

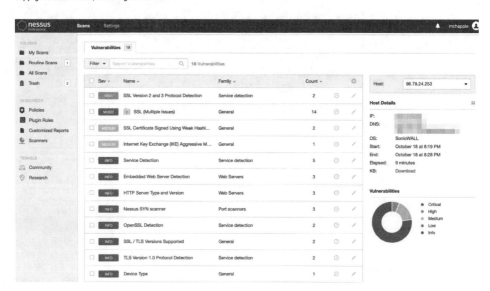

You can download a free limited version of Nessus at *https://www.tenable.com/products/nessus.*

OpenVAS. The **Open Vulnerability Assessment Scanner (OpenVAS)** is a free security scanning tool published under the GNU General Public License (GPL). The vulnerability testing plugins written for OpenVAS use the same Nessus Attack Scripting Language (NASL) as the Nessus scanner and, in fact, OpenVAS began as an offshoot of the Nessus project.

OpenVAS can deep-scan a network, looking for known issues that have not been patched in existing applications. It also scans for open ports. The configuration screen for an OpenVAS scan is shown in **FIGURE 12-7**.

OpenVAS scans provide detailed reports offering a breakdown of network vulnerabilities and the state of the environment in a format that even entry-level security professionals can understand. A sample OpenVAS report is shown in **FIGURE 12-8**.

You can find more information and live demonstrations of OpenVAS by visiting *http://openvas.org/*.

> **NOTE**
>
> Greenbone is the company behind the OpenVAS project. You may note in the figures that the tool used to access the OpenVAS scan is known as the Greenbone Security Manager. The terminology is somewhat confusing here, as the community still refers to this scanner as OpenVAS but many OpenVAS components now bear Greenbone branding.

FIGURE 12-7

The OpenVAS scan configuration wizard.

Courtesy of Greenbone Networks.

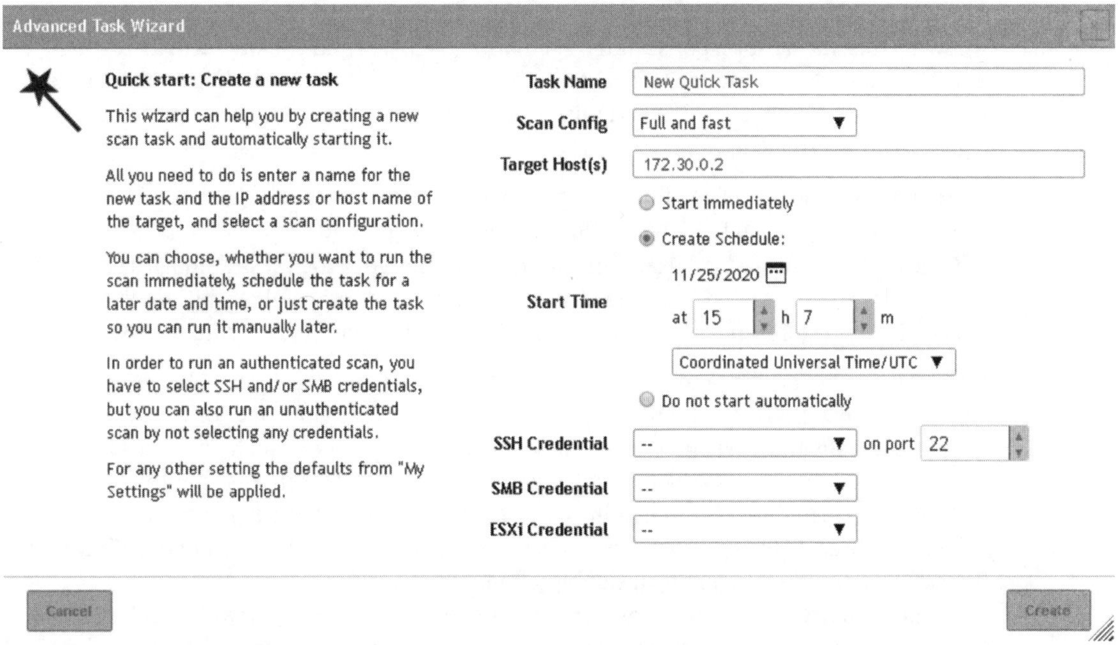

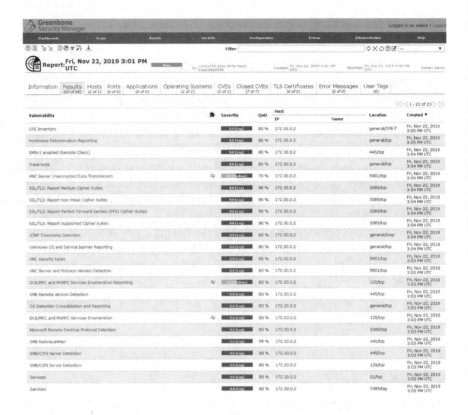

Unauthorized Access and Security Breach Attack Plan

Security breaches are inevitable. They can occur despite your best efforts to prevent them. Knowing this, incident response and remediation must be a part of any security testing effort. It is simply not enough to scan for known vulnerabilities, patch them, and assume your IT infrastructure is safe. When unauthorized access does occur, there are two stages to a good IT response:

- **Incident response**—The initial response to a security breach. The goal at this stage is to contain or shut down the attack before further damage is done.
- **Cleanup**—The process of examining a system or network to assess damage, removing any software installed during the attack, and looking for new vulnerabilities such as **backdoors**, or holes in a system's security that attackers create to facilitate repeat attacks.

Both of these are crucial and should be tested as part of an overall security assessment. The middle of a crisis is not when you want to discover that your network security expert hasn't read a **Bugtraq** alert in 5 years. Incident response testing usually involves bringing in or creating a penetration team, which will be discussed later in this chapter.

To subscribe to the Bugtraq mailing list, go to *https://www.securityfocus.com*.

Security breach drills are one way to test the ability of IT staff to respond to an incident. These drills can be open, blind, or double-blind.

In an open drill, everyone knows that the incident is a drill and that no real attack is taking place. This is the least intrusive type of security breach response test. In a blind drill, IT staff is not notified that a drill is taking place, but the testing team has full knowl-edge of the infrastructure. In a double-blind test, the IT staff is not given prior warning of the test. In addition, the testing team is not given information about the infrastructure. It must start from scratch just as an attacker would. This is the most accurate way to test breach response, because it most closely imitates a real attack.

Any security breach drill should end with an incident recap meeting involving man-agement, systems administrators, and testers. At the incident recap, the group should discuss what it learned from the tests, prioritize its findings, and begin the process of remediation.

Gap Analysis Within the Seven Domains of a Typical IT Infrastructure

Gap analysis is the process of identifying the difference between reality—the current state of an organization's IT infrastructure—and the organization's security goals. Every organiza-tion has a different ideal security level. Some organizations need the best, most secure infra-structure available. Others can forsake some level of security to gain cost savings and ease of use. Whatever that ideal level is, a gap analysis will inform IT of what improvements need to be made in order to achieve it.

A thorough gap analysis covers all seven domains of a typical IT infrastructure (shown in **FIGURE 12-9**) and examines security in each of them.

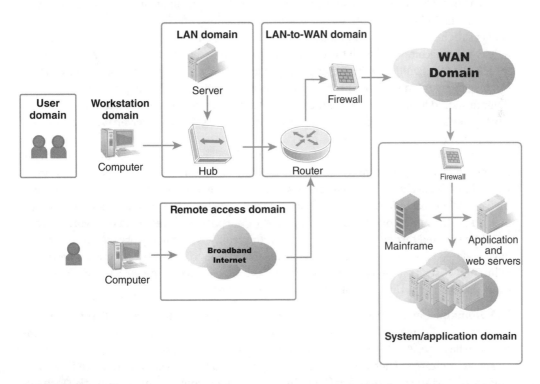

FIGURE 12-9

The seven domains of a typical IT infrastructure.

User Domain. Gap analysis in the User Domain focuses on user training and day-to-day practices, and how the practices affect IT security. If users are required to attend an annual security workshop on secure password creation, for example, but then use the same insecure passwords they used before the training, this represents a gap in security that should be addressed through better training and technical enforcement methods.

Most users do not willfully follow insecure practices. In most cases, they simply do not understand the purpose behind security procedures, or they do not know how to follow them successfully. Most users' highest priorities are convenience and task efficiency. They simply want to do their jobs as easily and quickly as possible. Users often perceive security measures as an obstacle to those goals. Creating, memorizing, and typing a complex password with eight or more characters, uppercase and lowercase letters, and numeric and special characters, is more difficult and time consuming than a simple four-character password or no password at all. Similarly, it is intuitive for many users to prop open a security door, especially if they are moving equipment in and out of a server room. It is inconvenient, from the users' perspective, to keep entering a password every time they go in and out of the server room, especially if they are carrying heavy equipment.

An effective training program that generates user buy-in to security practices bridges the gap between users' legitimate need for convenience and efficiency with the demands of a secure infrastructure.

Workstation Domain. Because the number of workstations in an organization can be very large, automated vulnerability scanners are often the most efficient way to perform a gap analysis in the Workstation Domain. The data derived from a vulnerability scan is useful only when it is compared with the organization's stated security goals. Many vulnerability scanners find vulnerabilities that can be exploited only from within the local network because the workstations are protected by the network firewall. The gap analysis in this domain should focus on vulnerabilities on workstations that could spread to the local network. They should be run on a regular basis because the state of any given workstation can change at any time.

For example, users—despite thorough training—will occasionally open an email attachment or load a webpage that contains a virus. Many viruses are designed to hide on a system and spread themselves across a local network until a trigger event causes them to deploy their malicious payload. The original user may not even be aware that he or she clicked on a malicious attachment or webpage. Ideally, every data packet downloaded to a workstation should be passed through a virus scanner, but the reality is that many organizations do not have updated virus scanners or users have disabled them to save time. Running a periodic vulnerability scan on the Workstation Domain is a second layer of defense in case a malicious program slips through automated virus scanning.

LAN Domain. Gap analysis in the LAN Domain focuses on the network itself. How are resources on the network secured, and could those security measures be bypassed by someone who has access to the network, either internally or remotely?

For example, many networks are set up with a firewall to prevent unauthorized users outside of the local area network (LAN) from accessing resources on the network. Once inside the firewall, however, there can be a false sense of security that leads to insecurely protected resources. Consider a file server located behind the firewall. Because it is not exposed to outside attack, systems administrators consider it relatively safe and focus their attention on other vulnerabilities. Unfortunately, if strict access controls are not implemented on the file server itself, as well as on individual folders and files on the server, a low-level user could easily stumble upon sensitive information such as product designs or financial reports, which they could then disclose intentionally or unintentionally outside of the organization.

LAN-to-WAN Domain. The LAN-to-WAN Domain is where tools such as a port scanner come into play. This is where you will test an attacker's ability to gain privileged access to the organization's private network through openings between the LAN and the wide area network (WAN).

Many servers come with a default configuration that leaves various ports open, such as those used by web or File Transfer Protocol (FTP) server software. If those services are not used on a machine, the ports should be closed before the machine goes into production. Unfortunately, many systems administrators forget to do this, leaving an open door for an attacker to gain access from the WAN—usually the Internet—to the LAN. A port scanner will alert systems administrators to ports that have been left open unnecessarily.

WAN Domain. Resources on the WAN include cloud computing and web applications. These must be analyzed separately from locally hosted applications because they generally exist on the public Internet, which exposes applications to a host of new threats and vulnerabilities. Some of the most prominent vulnerabilities are code injection and buffer overflow errors. **Code injection** is an attack where the hacker inserts malicious code into an input field, usually on a web application. If the application is not coded securely, the server will execute the malicious code.

Consider a contact form on an organization's website. It is a simple application that allows website visitors to send a message to various departments within the organization. The user selects a department, and types his or her name and a message into a web form. The information is stored in a database table. Every 10 minutes, a script runs on the web server that pulls new comments from the database, reformats them, and emails them to the correct department.

As long as users do the expected, and enter a name and message into the form, the system works well. Unfortunately, if a malicious user finds this form, he or she could enter the following line of text in the message field:

```
This is a message for IT security"; drop table comments;
```

The web server would interpret the input as a database command:

```
Insert into comments "This is a message for IT security"; drop
table comments;"
```

The web server will send that line of code to the database, which would interpret it as three lines of code:

```
Insert into comments "This is a message for IT security";
drop table comments;
"
```

The trailing end quote would throw a syntax error, but not until after the crucial command, `drop table comments`, was executed. This command would delete the entire comments table from the database. This type of attack is common on web applications. It is possible because of lax input validation, which is something that a good web application security scanner will look for.

Remote Access Domain. Allowing remote access to internal resources adds a level of complication to any IT infrastructure and can lead to gaps in an otherwise secure system. Gap analysis in the Remote Access Domain focuses on the access controls that authorize remote users on the internal network and the encryption methods and IP tunneling that allow data to be sent securely over the public Internet to a remote worker.

There are many areas where a gap analysis could uncover vulnerabilities in the Remote Access Domain. Lost or stolen challenge-response tokens are a common problem for remote access. If a lost or stolen token cannot be disabled promptly, that represents a significant vulnerability in the Remote Access Domain. A gap analysis in this domain should examine the average time lapse between the point a device is missed and the point at which it is disabled.

System/Application Domain. Gap analysis on systems and applications focuses on insecure code in the application, the operating system, or the libraries and programming languages that connect the two. In the System/Application Domain, you will be looking for vulnerabilities that can lead to buffer overflows, SQL injections, and other common application-level attacks.

Unfortunately, many application-level vulnerabilities are not the fault of insecure code written in-house. The vulnerabilities exist in the programming languages and libraries that developers rely on. Libraries and functions within programming languages exist so that developers can concentrate on the high-level functionality of their applications and not get bogged down by the low-level details of file management or database communication. Unfortunately, when a vulnerability exists in low-level libraries, that vulnerability filters up into the application, where it can be exploited by malicious users.

New vulnerabilities are constantly surfacing, so it is important for developers and systems administrators to know exactly which libraries are in use and to keep up to date on new vulnerability announcements.

Selection of Penetration Testing Teams

Penetration testing is the most accurate way to assess an infrastructure's true vulnerability, because it simulates the actual attack. It can also be the most dangerous to both the targeted organization and the penetration team itself.

Penetration testing is an **intrusive testing method**. Because penetration testers use the same tools and methods actual attackers use, systems and networks can be taken down during a test. Because one of the greatest advantages to penetration testing is that it tests both the security of the infrastructure and the readiness of the incident response team, it is usually necessary to conduct the test during normal work hours when an outage could affect productivity. Even if the attack is carried out after hours, which tests the incident response team's ability to deal with an attack at those times, it could take some time to bring the network back online. Management should be aware of these possibilities and sign off on them before a penetration test begins.

Penetration testing is risky for the attacking team as well. If the incident response team—or even ordinary employees, if the testing involves social engineering—is well prepared, it may call in security or law enforcement authorities. This would be a normal and approved response, especially to an intruder in the building. Penetration testers should be prepared to step out of their role as attacker and prove their identity and authorization at a moment's notice. Every member of a penetration team should carry a copy of the authorization memo, signed by a member of upper management, which states that a penetration test has been authorized and exactly which methods the test will include.

Consider the case of a penetration testing team in Britain. They were hired by a media organization doing a story on how easy it is to steal automated teller machine (ATM) card numbers and personal identification numbers (PINs). The team was led to believe the bank that owned the specific ATMs they tested had sanctioned their activities. Unfortunately, this belief was incorrect. The team installed surveillance cameras near an ATM and a fake card reader on top of the legitimate one. The media organization filmed all of their activities and released that footage as part of an investigative report. After the report was aired, the members of the penetration team were arrested on charges of identity theft and credit card fraud, and the footage taken by the media was used as evidence against them.

 NOTE

A penetration team's authorization memo is often called a **get out of jail free card**. This memo, and the authorization it describes, is the only real difference between legal penetration testing and illegal hacking or computer crimes.

The members of the penetration team were very good at their job. Their only failure was in trusting the organization that employed them and not having a legal waiver indemnifying them against all liability and legal action as a result of their activities.

Red Team

The term "red team" originated in military war-gaming parlance. In this context, the red team is the attacker in a war game. Both the attacker and the defender know that the war game is taking place. The red team knows that the defenders expect them but do not know how they've prepared. In penetration testing, the **red team** may be made up of systems administrators from other departments within the organization or of external penetration testers.

Blue Team

The blue team in a war game is the defending team. It may not know how the red team will attack, but it knows to expect some sort of attack. In penetration testing, the systems administrators and general IT staff are considered the **blue team**.

Tiger Teams

A **tiger team** is the most common type of penetration tester. Tiger teams are almost always external testers who operate in a double-blind penetration test. The target, with the exception of upper management, who authorized the test, is unaware that the test is taking place, and the testing team is given no information about the infrastructure. The tiger team is left to discover what it can about the infrastructure prior to launching the actual attack, and the IT staff must detect and respond to the attack.

Performing the Access Control System Penetration Test

A penetration test is any simulated attack scenario. It could be purely technological, it could focus on uncovering weaknesses to social engineering tactics, or it could take a holistic approach and use any and all tactics and tools available to penetrate the organization's defenses. Because this type of testing is inherently invasive and simulates as close as possible the methods of an actual attack, it is important that all parties have a clear outline of what will be done, what restrictions (if any) must be followed, and what the tests are designed to uncover. If there is any miscommunication between the testers and the organization's management team, a useful penetration test could easily become a crisis situation.

For example, suppose an organization hired a security consulting firm to conduct a penetration test against its IT infrastructure. During the planning stage, management neglected to mention that they would be launching a new customer-facing website during the window allowed for the penetration test. The penetration test proceeded, and the test attack interrupted service during the website launch. Management was understandably upset that a test scenario disrupted a major website launch. The penetration testers had no idea that this particular website was any more important than any other hosted on the organization's servers. All this would have been avoided had the penetration test team known that the new website was off-limits, and if management had known exactly what the penetration test team planned to do.

FYI

Good communication between the penetration testing team and the organization is crucial, especially when determining the scope and timing of the test. Some methods used by penetration testing teams can result in systems crashing and network slowdowns due to increased traffic. It is important for the penetration team to know at what times this type of test is acceptable and when it is not. An organization will not want its customer-facing eCommerce website, for example, to be brought down during peak ordering times.

Any penetration test should follow a well-planned methodology that has been approved by upper management. The basic stages of a penetration test are:

- **Planning and preparation**—This is the most crucial stage in any penetration test. In the planning stage, penetration testers and organization management should meet to determine the goals, scope, and methodology of the penetration test. Without a clear indication of what the penetration test should accomplish, it is likely to produce nothing but a list of exploitable vulnerabilities without any prioritization or guidelines for the organization.

During this stage, appropriate legal documents must be created to protect the penetration testers. As part of the testing, penetration testers engage in activities that would otherwise be considered illegal, and it is possible that confidential information will be compromised. The testing contract should elaborate on how such confidential information will be handled and either returned or disposed of after the test. It should also contain a liability waiver to protect the testers from legal ramifications in the case of accidental or intentional damage to systems or data during the test.

- **Information gathering**—During the information-gathering stage, the penetration testing team uses nonintrusive methods to discover as much as it can about the target network. In this stage, port scanners and online tools such as Netcraft (*www.netcraft .com*) are invaluable. They give the penetration team a good sense of which parts of the network are potential targets and which systems are detectable. The team will use this information later during the actual penetration attempt.

- **Vulnerability detection**—Once the penetration team knows something about the target network, it can begin to probe for vulnerabilities using nonintrusive vulnerability scanners. The information gathered at this stage helps the team choose specific attack vectors and target systems during the penetration attempt.

- **Penetration attempt**—During the penetration attempt, testers may use a variety of methods and tools to gain unauthorized access to systems and networks. Social engineering may be a key method, if it is allowed under the terms of the contract with the organization. The penetration team may also attempt to defeat physical security to gain access to facilities such as data centers. The testing team must keep detailed records of every action it takes as a guide for the clean-up process.

- **Analysis and reporting**—Once the penetration test is complete, the testing team analyzes the gathered data and writes a report for the organization. The final report should contain a summary of the testing methods used and their success or failure on various targets, a detailed listing of all information gathered during the testing, a list that describes all vulnerabilities found, and recommendations for remediation.

- **Clean-up**—During penetration testing, the team may create new user accounts, modify configuration or data files, and make other changes to the environment. Once the test is complete, the testing team has the responsibility to undo any changes it made to the environment.

 TIP

Always consult legal counsel before conducting any penetration test, even on your own organization.

These basic steps will help ensure an accurate, safe penetration test that produces actionable results for the organization. The basic goals of any penetration test are to assess three areas: whether policies and standards are followed, whether an appropriate baseline is achieved throughout the infrastructure, and whether countermeasures and access control systems are implemented properly. The next three sections discuss these goals in detail.

Assess if Access Control System Policies and Standards Are Followed

Every organization should have policies and standards for access controls. Simply having standards is not enough to secure an infrastructure—those standards must be implemented and followed consistently. A good penetration test attempts to uncover inconsistencies and exploits them to demonstrate this weakness in the organization's infrastructure.

Social engineering methods are often used to find weaknesses in policy and in implementing standards. Often, a lax attitude toward security and a lack of understanding of how policies and standards contribute to an organization's overall security posture lead to employees who take shortcuts and circumvent access controls. They may hold or prop open the doors to sensitive areas, reuse passwords, or share privileged accounts. A good penetration testing team will use social engineering and other methods to discover these weak areas.

Assess if the Security Baseline Definition Is Being Achieved Throughout

During the planning phase, a security baseline is defined. The baseline is the minimum level of security that is acceptable to the organization. Whether that baseline is achieved throughout the organization is a question answerable by a good penetration test.

For example, if the organization has determined that no outside access should be permitted to the Intranet as one baseline for access control systems, penetration tests may scan for open ports on the intranet server and attempt to gain remote access.

Assess if Security Countermeasures and Access Control Systems Are Implemented Properly

Access control systems are often complex and sophisticated systems. Unfortunately, vulnerabilities often hide in those complexities. Security countermeasures are not always well understood by IT staff, and access control systems can be misconfigured in such a way as to allow false positives. Penetration tests probe access control systems and attempt to force a false positive. If they are successful, penetration tests will also exercise security countermeasures and ensure that they are effective.

Preparing the Final Test Report

The major deliverable from any penetration test is the analysis and report delivered to the organization. This report—and prior authorization—is all that really separates penetration tests from hacking. The first section of the final test report must include a detailed description of the penetration test team's activities, including which methods were used and what areas of the infrastructure were targeted. The next section should contain details of the vulnerabilities they found and what areas were adequately hardened and resisted their attacks. The final section of the report should contain the test team's final analysis, prioritization of risk, and recommendations for hardening.

The organization uses this report to guide security activities so that the vulnerabilities that represent the most significant risks are addressed. The report is also used to determine budgets for future infrastructure upgrades.

Identify Gaps and Risk Exposures and Assess Impact

In the first section, the penetration testers describe each of their activities and elaborate on any gaps and vulnerabilities they were able to exploit. They combine this information with knowledge of the organization's security goals to assess the impact of the gaps and vulnerabilities found during testing.

Once those gaps have been identified, they must be prioritized by risk exposure. It is important to keep in mind that the organization has limited resources—time, money, and personnel—available to close security holes, so the testing team's findings must be presented in a way that makes it easy to decide where to spend those resources.

Develop Remediation Plans for Closing Identified Security Gaps Prioritized by Risk Exposure

Once the gaps in an organization's infrastructure are identified, the next step is to develop remediation plans for closing the most important gaps. These plans will vary depending on the gaps identified and should always involve retesting to ensure that the gaps have been adequately closed. Remediation plans should be listed in order of risk exposure.

Prepare Cost Magnitude Estimate and Prioritize Security Solutions Based on Risk Exposure

Remediation of security gaps can be costly in terms of time, effort, and monetary costs. The final section of a penetration test report should include a breakdown of the costs of remediation, in order of risk exposure. Once the costs have been broken down, an executive summary is a useful tool to include. This summary will give a quick overview of the bottom line: what will it cost the organization in terms of time, effort, and money to close the most important security gaps in its infrastructure?

CHAPTER SUMMARY

Testing in various forms is an important tool for identifying vulnerabilities and security gaps in an organization's IT infrastructure. Ideally, a testing plan should include both intrusive and nonintrusive testing methods, as each will provide a different view on the infrastructure. For the protection of the testers, intrusive tests should be conducted only with the full approval of upper management as well as legal documentation of that support.

Once security testing is complete, a detailed report of the testers' findings as well as recommendations for remediation will be an invaluable guide for improving the overall security of an organization's IT infrastructure.

KEY CONCEPTS AND TERMS

Analysis and reporting
Automated testing
Backdoor
Blue team
Boundary conditions
Bugtraq
Clean-up
Code injection
Common Criteria
Gap analysis

Get out of jail free card
Hardening
Host discovery
Integration testing
Intrusive testing methods
Load testing
Nessus
Nmap
Nonintrusive testing
   methods

Open Vulnerability Assessment
   Scanner (OpenVAS)
Penetration attempt
Penetration testing
Port scanning
Red team
Tiger team
Unit testing
Vulnerability detection

CHAPTER 12 ASSESSMENT

1. It is necessary to consider security issues during every phase of the software development life cycle.

   A. True
   B. False

2. What occurs during the sunset phase of a security system's life cycle?

   A. Electronic media is wiped clean.
   B. Paper documentation is shredded or archived.
   C. Old equipment is destroyed or disposed of in a secure manner.
   D. All of the above

3. Which of the following are primary activities for an information security team? (Select two.)

   A. Researching new exploits
   B. Monitoring/incident handling
   C. Testing
   D. Upgrading security systems

4. Port scanning is an example of _____ testing.

5. Penetration testing is an example of _____ testing.

6. Which of the following tests is the most accurate way to test security incident response?

   A. Open
   B. Blind
   C. Double-blind
   D. Automated

7. Gap analysis in which domain focuses primarily on the effectiveness of an organization's training program?

   A. User
   B. Workstation
   C. LAN
   D. LAN-to-WAN
   E. WAN
   F. System/Application
   G. Remote Access

8. A web application security scanner is a good tool to use when testing which domain?

   A. User
   B. Workstation
   C. LAN
   D. LAN-to-WAN
   E. WAN
   F. Remote Access

9. Penetration testing is a risky operation for both the organization and the testers.

 A. True
 B. False

10. Which penetration testing team may be composed of systems administrators in other departments of an organization?

 A. Red
 B. Blue
 C. Tiger
 D. Orange

11. Which penetration testing team is composed of systems administrators who defend the network and respond to the activities of the penetration testers?

 A. Red
 B. Blue
 C. Tiger
 D. Orange

12. Which penetration testing team is given no prior knowledge of the IT infrastructure and uses the same tools and strategies that an actual attacker would use?

 A. Red
 B. Blue
 C. Tiger
 D. Orange

13. The clean-up phase of a penetration test is the responsibility of which individual or group?

 A. Systems administrator
 B. Upper management
 C. Penetration testing team
 D. Help desk

14. A penetration test report should include which of the following? (Select three.)

 A. Description of gaps and risk exposures found during the test
 B. List of passwords uncovered by the penetration testing team
 C. Remediation plans for closing security gaps
 D. Cost analysis and solution prioritization based on risk exposure

FIGURE 13-1

The C-I-A triad represents three criteria for maintaining secure information.

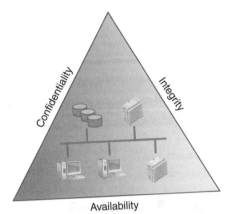

Confidentiality

According to the Committee on National Security Systems Instruction No. 4009 (CNSSI-4009), confidentiality is "The property that information is not disclosed to system entities (users, processes, devices) unless they have been authorized to access the information." In other words, information must be viewed, used, or copied only by individuals who have the proper level of access as well as a legitimate need to access the information. A confidentiality breach occurs when an unauthorized individual gains access to sensitive information.

If someone watched over your shoulder while you were entering your automated teller machine (ATM) PIN, a confidentiality breach occurred. Confidentiality breaches can also happen when hardware containing sensitive information is lost or stolen. Any time an unauthorized user can access confidential information, a breach has occurred.

Confidentiality is maintained through proper use of access controls such as limiting access to information to a need-to-know basis and properly assigning security levels to information.

Integrity

CNSSI-4009 defines integrity as "The property whereby an entity has not been modified in an unauthorized manner." Data integrity refers to the principle that information cannot be changed, created, or deleted without proper authorization; however, integrity in the C-I-A triad goes beyond that. It is also the requirement that the path on which the information travels and the location where it rests are also secure.

Information integrity refers to the ability to trust that the information received is the same as the information originally created. It is also the ability to trust that a document stored in multiple locations contains the exact same information.

Data integrity isn't just concerned with information security. Accidental data loss and data corruption through transmission are also major causes of integrity failure. Coping with accidental loss and corruption is one of the areas where IA moves beyond information security into information verification.

Availability

CNSSI-4009 defines availability as "The property of being accessible and useable upon demand by an authorized entity." In other words, information is accessible when it is needed. This requires that the network and systems used to store the information are working correctly. Availability can be compromised by accidents and system failure as well as malicious attacks. A hard drive or network card failure can cause a breach of availability, as can denial of service (DoS) attacks.

The Five Pillars

The five pillars of IA were developed by the National Security Telecommunications and Information Systems Security Committee (NSTISSC). Detailed in CNSSI-4009, it is an expansion of the C-I-A model.

The three tenets of the C-I-A model make up the foundation of the five pillars of IA. Two further tenets were added to better model the situation that complex organizations face when dealing with IA. CNSSI-4009 defines IA as "Measures that protect and defend information and information systems by ensuring their availability, integrity, authentication, confidentiality, and nonrepudiation. These measures include providing for restoration of information systems by incorporating protection, detection, and reaction capabilities." Authentication and nonrepudiation are the two factors added to the traditional C-I-A framework.

13

The McCumber Cube

In the early 1990s, the C-I-A triad model was expanded by John McCumber into a cube to look deeper at IA. McCumber took the C-I-A framework and added two more triads to it, forming a multidimensional cube as shown in **FIGURE 13-2**. The concept behind the cube was to allow an organization to look at all aspects of IA fully, without overemphasizing any one aspect. McCumber proposed three dimensions of IA:

- **Goals**—These are represented by the C-I-A triad.
- **Information states**—These describe where data are located at any given moment.
- **Safeguards**—These refer to what is being done to secure data.

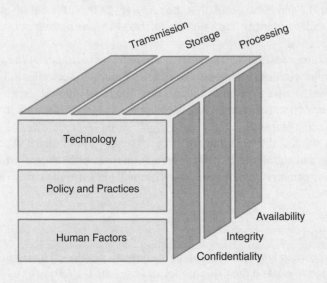

FIGURE 13-2

The McCumber cube, by Munawar Hafiz, illustrates a deeper understanding of information assurance.

There are three information states in the cube: transmission, storage, and processing. Storage and transmission are just other terms for data at rest and data in motion. The processing state refers to the time when data are being acted upon by a system. This is a data state that is often overlooked.

Another dimension of the cube includes safeguards. These include the policies and practices in place to secure information. Human factors such as information security training, and technological safeguards like antivirus software, intrusion detection systems, and firewall systems are included in the concept of safeguards.

In addition to the three triads, there is a fourth dimension: time. According to the cube framework, all three triads must be addressed in connection with each other over time. Understanding the interdependencies of these factors over time is essential to IA.

Some organizations use an expanded McCumber cube model that replaces the C-I-A triad with the five pillars of IA on the goals dimension of the cube.

Authentication

CNSSI-4009 defines authentication as "The process of verifying the identity or other attributes claimed by or assumed of an entity (user, process, or device), or to verify the source and integrity of data." This entails knowing that those who access the information are who they say they are. Authentication can be achieved through the three tests of what you know, what you have, and what you are. An example of an authentication breach is if an unauthorized user accesses a system using an authorized username and password obtained through illegitimate means.

Nonrepudiation

Nonrepudiation is defined in CNSSI-4009 as "Assurance that the sender of information is provided with proof of delivery and the recipient is provided with proof of the sender's identity, so neither can later deny having processed the information." With this concept, both the sender and the receiver are accountable for the information. To implement nonrepudiation, there must be a way for the sender to verify that the receiver got the information and for the receiver to verify the sender's identity. With nonrepudiation in place, neither side can deny actions they took on the data.

A good example of nonrepudiation can be seen in a banking wire transfer. When a wire transfer is sent, the sender verifies its credentials with the Federal Reserve Bank. The Federal Reserve then moves the wire transfer to the receiver. The recipient of the wire verifies receipt of the transfer, and the amount received, back to the sender. This way, the banking system can mitigate the risk of fraud.

Since their creation in 2001, the five pillars of IA have become the standard IA framework for U.S. governmental organizations. Inside the government, these pillars are utilized based on sensitivity, threat, and other risk management decisions. They form the core of any governmental IA operation.

The Parkerian Hexad

The Parkerian hexad, shown in **FIGURE 13-3**, is an IA framework developed by Donn B. Parker in 2002. It was developed to expand the C-I-A model and uses the C-I-A triad as a base. This

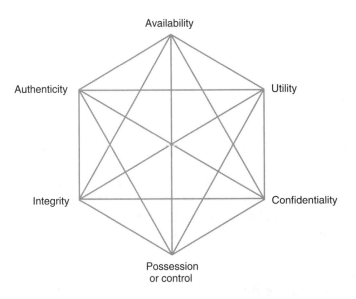

FIGURE 13-3
The Parkerian hexad.

was developed in response to the limitations of the C-I-A framework. Parker described these elements as fundamental and nonoverlapping. Most security breaches compromise more than one element at a time.

The three additional elements of the hexad are possession or control, authenticity, and utility. Next, you will look at each of these aspects.

Possession or Control

Possession or control is related to confidentiality. It is the concept that control of the information can be breached without a confidentiality breach. For example, suppose a flash drive containing the master copy of sensitive data is lost. The possession of those data is now breached, but until they are accessed, they are still confidential. The basis of control is preventing contact with confidential information by unauthorized users. This idea also covers unauthorized copying of or use of intellectual property. An example of a breach of possession is the piracy of copyrighted music files.

Authenticity

Authenticity is the appropriateness of the labeling of information. Does the information correspond correctly to its intended meaning? The idea behind this element is to avoid garbled data and fraud. A breach may be caused by an incorrect address in an email database.

Utility

Utility describes the usefulness of data. Information that is stored in an obsolete format that can no longer be read would be a breach of utility. Encrypted information with a lost encryption key is also an example of a utility breach.

The hexad and the five pillars of IA both expand upon the C-I-A model. It is important to remember that these are just frameworks or guidelines. Even the C-I-A model, which is the simplest of the three, is a useful guideline for IA. These frameworks give an organization a starting point for developing a robust IA infrastructure. These models are not to be taken literally but used as a tool to craft your own organization's IA policies and procedures.

How Can Information Assurance Be Applied to Access Control Systems?

As you have seen in the descriptions of various frameworks, access control is essential to IA, and IA concepts should be applied to an organization's access control infrastructures. Information assurance models are a guideline to use when building or sourcing an access control system. When designing any access control system, you should first determine which information assurance model best represents your organization's IA requirements. From there, you can determine specific requirements based on the chosen IA model. These requirements will be the basis for choosing or designing an access control system that ensures confidentiality, integrity, and availability at the very least.

Access Controls Enforce Confidentiality

One of the primary functions of any access control system is to allow or deny access to resources and data. However, by denying access to unauthorized users, the system maintains data confidentiality. Those users without authorization to a given data object cannot view it. Depending on how the access control system is configured, an unauthorized user may not even be aware that a data object exists.

Access Controls Enforce Integrity

Access controls prevent the loss of data integrity by preventing unauthorized users from modifying data objects either accidentally or intentionally. If the user does not have modify or write privileges on a file, that user cannot make changes to the data contained within the file.

Access Controls Enforce Availability

By enforcing confidentiality and integrity, access control systems can also ensure availability. A strong access control system will prevent all but the most determined attacker from destroying data or compromising the servers and networks that make that data available to authorized users.

Training and Information Assurance Awareness

Simply implementing technological access controls is not sufficient to ensure information assurance. Managers, staff, systems administrators, and security engineers must be constantly aware of the information assurance implications of their actions and vigilant as they watch for signs of attack.

Often, the first people to notice an anomaly are the staff members who use a resource every day. They are the ones who will notice that the database is slower than usual or that a web application is not behaving as expected. Without some training in the basics of information assurance, those staff members may not realize the importance of their observations, and those observations may go unreported.

What Are the Goals of Access Control System Monitoring and Reporting?

Simply having an access control system is not enough to secure sensitive information and resources. Those access control systems must be continuously monitored to ensure they are working properly and that no unauthorized user has been granted access. Access control reporting can take the form of real-time alerts sent to systems administrators notifying them of a breach in progress or after-the-fact tabulations of access control activity over a period of time.

There are several primary goals achieved through monitoring and reporting on an access control system:

- **Accuracy:** To be useful, a monitoring system must have a high level of accuracy. Authorized users must be granted access reliably, and unauthorized users must be denied access. Unfortunately, no system is 100% accurate and will have a rate of both false positives and false negatives. **False positives** occur when a system labels normal activity as anomalous. **False negatives** occur when a system overlooks anomalous activity.
- **Variety:** A monitoring system must be able to detect many types of suspicious activity.
- **Timeliness:** The system must report suspicious activity quickly enough for systems administrators to cut off an attack in progress.
- **Ease of use:** The system's reporting facility must create reports that are easy to read and understand.

An **intrusion detection system (IDS)** is a hardware- or software-based solution that monitors network traffic, looking for signs of a security breach. Intrusion detection systems are based on several models of anomalous behavior:

- **Anomaly detection:** Anomaly detection operates on two core principles: What is known is good, and what is unusual is bad. Therefore, any activity that is unknown must be reported as suspicious. Early anomaly detection systems were based on statistical models of system behavior. Any activity that fell outside of a standard deviation from that model was considered anomalous. Later, models were proposed that were based on logic-based descriptions of system behavior. Modern anomaly detection applications use a hybrid approach to compute an anomaly score. Any activity that generates a score higher than a predetermined acceptable level is flagged. An IDS based on anomaly detection requires a period of training to create a baseline of normal system behavior.
- **Misuse detection:** This model operates on a simple premise: What is bad is known. This type of IDS compares activity with a **blacklist** of known suspicious events. This type of intrusion detection has the benefit of being useful immediately upon installation. A misuse detection IDS includes a large database of known attack signatures. The system

compares system activity with these attack signatures and triggers an alert on a matching event.

- **Specification detection:** This model is similar to misuse detection, except that it operates on a **whitelist** principle instead of a blacklist. Whitelist principles are: We know what is good, and what is not good is bad. Any behavior that does not correspond to predefined specifications must be considered suspicious. A specification detection system will describe the range of normal system and application behaviors and will trigger an alert on any activity that does not fall within normal ranges.

The major difference between specification detection and anomaly detection lies in how each system knows what normal behavior is. An anomaly detection system observes system behavior over a period of time and then uses statistical and logical models to create a baseline. A specification detection IDS uses a behavior modeling language to describe what activities and behaviors developers and systems administrators expect under normal circumstances.

What Checks and Balances Can Be Implemented?

Many access control breaches originate internally. To guard against this risk as well as the risk of external attack, a system of checks and balances should be in place. This way, even a trusted internal user, such as a systems administrator, will know that his or her activities are monitored and any unusual behavior will be noticed.

Track and Monitor Event-Type Audit Logs

Event-type audit logs record specific events on a system. Tracking the events recorded in these audit logs ensures that the events leading up to a security breach, the events that comprise the breach, and any after effects of the breach are understood. No security breach happens in a vacuum. There are discernable events that create favorable conditions for an attack. Careful monitoring of event logs can give hints that an attack is about to take place and allow you to stop it before it happens. Tracking the events before, during, and after an attack can give systems administrators valuable information to reduce the risk of similar attacks in the future.

There are three levels of events:

- **System-level events:** These focus on user logon attempts, system resource usage, and other low-level events that affect the integrity of the entire system.
- **Application-level events:** These are specific to a given application, including error messages, file modifications, and security alerts within the application.
- **User-level events:** These are initiated by individual users and include authentication attempts, commands and applications used, and security violations. This type of event log is discussed in the next section.

Each of these event types holds valuable information about potential and actual security breaches. An example of Event Viewer log information from a Windows Server system appears in **FIGURE 13-4**.

Windows Server Event Viewer.

Used with permission from Microsoft.

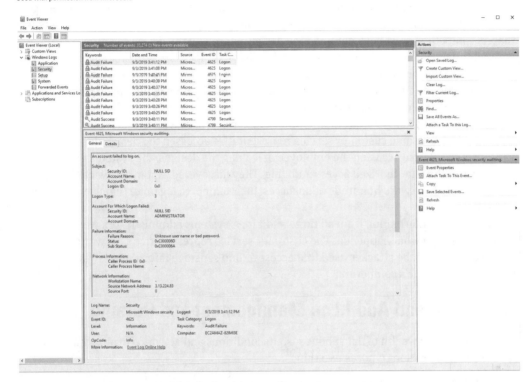

Track and Monitor User-Type Audit Logs

User audit logs store information on authentication attempts, resources used, commands and applications run, and security violations committed by users. Most importantly, this type of log provides accountability because it ties specific actions to individual users. When suspicious activity is detected in the event audit log, it can be cross-referenced with the user log to determine who was logged onto the system at the time of the breach, and what he or she was doing.

Track and Monitor Unauthorized Access Attempts Audit Logs

Unauthorized access attempts are a key signal that an attack may be in progress. A single failed access attempt is likely just a typing error on the part of a legitimate user, but 10 failed access attempts signal an attempt at password cracking. The information stored in this audit log can be combined with the user and event logs to give a complete picture of the system before, during, and after an attack.

Consider the case of Acme Communications, a mobile phone manufacturer. The company stores proprietary and experimental product designs, project plans, and long-term strategy documents on a file server. The file server is located behind a firewall and protected by an intrusion detection system and is relatively secure against an attack from outside the organization.

In a press release, the company's major competitor announces that it has a working prototype and will release a consumer model with many of the same features and cutting-edge technology that Acme has spent the past 3 years developing. It is clear to Acme management that its competitor must have obtained the designs stored on the file server.

While analyzing the audit logs, systems administrators locate several instances of access to product design documents on the file server over several months originating from a workstation in the customer service department. Normally, there would be no reason for anyone outside of engineering to access those documents.

Digging further, the systems administrator cross-references with the user audit log and discovers that the same customer service representative accessed the design documents in each instance. Before accusing the employee of leaking the designs, the systems administrators checked the unauthorized access audit log. They discovered that in the weeks before the first incident, there were hundreds of unsuccessful attempts to log on to that user's network account.

By analyzing information from all three audit logs, systems administrators were able to get a clear idea of what happened. The customer service representative's network account was breached, and the attacker used that access to find sensitive information, which was then leaked to Acme's competitor.

Audit Trail and Audit Log Management and Parsing

Log files contain a wealth of data about system conditions and activity. Turning that data into useful information requires two things:

- **Log file management:** A system of storing and rotating log files. The data recorded and stored in log files may be necessary legal evidence when the time comes to prosecute the attacker in a security breach. Because of this, log files should be kept for at least the length of time allowed under the statute of limitations in your jurisdiction. However, keeping several years' worth of log files on a production server is unwieldy. Log files should be backed up regularly and deleted from production servers to conserve space.
- **Log file parsing: Parsing** is the process of translating and reformatting raw log files into useful reports. In the middle of an attack, systems administrators do not have time to dig through raw log files. They need specific, actionable information in an easy-to-use format.

An **audit trail** is a series of events gleaned from parsed log file reports over a period of time. These events generally revolve around a specific user or a larger event such as a security breach. An audit trail is a useful tool in piecing together the events leading up to and including a security breach.

Audit Trail and Audit Log Reporting Issues and Concerns

Once log files are effectively managed and parsed, they must be analyzed. On a production system, the auditing system can produce gigabytes of data per day—too much data to be effectively analyzed in its raw state. Trying to manually analyze that much raw data would take an excessive amount of time, and it would quickly become difficult to separate the important from the trivial log entries.

To avoid these problems, it is crucial to follow an effective and efficient analysis system that allows systems administrators to manage such large amounts of data. A good analysis system will overcome these issues:

- **Time:** Digging through log files looking for signs of malicious activity that may or may not exist is a tedious and time-consuming task. Automated analysis and reporting can help by putting all those data into a more easily understood format. Procedures that dictate a regular log analysis can also help remind systems administrators to spend the necessary time on this task.
- **Normalization: Normalization** is the process of translating log files from various systems into a common format. This allows administrators to easily compare and correlate events from a UNIX-based web server and a Windows-based domain controller, for example. Normalization also ensures that system-specific information, such as times and IP addresses, is correlated across multiple log sources.
- **Prioritization: Prioritization** is the process of determining which log files and/or entries are important and may require action and which are less important or informational only. Knowing what to look for makes the job of analyzing log files more efficient because it allows administrators to quickly discard log entries that are not of immediate interest. Most of the time, log file analysis is done to answer a specific set of questions:
  - Are we now or have we recently been under attack?
  - Did the attack succeed?
  - How extensive is the damage from the attack?
  - Has this ever happened before?
- **Tunnel vision:** The downfall of prioritizing is that some very interesting and important data can be overlooked because they do not directly answer the immediate questions. You might know what a DoS attack looks like in the logs. However, if you are looking specifically for a DoS attack, it is easy to miss the warning signs of a code injection attack.

Automated log analysis software can help make this task more manageable but ultimately there is no substitute for time and expertise. Good systems administrators who are not rushed can often find a crucial piece of evidence in the log files that allows them to prevent an attack before it starts.

Security Information and Event Management (SIEM)

A **security information and event management (SIEM) system** is a software solution that attempts to solve several of the issues discussed in the previous section. It is designed to centralize storage and normalize log files from a wide variety of applications and devices. Most include real-time analysis and notification features that alert systems administrators immediately if the SIEM recognizes an attack in progress.

SIEMs also simplify the task of manually analyzing log files because they give a consistent interface and the ability to cross-reference logs from a variety of devices, such as a firewall, router, web server, and an intrusion detection system.

Integrating the SIEM with applications is more difficult due to a lack of standard auditing policies. Even if applications developed in-house follow a strict auditing and logging policy, third-party applications may not. The SIEM cannot analyze logs that were never created. An application without an audit trail or with logs that are never monitored is an obvious target for an attacker.

Consider the case of a pharmaceutical company running a Windows web farm. The servers generated a large amount of data every day—far too much for systems administrators to analyze manually. For years, those logs had simply been rotated and overwritten. The company decided to implement a web-based email system and realized it needed to pay more attention to security on its web servers. Personnel implemented an SIEM solution and quickly discovered that probe attacks against their web servers were being launched from a foreign university every 15 minutes. Without the SIEM, the pharmaceutical company would not have realized it was under scrutiny until it was too late to prevent an attack.

Best Practices for Performing Ongoing Access Control System Assurance

Whether access control system assurance is done for regulatory compliance or simply because it is good business practice, there are some best practices to make the task more effective:

- **Follow a defined model:** The C-I-A triad, five pillars of IA, and Parkerian hexad are all well-known and tested models of information assurance.
- **Use access controls to enforce IA:** Regardless of which model you use, your organization should choose and develop access control systems that will enforce the key tenets of confidentiality, integrity, and availability.
- **Implement an IDS:** An intrusion detection system is a key tool for recognizing and stopping an attack in progress.
- **Make audit trail analysis a priority:** Log files and audit trails that are rarely analyzed are the digital equivalent of a paperweight. They are of limited use and take up a lot of space. Tools such as SIEMs make this task easier.
- **Implement an ongoing training policy:** This will ensure that all personnel, not just security engineers, are aware of information assurance concepts and know how to recognize potentially important anomalies as they encounter them.

Following these best practices will help you implement information assurance within your organization.

Case Studies and Examples

Information assurance can be a difficult concept to understand in practical terms. In this section, you will read about how information assurance is implemented in real-world situations.

Private Sector Case Study

The human element of IA is an important and often overlooked factor. As previously mentioned, training is an important aspect of implementing IA and a vital part of any IA program. Here, you'll learn how implementing a training program assisted an organization in securing its environment and strengthening its IA.

Acme Tech Systems is one of the largest providers of IT services, systems integration, and training to the U.S. government. Nearly 80% of Acme's business is with the U.S. Department of Defense and other U.S. federal government agencies.

Due to the nature of its work, Acme always had IA as a priority. The nature of the information Acme deals with is often classified and highly confidential. Unfortunately, in early 2015, Acme's systems were being targeted at an increasing rate. Acme's research showed that its network was being attacked over 1,000 times an hour, and a number of those attackers were getting through Acme's perimeter defenses. Acme recognized that its critical information was being exposed to malicious users all over the world.

Improving the security of Acme's network was a daunting task, and the small security team was often overwhelmed by the size and complexity of the system. Although a number of initiatives were started to further secure the system, a training program was seen as one of the most successful. Acme decided the best way to assist the security team was to have all of Acme's systems administrators (SAs) acquire at least a basic knowledge of information security.

This was a challenge, with nearly 3,000 SAs to train. Acme implemented a two-phase program with computer-based training courseware and instructor-led courses, most of which consisted of hands-on labs. In fact, 60% of the course work was lab-based. This gave the SAs invaluable practice preventing hackers from accessing the network. The courses helped Acme's SAs learn the skills and develop the tools needed to help them identify system vulnerabilities and implement countermeasures.

The results of the training were immediate. Within months of implementing the program, the number of successful attacks decreased by half. The training also provided valuable feedback to help strengthen Acme's overall network further. Ongoing training allows the SAs to stay current with the tricks malicious users employ as well as with current security trends.

By enhancing the security awareness of all of its SAs, Acme was able to ensure the confidentiality and integrity of its critical information. By maintaining an ongoing training program, Acme is able to verify that it will have a strong IA infrastructure going forward.

Public Sector Case Study

A major university medical center recently piloted its new teleradiology program. The program allowed radiologists and physicians to share and view patient images digitally. Due to concerns over the Health Insurance Portability and Accountability Act (HIPAA) compliance, the medical center embarked on an information assurance risk assessment project during the planning phase of the teleradiology program.

The information assurance risk assessment project was carried out in three phases: Organizational View, Technological View, and Strategy and Plan Development. In each of these phases, a multidisciplinary team of senior management, operational management, IT staff, and clinical staff participated in workshops, discussions, and information-gathering activities. The result of this multidisciplinary approach was that the medical center identified areas of its planned teleradiology project that were inherently insecure before those insecurities were introduced into actual practice. The IA process led to better project planning and a more successful end result.

In Phase I, Organizational View, members of the team met to determine the most critical resources involved in the teleradiology project. They initially brainstormed over 30 resources including people, patient images, servers, and laptops. They narrowed the list to the five most critical and focused the rest of their efforts on those resources.

The analysis team gathered opinions on the following:

- Critical assets
- Threats to those assets
- The relative importance of confidentiality, integrity, and availability of those assets
- The medical center's existing practices that either supported or undermined information assurance

The team met for extensive debate and discussion of these topics and eventually came to a consensus.

In Phase II, Technological View, the IT staff on the team conducted a vulnerability scan on the IT infrastructure and reported its findings back to the rest of the team members.

In Phase III, Strategy and Plan Development, the team integrated and analyzed all of the data gathered in the first two phases. From this analysis, they conducted a formal risk analysis, identifying, categorizing, and prioritizing the impact of various types of breaches on the five critical assets identified in Phase I.

From there, the team created an information security risk management plan. The plan was broken down into three parts: action items, mitigation plans, and protection strategy. The action items were tasks that could be undertaken immediately, with no need for new staff, policies, or funding, which would result in a significant improvement in the overall security outlook for the project. Some examples of action items included changing default passwords and deleting user accounts for former employees.

The mitigation plans focused on high-impact threats to critical assets and included methods to recognize, resist, and recover from a security incident. These plans were designed to have a broad impact on critical assets as well as secondary ones.

The final section of the risk management plan was the protection strategy. This section detailed plans to improve the medical center's overall information security stance by implementing best practices for information assurance.

The information assurance risk assessment provided valuable insight to the medical center and allowed the teleradiology department to prevent security issues in the planning stages. For example, the team's original plan had been to instruct radiologists to use their personal computers to manage patient images after hours. During the risk assessment project, the team identified three high-priority concerns surrounding the use of personal computers:

- **Technical support:** IT staff could not effectively troubleshoot or support equipment privately owned by individual radiologists. This could affect the availability of patient images in the event of a computer crash.

- **Threats to confidentiality of patient images:** Radiologists' home computers were often located in public areas of the home where family members and guests could easily look over the radiologists' shoulder and view protected health information. This constituted a serious breach of HIPAA regulations.
- **Threats to integrity of patient images:** Because images would be stored on home computer hard drives, there was the potential for those images to be altered using photo manipulation software.

To mitigate these concerns, the medical center decided to purchase dedicated laptops for use by on-call radiologists.

Critical Infrastructure Case Study

Availability is one of the three components of the C-I-A model of information assurance, and in the case of access controls, it is a vitally important component. Consistent and quick availability of the information allows physical security to work efficiently. Take a look at how the U.S. Coast Guard handles the availability of information to maintain the security of Hawaii's ports.

To deal with availability of IA, the Coast Guard implemented a centralized, IP network-based access control card system. Through a secure website, many state and federal agencies, including the Coast Guard, Hawaii's Department of Transportation, and customs and immigration authorities, as well as private maritime organizations and others, can share information related to all activities and data for the port. This allows the Coast Guard to have a centralized clearinghouse for all expected activity and focus its security efforts.

This system, referred to as the Hawaii Integrated Maritime Information System (HIMIS), allows authenticated users to access and update information. This enables quick information sharing and real-time data to enhance the Coast Guard's security practices. This information can be entered both in flexible custom reports and on nautical charts.

The high availability of the HIMIS system greatly enhances the Coast Guard's ability to secure the Hawaiian ports.

13

Access Control
Assurance

CHAPTER SUMMARY

Information assurance is a guideline for planning, implementing, and assessing a secure IT infrastructure. This chapter examined several models, including the C-I-A triad, five pillars of IA, and Parkerian hexad. An organization should choose the one that most accurately reflects its IA requirements.

Ideally, every component of infrastructure should be evaluated for its contribution to information assurance on critical resources. Staff members, both technical and non-technical, should participate in regular training on information assurance concepts so they are aware of the security implications of their decisions and are able to recognize important anomalies when they occur. When security incidents do occur, careful analysis and cross-referencing of various audit logs provides key information about the incident. This information is a valuable resource for preventing similar breaches in the future.

KEY CONCEPTS AND TERMS

Audit trail
Blacklist
False negative
False positive

Intrusion detection system (IDS)
Normalization
Parsing
Prioritization

Security information and event management (SIEM) system
Whitelist

CHAPTER 13 ASSESSMENT

1. According to the C-I-A triad, the three pillars of information assurance are _____, _____, and _____.

2. Nonrepudiation provides the sender of information with which of the following?
   A. Read receipt
   B. Notification that the message was deleted without being opened
   C. Proof of delivery
   D. Notification that the message was forwarded to a third party by the original recipient

3. The Parkerian hexad adds which elements to the C-I-A triad? (Select three.)
   A. Possession or control
   B. Nonrepudiation
   C. Authenticity
   D. Utility
   E. Authentication

4. Only security engineers need training in information assurance.
   A. True
   B. False

5. Timeliness is an important goal of any access control monitoring system.
   A. True
   B. False

6. Intrusion detection systems that operate on the principle of misuse detection compare activity with a _____ of known suspicious events.

7. Intrusion detection systems that operate on the principle of specification detection use a _____ to identify normal ranges of behavior.

8. Which events in an audit log report user logon attempts and system resource usage?
   A. System-level
   B. Application-level
   C. User-level
   D. Unauthorized access-level

9. Which events in an audit log report user authentication attempts, commands and applications used, and security violations committed by users?
   A. System-level
   B. Application-level
   C. User-level
   D. Unauthorized access-level

10. Which events in an audit log report error messages, file modifications, and security alerts generated by individual applications?

    A. System-level
    B. Application-level
    C. User-level
    D. Unauthorized access-level

11. What is normalization?

    A. The process of rotating older audit logs into long-term storage
    B. The process of translating log files from various systems into a common format
    C. The process of separating normal events from anomalies
    D. The process of analyzing log files

12. Automated audit log analysis software makes manual log analysis unnecessary.

    A. True
    B. False

13. An SIEM is which type of tool?

    A. Access control
    B. Risk analysis
    C. Audit log analysis
    D. Training

13

Access Control Laws, Policies, and Standards

WHILE MANY ORGANIZATIONS adopt access controls to achieve business objectives, these mechanisms are also adopted for many other reasons. This chapter examines the laws and regulations governing information security and the ways that complying with these regulations drives the use of access controls. This chapter also discusses how organizations use policies, standards, procedures, and guidelines to achieve control objectives.

You will read in this chapter what happens when access controls fail. Security breaches can have serious implications ranging from loss of profitability to fines and prison time. The goal of this chapter is to highlight the important role access control plays in the larger scheme of business, governmental regulation, and the operation of critical infrastructures such as the electricity grid.

Chapter 14 Topics

This chapter covers the following topics and concepts:

- U.S. compliance laws and regulations concerning IT
- Access control security policy best practices
- Where access control fits into an overall IT security framework
- Examples of access control policies, standards, procedures, and guidelines

Chapter 14 Goals

When you complete this chapter, you will be able to:

- Explain the major U.S. compliance laws and how they affect IT
- Utilize best practices to create secure access control systems
- Understand how access control fits into an overall IT security framework
- Use examples and case studies to design your own access control policies, standards, procedures, and guidelines

U.S. Compliance Laws and Regulations

Modern corporations are required to be compliant with various government standards. Depending on the industry and the organization, various laws like the Health Insurance Portability and Accountability Act (HIPAA) for the healthcare industry and Sarbanes-Oxley (SOX) for public companies shape the business landscape, requiring organizations to adhere to these standards. Compliance is necessary from an organizational standpoint. It also ensures that organizations implement more secure business practices. Secure business practices help organizations avoid the costs associated with security lapses. Another benefit is that secure business practices can enhance customer confidence by assuring customers that their private information is stored securely.

Creating and adhering to the requirements of these laws can be a difficult task initially. It is usually costly and time-consuming to build a compliant infrastructure. Once an organization creates a compliance framework as a way to protect its sensitive information, compliance with the applicable government regulations can become the priority it needs to be.

In IT, it is imperative that you keep up to date with regulatory compliance laws. Understanding which regulations affect your business can help create a strategy for designing your infrastructure to meet the regulations.

Your organization may already have various security measures in place to maintain compliance, but you must update and maintain them regularly. You must also keep thorough documentation of the systems and procedures that are in place. Your documentation shows the regulatory bodies which steps your organization has taken to be in compliance.

> **NOTE**
>
> Having controls already in place gives your organization a good start toward compliance. You should also set up auditing procedures to keep track of hardware, software, and other IT devices to understand what areas are at higher risk and need further protection.

Different industries need to deal with compliance in different ways. Companies in the financial and healthcare industries, for example, are more strictly regulated than companies in most other industries. Financial and healthcare companies should consider specialized software systems to help meet compliance and track compliance efforts. This is especially useful for companies that have periodic regulatory compliance audits.

Regulatory compliance is an important part of the modern business world. A company that complies with regulatory obligations builds consumer trust—consumers know their information and data are secure. Acting on regulatory requirements helps a corporation build and maintain a secure IT infrastructure, which saves it time and resources. In addition, keeping up to date with regulatory issues makes it easier to remain in compliance when laws and policies are updated in the future. The following sections cover several major regulations that may affect the organization or industry in which you work.

Gramm-Leach-Bliley Act (GLBA)

The GLBA, otherwise known as the Financial Modernization Act of 1999, is primarily aimed at the financial services industry. This not only covers banking but also insurance, securities, brokers, lenders, real estate settlement, tax preparers, and others.

NOTE

The **Gramm-Leach-Bliley Act (GLBA)** covers a wide range of businesses; however, not every type of business is included. GLBA specifically covers any institution that is significantly engaged in financial activities. This covers not only traditional financial institutions but also companies that offer self-financing as well as debt collectors. For example, a university that offers student loans falls under GLBA.

GLBA takes compliance and information security outside of an IT-only world and into the realm of the entire company, requiring every department to be responsible for the security of consumer privacy. Information technology is a major component of the process, but the overall implementation of the security processes is not the sole responsibility of IT.

Requirements

GLBA requires companies to "develop, implement, and maintain a comprehensive written information security program that contains administrative, technical, and physical safeguards that are appropriate to the size and complexity of the entity, the nature and scope of its activities, and the sensitivity of any customer information."

Companies are also required to implement a continuous risk management program. In this program, you must identify potential risks to your company's infrastructure and information. After your company meets GLBA's initial risk identification requirement, you must reassess for risks any time your business or technology changes. After the reassessment, you must update your written policies and procedures. Many companies use a configuration management policy to handle this process. These policies may require any IT project to go through a security audit and that you document the findings of the audit after project completion.

GLBA contains provisions for the protection of nonpublic personal information that financial institutions and their affiliates receive about individuals. The law regulates with whom and how the institution may share that information and provides consumers with the ability to opt out of some types of data-sharing arrangements.

A company's privacy policy is more than just a note on its webpage. GLBA requires that companies notify customers of the privacy policy and receive acknowledgment from the consumer. The notice must be conspicuous and delivered as part of the transaction. If the customer acknowledges receipt of the policy, the company has fulfilled part of its obligations. The notice must remain accessible, and the company is obligated to communicate any change in the same manner.

Companies are obligated to select and retain service providers that are capable of maintaining appropriate safeguards for nonpublic customer information at issue. Your service contracts with providers should require them to implement and maintain these safeguards.

One of GLBA's major components requires companies to have a security program in place that limits access to and protects a consumer's financial data. The institution must protect against any perceived threats to the security and integrity of the consumer's information. Additionally, the institution is obligated to protect against the unauthorized access or use of customer information or records.

GLBA and Access Control

When discussing GLBA in terms of access control policy, an organization should define who can access data and for how long. Any access to sensitive data must be logged to provide accountability to the company and deter misuse of the information.

Data security goes beyond storage and encompasses all aspects of an organization's policies, procedures, and equipment where you hold sensitive data. A company's storage systems must protect against unauthorized access. The company should always know who is accessing the data, when, and why. Technical solutions and strict policies and procedures are all tools your company should use to protect sensitive customer information and prevent legal liabilities.

Health Insurance Portability and Accountability Act (HIPAA)

The **Health Insurance Portability and Accountability Act (HIPAA)** of 1996 has two main parts. Title I protects health insurance coverage for workers and their families if they change or lose their job. Title II, known as the Administrative Simplification provisions, requires the establishment of national standards for electronic healthcare transactions and national identifiers for providers, health insurance plans, and employers. It also addresses security and privacy of health data. Title II has the most significant impact on IT departments.

The following Title II rules directly affect an IT department:

- Privacy Rule
- Transactions and Codes Set Rule
- Unique Identifier Standards Rule
- Security Rule
- Enforcement Rule

Privacy Rule

The Privacy Rule took effect on April 14, 2003. It regulates the use and disclosure of protected information held by covered entities. It establishes regulations for the use and disclosure of **protected health information (PHI)**, which is any information that concerns health status, health care, or any payment for health care that can be linked to the individual. This is interpreted very broadly and includes all of an individual's medical records and payment history.

 NOTE

HIPAA-covered entities include health plans, healthcare clearinghouses, and healthcare providers who engage in certain electronic transactions

If HIPAA applies to your organization, you must protect this medical information, which may be disclosed only in the following circumstances:

- To the individual within 30 days of a request
- When the covered entity has obtained the written permission of the individual
- When required by law
- To facilitate treatment, payment, or healthcare operations

When disclosing PHI, it's the covered entity's responsibility to disclose the minimum amount of information necessary. If your organization is a covered entity, you must secure all communications and transmission of PHI.

Transactions and Codes Set Rule

The Transactions and Code Set Rule of HIPAA requires a common standard for the transfer of all health information between healthcare providers and the organizations that process payment for these services. Before HIPAA, different entities had different methods to exchange information. This was a cumbersome and expensive system for healthcare providers. With HIPAA, all payees must accept a common standard for electronic data.

Unique Identifier Standards Rule

The Unique Identifier Standards Rule handles the creation and use of unique identifiers for providers, health plans, employers, and patients. The identifiers are as follows:

- The employer identifier, which is based on the IRS-assigned Employer Identification Number
- The patient identifier, which will be a standard unique way of identifying patients; currently on hold due to privacy legislation
- The national provider identifier, which was originally developed for the Medicare system
- The health plan identifier, which is a nine-digit number with a check digit developed for HIPAA

Security Rule

The Security Rule is a complement to the Privacy Rule that covers how PHI is secured. The Security Rule deals specifically with **electronic protected health information (EPHI)**. It lays out three layers of security safeguards required for compliance: administrative, physical, and technical. For each type, the rule specifies various standards and implementation specifications.

If your organization is a covered entity, you must follow these administrative safeguards:

- Adopt a written set of privacy procedures and designate a privacy officer who is responsible for developing all required procedures.
- Reference policies and procedures to ensure organizational buy-in and management oversight to comply with documented security controls.
- Identify employees or groups of employees who have access to EPHI in your procedures.
- Restrict access to EPHI to only those employees who need the information for their job function.
- Address access authorization, modification, and termination in your procedures.
- Show that you are providing ongoing PHI training to employees.
- Ensure that all of your third-party vendors have a framework in place to comply with HIPAA regulations.
- Implement contingency plans for responding to emergencies and ensure you have backup and recovery procedures in place for all PHI.
- Perform internal audits to review HIPAA compliance.
- Implement procedures for addressing and responding to security breaches.

> **NOTE**
>
> When information flows over a public network, you must apply some form of encryption. If the information is on a closed network, existing access controls are sufficient and encryption is optional.

Be sure to put these technical safeguards into action:

- Protect information systems containing PHI from intrusion.
- Ensure the PHI contained within your systems is not changed or erased in an unauthorized manner.
- Use data corroboration, such as check sum, message authentication, and digital signatures, to ensure data integrity.
- Authenticate the identity of all entities which whom your organization communicates. You can do this with password systems, two- or three-way handshakes, telephone callbacks, and token systems.
- Document all of your HIPAA procedures, and make this documentation available to the government to determine compliance.
- Include a written record of all configuration settings on all components of the network in information technology documentation.
- Implement documented risk analysis and risk management programs.

You must ensure the following physical safeguards:

- Put controls in place to govern the addition and removal of software and hardware to the environment.
- Carefully control and monitor access to equipment containing EPHI.
- Limit access to equipment and software to authorized individuals.
- Create physical access controls that consist of facility security plans, maintenance records, visitor records, and escorts.
- Incorporate proper security policies for workstations that access EPHI.
- Train contractors or third-party agents on their physical access responsibilities.

Enforcement Rule

The HIPAA Enforcement Rule was created in February of 2006 by the Department of Health and Human Services (HHS). It is the final rule that details the basis and procedures for imposing civil monetary penalties on covered entities that violate HIPAA.

This rule is a unification of the patchwork of existing rules and regulations that governed the enforcement of different parts of HIPAA. The HHS Office for Civil Rights (OCR) is responsible for enforcing the Privacy Rule, and the Centers for Medicare and Medicaid Services (CMS) is responsible for the Security Rule. The Enforcement Rule brings together and extends all of the other rules, resulting in a unified comprehensive policy on enforcement of compliance.

The rule requires HHS to try to resolve compliance issues in an informal manner before resorting to monetary penalties. In the informal process, the covered entity must submit a corrective

> **NOTE**
>
> The **Health Information Technology for Economic and Clinical Health (HITECH) Act** of 2009 extended HIPAA to include an update to the civil and criminal penalties section and requires notification of the information owner if any breach causing the disclosure of PHI occurs.

action plan to show how it is going to remedy the noncompliance. If these means do not work, HHS proceeds to the civil monetary penalty phase.

Civil penalties in the Enforcement Rule are $100 per violation up to a maximum of $25,000 for all violations of an identical requirement or prohibition during a calendar year. The Enforcement Rule identifies the following three factors to be used in calculating the number of violations:

- The number of times the covered entity takes the prohibited action
- The number of people affected
- The duration of a violation in days

HIPAA compliance is an all-encompassing endeavor. It requires every level of an organization to be on board. By fully understanding your business model and goals, you can help your company to comply with HIPAA, ensuring your organization is a more secure environment for customer information. Organizations must realize that HIPAA is not just an IT issue; HIPAA affects every aspect of the organization. Anything from failing to utilizing network security to failing to implement an awareness program can result in an organization being out of compliance.

Sarbanes-Oxley (SOX) Act

The Sarbanes-Oxley (SOX) Act of 2002 was created to protect investors by improving the accuracy and reliability of the financial disclosures of publicly traded companies. SOX accomplishes this by strengthening existing penalties and making corporate officers personally responsible for the disclosures. It imposes harsher punishment, large fines, and prison sentences for any individual who knowingly alters or destroys information with the intent to obstruct an investigation. This affects IT departments in the form of record retention policies and access to an organization's electronic records such as email and accounting system data.

SOX contains 11 titles that describe specific mandates or requirements for financial reporting:

- **Title I: Public Company Accounting Oversight Board (PCAOB)**—Provides independent oversight of public accounting firms. The PCAOB exists to prevent third-party accounting firms from using fraudulent accounting practices on behalf of their clients. The PCAOB's Auditing Standard No. 5 specifies a top-down approach that might limit the scope of review of IT systems.
- **Title II: Auditor Independence**—Establishes standards that require external auditors to be completely independent from the firms they audit, which limits conflicts of interest.
- **Title III: Corporate Responsibility**—Mandates that executives must take individual, personal responsibility for the accuracy and completeness of corporate financial reports. It also deals with the integrity of financial data contained within those reports.

- **Title IV: Enhanced Financial Disclosures**—Describes enhanced reporting procedures required for financial transactions. Also requires internal controls that ensure that financial reports and disclosures are accurate.
- **Title V: Analyst Conflicts of Interest**—Establishes standards designed to prevent conflicts of interest among securities analysts and to improve investor confidence in analysts' reporting.
- **Title VI: Commission Resources and Authority**—Defines the conditions under which the Securities and Exchange Commission (SEC) has the authority to censure or bar securities professionals from practice.
- **Title VII: Studies and Reports**—Defines the studies the Comptroller General and the SEC are required to perform and report upon.
- **Title VIII: Corporate and Criminal Fraud Accountability**— Imposes documentation retention requirements on companies and auditors. It also describes specific criminal penalties for manipulation, destruction, or alteration of financial records.

> **NOTE**
>
> The Securities and Exchange Commission (SEC) is an independent agency of the U.S. government that holds primary responsibility for enforcing the federal securities laws and regulating the securities industry, the nation's stock and options exchanges, and other electronic securities markets.

- **Title IX: White Collar Crime Penalty Enhancement**—Increases the criminal penalties associated with white-collar crimes and conspiracies.
- **Title X: Corporate Tax Returns**—States that the chief executive officer should sign the company tax return.
- **Title XI: Corporate Fraud Accountability**—Identifies fraud and records tampering as criminal offenses and specifies penalties for those offenses.

SOX regulations, especially parts I, III, IV, and VIII, have a direct impact on corporate IT. Your organization needs to secure financial data with strong access controls to guarantee its integrity. If your company is a public entity, you are obligated to secure financial data so it is not modified or removed by anyone.

The role of IT in a SOX environment comes in the form of controls. You must put controls in place to handle how information is generated, accessed, collected, stored and processed, transmitted, and used throughout the organization. Implementing controls makes your organization more efficient and protects the integrity of those data.

> **NOTE**
>
> The main role of SOX is to stop internal fraud. Internal fraud is one of the most difficult crimes to stop because the perpetrators understand the systems and controls in place. The layered controls and external independent audits mandated by SOX are not foolproof but will make the organization more resilient.

14

Access Control Laws, Policies, and Standards

For example, SOX Section 404 requires publicly traded companies to have policies in place to secure, document, and process any information dealing with financial results. This requires IT to have strict procedures when dealing with the electronic versions of these documents. You must have these controls and procedures certified by an outside auditing firm.

Family Educational Rights and Privacy Act (FERPA)

The **Family Educational Rights and Privacy Act (FERPA)** of 1974 is a federal law that protects the privacy and ensures the accuracy of student educational records. Educational institutions are required to protect educational records by adhering to the strict guidelines set in the act. The faculty and staff must be familiar with FERPA before they may release any student's educational record. This regulation requires physical access controls, requiring people to adhere to established regulations.

FERPA establishes a student's right to know the information, location, and purpose of an educational record. Information in that record must be kept confidential unless the student has explicitly given permission for its disclosure. Educational institutions must control access to a student's record by physical, logical, and administrative processes and procedures.

Educational records may appear in the following forms:

- Written documents stored in the students' folders
- Computer media
- Microfilm and microfiche
- Video tapes, audio tapes, or CDs
- Film
- Photographs
- Any record that contains personally identifiable information

The following items are exempt from FERPA:

 NOTE

Some information that's exempt from FERPA, such as medical records, is covered by other federal regulations. Safeguards must be in place to guard against disclosure of that information, even though it is not covered by FERPA.

- Private notes made by faculty or staff for the purpose of assisting memory; as long as they are kept in the sole position of the maker, they may be shared with substitute teachers
- Law enforcement records
- Medical records
- Statistical data that do not contain personally identifiable information
- Pregraded materials before the final grade is determined by the faculty

There are two types of educational records under FERPA, each with its own rules for disclosure:

- **Directory information:** May be released by the educational institution without the written consent of the student. **Directory information** includes name, address, phone number, email address, dates of attendance, degree earned, enrollment status, and field of study. Students have the right to limit the release of directory information. This can be done by submitting a formal written request to the school to limit disclosure.
- **Non-directory information:** Any educational information not explicitly considered directory information. Nondirectory information may not be disclosed to any party including the parent or guardian of the student without the student's written consent. Faculty and staff can only access nondirectory information for legitimate academic purposes.

To protect student privacy and maintain compliance with FERPA, an educational institution must implement administrative and technical safeguards to disclosure. To ensure compliance, an institution must get a student's written consent for the release of any educational information. Administrative measures can consist of consent forms that outline the specific records being disclosed, with a space for the student's signature. Technical safeguards need to be both physical, such as a locking cabinet; and logical access controls on all electronic documents. Procedures and controls must be in place to prevent unauthorized access to the educational records.

Communications Assistance for Law Enforcement Act (CALEA)

The **Communications Assistance for Law Enforcement Act (CALEA)** of 1994 requires that telecommunications carriers and the makers of equipment used by the telecommunications industry take steps to facilitate the electronic surveillance activities of law enforcement agencies.

Firms subject to CALEA must cooperate with legitimate law enforcement requests to conduct electronic surveillance on an individual and provide detailed calling records of individuals under investigation. This normally involves providing law enforcement officers with a network tap that enables their surveillance activities. In addition, it may include the provision of detailed communications records gathered by either a pen register or a trap-and-trace device. Pen registers are used to capture the destination address information for outbound electronic communications. Trap-and-trace devices are used to capture the source information of inbound electronic communications.

Children's Internet Protection Act (CIPA)

The **Children's Internet Protection Act (CIPA)** is the federal law enacted in 2000 that addresses Internet access in public schools and libraries. Any school or library using the federal E-Rate program is subject to CIPA. E-Rate offers discounts to libraries and schools ensuring that they have affordable access to modern telecommunications and information services.

CIPA deals with the implementation of protection systems meant to handle inbound threats, such as viruses and spam, and outbound information leaks. Failure to be in compliance will result in a loss of federal funding.

The safety measures that are required by this regulation are as follows:

- Filter or block pictures that are obscene, contain child pornography, or are harmful to minors on computers that minors can access.
- Adopt a policy addressing the following:
  - Access by minors of inappropriate materials
  - The safety and security of minors when using electronic communications such as email
  - Unauthorized access, including hacking and other unlawful activities by minors
  - Unauthorized disclosure of personal information regarding minors
  - Restricting minors' access to materials that are harmful to them

Having effective access controls is imperative for entities covered by CIPA. Other security safeguards are also necessary, which include web filtering, firewalls, virus and spyware protection, and monitoring systems. These regulations affect all Internet-accessible computers in the covered entities including staff, administrative, and student workstations. There are provisions within CIPA to permit disabling of these safeguards for adults conducting research or for other lawful purposes.

Food and Drug Administration (FDA) Regulations

Title 21 CFR Part 11 of the Code of Federal Regulations (**21 CFR Part 11**) deals with Food and Drug Administration (FDA) guidelines on electronic records and signatures. This title requires industries that fall under FDA regulation to implement controls such as audits, audit trails, electronic signatures, and policies for software and systems that process electronic data.

21 CFR Part 11 calls for all FDA-regulated organizations to implement the following:

NOTE

21 CFR Part 11 applies to any organization involved with the production of food, prescription and nonprescription drugs, medical devices, cosmetics, dietary supplements, veterinary medicines, and other related fields. The goal of this regulation is to define standards for electronic records and signatures, which are considered equivalent to paper records and handwritten signatures.

- System access limited to authorized individuals
- The use of operational system checks
- The use of authority checks
- The use of device checks
- Appropriate education and task training for anyone who develops, maintains, or uses electronic systems
- Appropriate controls for documentation in place
- Controls for both open systems and closed system requirements related to electronic signatures

In addition, there are requirements for entities that keep paper copies of all records. Organizations can use paper copies for regulatory purposes, but the paper copies must be certified as being complete and accurate.

Other sections of FDA regulations may be applicable to healthcare organizations. For example, manufacturers of medical devices are governed by 21 CFR Part 806, which covers reports and records, while 21 CFR Part 802 applies to the quality controls around medical devices.

North American Electric Reliability Council (NERC)

The **North American Electric Reliability Council (NERC)** handles regulation of energy and utility companies. NERC was created in 1968 to ensure that the North American energy network is secure, adequate, and reliable. IT security is mostly concerned with the creation of guidelines for strong access controls and processes.

Physical guidelines include physical protective measures for all critical infrastructures. A physical barrier must be in place, access points identified and controlled, and all access must be logged, either electronically via video or written in a logbook.

Electronic security guidelines include procedures meant to provide protective measures for assets. If your organization falls

NOTE

Compliance with NERC standards requires dealing with physical, electronic, and personal security as well as training and awareness programs. NERC also requires documentation and auditing of all protective measures of critical resources.

within this industry, you should ensure you've accurately inventoried your systems, limited access to systems by role, created an electronic security perimeter, and implemented account management procedures. These procedures include audits, passwords, and network security policies. You are also required to create a disaster recovery plan that includes backup and data restoration strategies and the documentation of spare parts and equipment. You must document all procedures, which can be subject to yearly audits and reviews.

You must also have requirements in place to handle background checks for employees and contractors. You are required to document procedures for contractor and vendor risk assessments.

It is also mandatory that you provide training for anyone with access to the energy or utility infrastructure, including contract workers, employees, and vendors.

Homeland Security Presidential Directive 12 (HSPD 12)

The **Homeland Security Presidential Directive 12 (HSPD 12)** was issued in August of 2007 and was initiated to enforce the standardization of security identification credentials for government employees and contractors. This standard covers both physical and logical access to government resources.

The standard is broken into two parts with the requirements of Part 2 built upon the requirements of Part 1.

Part 1

Part 1 covers common identification, security, and privacy requirements. The minimum requirements for a federal personal identification system include personal identity proofing, registration, and issuance process for employees and contractors.

To comply with Part 1, an organization must:

- Adopt and accredit a registration process in line with National Institute of Standards and Technology (NIST) standards.
- Initiate the National Agency Check with Written Inquiries (NACI) or other suitability or national security investigation prior to credential issuance.
- Include language implementing the standard in all contracts with third-party vendors and contractors.
- Verify that all current employees and contractors have gone through the appropriate background checks and develop a plan for those who have not.

Part 2

Part 2 deals with the uniformity and portability of identification. This contains detailed specifications to handle technical interoperability of identifications between departments and agencies. This includes card elements, system interfaces, and security controls required to store and retrieve data from the identification card.

All U.S. government departments and agencies must deploy products and systems that meet these requirements to comply with Part 2:

- Issue and require the use of identification credentials for all employees and contractors, compliant with Part 1 of the standard.

- Implement the technical requirements of the standard for card hardware in the areas of personal authentication, access controls, and card management.
- Use the appropriate card authentication mechanism with the additional reliance on visual authentication, depending on the level of risk in the facility accessed.
- Use digital certificates to verify authentication.

These standards exist to make it easier for governmental agencies to exchange information securely and reliably.

Americans with Disabilities Act (ADA)

The **Americans with Disabilities Act (ADA)** includes provisions ensuring that everyone has equal access to public accommodations, regardless of any disability they might have. While this regulation is not directly germane to cybersecurity, federal compliance officials should be aware that ADA Section 508 does govern accessibility to websites run by the federal government.

Access Control Security Policy Best Practices

Best practices cover the policies, standards, procedures, and guidelines for a given topic. This section covers best practices for access controls, which can help your organization implement a strong access control environment.

Private Sector—Enterprise Organizations

Access control security policies are generally different for enterprise-level organizations than they are for smaller organizations. An enterprise organization may have employees across a wide geographic area, even in multiple countries. These organizations often have a complex organizational structure with several fairly autonomous divisions, each with their own critical assets and access control policies.

Security policies for enterprise organizations must take this complexity into account and balance the business needs of each division with the access control and security needs of the organization as a whole. In this section, you will learn more about how large enterprises manage access control.

Defining an Authorization Policy

An authorization policy is a high-level document that defines how an organization will assign and enforce access control rights. It is important to write a formal authorization policy rather than simply implement random access controls. A written policy defines a high-level strategy for access control security and identifies the organization's security goals and compliance obligations.

An authorization policy should also take into account the fact that access controls do not exist in a vacuum. Access controls for systems are dependent on physical access controls, and application security is interrelated with systems and data security. An authorization policy defines these relationships and ensures that steps taken to secure one element of an organization's infrastructure will promote the security of all of the other elements as well.

Access Control for Facilities

Securing the data center or other facility that stores sensitive resources is a vitally important part of an access control plan. You can encrypt and protect a database server that holds customer records with a multistage authentication system, but what happens if someone physically steals it? The data is unavailable to those with legitimate access.

An authorization policy for facilities should dictate the following points:

> **NOTE**
>
> The authorization policy should also anticipate and account for employees who may find the entry system inconvenient and disable it by propping doors open. To compensate, the policy may specify repercussions for employees who undermine the locking mechanisms or simply call for automatically closing and locking doors.

- **Appropriate entry system access controls:** An authorization policy should specify which areas should be locked at all times and may dictate whether a one-, two-, or three-stage locking mechanism is appropriate given the resources in that area. For example, a data facility housing an organization's database servers may justify a two- or three-stage locking mechanism that incorporates both a token and a biometric authentication mechanism. You would elaborate on the specific implementation details of what type of biometric system to use in a separate, lower-level document.

- **Secondary locks on equipment and storage cabinets within the facility:** To further secure specific pieces of equipment, such as a database server that stores mission-critical data, the policy may call for secondary locks on that equipment. This section of the policy should also dictate which employees should be given keys to that equipment.

- **Prevention of social engineering:** The authorization policy should specify goals for the prevention of social engineering. These goals should focus primarily on training employees and on their acceptance of their role in preventing social engineering attacks.

Access Control for Systems

Once you dictate how to secure the data center or other facility, you should secure the systems within that data center as well. This is doubly important for systems that are not stored in a dedicated facility with strong physical security.

A good authorization policy includes goals for securing systems. Some points to include are:

- Limit access to those employees who have a legitimate need for resources. Which employees need access to specific resources varies by organization. In general, if an employee does not need access to a system in order to perform his or her duties, you should not grant access regardless of the employee's position.

- Describe a strong password policy that includes password length requirements, use of several types of characters (uppercase and lowercase, numeric, and special characters), and change frequency. In this section, you should be careful to balance the employees' need for passwords that are easy to remember and the ideals of robust passwords. If the policy dictates that users should change their passwords weekly, for example, employees might begin reusing old passwords, use the same password with a minor change, or simply write them down. These practices make it easier for employees to remember their frequently changing passwords. They also make those passwords less secure, defeating the purpose of the policy.

Access Control for Applications

Applications are one of the most common sources of vulnerability in any system. They are often designed with functionality in mind, not security. This can lead to security testing as an afterthought. Because you cannot control the practices of various software vendors, your access control policy should include as many precautions as possible on the systems end to safeguard the environment for which you are responsible.

Key elements to include in the policy are:

 TIP

You should detail the actual methods for testing and securing third-party applications in a lower-level document. Keep the policy document generic so that it can remain in effect for many years. If the policy dictates specific testing procedures, you would have to update it as technology evolves.

- **Standard testing procedures for any third-party application installed in the environment:** The authorization policy should dictate that all access controls within applications be examined and tested for security. You should replace applications that do not handle access controls securely—for example, by storing application user data in an unprotected flat file or unencrypted database table—with more secure alternatives, update to a newer version, or secure on the systems end.

- **Limiting application access:** Many organizations seek to avoid operational issues by running applications under an administrative account. While this may be expedient, it can also cause serious problems if the application is compromised by granting an attacker administrative access to the underlying operating system. Organizations implementing applications should follow the principle of least privilege and install software with an account that has only the specific permissions necessary to run the application.

Access Control for Data

Data access is the core of any authorization policy. Access control for facilities, systems, and applications exists to protect the data stored in those facilities and systems, and the applications used to access and process those data. An authorization policy for data should include these points:

- **Specify which data should be encrypted**—Passwords are an obvious example, but other data may also justify encryption, depending on the organization's regulatory compliance needs and other factors. The authorization policy should not dictate specific data elements to be encrypted but rather should provide criteria for encrypted data. For example, a policy might specify that you must encrypt any data defined as protected health information under HIPAA. This allows systems engineers and database administrators to decide whether a specific data element qualifies for encryption, even if that data did not exist when you wrote the policy.

- **Enforce the principle of lowest possible access**—This states that if read access is sufficient for an employee to perform a necessary task, the employee should not be granted read-write access.

Access Control for Remote Access

Providing remote access capabilities can greatly increase employees' productivity by allowing them to do their jobs wherever they need to be, from a hotel room to a job site. However, with increased levels of access come new access control challenges. When every person who connects to the internal network does so from a workstation on that network, you don't have to worry about communications being hijacked. When employees gain remote access, they can use any Internet connection to access the internal network via a virtual private network (VPN). Because you have no control over those Internet access points, you should always assume the worst—that they are being actively monitored by hackers.

Including the following points in an authorization policy will provide direction for implementing specific controls to secure remote access:

* Provide remote access only to those employees who have a legitimate need to work off-site. Grant it on a temporary basis for those who travel or work offsite occasionally.
* Grant access to the VPN through a two-stage authentication process that includes both a strong password and a token device. You should document specific password creation guidance in a separate password policy document.
* Outline specific guidelines in your authorization policy on acceptable activity while connected to the VPN.

Public Sector—Federal, State, County, and City Government

In the public sector, the use of best practices is often required. In the case of access control, best practices are essential to an organization's information technology infrastructure. In the public sector, you are required by regulation to create access controls to prevent unauthorized access and disclosure to both logical and physical assets. Establishing documented policies, procedures, and safeguards to address the regulations is also often mandatory. Best practices can help meet these regulatory requirements, and groups like NIST often provide organizations in the public sector with a road map to compliance.

The Federal Information Security Management Act (FISMA) of 2002 sets forth specific requirements for implementing best practices in federal government agencies. In the public sector, best practices are more than simply recommended guidelines or strategies for successful access control. These legally mandated practices include:

* Conducting periodic risk assessments to ensure that security activities and resources address the highest priority risks an organization faces at the present time.
* Implementing policies and procedures based on the most recent risk assessment.
* Creating plans for the security of networks, systems, and other resources.
* Conducting employee and contractor training to ensure that all personnel who interact with sensitive data are aware of the security implications of their activities and know how to comply with policies designed to minimize those risks.
* Testing periodically to ensure that policies and procedures designed to lower risk are working correctly.

 TIP

Design policies and procedures to lower risks to an acceptable level and ensure that information security is addressed throughout the life cycle of applications and systems.

NOTE

Test policies and procedures annually, at a minimum. The frequency with which you perform tests within a 12-month period depends on the risk involved.

NOTE

The Department of Defense Information Assurance Certification and Accreditation Process, or DIACAP, is designed to ensure that risk management is a fundamental concern for all information systems within the Department of Defense. It sets out best practices for evaluating the validity of information, ensuring that data have not been tampered with.

- Creating processes to address any shortcomings in the organization's information security policies, procedures, and practices.
- Implementing processes for detecting, reporting, and responding to security incidents.
- Incorporating continuity plans for the organization that will allow critical operations to continue in the event of a disaster, including but not limited to natural disasters, serious security incidents, and other crises.

The best practices required by governmental regulations are similar in practice and intent to those used in the private sector.

Critical Infrastructure, Including Utilities and Transportation

Modern society depends on complex systems to work. These systems are known as critical infrastructure. Critical infrastructure provides essential services necessary for modern life. This includes water supply; roads, rail, and other transportation networks; sewers; the energy grid; emergency services; communications networks; governmental and military facilities; and more. Best practices for how to handle failure in this infrastructure are critical.

Critical infrastructure assets can fall under the public or private sector. The water supply system is clearly within the public sector domain, while most communications networks are owned by companies in the private sector. Transportation systems often fall under both public and private sectors. Consider Amtrak, for example. It is a private company but it is heavily subsidized by the government. When implementing best practices for critical infrastructure, choose the best practices that apply based on the infrastructure in question.

There are some special considerations to keep in mind when you deal with critical infrastructure, especially with the devices and systems that control elements of that infrastructure. The next section deals with these special considerations in greater depth.

Supervisory Control and Data Acquisition (SCADA) Process Control Systems

NOTE

A SCADA system includes hardware, controllers, networks, user interfaces, software, and communications equipment, used together to monitor and manage utilities. SCADA systems have monitors both in close proximity to the control center and offsite.

Supervisory control and data acquisition (SCADA) process control systems are at the heart of much of society's critical infrastructure. SCADA systems monitor and control telecommunications, water and waste control, energy, and transportation, among other industries and utilities. SCADA devices use local area network (LAN), wide area network (WAN), and wireless communications infrastructures for monitoring and control purposes. These systems can be very complex. The systems are used for everything from monitoring the temperature in a room within an electrical substation to monitoring all of the activity in a waste management plant. Access controls to these devices are critical.

SCADA systems have the ability to monitor and control utility systems in real time. The monitoring provides readings from meters and sensors to a central facility through devices called **remote terminal units (RTUs)** to the user interface at regular intervals. The operator at the central facility is able to interact with the SCADA system to modify or override settings as necessary.

This interface, called a **human machine interface (HMI)**, is where the operator views the data that are received and processed. The HMI is connected to a database that gathers information from the RTUs. **Programmable logic controllers (PLCs)** are also connected to this system. PLCs are designed to generate graphs on logistical information and trends. They also provide access to troubleshooting guides. These devices allow SCADA operators to efficiently monitor and manage the infrastructure.

SCADA systems are a point of risk for the utilities that use them. These systems were often designed with the assumption that they would not be connected to outside networks. They were also designed with misplaced faith in the practice of security through obscurity. The designers of SCADA systems also relied on logical security and did not consider physical security. This has resulted in a critical system that is inherently insecure.

The ISA Security Compliance Institute (ISCI) publishes industry standard guidelines that may be used to certify secure SCADA devices. Devices meeting the ISCI requirements may be awarded the ISASecure Certified Device designation. It is imperative that organizations understand the limitations of SCADA system security. You must physically secure devices and WANs. Strong access controls, such as the following, in both the physical and logical realm are necessary:

- Physical security on collection points
- Encrypted communications between collection points, controllers, and the central hub
- Two-way authentication between remote points and a centralized controller
- Easily managed user rights for removing or modifying users
- Segregation of SCADA systems from the rest of the network systems

Following these practices will make SCADA systems more secure and lessen the risk of a security breach.

Threats and Vulnerabilities

It is imperative to conduct a threat and vulnerability assessment of critical infrastructures. Some of the more difficult to handle are those threats and vulnerabilities related to interdependencies and interoperability of the various systems. Understanding these interdependencies is essential to securing the most critical systems. Identifying single-point vulnerabilities is also essential to risk mitigation.

One of the first steps you must take when analyzing risk and developing a mitigation plan is to identify which assets are more critical. Determining which systems rely on each other

 TIP

Critical infrastructures are threatened by more than just manmade threats. Natural events can also seriously threaten critical infrastructures. Any plan developed to protect these systems must account for all threats.

is vital. If a water treatment plant is damaged, how will that affect other services? It is essential that you identify critical points that can cause multiple systems to fail.

Redundancy for these critical systems is also vital to risk mitigation. They must be completely separate systems. Two power lines running on the same path do not achieve redundancy. One event, whether it's natural or unnatural, could take out both systems. To mitigate risk, infrastructure design must avoid single points of failure.

IT Security Policy Framework

Organizations have policies and procedures in place for various business units such as accounting and human resources. They also have essential policies for information security and access. The challenge for IT departments is to establish and continually update access control policies in an evolving technology and business environment. Creating and documenting standards for logical and physical security of the organization is essential in the protection of the organization's infrastructure as shown in **FIGURE 14-1**.

The size of the organization, the types of information used, and the industry in which the company exists are all factors to consider when building an IT security policy framework. This framework must address both logical and physical security. The human aspect of security is vital as well. Without training and awareness programs, the best defense can fail. At the heart of these systems is a strong access control policy.

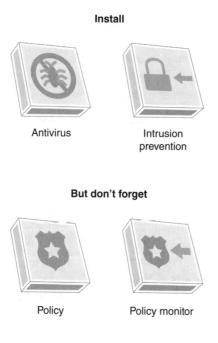

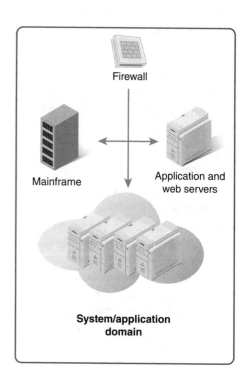

FIGURE 14-1

Protecting the infrastructure through logical and physical security policies and procedures.

Before discussing security policy frameworks, it is helpful to define a few terms that are often used interchangeably:

NOTE

Failure to require strong access controls in a company's security policy framework will contribute to vulnerabilities and breaches in the system. These breaches may result in the disclosure and loss of valuable information and assets and can expose the organization to civil and legal penalties.

- **Policy**—A policy is a document that describes specific requirements or rules that must be met in a given area. An organization's acceptable use policy typically describes what is and is not acceptable use of the organization's computing resources.
- **Standard**—A standard is a collection of requirements that must be met by anyone who performs a given task or works on a specific system. An organization might have a standard that describes the specific tests that must be performed before an application can be released to the production environment.
- **Guideline**—A guideline is a set of suggestions and best practices for meeting standards and policies. An organization might have strong password guidelines that describe the use of mnemonic devices or passphrases for creating strong passwords. Guidelines are strongly recommended practices but do not carry the weight of a mandatory requirement. An employee could use a random password generator to create a strong password, and thus meet the organization's strong password policy without following the guidelines laid out for choosing passwords.
- **Procedure**—A procedure is a set of specific steps to be taken to achieve a desired result. Procedures are often written to ensure that tasks are completed in the same way each time, preventing unexpected problems. For example, an IT department might have a procedure for changing a password on a workstation. That procedure will include a step-by-step workflow with enough detail that anyone in the IT department could follow and expect the password to be changed correctly. Well-written procedures eliminate the problem of critical information being stored in one individual's mind. If that individual leaves the organization, the information is lost.

A policy is a general-purpose document that describes high-level organizational rules and requirements. A standard is a more specific implementation of a policy. Guidelines are strong suggestions for implementing policies and standards. Procedures are step-by-step outlines for completing a specific task as outlined in the guidelines and standards.

Which Policies Are Needed for Access Controls?

The specific policies needed for access controls vary by organization, but in general, organizations should have policies that describe which users have access to sensitive systems and data, for what purpose, and for how long.

The following are common organization policies:

- **Acceptable use policy (AUP):** Describes what tasks can and cannot be performed using the organization's computing resources
- **Password policy:** Describes the organization's requirements for strong password creation and maintenance

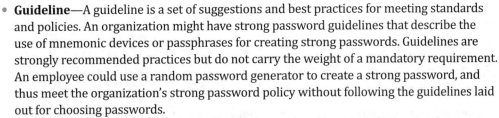

- **Account management policy:** Describes how new accounts are to be created and secured, and old accounts deleted
- **Remote access policy:** Defines standards for connecting to the organization's network offsite

These policies provide a basis for an organization's access control systems. You should base them on the organization's business needs and risk assessment.

What Standards Are Needed to Support These Policies?

A standard is a set of detailed processes or methods for implementing technology, hardware, or software solutions. Access control standards are the rules that an organization uses to control access to its IT assets. You need these standards for all points in access control from creation of the users, to granting and revoking rights, to user removal. Standards are important guides for evaluating an organization's compliance with regulation.

Standards documents, established by collective agreement and approved by management, provide for common repeatable rules. This helps to safeguard access controls and policies. This allows an organization better control in protecting its infrastructure and assets. Some common standards documents that many organizations use are:

- **User account standard:** Describes the various types of user accounts on specific systems and networks
- **Identification standard:** Describes how user IDs will be defined based on the individual's name, job function, or other identifying information
- **Remote access standard:** Describes the specific tools to be used to implement the organization's remote access policy
- **Application development standard:** Describes the security precautions that must be designed into any application developed in-house

Every organization will have a unique set of standards based on business needs. These are the most common standards that most organizations use.

Which Procedures Are Needed to Implement These Policies?

You must establish access control procedures by outlining the steps needed to access organizational IT assets. Procedures should be included that detail authentication, account management, password management, and remote access. Additionally, you will need access determination policies and systems to restrict unauthorized access.

Procedures outlining specific steps for each process should be developed and used. The following is an example of an access request change procedure:

1. User fills out an access request form.
2. IT receives the form and passes it to the correct authority for approval.
3. The form is reviewed and authorization is granted or denied.
4. IT implements the access rights modification.
5. After signoff, IT files the request in the user's file to verify access and to provide information to an audit, if required.

This is a simple example of a procedure. Having explicit procedures is vital for the efficient and consistent application of an access control policy. Without written procedures, the risk of mistakes and errors in an organization's access controls grows dangerously high.

What Guidelines Are Needed for Departments and End Users?

Guidelines are a collection of suggestions and best practices relating to a standard or procedure. A guideline doesn't necessarily need to be met but compliance is strongly encouraged. Any access control policy in an organization will make reference to guidelines that are in existence in the organization. Although these actions are strongly encouraged, it is important to remember that these are not fixed rules. Guidelines are best viewed as recommendations.

An organization can have various guidelines for department and end users relating to access control policies. All of the information pertaining to the guideline should be included within a policy or procedure that a department or end user is required to follow. Inclusions into these official documents will lend weight to the guideline and allow a system to easily get them to the end users.

Some examples of departmental guidelines are:

- Department heads and managers should review access control systems periodically but not less than annually.
- User accounts should be disabled after 30 days of inactivity.

Some examples of individual guidelines are:

- Individuals should periodically review access control policies, standards, procedures, and guidelines.
- Individuals should not store critical information in their email accounts. Rather, critical information should be stored as documents on the file server.
- Users should not write down their passwords or base them on personally identifiable information. Instead, they should use a mnemonic to create a strong password that is also easy to remember.

Both individual and departmental guidelines should be written as helpful guidance for compliance with more official documents such as policies, standards, and procedures.

Case Studies and Examples

You have seen different types of access control policies and the way standards and procedures are used to implement them. Now, let's look at some real-world examples of access control policies being used.

Private Sector Case Study

A large, private pharmaceutical corporation created a new public entity called Acme, a medical device company. Acme's staff already had experience with HIPAA and knew that it would have to set up procedures and policies to enforce compliance. As a new public company, however, it would also have to deal with SOX and a new set of regulations.

Acme was at an advantage from the start with staff already experienced in HIPAA. Not only was the business intelligence in place on how to navigate HIPAA regulations but there was also already compliance buy-in at the employee and management level. A multi-departmental team was created to bring the company into compliance. This could have been a major hurdle for the company, but it was easily achieved.

HIPAA polices were cloned from the former parent company, compliance forms created, and electronic and physical document repositories were created to store compliance documents. The company secured these repositories with physical and logical access control policies. They also developed automated processes for storing, updating, and removing documents. Access was limited to a strict need basis, with a role-based access control (RBAC) system put in place to determine if users had rights to access or modify documents. Regulations were created for handling EPHI. The staff created training documents for new hires. The compliance team also identified and trained privacy officers in all of Acme's business units. By leveraging existing business knowledge, HIPAA compliance was quickly achieved and the compliance team could focus on a brand new set of regulations with Sarbanes-Oxley.

> **NOTE**
>
> Role-based access control (RBAC) is an alternative to traditional discretionary access control (DAC) and mandatory access control (MAC) policies. RBAC is becoming more common, particularly for commercial applications. It uses individual and group roles as the basis for organizing access.

SOX was a brand-new challenge. The first step toward compliance for Acme was to research the new regulations. Already having a business culture that was accustomed to the need for regulatory compliance was a big advantage. The team quickly realized they could expand and reuse many of the HIPAA policies to gain SOX compliance as well.

They created new classes of information and roles in the access control systems. The document repositories already had the necessary safeguards in place to protect SOX documents, so they created a new class of document in both the physical and logical repositories. Compliance officers were already in place in the form of HIPAA privacy officers. They further trained these individuals to be aware of SOX regulations and how they affected the officers' department. Acme's vendors posed the biggest challenge with SOX compliance. Acme needed to find and develop new business relationships with auditing and accounting vendors who were SOX compliant.

> **NOTE**
>
> The new roles and permissions created to achieve SOX compliance were auditors (read documents, view change logs), document owners (create, modify, and remove draft documents), compliance officers (promote a draft to an official document), and document consumers (read official documents).

Once an organization has management and employee buy-in with the need for compliance, it can attain regulatory compliance with a minimum of cost and effort. The heart of any compliance effort is a strong access control policy, both physical and logical. You cannot achieve compliance without robust access controls, as documents cannot be trusted.

Public Sector Case Study

The Los Angeles County Department of Health Services handles and distributes a dozen serious health alerts monthly. These alerts go to physicians, hospitals, and emergency response agencies in Los Angeles County.

These alerts range from disease outbreaks, to epidemic and pandemic warnings, to bioterrorist alerts. The department has to ensure that these sensitive data reach the correct people in a timely manner without an information leak. If the information is leaked to the wrong outlets, it could cause a panic.

To handle this task, the department implemented a RBAC-controlled messaging system. This supports the county's distributed network and validates users in a collaborative health alert network.

"Physicians and other health care providers need to know they can send us information on their patients, and it's going to be a secure transmission," explains bioterrorism IT coordinator David Cardenas, who oversees security for the county's Bioterrorism Preparedness and Response Unit and Acute Communicable Disease Control.

The system implemented in Los Angeles encrypts the information with a two-way authentication system for validating both the message sender and the receiver. The RBAC allows the department to handle who can send and who can receive, as well as what each user sends and who he or she can send to. This level of granularity allows the system's operators to determine which messages go to which recipients as well as how and when they arrive, which helps protect against information leakage.

The entire system is behind a firewall for further protection and is set up in a redundant load-balanced cluster. This allows for a backup system in the case of a system failure.

Heath alert communications must be secure and timely; employing a role-based authentication messaging systems allows the department to achieve both of these goals.

Three Essential Roles for This Approach to Access Control

Three roles are required in this access control scenario: A Creator can create draft alerts. Creators may be physicians, emergency response personnel, or the Centers for Disease Control and Prevention. The Distributor role is held by the Los Angeles Department of Health Services, and is responsible for promoting draft alerts to official alerts and distributing official alerts to consumers. The Consumer role is reserved for any individual or organization that receives official alerts. Many consumers are also Creators.

Critical Infrastructure Case Study

A Washington-based company is developing and constructing seaport gate control systems to be installed in Florida's deepwater seaports. They are installing thousands of access control readers to manage physical access. These readers utilize identification badges and biometrics to handle access.

Access control to port facilities is a major problem. On a normal day, employees, truck drivers, and vendors all show up needing different levels of access. The current access control process is to check driver's licenses against paperwork. Although this system is relatively secure, it is a time-consuming process subject to human error.

In the new system, the security policy requires that companies and individuals apply for access. The state will then perform background checks. When an individual is cleared, a smart card will be issued. The smart card will contain the individual's credentials as well as a photograph and fingerprint. Each smart card is designed to work at all of the state's seaports so that once a user is registered into the system, granting access to any, some, or all of the ports is an easy task. The smart cards grant users contactless access to the ports, greatly reducing the time it takes to pass through the security points. This is a major benefit and increases the efficiency of the ports. The smart card solution also brings the ports closer to compliance with HSPD 12.

CHAPTER SUMMARY

In this chapter, you read about several scenarios in which access control is mandated by law and others in which controlling access to information is critical to achieving basic business goals. You learned about best practices, standards, policies, and procedures for implementing an access control policy. Finally, you explored several case studies that illustrate the concepts discussed in this chapter.

KEY CONCEPTS AND TERMS

21 CFR Part 11
Americans with Disabilities Act (ADA)
Best practice
Children's Internet Protection Act (CIPA)
Communications Assistance for Law Enforcement Act (CALEA)
Directory information
Electronic protected health information (EPHI)

Family Educational Rights and Privacy Act (FERPA)
Gramm-Leach-Bliley Act (GLBA)
Health Information Technology for Economic and Clinical Health (HITECH) Act
Health Insurance Portability and Accountability Act (HIPAA)
Homeland Security Presidential Directive 12 (HSPD 12)

Human machine interface (HMI)
North American Electric Reliability Council (NERC)
Programmable logic controller (PLC)
Protected health information (PHI)
Remote terminal unit (RTU)
Sarbanes-Oxley (SOX) Act
Supervisory control and data acquisition (SCADA)

CHAPTER 14 ASSESSMENT

1. In IT, it is imperative that you keep up to date with regulatory compliance laws.
   A. True
   B. False

2. The Gramm-Leach-Bliley Act regulates which industry?
   A. Health Care
   B. Energy
   C. Financial services
   D. Automobile
   E. Education

3. A company regulated by GLBA is only required to protect against proven security threats, not perceived threats.
   A. True
   B. False

4. HIPAA regulates which industry?
   A. Health care
   B. Energy
   C. Financials
   D. Automobile
   E. Education

5. Protected health information is interpreted very broadly and includes all of an individual's medical records and payment history.

A. True
B. False

6. The HIPAA Security Rule requires a set of _____, technical, and physical safeguards to electronic protected health information (EPHI).

7. The Sarbanes-Oxley Act regulates all _____ companies.

8. The Family Educational Rights and Privacy Act establishes a student's right to know the information, location, and purpose of an educational record.

A. True
B. False

9. Which regulation defines a standard for electronic records and signatures?

A. Children's Internet Protection Act
B. 21 CFR Part 11
C. HIPAA
D. Sarbanes-Oxley
E. HSPD 12

10. A(n) _____ policy describes the actions that users may and may not take using the organization's IT resources.

11. _____ are a collection of suggestions and best practices.

ENDNOTE

1. *Federal Register*, 16 CFR Part 314, 67 (100): 36488.

Security Breaches and the Law

A CCESS CONTROLS EXIST to reduce the risk of unauthorized access to valuable information and resources. The consequences of unauthorized access can be serious—loss of reputation, financial losses, and even the loss of life if military or infrastructure resources are compromised. In this chapter, you will discover the ways that compromised access controls can result in security breaches. You will also discover the legal implications of security incidents.

Chapter 15 Topics

This chapter covers the following topics and concepts:

- U.S. federal and state laws that deter information theft
- The costs of inadequate access controls
- How access controls fail
- A security breach
- Case studies and examples

Chapter 15 Goals

When you complete this chapter, you will be able to:

- Discuss the U.S. federal and state laws passed to deter information theft
- Understand the costs associated with inadequate access controls
- Explain how access controls can fail
- Discuss security breaches and their implications

Laws to Deter Information Theft

Espionage between organizations used to require a physical act, such as stealing paper documents and making physical copies. Identity theft was a factor only if someone lost a wallet or if it was stolen. Although information technologies such as networked file servers, tablets, and web-based applications have made data easier to manage, IT has also made that information far more vulnerable.

Federal and state laws have been created to act as deterrents to information theft. These laws require organizations to take steps to protect the sensitive data stored, processed, or transmitted by their IT infrastructure. There are penalties for both stealing information and failing to follow the regulations in safeguarding it.

These laws add other considerations with which organizations must comply. Organizations must protect data from **breaches**; they must also be able to tell if an information breach has occurred. An organization may have a legal obligation to inform all stakeholders about breaches that have occurred and any information that may have been compromised.

U.S. Federal Laws

The technology breakthroughs of the information age have allowed organizations to be more productive and automate many interactions with consumers and stakeholders through the Internet. This has had unfortunate drawbacks; individuals can now use the Internet to gain unauthorized access to an organization, putting sensitive data at risk. An IT professional must be aware of these risks, as well as the numerous laws and regulations affecting the organization.

Various regulations define an organization's obligation to secure information. This section explores a few laws that cover unauthorized access of that information: the Computer Fraud and Abuse Act and the Digital Millennium Copyright Act.

Computer Fraud and Abuse Act (CFAA)

The **Computer Fraud and Abuse Act (CFAA)** is a federal criminal statute designed to protect electronic data from theft. The CFAA was enacted in 1984 and was designed to protect classified information maintained on governmental computer systems as well as financial and credit information maintained at financial institutions.

In 1994 and again in 1996, Congress expanded CFAA to cover any computer used in interstate commerce. The law was also amended to allow for private civil actions to help individuals injured in criminal activity that the CFAA prohibits. In 2002, the law was further expanded to cover a system located outside of the United States that is used in a manner that affects interstate or foreign commerce activities within the United States. The most recent amendment to the CFAA occurred in 2008 with the passage of the Identity Theft Enforcement and Restitution Act. This act revised CFAA to include provisions regulating spyware and cyberextortion. It also now requires identity thieves to pay restitution to their victims and forfeit any computer equipment used in identity theft.

The expansion of the CFAA has been an effective tool in protecting data stored on computers. This has allowed different types of civil actions to be brought against various activities. Here are some examples:

- Obtaining information from a computer through unauthorized access
- Trafficking in a computer password that can be used for unauthorized access
- Intentionally damaging computer data
- Stealing the identity of an individual

The CFAA allows an organization or individual affected by theft or destruction of data to seek relief and restitution from the courts as well as forces the return of stolen information. The CFAA also allows organizations to prevent the use of stolen information by their competitors in the marketplace. In this manner, the CFAA protects the rights of organizations and individuals that need to safeguard their sensitive information and processes from their competitors.

CFAA is based on unauthorized access to computers and information. "Unauthorized access" can be defined as using a computer to obtain or alter information in a system that the individual does not have a legitimate right to obtain or alter. For example, suppose an employee accesses and sends valuable company information through the Internet to a competitor right before his termination in hopes of obtaining a position with the competitor. The employee in this scenario could argue that the CFAA does not apply because he had legitimate access to the computer and data at that time. Under the CFAA, however, the courts would probably not agree with this assertion. A court could hold that the employee's legitimate access ended when he no longer held the best interest of the company in mind. When the employee accessed and sent the proprietary information to the competitor, he lost authorization to the data.

Digital Millennium Copyright Act

The **Digital Millennium Copyright Act (DMCA)**, passed in 1998, is the implementing legislation that facilitates the United States' participation in **World Intellectual Property Organization (WIPO)** treaties. DMCA has two major provisions of interest to IT professionals. First, it makes it a crime to bypass technological mechanisms used to enforce copyright provisions or sell equipment designed to bypass those mechanisms. Second, it introduces requirements for Internet service providers to receive and respond to copyright infringement complaints.

> **FYI**
>
> There are exceptions to the DMCA. It allows for legitimate research of reverse engineering for interoperability requirements. For example, a research team could legally attempt to figure out how access control measures were coded for the purposes of allowing third-party applications to interface with the access controls. There is also an exception if prior approval from a legitimate authority has been granted to try to break through an access control measure. Another exception is the manufacturing and sale of parental control systems to allow parents to restrict what their children view on the Internet. There are also exceptions for some government activities and legitimate law enforcement actions.

Copyright Technology Protection

The DMCA prohibits unauthorized disclosure of data by circumventing an established technological measure of the organization. Technological measures include things like product keys for software, CD and DVD copy protection, system passwords, and so on. The DMCA also prohibits the manufacture or sale of programs or devices designed to break access control measures of an organization.

The idea behind the DMCA is that unless it is illegal to break implanted technology, malicious users could manipulate access control solutions and violate copyright laws without consequence. DMCA provides for legal liabilities and attempts to ward off malicious users while providing incentives for organizations to implement access controls.

For example, let's take a look at the case of *Universal City Studios v. Reimerdes*, in which eight motion picture studios employed the DMCA against a defendant who posted DVD decrypting software on his website.

Upon the advent of DVDs, movie studios were concerned with the piracy aspect of the new technology. Unlike analog video, digital video can be replicated without any degradation in video quality. In the mid-1990s, the Content Scramble System (CSS) was created in partnership with the consumer electronics industry to help defend against piracy.

CSS provides encryption to a DVD's sound and graphics files according to predefined algorithms, making it supposedly impossible to replicate a legitimate studio-sanctioned DVD. This technology was then licensed to consumer electronics manufacturers for use in creating DVD players for retail sale.

In the fall of 1999, a teenager was able to crack the encryption. He reverse-engineered an officially licensed DVD player. This allowed for the creation of a computer program capable of decrypting the DVDs. This program allowed the DVDs to be viewed on noncompliant computers. It also allowed the decrypted files to be copied. The software was then posted on the Internet, where it could be downloaded from hundreds of sites.

The movie studios, using the DMCA, sought a legal solution to the problem. Using the anti-circumvention provisions of the DMCA, the courts found that the software generated to break the encryption on the DVD players constituted technology and was designed to circumvent the technology implemented by the studios for the copyright protection of their proprietary DVDs. As a result, the court ruled in favor of the studios using the DMCA.

ISP Requirements

DMCA also requires that Internet service providers (ISPs) receive and respond to copyright complaints in a timely manner. ISPs who meet the requirements of DMCA qualify for safe harbor status, which protects them from prosecution for the activities of their customers. The DMCA requires ISPs to:

- Block access to any potentially infringing material when they receive proper notice from a copyright owner.
- Notify users of their policy regarding copyright infringement and the consequences that may occur if users engage in unlawful activity.
- Implement measures to terminate the access of repeat infringers.

The specific provisions of DMCA vary depending upon the services provided by the ISP.

State Laws

All U.S. states now have laws that apply to unauthorized access to confidential information. Because they have many parts in common, this section covers one law in depth. The **California Identity Theft Statute** will give you a basic understanding of state laws designed to protect data.

The California Identity Theft Statute requires businesses operating in California to notify customers when the business has reason to believe that personal information has been disclosed through unauthorized access. Personal information is defined as a Social Security number (SSN), driver's license number, or physical address maintained in digital form.

As soon as an organization realizes that there has been an unauthorized disclosure, the organization must notify the owner of the information that a breach has occurred. The law further provides for any individual damaged by the breach to bring a lawsuit to recover any loss incurred due to the information disclosure and failure of the organization to issue a timely notification.

> **■ NOTE**
>
> Identity theft is one of the fastest growing crimes being committed on the Internet. Data thieves sell personal information to criminals, who then open credit card accounts, purchase products, or commit to other financial obligations using the stolen identities. Early notice that identity theft has occurred and action by individuals to protect themselves following a security breach will help reduce the impact of this type of criminal activity.

The purpose of the California Identity Theft Statute is to provide sufficient notice to individuals whose personal information has been stolen so they can take appropriate actions in a timely manner to prevent further damage by the data thieves.

The following are some of the elements of the California Identity Theft Statute that apply to data access and handling:

- Any person who, with the intent to defraud, acquires, transfers, or retains possession of personally identifying information of another person, is guilty of a crime punishable by up to $1,000 and 1 year in jail.
- Businesses are required to take reasonable steps to destroy all records containing personal information by shredding, erasing, or modifying the information to make it unreadable.
- Businesses and governmental agencies must notify individuals when any of the following unencrypted personal information has been accessed in a computer security breach: SSN, driver's license number, account number, credit card number, or debit card number.

Furthermore individuals, commercial entities, and certain governmental entities including public universities and colleges may not:

- Publicly display or post SSNs.
- Print SSNs on ID cards or badges.
- Require people to transmit SSNs over the Internet unless the connection is secure or the number is encrypted.

> **▶ TIP**
>
> The California Identity Theft Statute, used as an example in this section, is representative of many states' identity theft laws. Some of these laws, including California's go so far as to explicitly criminalize identity theft. If you are in a position to safeguard personally identifiable information, research the specific laws that apply in your state. You can begin by visiting your state's Office of the Attorney General website.

- Require people to use their SSN to log on to the Internet without a password.
- Print SSNs on mailed documents unless required by state or federal law.
- Embed or encode SSNs on a card or document where it cannot otherwise be printed. This includes chips, radio frequency identification (RFID), magnetic strips, and barcodes.
- Mail SSNs where the number is visible without opening the envelope.

Financial institutions are prohibited from sharing or selling nondirectory personally identifiable information without obtaining the consumer's consent.

Cost of Inadequate Front-Door and First-Layer Access Controls

Computer systems and data are essential to our modern lives. The safeguards securing these assets are both logical and physical. Many times, the need for physical security in a computing environment is overlooked. Unauthorized access to sensitive data and physical assets can create a significant risk for an organization.

The direct and indirect cost to an organization can be substantial. Direct costs come in the form of the cost to replace hardware, upgrade hardware and software, time and resources needed to reinstall and reconfigure the systems, as well as possible legal liabilities of having inadequate access controls. Indirect costs can come in the form of lost orders, lost customers, lost production, loss of competitive advantage, and possible legal liabilities.

Here are some examples of security policies that would be effective in limiting physical access to protect the data and assets of an organization:

* All physical security must comply with all applicable regulations such as building and fire codes.
* Access to secure computing facilities will be granted only to individuals with a legitimate business need for access.
* All secure computing facilities that allow visitors must have an access log.
* Visitors must be escorted at all times.

Access Control Failures

Every organization has sensitive areas and information that should be protected. If this information is left unsecured, it is hard to claim that access is unauthorized. Most responsible organizations implement some type of access control. Unfortunately, even the most thorough and vigilant system can fail. There are two primary causes of access control failures: people and technological factors.

People

Even the most strict and thorough access control policies are prone to human error. This was vividly demonstrated in 2010 when a Virginia couple slipped past security and into a state dinner at the White House. The couple was subjected to all of the normal security screening procedures and was never a threat, but they were not on the guest list. They got in due to human error—the guard at the entry gate did not follow proper procedure and verify the couple was on the guest list.

Although the couple was not a threat and the situation was humorous, this type of failure could pose a grave risk. They could have been spying for a foreign government or planning an attack on the dignitaries attending the event. This is a perfect example of failure in the human element of access control. An organization can have sound access control procedures, but without proper training and buy-in from all employees, the system can easily be defeated.

In the White House example, there were multiple layers of defense in place, including metal detectors and bomb-sniffing dogs. This ensured that even if someone got through, that person would not be armed. This does not mean that they could not be a threat. This is also true in computer security. Network antivirus solutions may keep malware from infecting other systems, but a connection from an unauthorized laptop could still be a threat.

The party crashers are also a good example of social engineering. They dressed properly and acted with confidence that they belonged. These types of attacks along an organization's human vector are all too common.

In another example, a penetration testing team, called a tiger team, was testing the security and integrity of a major financial institution's customer data. The corporation had an IT office in a major metropolitan skyscraper. The bottom floor had a publicly accessible restaurant, automated teller machines (ATMs), and washrooms. Dressed as a maintenance man, one of the tiger team members hung an out-of-service sign on the public washroom.

Another tiger team member, dressed as a businessman with a briefcase, talked his way past the security at the door into the secure area of the office complex under the pretext of needing to use the washroom. This was a clear violation of security protocol. This access control failure was compounded by allowing the man to go to the washroom unescorted. Once in the washroom, the intruder accessed network cables in the drop ceiling and inserted a wireless access point into the network. From there, another member of the team sitting in the restaurant used his laptop to access the wireless network.

> **NOTE**
>
> Penetration testing, especially using an independent third party, is an invaluable tool in assessing the robustness of an organization's access controls. It allows an organization to take an honest look at its access control polices without excessive risk.

While inside the network, the team didn't have access to the system yet—but was able to access unencrypted data, like customer debit card numbers and Windows password hashes in the supposedly secure internal network. Although there were intrusion detection systems and network-based antivirus systems running, passively sniffing network data did not trip any alarms. They were able to compromise hundreds of customer card accounts in a few minutes and leave undetected, all because of a failure in the human element of physical access control procedures. Luckily, in this example, it was a tiger team working for the financial institution and not malicious data thieves. If this had been a real incident, it would have been a major problem for the institution. Needless to say, this caused the team in charge of securing this information to reevaluate its security assumptions.

Rogue Internal Operatives

Another aspect in the human vector of access controls is rogue internal operatives. Disgruntled employees can pose a major threat to information security in the forms of theft, sabotage, vandalism, and more. The best way to handle these threats is by embracing a least-privileged access control policy. If you limit users to the least amount of access that they need to accomplish their tasks, the damage they can do is limited.

Other People-Related Threats

There are other internal threats besides disgruntled users; here are some other common threats:

- **Phishing and spear phishing attacks:** These are emails and websites crafted to trick a user into installing malicious code. They look like legitimate emails and websites but redirect the user's information to the attacker. Spear phishing attacks are targeted at a specific individual or organization.

- **Poor physical security on systems:** A hard drive, flash thumb drive, and even an entire laptop can vanish quickly if left unattended.
- **Physically stored passwords:** A password stored on a slip of paper can easily allow for unauthorized access to an organization's systems.
- **File-sharing and social networking sites:** As more and more people use these online services, they are becoming a major vector for social engineering attacks.

The best way to handle the human element in access control is through training and organizational buy-in. Every employee—at all levels of an organization—needs to adhere to security procedures or the access control system is useless.

Technology

Sometimes the best access control systems can be bypassed due to a failure in technology. No computer system is bug-free. Anything from an organization's operating system to its choice in web browser or instant messaging client could be an access point for unauthorized access to its systems. Let's look at some technological failures that could lead to unauthorized access.

Microsoft Windows operating systems prior to Windows Vista had the possibility of running very weak password encryption. Passwords in Windows NT, 2000, and XP of fewer than 15 characters long were stored in a file called a **LAN Manager (LM) hash**. This file employed **Data Encryption Standard (DES) encryption**; unfortunately, it did so in a predictable manner. This allowed for quick-and-easy brute-force attacks on the password files. Some systems could be accessed by brute force in a matter of seconds. Starting with Windows 2000, administrators have the ability to turn off LM passwords and use a more secure **NT LAN Manager (NTLM) hash** to handle user access.

UNIX/Linux systems had a similar issue in the late 1990s. Password hash files and the **hash salt** were stored together in an unencrypted file. Using that file, a malicious user could brute-force a password offline very quickly. The common acceptance of a more secure **shadow password file**, which provided an alternative by storing password hashes in a location unavailable to end users, solved the problem and is a very common element found in UNIX/Linux implementations today.

Web browsers are a major vector for unauthorized access. Every major browser including Firefox and Internet Explorer has had bugs that allow for the arbitrary execution of code. These bugs have been exploited to allow malicious users access and elevated rights on compromised systems. A system could be compromised just by being used to view a contaminated website.

Servers, especially web servers and other public-facing systems, are another common entry point for unauthorized access. Not only are web servers a risk due to the possibility of unsecure code being hosted but some of the languages used on the web

> **NOTE**
>
> Even in the realm of physical access control, technology can be the failure point. Recently, security researchers discovered that biometrics are not as secure as previously thought. The researchers demonstrated that most fingerprint scanners could be defeated with nothing more than a gummy bear.

15

servers have also had security flaws. Both PHP and .NET have had arbitrary code execution bugs that allow malicious users to access the web server.

Radio Frequency Identification (RFID) badges can also be a vector for unauthorized access. A malicious user could use an inexpensive reader to pull information off an ID badge and then flash a new chip with the cloned information. Security researchers have already demonstrated this technique by cloning the new RFID-enabled U.S. passports.

You have seen how both technology and humans can be the cause of unauthorized access. It is important to take steps to mitigate these possibilities, never relying on just one method to secure sensitive information.

Access Control and Privacy Assessments

A **privacy impact assessment (PIA)** is a comprehensive process for determining the privacy, confidentiality, and security risks associated with the collection, use, and disclosure of personal information. It also describes the measures used to mitigate and, if possible, eliminate identified risks. The PIA process makes sure measures intended to protect privacy and security of personal information are considered at the beginning of a new program or initiative. A PIA also communicates to the public how their privacy is protected and information kept secure.

A PIA is required in the public sector for any new system that handles personally identifiable information (PII). To be successful, it is important that the PIA looks at the system in a systematic manner. It should:

- Identify the key factors involved in securing PII
- Emphasize the process used to secure PII as well as product
- Have a sufficient degree of independence from the project implementing the new system
- Have a degree of public exposure
- Be integrated into the decision-making process

> **NOTE**
>
> In the public sector, it is mandatory for all PIAs to be published.

An important aspect of a PIA is looking at the access controls that will be used to secure the data. The assessment needs to not only look at the physical and logical access controls that will be put into place but it also needs to look at how the access control policies are implemented. Questions like "Who has rights to the information?" and "How will access be granted and removed?" need to be asked. In a thorough PIA, the administrative, physical, and technological access control policies must be described. This is required in all PIA generated by governmental organizations.

Not only are access control systems vital to securing privacy but new access control systems should also go through the PIA process as well. This is especially true in the case of physical access control.

Let's look at the example of an ID badge system. What information is stored on the ID—just name or name and ID number? Is the information electronically readable and if so by what means? What does the employee ID number consist of? Organizations should follow best practices for privacy protection. For example, they should never use PII, such as a Social Security number, as an employee identification number. Instead, best practice dictates using a random or sequential number as the employee ID. Starting an RFID badge project with a valid PIA ensures that the security of this information is addressed throughout the project.

Structure of a PIA. A typical PIA includes the following sections:

- **Summary of the system under analysis:** This section should include a physical or logical description of the particular system being analyzed, such as an RFID badge system, and its intended purpose. This section should also include the owner or stakeholders of the system, where the project is in its life cycle (planned, implemented, and so on), and how it will interact with the rest of the infrastructure.
- **List of information to be collected:** Include specific examples of all information that will be collected or affected by the system.
- **Description of how the information will be collected:** Include specific plans for collecting personal information. This section may contain copies of questionnaire forms, telephone scripts, or other tools.
- **Explanation of why personally identifiable information is necessary:** Use this section to justify the collection and use of personally identifiable information. If the organization's goals could be achieved without the use of personally identifiable information, it should not be collected or used.
- **Explanation of how the information will be used:** Include a specific description of how each piece of information will be used. Information should not be used except in ways described in the privacy impact assessment.
- **List any new information the system will create through aggregation:** For example, if biometric data such as fingerprints or photographs are stored in database A and names, phone numbers, and addresses are stored in database B, and the proposed system will link the two databases, this needs to be explained in this section of the PIA.
- **List of groups, organizations, and individuals with whom the information will be shared:** Include both those within the organization and external entities.
- **Opt-out opportunities:** This should feature an explanation of all chances individuals will have to opt-out or object to the collection of information about themselves.
- **Description of any information that will be provided to the individual:** This section will generally include the privacy statement and specifics on how that information will be provided, such as a hard copy or in electronic format.
- **Description of the access controls that will be adopted to secure the information:** This section should include administrative policies, physical security, and logical access controls.
- **Description of any potential privacy risks involved in collecting, using, and sharing information:** This section should also include analysis of any risk involved in providing individuals the chance to opt-out, notifying individuals of the collection of information. Finally, this section should include an evaluation of the risks posed by the proposed security measures.

By carefully and thoughtfully completing each of these sections, you should have a thorough PIA that accurately assesses the privacy impact of a proposed access control solution.

Security Breaches

Information security breaches take many forms. These include lost or misplaced data media, stolen laptops and cell phones, hacked systems, data lost or stolen in transit, information taken by rogue employees, and more. Damage done by a security breach can be measured in both tangible and intangible terms.

Tangible damage is calculated based on estimates of lost business, lost productivity, labor and material costs to repair the breach, labor and legal costs associated with the collection of forensic evidence, and the public relations costs to prepare statements. Increases in insurance premiums and legal costs related to defending the organization in liability suits can also be tangible damages.

The intangible damages refer to costs that are difficult to measure or calculate. Much of this cost is due to a loss of competitive advantage due to the breach. This can stem from a loss of customer confidence, bad press, or the possibility of proprietary information falling into the hands of competitors.

Kinds of Security Breaches

There are a number of different types of security breaches. This is also a moving target as technology evolves. Here are some of the types of security breaches an organization may have to face:

- **System exploits**—These include Trojan horse programs, computer viruses, and other malicious code.
- **Eavesdropping**—This is the act of passively gathering information. Eavesdropping can take the form of sniffing network and wireless traffic, intercepting Bluetooth traffic, and even using equipment to remotely pull information from monitors due to electromagnetic fields (EMFs).
- **Social engineering**—This is an exploitation of human nature and human error as discussed previously.
- **Denial of service (DoS) attacks**—These are purely damaging attacks, meant to render a system unusable.
- **Indirect attacks**—This involves using a third party's system to launch an attack. Distributed denial of service (DDoS) attacks are an example of this. Rather than directly attacking the target, hackers first compromise other systems and use those to launch their primary attack.
- **Physical attacks**—These range from the technological aspects of unauthorized access to the utilization of devices like keystroke loggers, to outright theft of equipment.

This isn't a comprehensive list, and new vectors of attack are always being developed, but it does give you an idea of what the IT security field is facing.

Why Security Breaches Occur

The why of a security breach is almost as diverse as the how, but can be generalized into two categories: monetary gain and vandalism of systems.

Hackers and Crackers

Hackers have historically been known as white-hat hackers or ethical hackers—the good guys. They hack into systems to learn how it can be done, but not for personal gain. Crackers have been known as black-hat hackers or malicious hackers—the bad guys. They hack into systems to damage, steal, or commit fraud. Many black-hat hackers present themselves as white-hat hackers, claiming that their actions are innocent. However, most mainstream media put all hackers in the same black-hat category. The general perception is that all hackers are bad guys.

Be aware though that Linux users and the open source communities think of themselves in a positive way as hackers—people who just want to create better software. The Linux world defines people who are threats to information security as crackers.

Financial gain takes numerous forms. Intruders in a system could look for valuable data to sell, personally identifiable information to steal and use, or physical equipment to resell. Insider information to gain an advantage in stock trading is also often targeted. Accounting and human resources are also tempting targets. There have been cases of direct deposit information being tampered with, causing paychecks to be deposited into the incorrect account. DoS and DDoS attacks have even been used in extortion.

Monetary gain motives may not even involve the organization attacked, just their servers. Spam remailers commonly get installed during web server security breaches. Malicious code can also be injected into a company's website to try to infect customer computers for identity theft purposes.

Vandalism is the other major category for security breaches. This can be as harmless as kids having "fun" or trying to make a name for themselves among their peers, to groups making a political statement, and even individuals and groups protesting an organization.

> **NOTE**
>
> A spam remailer is a hidden mail server that is used to relay spam so its origins are obscured.

> **NOTE**
>
> Monetary gain and vandalism can overlap. During the early stages of the U.S. war in Iraq, a group of Middle Eastern hackers were defacing websites of U.S. companies with anti-American messages. While they were in the systems, they also installed spam remailers to help fund their group.

Implications of Security Breaches

Computer security is a critical issue for any organization. A breach in system security that damages an organization's computer systems can result in financial costs, loss of customer trust, and legal penalties.

There is also the possibility of ongoing system security issues. Did the intruders build themselves some additional backdoors for later access?

What disclosure must happen after the breach? Depending on the industry and what was taken, an organization may be obligated to disclose the breach to the public. This must be done in a timely manner, especially if customer data were accessed. Not only is it a good business practice—allowing customers a chance to ward off identity theft—it may also be legally mandated.

An organization will also have to take a long look at its security procedures. Did the technology that was used fail? If so, what will it take to mitigate the issue, and does the organization need to upgrade or change systems?

Was it due to a human failure? If it was human error, more awareness training may be needed. If it was due to malicious users or rogue employees, access audits may be in order to make sure that no one has access to information that they do not need.

The breach may also be due to a failure in procedure. If this is the case, new procedures must be developed.

The Impact of a Security Breach Can Be Significant

A credit card processing company called Acme Credit Card Processing received notice from two of the larger card issuers that fraudulent credit card purchases were occurring. Prior to receiving the notification, Acme did not know that there was an issue.

After some investigation, the problem was discovered in Acme's system. A spyware program was loaded onto Acme's system that originated with a spear phishing attack. A well-crafted email was sent to an employee who clicked a link that infected his system with malicious code. The malicious program was able to pull the credit card information off Acme's system for every card that they processed. This information was sent to a remote system, where data thieves were able to use the information to clone credit cards. Any consumer who used a credit card somewhere that utilized Acme's processing could potentially be affected.

The impact to Acme was significant. There was the cost of removing every trace of the spyware, both in monetary and time resources. Acme had to pay fines due to various industry and legal regulatory groups. Acme also had to communicate the breach to all consumers affected. There was also the impact to Acme's reputation. Secure transactions are vital for a processing company. A number of merchants who used Acme's services moved to other processing companies. Acme enhanced its email security and launched a user awareness program in an attempt to prove to customers that security breaches of this nature would not happen again.

Financial Impact of Security Breaches

As discussed above, the costs of a security breach to an organization can come in both direct and indirect forms. The direct costs to a financial breach can be easily identified. They come in the form of equipment replacement costs, security upgrades and enhancements, additions, and other monetary costs paid to repair the damage done.

 NOTE

The indirect costs of a security breach can be difficult to identify. The costs of contacting all of the individuals affected by the security breach, defending the organization from legal action, and loss of reputation are some examples of these costs.

Monster.com security breach. In 2007, Monster.com discovered that intruders had obtained personal information from 1.3 million résumés stored there. The breach affected both Monster.com and USAJobs.gov, a government jobs site that Monster.com runs for the United States government. Monster.com officials estimate that it cost $80 million to upgrade security on the sites. These upgrades included better monitoring of site access and stricter access controls and intrusion prevention systems.

TJX security breach. The TJX Companies, Inc., which operates stores such as T.J.Maxx and Marshalls, disclosed a massive security breach in 2007. The customers affected by the security breach were offered free credit monitoring at the expense of the organization. TJX also had to settle a civil suit with MasterCard for an additional $24 million. In addition, TJX is still the defendant in other litigation and claims on behalf of customers and other credit card companies who were damaged as a result of the computer intrusions. Besides the millions in legal liabilities, there are also untold costs in lost reputation and customer trust. Unknown numbers of former customers will no longer shop at T.J.Maxx due to the loss in consumer confidence.

New York Times security breach. In 2013, *The New York Times* and other major media outlets announced that Chinese hackers had infiltrated their internal systems, seeking information on confidential sources within the Chinese government. While the direct financial impact of this type of attack is hard to quantify, it is likely that it had a chilling effect on potential future sources who may question the newspaper's ability to maintain confidentiality.

Equifax security breach. In September 2017, the credit-reporting agency Equifax announced that it had been the victim of a data breach that exposed the sensitive personal information of over 147 million individuals. Attackers were able to exploit an exposed vulnerability in the Apache Struts service running on Equifax servers and used it to exfiltrate massive amounts of personal information. In July of 2019, the Federal Trade Commission announced a settlement with Equifax that included $425 million in compensation to the victims of the breach.

The impact to an organization's market share due to a security breach is an additional cost. There are recovery costs to regain market share, rebuild reputation, and restore customer and shareholder confidence. The continuing potential damage to an organization could be significant if its customers and stakeholders feel that they can no longer trust the access control safeguards in place to protect sensitive information.

Information assurance is critical for any organization. An organization's data are key assets and must be treated as such. Access control safeguards are essential to ensure that measures are in place to prevent unauthorized access. If data are accessed, there must be mechanisms in place to identify what was accessed. TJX executives, in their initial communications, advised that they did not have enough information to estimate the extent of the data loss. Without robust auditing to determine the extent of a breach, affected customers cannot be alerted in a timely manner, which causes more legal liabilities. An organization needs both strong access controls and auditing mechanisms; a failure in these systems can lead to staggering direct and indirect financial losses.

Case Studies and Examples

Security breaches can have serious consequences for an organization. They can rely on lax physical security, inadequate logical access controls, or a combination of both. In this section, we look at case studies of breaches that occurred in the private sector, the public sector, and in critical infrastructure applications.

Private Sector Case Studies

The following case studies highlight examples of failures in both logical access controls and physical security.

LexisNexis

LexisNexis is a major information clearinghouse of newspaper, magazine, and legal documents. Customers can search the system for basically any published information. In early 2005, a number of teenage hackers were able to gain access to the system. They exposed personal information of over 300,000 individuals. Names, addresses, and SSNs were exposed in the breach. This was a failure in logical access controls on a major level.

The breach started with the account of a police officer in Florida. One of the teenagers, posing as a 14-year-old girl in a chat session, convinced the officer to download and open a Trojan horse file, claiming it was a photo. This gave the hackers access to the officer's system. While browsing his files, they discovered a logon into a LexisNexis subsidiary, called Accurint, a law enforcement information database. The hackers started to search the database for themselves and celebrity information.

The hackers realized that they needed more access to effectively explore the system. They called Accurint and, posing as administrators with LexisNexis, they got account logins and passwords for an account with enhanced rights.

They used their new access to create accounts for friends and search the system. They were able to pull at least 30,000 accounts, possibly as many as 300,000, gaining names, addresses, phone numbers, and SSNs. Luckily the teens were "joyriding," and none of the information was sold or utilized in identity theft, but the possibility was there. There were at least 57 separate breaches connected to this incident.

LexisNexis had to offer identity theft monitoring to all of the affected customers. In addition, they claimed to strengthen their customer account and password administration to make sure a breach could not happen again. LexisNexis went so far as to claim their new system was watertight.

Bank One

Bank One, a major Midwest bank that is now owned by JPMorgan Chase, lost around 100 employee laptops due to a failure in physical access controls. The office had one access point that was controlled with an RFID badge system. The badge system was slow, taking around 30 seconds to a minute to unlock the door. This led to impatient employees at this location assisting each other by piggybacking at the door. Employees would badge in and then hold the door open for the other employees behind them. This security flaw was further exacerbated by a lack of security cameras at the door. Most employees were using laptops at this location, with no security cables or locking docking stations.

In the early 2000s, during an all-hands off-site meeting, thieves gained access to the office and stole approximately 100 laptops. After the incident, measures were taken to enhance the physical access controls at the location. Cameras were added at the entry point, and the badge system was modified so that employees had to badge in and out of the building. Policy changes were also enacted. The act of piggybacking was banned, and this was added to the code of conduct.

Public Sector Case Study

Sometimes, security breaches happen not because of external attacks but due to internal failures. Let's take a look at an example from the United Kingdom (U.K.).

On November 22, 2007, the U.K. government admitted that one of its departments, Her Majesty's Revenue & Customs (HMRC), had lost in the mail two CDs containing the unencrypted personal details of 25 million U.K. residents.

In response to a request by the National Audit Office (NAO), a junior member of HMRC's staff was instructed to send details of child benefit recipients to the NAO. The details were burned onto two CDs as unencrypted files and then sent to the NAO using regular mail. At the time, this was standard procedure at HMRC. To compound the security lapses, HMRC decided it was too costly to remove unneeded information from the files before they were sent. This included addresses and bank account information. NAO explicitly requested that the bank account information be removed, and HMRC ignored the request.

The U.K. Data Protection Act of 1998 specifies that if information is to be sent, it must be subject to safeguards, and only the necessary data required for processing may be sent. In this case, HMRC violated both points of this law.

Once the data loss became apparent, HMRC started an investigation of the loss. They attempted to track down the CDs and contacted law enforcement for assistance. Instead of immediately reporting the data loss to the public, HMRC waited 10 days, plenty of time for accounts to get compromised.

The fallout from this breach has been major: The Information Commissioner's powers have been expanded, his office can now audit departments at will, and they have enforcement powers. Due to the loss of public confidence in the HMRC, other projects have been put on hold, most notably the national ID card program. There was also the cost of the search for the disk and affected citizens needing to close existing bank accounts.

Critical Infrastructure Case Study

Security breaches do not always come from targeted attacks. Untargeted, general attacks can also cause a security breach in an organization. Let's look at the CSX Corporation virus incident of August of 2003.

The SoBig computer virus infected CSX Corporation's computer network at its headquarters in Jacksonville, Florida. These infected systems flooded the internal network with infection attempts and spammed the equivalent of an internal DDoS attack. No critical systems were infected, but the network congestion disrupted signal dispatching and other mission critical systems.

Freight trains were delayed. At least 10 Amtrak long-distance trains were canceled or delayed up to 6 hours, and commuter trains in Washington D.C. were canceled. Half-hour delays continued for the next few days. The initial damage ran into the millions in late delivery penalties and customer refunds, and millions more were spent updating and expanding the antivirus and network systems to mitigate any further issues.

CHAPTER SUMMARY

Now that you understand the impact of a security breach and how attackers often combine several attack vectors in a single breach incident, you will be able to design access controls that mitigate those attack vectors. You will also be less likely to underestimate weak access controls.

KEY CONCEPTS AND TERMS

Breach
California Identity Theft Statute
Computer Fraud and Abuse Act (CFAA)
Data Encryption Standard (DES) encryption

Digital Millennium Copyright Act (DMCA)
Hash salt
LAN Manager (LM) hash
NT LAN Manager (NTLM) hash
Privacy impact assessment (PIA)

Radio Frequency Identification (RFID) badge
Shadow password file
World Intellectual Property Organization (WIPO)

CHAPTER 15 ASSESSMENT

1. Information security falls strictly under the jurisdiction of federal law—state law does not restrict information security practices.

A. True
B. False

2. The CEO of a major company received an email message requesting her password. The message claimed to be from the organization's help desk, but it was actually sent by an attacker. What term best describes this attack?

A. Phishing
B. Eavesdropping
C. Denial of service
D. System exploit

3. Under DMCA, Internet service providers must immediately block access to content that infringes on the copyright of another individual or group upon receiving proper notice from the copyright owner.

A. True
B. False

4. A(n) _____ is a comprehensive process for determining the privacy, confidentiality, and security risks associated with the collection, use, and disclosure of personal information.

5. Which of the following are effective physical security policies?

A. All physical security must comply with all applicable regulations such as building and fire codes.
B. Access to secure computing facilities will be granted only to individuals with a legitimate business need for access.
C. All secure computing facilities that allow visitors must have an access log.
D. Visitors must be escorted at all times.
E. All of the above.

6. What are the two primary causes of access control failure discussed in the chapter? (Select two.)

A. People
B. Planning
C. Technology
D. Follow-up analysis

7. Which of the following are types of security breaches? (Select all that apply.)

   A. System exploits
   B. DoS attacks
   C. PII
   D. Eavesdropping
   E. Social engineering

8. Anything from an organization's operating system to its choice of web browser or instant messaging client could be an access point for unauthorized access to the systems.

   A. True
   B. False

9. When should a privacy impact assessment be performed?

   A. During the planning stages of a new system
   B. After a new system is designed
   C. After a new system is implemented
   D. After a security breach

10. The two most common motives for a security breach are monetary gain and _____.

11. A security breach can result in criminal penalties as well as financial losses.

   A. True
   B. False

Answer Key

CHAPTER 1 Access Control Framework

1. Policies 2. B 3. C 4. A 5. Unknown 6. B 7. D 8. C 9. B
10. D 11. A 12. Administrative 13. B 14. Behavioral

CHAPTER 2 Business Drivers for Access Controls

1. A 2. Confidential 3. A 4. A 5. A 6. B 7. A 8. A 9. A

CHAPTER 3 Human Nature and Organizational Behavior

1. Status, wealth 2. A 3. F 4. C 5. A 6. B 7. Disgruntled 8. E
9. A 10. A and C 11. Two-person control 12. A 13. B 14. A

CHAPTER 4 Assessing Risk and Its Impact on Access Control

1. Probability of occurrence 2. A 3. Quantitative 4. B 5. B 6. A
7. A, B, and C 8. B 9. B 10. A 11. A 12. B 13. B 14. $150,000
15a. $1.5 million 15b. 10% 15c. $150,000 15d. 3 15e. $450,000

CHAPTER 5 Access Control in the Enterprise

1. D 2. Mandatory access control (MAC), discretionary access control
(DAC), role-based access control (RBAC), attribute-based access control
(ABAC) 3. B and C 4. B 5. B, C, and E 6. A 7. A and C 8. C 9. C
10. A 11. A 12. C 13. A 14. C 15. B

CHAPTER 6 Mapping Business Challenges to Access Control Types

1. A 2. Risk avoidance 3. Risk acceptance 4. Risk transference
5. Risk mitigation 6. Integrity 7. A 8. Sensitive 9. D 10. C
11. B 12. B 13. View full record

CHAPTER 7 Access Control System Implementations

1. B 2. ISO 3. A 4. B and C 5. D 6. Federal Financial Institutions
Examinations Council (FFEIC) 7. A 8. C 9. NIST

CHAPTER 8 Access Control for Information Systems

1. Industrial control system (ICS) 2. B 3. ACL 4. System-audit
5. Binary large objects, or BLOBs 6. B 7. A 8. A 9. B 10. Linux
11. B 12. A and C

CHAPTER 9	Physical Security and Access Control

1. B   2. C   3. B   4. B and D   5. D   6. A   7. Dark   8. D   9. Physiological, behavioral   10. B   11. The point at which Type I and Type II errors are equal   12. D   13. A   14. D   15. B

CHAPTER 10	Access Control Solutions for Remote Workers

1. B   2. Authentication, Authorization, and Accounting   3. B   4. B, C, and E   5. A   6. C   7. A, C, and D   8. B   9. A   10. D   11. Two-way   12. Three-way   13. C   14. B

CHAPTER 11	Public Key Infrastructure and Encryption

1. B   2. B   3. B and C   4. A   5. B   6. A, B, and C   7. Certificate Practice Statement (CPS)   8. C   9. C   10. B and E

CHAPTER 12	Testing Access Control Systems

1. A   2. D   3. B and C   4. Nonintrusive   5. Intrusive   6. C   7. A   8. E   9. A   10. A   11. B   12. C   13. C   14. A, C, and D

CHAPTER 13	Access Control Assurance

1. Confidentiality, integrity, availability   2. C   3. A, C, and D   4. B   5. A   6. Blacklist   7. Whitelist   8. A   9. C   10. B   11. B   12. B   13. C

CHAPTER 14	Access Control Laws, Policies, and Standards

1. A   2. C   3. B   4. A   5. A   6. Administrative   7. Publicly traded   8. A   9. B   10. Acceptable Use   11. Guidelines

CHAPTER 15	Security Breaches and the Law

1. B   2. A   3. B   4. Privacy impact assessment   5. E   6. A and C   7. A, B, D, and E   8. A   9. A   10. Vandalism   11. A

Standard Acronyms

3DES	triple data encryption standard		**DES**	Data Encryption Standard
ACD	automatic call distributor		**DMZ**	demilitarized zone
AES	Advanced Encryption Standard		**DoS**	denial of service
ANSI	American National Standards Institute		**DPI**	deep packet inspection
AP	access point		**DRP**	disaster recovery plan
API	application programming interface		**DSL**	digital subscriber line
B2B	business to business		**DSS**	Digital Signature Standard
B2C	business to consumer		**DSU**	data service unit
BBB	Better Business Bureau		**EDI**	Electronic Data Interchange
BCP	business continuity planning		**EIDE**	Enhanced IDE
C2C	consumer to consumer		**FACTA**	Fair and Accurate Credit Transactions Act
CA	certificate authority		**FAR**	false acceptance rate
CAP	Certification and Accreditation Professional		**FBI**	Federal Bureau of Investigation
CAUCE	Coalition Against Unsolicited Commercial Email		**FDIC**	Federal Deposit Insurance Corporation
			FEP	front-end processor
CCC	CERT Coordination Center		**FRCP**	Federal Rules of Civil Procedure
CCNA	Cisco Certified Network Associate		**FRR**	false rejection rate
CERT	Computer Emergency Response Team		**FTC**	Federal Trade Commission
CFE	Certified Fraud Examiner		**FTP**	file transfer protocol
CISA	Certified Information Systems Auditor		**GIAC**	Global Information Assurance Certification
CISM	Certified Information Security Manager		**GLBA**	Gramm-Leach-Bliley Act
CISSP	Certified Information System Security Professional		**HIDS**	host-based intrusion detection system
CMIP	Common Management Information Protocol		**HIPAA**	Health Insurance Portability and Accountability Act
COPPA	Children's Online Privacy Protection		**HIPS**	host-based intrusion prevention system
CRC	cyclic redundancy check		**HTTP**	hypertext transfer protocol
CSI	Computer Security Institute		**HTTPS**	HTTP over Secure Socket Layer
CTI	Computer Telephony Integration		**HTML**	hypertext markup language
DBMS	database management system		**IAB**	Internet Activities Board
DDoS	distributed denial of service		**IDEA**	International Data Encryption Algorithm

IDPS	intrusion detection and prevention	**RSA**	Rivest, Shamir, and Adleman (algorithm)
IDS	intrusion detection system	**SAN**	storage area network
IEEE	Institute of Electrical and Electronics Engineers	**SANCP**	Security Analyst Network Connection Profiler
IETF	Internet Engineering Task Force	**SANS**	SysAdmin, Audit, Network, Security
InfoSec	information security	**SAP**	service access point
IPS	intrusion prevention system	**SCSI**	small computer system interface
IPSec	IP Security	**SET**	Secure electronic transaction
IPv4	Internet protocol version 4	**SGC**	server-gated cryptography
IPv6	Internet protocol version 6	**SHA**	Secure Hash Algorithm
IRS	Internal Revenue Service	**S-HTTP**	secure HTTP
(ISC)²	International Information System Security Certification Consortium	**SLA**	service level agreement
		SMFA	specific management functional area
ISO	International Organization for Standardization	**SNMP**	Simple Network Management Protocol
		SOX	Sarbanes-Oxley Act of 2002 (also Sarbox)
ISP	Internet service provider	**SSA**	Social Security Administration
ISS	Internet security systems	**SSCP**	Systems Security Certified Practitioner
ITRC	Identity Theft Resource Center	**SSL**	Secure Sockets Layer
IVR	interactive voice response	**SSO**	single system sign-on
LAN	local area network	**STP**	shielded twisted cable
MAN	metropolitan area network	**TCP/IP**	Transmission Control Protocol/Internet Protocol
MD5	Message Digest 5		
modem	modulator demodulator	**TCSEC**	Trusted Computer System Evaluation Criteria
NFIC	National Fraud Information Center		
NIDS	network intrusion detection system	**TFTP**	Trivial File Transfer Protocol
NIPS	network intrusion prevention system	**TNI**	Trusted Network Interpretation
NIST	National Institute of Standards and Technology	**UDP**	User Datagram Protocol
		UPS	uninterruptible power supply
NMS	network management system	**UTP**	unshielded twisted cable
OS	operating system	**VLAN**	virtual local area network
OSI	open system interconnection	**VOIP**	Voice over Internet Protocol
PBX	private branch exchange	**VPN**	virtual private network
PCI	Payment Card Industry	**WAN**	wide area network
PGP	Pretty Good Privacy	**WLAN**	wireless local area network
PKI	public key infrastructure	**WNIC**	wireless network interface card
RAID	redundant array of independent disks	**W3C**	World Wide Web Consortium
RFC	Request for Comments	**WWW**	World Wide Web

Glossary of Key Terms

21 CFR Part 11 | A title in the Code of Federal Regulations that deals with U.S. Food and Drug Administration (FDA) guidelines on electronic records and signatures. This title requires industries that fall under FDA regulation to implement controls such as audits, audit trails, electronic signatures, and policies for software and systems that process electronic data.

802.1x | An IEEE standard, which addresses authentication for Layer 2 (bridges and switches) devices when communicating on a network; a protocol that provides a framework for implementing authentication on a network.

A

Access | The ability of a subject and an object to interact.

Access control | The process or mechanism of granting or denying use of a resource; typically applied to users or generic network traffic.

Access control entry (ACE) | An element of the access control list.

Access control list (ACL) | A list of security policies that is associated with an object.

Access mask | In Windows-based systems, a value that specifies the rights that are allowed or denied in an access control entry (ACE) of an access control list (ACL).

Accounting | As part of AAA, provides the ability of a system to collect statistics on networks or users for auditing and billing purposes. Accounting enables the tracking of systems usage, start and stop times of resources, and number of packets, as well as other metrics that identify what was used and for how long.

Active Directory | The directory service for Microsoft Windows Server. Active Directory stores information about objects on the network and makes this information available for authorized systems administrators and users. It gives network users access to permitted resources anywhere on the network using a single sign-on process. It also provides systems administrators with an intuitive hierarchical view of the network and a single point of administration for all network objects.

Advanced Encryption Standard (AES) | A symmetric encryption algorithm that serves as an approved standard for encrypting U.S. government data.

Algorithm | A process that performs a sequence of operations.

Americans with Disabilities Act (ADA) | Regulation including provisions ensuring that everyone has equal access to public accommodations, regardless of any disability they might have.

Analysis and reporting | The penultimate stage in a penetration test, where the testing team analyzes the gathered data and writes a report for the organization once the penetration test is complete.

Annual rate of occurrence (ARO) | The number of times per year you expect a compromise to occur.

Annualized loss expectancy (ALE) | The total cost per year of the threat under assessment. ALE is calculated by multiplying the single loss expectancy (SLE) by the annualized rate of occurrence (ARO).

Application Layer | Provides services for an application program to ensure effective communication.

Asset value | The relative value, either in monetary terms or in overall impact, of the resource being protected by the access control system.

Asymmetric cryptography | Encryption approach that uses a pair of keys for each user: a public key and a private key.

Assessment | Documenting rules, procedures, and guidelines to be tested against a system.

Asymmetric encryption | A type of encryption in which an encryption key (the public key) is used to encrypt a message and another encryption key (the private key) is used to decrypt the message.

Attacker | Someone trying to compromise information or data.

Attribute-based access control (ABAC) | Access control policy where the policy is a function of a subject's characteristics.

Audit trail | A series of events gleaned from parsed log file reports over a period of time.

Authentication | The process of confirming the identity of a user. Also, ensuring that a sender and recipient are who they say they are.

Authentication factor | A way of confirming the identity of a subject. The three authentication factors are something you know, something you have, and something you are.

Authentication Header (AH) | An IPSec authentication protocol that is used to prove the identity of the sender and ensure the data has not been tampered with.

Authentication server | The server that validates requests for network access, using the RADIUS or EAP protocols.

Authentication service | The service provided through Kerberos that identifies users on a computer system. The authentication service is part of the Key Distribution Center.

Authentication, Authorization, and Accounting (AAA) | Network services that provide security through a framework of access controls and policies, enforcement of policies, and information needed for billing purposes.

Authenticator | A message that is part of the Kerberos authorization process and is composed of the client ID and timestamp.

Authorization | The decision to allow or deny a subject access to an object. After a user has been authenticated, for example, authorization determines if the user has the rights to perform specific actions on the network or system.

Automated testing | The use of software to control the execution of a test suite.

Availability | Ensuring a system is accessible when needed.

Automatic declassification | The process for U.S. government documents over 25 years old. Unless they meet strict criteria, documents are automatically declassified after the department that owns the documents reviews them. The documents are moved to the publicly accessible shelves of the national archives.

B

Backdoor | A hole in system or network security placed deliberately, either by system designers or attackers. A way of quickly bypassing normal security measures.

Baseline | A normal level of measurement.

Bell-LaPadula Model | A model that defines basic principles of access controls.

Best practice | A documented method or system of achieving a specific result in an effective, efficient manner. Best practices generally take lessons learned from individuals or groups so that others can complete similar tasks in a more efficient manner.

Binary large object (BLOB) | A collection of binary data stored in a relational database.

Biometrics | An authentication system based on physical characteristics or behavioral tendencies of an individual.

Blacklist | A list of known malicious behaviors that should be automatically denied.

Blue team | In a penetration test, the blue team consists of IT staff who defend against the penetration testers. They are generally aware that a penetration test is happening, but do not know what methods the penetration testers will use.

Bollards | Short vertical posts designed to control traffic and prevent vehicular attacks on a building.

Boundary conditions | The outermost extremes of test conditions.

Breach | A confirmed event that compromises the confidentiality, integrity, or availability of information.

Bring Your Own Device (BYOD) policies | Allows users to access corporate systems and data using personally owned devices.

Bugtraq | An industry mailing list provided by Symantec that reports new vulnerabilities as they are discovered.

Business continuity | The ability of an organization to maintain critical functions during and after a disaster.

Business to business (B2B) | Activities that occur between two or more businesses.

Business to customer (B2C) | Activities that occur between a business and a customer.

California Identity Theft Statute | Requires a business operating in California to notify customers when it has reason to believe that personal information has been disclosed through unauthorized access.

Card holder unique identification (CHUID) | A unique number that identifies an individual in possession of a smart card.

Certificate authority (CA) | An entity, usually a trusted third party, that issues digital certificates.

Certificate Practice Statement (CPS) | A formal statement that provides details on the business processes used by the CA to verify the identity of certificate owners prior to issuing the certificate, revoking digital certificates, renewing expired certificates, and other certificate practices.

Certificate revocation list (CRL) | The certificate authorities' list of invalid certificates.

Challenge Handshake Authentication Protocol (CHAP) | Provides authentication over a PPP link.

Child object | An object that inherits certain characteristics, such as access controls, from a parent object.

Children's Internet Protection Act (CIPA) | A U.S. law passed in 2000. It requires schools and libraries receiving E-Rate funds to filter some Internet content. The primary purpose is to protect minors from obscene or harmful content.

Classification scheme | A method of organizing sensitive information into various access levels.

Clean-up | The last stage in the penetration test, where the testing team has the responsibility to undo any changes it made to the environment once the test is complete.

Clearance | The level of information an individual is authorized to access.

Cleartext | Information that has no cryptographic protection applied to it.

Cloud services | Applications or IT services delivered over the Internet rather than in a typical client/server model on a local area network. Yahoo Mail, Google Docs, and Mozy online backup are examples of cloud services.

Code injection | An attack in which malicious code is introduced into an application. This type of attack is possible because of lax input validation in the target application.

Commercial off-the-shelf (COTS) | Commercially available hardware or software that is available for immediate use in an enterprise environment.

Common Access Card (CAC) | The smart card authentication devices used by the U.S. Government in military organizations.

Common Criteria | Abbreviation of Common Criteria for Information Technology Security Evaluation.

Common Criteria for Information Technology Security Evaluation | ISO/IEC 15408 standard for computer security.

Communications Assistance for Law Enforcement Act (CALEA) | A law requiring that telecommunications carriers and equipment makers take steps to facilitate the electronic surveillance activities of law enforcement agencies.

Compartmentalization | The practice of keeping sensitive functions separate from nonsensitive ones.

Complete mediation | Approach in which access control decisions are not cached for later use. Each attempt to access an object should be verified.

Compromise | Unauthorized access and release of information.

Computer Fraud and Abuse Act (CFAA) | A federal criminal statute designed to protect electronic data from theft.

Confidential information | This is the lowest level of sensitivity in the U.S. government classification scheme. Confidential information would damage security if it was disclosed. This information may be handled only by personnel with security clearance, may not be disclosed to the public, and must be disposed of in a secure manner.

Confidentiality | Ensuring that only the intended recipient can read the data.

Control | A technical, physical, or administrative process designed to reduce risk.

Controlled Unclassified Information (CUI) | Information that has not been classified by the U.S. government but is pertinent to the national interests of the United States or to the important interests of entities outside of the federal government or under law or policy requires protection from unauthorized disclosure, special handling safeguards, or prescribed limits on exchange or dissemination.

Cost of impact | What an organization would lose if an asset were unavailable. For example, a particular organization might lose $50,000 per hour in lost productivity if its internal network went down.

Cost of replacement | What it would cost an organization to replace an asset if it were stolen or compromised.

Counter Mode Cipher Block Chaining Message Authentication Protocol (CCMP) | Encryption approach used in the WPA2 standard to provide strong security.

Credentials | Used to control access to resources.

Crossover error rate (CER) | The point at which Type I errors and Type II errors in an access control system are equal.

Cryptography | Used to protect data so that it cannot be easily read or understood.

Cryptosystem | The hardware or software system that transforms the cleartext into ciphertext.

Data at rest (DAR) | Stored data. The data may be in archival form on tape or optical disc, on a hard disk, or sitting in a system's buffers.

Data Encryption Standard (DES) encryption | A method of scrambling data for security purposes. Published in 1974, it has since been broken and is no longer considered highly secure.

Data in motion (DIM) | Data as it travels from one place to another, such as over a network.

Data Link Layer | Network components that interconnect network nodes or hosts.

Declassification | The process used to move a classified document into the public domain.

Default deny | The base assumption of any access control mechanism should be that the access is denied unless it was explicitly authorized.

Defense-in-depth strategy | The approach of using multiple layers of security to protect against a single point of failure.

Delegated access rights | Access rights that are given to a user by the owner of an object.

Denial of service (DoS) attack | An attack against a system that limits it from doing the tasks it is intended to do.

Diffie-Hellman key exchange | A protocol or an algorithm allowing two users to exchange a secret key over unsecure communications.

Digital certificate | A data structure used to bind an authenticated individual to a public key.

Digital Millennium Copyright Act (DMCA) | A U.S. copyright law that enacts criminal penalties for breaking or distributing technology designed to break digital rights management technologies.

Directory information | Information about a student that an educational institution may release without the written consent of the student. Directory information includes a student's name, address, phone number, e-mail address, dates of attendance, degree earned, enrollment status, and field of study.

Disaster recovery | Refers to efforts to bring an organization back online after a natural or man-made disaster.

Discretionary access control (DAC) | An access control system where rights are assigned by the owner of the resource in question.

Discretionary access control list (DACL) | Controls access to an object.

Disgruntled employee | An employee who is angry or dissatisfied, usually with some aspect of his or her employment.

Domain administrator | A user with full rights over all computers in a Windows domain.

Domain Validated (DV) | Certificates that confirm that the certificate was issued to someone controlling the DNS domain included in the certificate.

Dual conditions | One of two aspects in separation of privileges. They are most often implemented through two-stage authentication methods, which require both a biometric scan or token device and a password to grant access.

E

EAP with Flexible Authentication via Secure Tunneling (EAP-FAST) | Proprietary Cisco implementation of EAP authentication that provides mutual authentication but does not use certificates.

EAP with Message Digest 5 (EAP-MD5) | A type of EAP that uses the outdated MD5 hash protocol and is no longer recommended for use.

EAP with Transport Layer Security (EAP-TLS) | A type of EAP that uses certificate-based authentication in conjunction with the standard TLS protocol and is a strong, secure authentication choice.

EAP with Tunneled Transport Layer Security (EAP-TTLS) | A type of EAP that uses TLS to provide network authentication.

Economy of mechanism | Access control mechanisms should be as simple as possible, using as few components and procedures as necessary to meet the requirements.

Electronic protected health information (EPHI) | Information about an individual's health care stored in an electronic format.

Elliptic Curve Cryptosystem (ECC) | Provides a stronger cryptographic result with a shorter key.

Encapsulated Security Payload (ESP) | Authentication and encryption protocol for IPSec that encrypts Internet Protocol (IP) packets and ensures their integrity.

Encryption | The process of applying an algorithm to cleartext (or plaintext) data, resulting in a ciphertext.

Explicitly delegated rights | Access rights that are actively given to a user by an object owner.

Exposure factor (EF) | The expected amount of damage that an asset would incur if a risk materialized; normally described as a percentage.

Extended TACACS (XTACACS) | A client/server protocol developed in 1990 by Cisco; an extension of TACACS.

Extended Validation (EV) | Certificates that provide the strongest degree of trust, verifying the physical presence of the certificate subject.

Extensible Authentication Protocol (EAP) | A framework enabling multiple authentication mechanisms over various connections.

F

Failure to capture rate | The percentage of an individual's authentication attempts that fail because the system is unable to obtain the information necessary to make an authentication decision; also known as failure to acquire rate.

Failure to enroll rate | The percentage of failed attempts to create a sample data set for an individual, divided by the total number of attempts to enroll users.

False acceptance rate | The percentage of imposters that will be recognized as authorized users.

False negative | Occurs when an intrusion detection system overlooks anomalous activity.

False positive | Occurs when an intrusion detection system labels normal activity as anomalous.

False rejection rate | The percentage of attempts by legitimate users that are rejected by the system.

Family Educational Rights and Privacy Act (FERPA) | An act of Congress to protect the privacy of education records. It applies to all educational institutions receiving funding from the U.S. Department of Education.

Federal Information Security Modernization Act (FISMA) | Legal standard that sets forth security requirements for all federal government agencies.

Federation | An approach where one organization depends on the identity information provided by another organization.

FOIA request | See **Freedom of Information Act request**.

Forest | The outermost boundary of an Active Directory service. A forest may contain several domains.

Freedom of Information Act (FOIA) | A law enacted in 1966. It states that any person has a right of access to federal agency records, and that federal agency records must be made available to the public unless they are specifically exempt from public release.

Freedom of Information Act request | An attempt by a member of the general public to get a document declassified. The act allows for full or partial disclosure of the document; if the owning organization refuses the request, the decision can be appealed in a judicial review.

G

Gap analysis | The process of identifying the difference between reality—the current state of an organization's IT infrastructure—and the organization's security goals.

Generic Routing Encapsulation (GRE) | A tunneling protocol that encapsulates packets inside Internet Protocol (IP) tunnels.

Get out of jail free card | The authorization memo, signed by a member of upper management, that states that a penetration test has been authorized and exactly what methods the test will include. Every member of a penetration testing team should carry a copy of this memo at all times to avoid misunderstandings with security and law enforcement.

Gramm-Leach-Bliley Act (GLBA) | An act of Congress that allowed banks, investment firms, and insurance companies to consolidate. It also introduced some consumer protections, such as requiring credit agencies to provide consumers with one free credit report per year.

Group | A collection of users with similar access needs.

Guideline | A collection of suggestions and best practices relating to a standard or procedure. A guideline doesn't necessarily need to be met but compliance is strongly encouraged.

H

Hackers | People who break into a computer system without a legitimate right to obtain data or information.

Hardening | The process by which vulnerabilities are addressed to create a secure system.

Hash salt | Random data that are used as the basis for an encryption algorithm. The randomness of these data provides an additional layer of security to the encryption.

Health Information Technology for Economic and Clinical Health (HITECH) Act | Expanded and updated the civil and criminal penalties for HIPAA violations and requires notification if any breach occurs causing the disclosure of PHI.

Health Insurance Portability and Accountability Act (HIPAA) | Legislation passed in 1996 that protects the privacy and accessibility of healthcare information.

Heightened access | The ability of an attacker to log into a system under one level of access and exploit a vulnerability to gain a higher level of access.

History-based access control (HBAC) | A kind of contextual access control, which takes the past and present activity of the user into account when making access control decisions.

Homeland Security Presidential Directive 12 (HSPD 12) | A standard issued in August of 2007 to enforce the standardization of security identification credentials for government employees and contractors. This standard covers both physical and logical access to government resources.

Host discovery | The process of scanning the network to find out which Internet Protocol (IP) addresses are attached to vulnerable resources.

Human machine interface (HMI) | Place where the operator views the data that are received and processed. The HMI is connected to a database that gathers information from the RTUs.

Human nature | The sum of qualities and traits shared by all humans.

Hypertext Transfer Protocol Secure (HTTPS) | Secure protocol for use in encrypted web communications. Integrates Transport Layer Security (TLS) with the Hypertext Transfer Protocol (HTTP).

Identification | The process by which a subject or object identifies itself to the access control system. In the case of users, identification uniquely distinguishes an individual. In most cases, identification needs to be provided prior to authenticating the user.

Identification mode | The mode in which a biometric system compares live data with a database of known samples and returns one or more matching user profiles.

Identity and access management (IAM) | The process that combines identity management (allows people to confirm that a person is who they claim to be (authentication)) and access control (allows people to restrict their activities to authorized actions (authorization)) together.

Identity as a Service (IDaaS) | Outsourcing professional service to manage the access control implementation and maintain complex technical infrastructures.

Identity management | The process of creating, maintaining, and revoking user accounts and providing the mechanisms used to authenticate users.

Identity provider | The organization that provides the accounts in a federated identity system.

Identity-based access control (IBAC) | Access control decisions made by the system are based on the identity of the user.

Implicitly delegated rights | Rights that are inherited or otherwise passively assigned.

Industrial control system (ICS) | A mechanism used to control the output of a specific industrial process.

Information availability | Ensures that information is available to authorized users when they need it.

Information confidentiality | Ensures that private or sensitive information is not disclosed to unauthorized individuals.

Information integrity | Ensures that data have not been accidentally or intentionally modified without authorization.

Input control | Dictates how users can interact with data and devices that introduce new data into a system.

Integration testing | The process of testing how individual components function together as a complete system.

Integrity | Ensuring that the data has not been altered.

Internet Key Exchange (IKE) | Provides identification to communication partners via a secure connection.

Internet Layer | Provides services for connecting network resources across network domains.

Internet Protocol Security (IPSec) | A protocol that secures IP communications by authenticating and encrypting each IP packet.

Internet Security Association and Key Management Protocol (ISAKMP) | A protocol that provides the framework for the negotiation of algorithms, protocols, modes, and keys for IKE.

Intrusion detection system (IDS) | A combination of hardware and software used to analyze network traffic passing through a single point on the network. It is designed to analyze traffic patterns to find suspicious activity.

Intrusion prevention system (IPS) | A combination of a firewall and an IDS. An IPS is designed to analyze network traffic patterns and react in real time to block suspicious activity.

Intrusive testing methods | Security testing methods that exploit possible vulnerabilities to prove their existence and potential impact.

IP tunneling | Used to create secure pathways for data through a public network.

K

Kerberos | Provides a means of verifying identities of computer systems on an unprotected network. Kerberos is designed to provide strong authentication for client/server applications by using secret-key cryptography.

Key archival | Retaining a key that has been terminated. A copy is kept in a key storage for validating data that was protected by the original key.

Key distribution | Moving encryption keys from one point to another with two stages: initial and subsequent.

Key Distribution Center (KDC) | The service or server that acts as both the ticket granting service and the authentication service.

Key generation | The initial creation of encryption keys.

Key recovery | Restoring an encryption key after a failure has occurred to key storage.

Key storage | Storing the encryption keys after they are distributed.

Key termination | The destruction of encryption keys because they have reached the end of their life cycle or because a key has been compromised in some fashion.

Key usage | When encryption keys are in a production environment and being used for email, file transfers, secure connections, and so on.

Keyspace | The range of values that construct a cryptosystem key.

L

LAN Manager (LM) hash | The method used to store passwords of up to 15 characters in Windows operating systems prior to Windows Vista.

Layer 2 Tunneling Protocol (L2TP) | Sets up a point-to-point connection between two computer systems that can be transmitted over multiple types of networks.

Least astonishment | Security mechanisms should be as nonintrusive as possible, providing security while minimizing disruption to user activity.

Least common mechanism | The mechanisms used by different classes of users should be separated to the extent possible.

Least privilege | The principle in which a subject—whether a user, application, or other entity—should be given the minimum level of rights necessary to perform legitimate functions.

Least user access (LUA) | Requires that users commonly log into workstations under limited user accounts.

Lightweight Directory Access Protocol (LDAP) | Protocol used for the exchange of directory service information.

Lightweight EAP (LEAP) | A Cisco proprietary protocol used primarily on wireless networks.

Linux | A popular open-source operating system that is widely used in server environments.

Linux Intrusion Detection System (LIDS) | A patch to the Linux kernel and a set of administrative tools that attempt to enhance security.

Load testing | A way of measuring how software will perform with an average number of users, as well as how it will perform under extreme load conditions.

Local area network (LAN) | A network connecting computers and other assets in a small, physical location such as an office, home, or school.

M

Malware | Any form of malicious software, including viruses, Trojan horses, and spyware.

Mandatory access control (MAC) | An access control system where rights are assigned by a central authority.

Mandatory declassification review | Instigated when an individual attempts to get a document declassified. After the review request has been filed, the owning organization must respond with approval, denial, or the inability to confirm or deny the existence or nonexistence of the document. If the request is denied, the requester can appeal to the interagency security classification appeals board.

Media Access Control (MAC) address | A unique identifier assigned to every piece of hardware on a network.

Message Digest 5 (MD5) | An algorithm that applies a hash function to a message, creating a 128-bit message digest. This algorithm is used to ensure the data has not been changed in any manner.

Minimization of implementation | The mechanisms used by different classes of users should be separated to the extent possible.

Mitigation plans | Detailed plans about how to mitigate the vulnerabilities and risks described in the vulnerability assessment and threat assessment.

MS-CHAP | Microsoft's version of the CHAP protocol, which is used only in Microsoft-centric applications and comes in two different versions: MS-CHAPv1 and MS-CHAPv2.

Multifactor authentication | The identification process that involves multiple ways of confirming the identity of the subject.

Multilayered access control | The combination of more than one access control method to secure a single resource.

Multilayered approach | An approach that offers a reasonable overall level of security by implementing a set of complementary and overlapping security controls.

Multilevel security (MLS) system | A system that allows the computer system to simultaneously process information of different classification levels and ensures that a subject with the correct clearance can only access the information at his or her authorization level.

Multiple single level (MSL) environments | A system that does not allow different classification levels to commingle. A separate system should be used for each classification level.

N

Need to know | A major component in accessing sensitive information. It requires that the requester must also establish a justifiable need to see the information, and access should be granted only if the information is essential for the requester's official duties.

Nessus | A proprietary security scanner developed by Tenable Network Security. It is network-centric with Web-based consoles and a central server.

Network access control (NAC) | The use of policies within a network infrastructure to limit access to resources until the system proves that it has complied with the policy. Sometimes referred to as network admission control.

Network access server (NAS) | Provides a service to dial-in users. This server allows a computer system to connect to the network through either a phone line or the Internet.

Nmap | An open source port scanning and host detection utility. Nmap stands for Network Mapper.

Nonintrusive testing methods | Security testing methods that do not exploit possible vulnerabilities.

Nonrepudiation | The concept of ensuring an originator cannot refute the validity of a statement or document.

Normalization | The process of translating log files from various systems into a common format.

North American Electric Reliability Council (NERC) | Created in 1968 to ensure that the North American energy network is secure, adequate, and reliable. IT security is mostly concerned with the creation of guidelines for strong access controls and processes.

NTLM hash | A challenge-response authentication protocol used by NT servers when using the Server Message Block (SMB) protocol.

OAKLEY | A protocol that allows computer systems to exchange key agreement over an insecure network.

Object | *1.* Anything that is passively acted upon by a subject. *2.* The resource to which a subject desires access. Common objects are data, networks, and printers.

Online Certificate Status Protocol (OCSP) | A method for live, interactive verification of a certificate's status.

Open design | The security of an access control mechanism should not depend upon the secrecy of its design or the secrecy of details of its implementation, which is the opposite of security through obscurity.

Open Systems Interconnection (OSI) Reference Model | Divides the network infrastructure into seven layers.

Open Vulnerability Assessment Scanner (OpenVAS) | A free security scanning tool published under the GNU General Public License (GPL).

OpenID Connect | An alternative to SAML that works in a similar manner from the end user's perspective.

Orange Book | Orange-covered book that is part of the "Rainbow Series" published by the U.S. Department of Defense.

Organization Validated (OV) | Certificates that verify the identity of the business named on the certificate in addition to domain validation (DV).

Organizational unit (OU) | A logical structure that allows you to organize users, computers, and other objects into separate units for administrative purposes.

Organization-based access control (OrBAC) | A kind of access control that applies differing policies based on the user's organizational membership.

Output control | Dictates how users can interact with the output of data, either to a screen, printer, or another device.

Parent object | An object from which other objects inherit various properties, including access controls.

Parsing | The process of translating and reformatting raw log files into useful reports.

Passphrase | A phrase or sentence used in place of a password. Passphrases are often used as mnemonic devices to help remember complex passwords.

Pass-the-hash attack | Attack where the attacker gains access to hashed passwords and uses them to move laterally across the network.

Password | A secret combination of characters known only to the subject.

Password Authentication Protocol (PAP) | A data-link protocol that provides authentication over PPP.

Password cracking | Guessing or deciphering passwords.

Password hash | A password that is stored in its encrypted form.

Payment Card Industry Data Security Standard (PCI DSS) | The contractual obligation that requires that companies handling credit cards comply with a rigid set of security controls, including specific provisions surrounding access controls.

Penetration attempt | The stage after vulnerability detection in the penetration test, which asks testers to use a variety of methods and tools to gain unauthorized access to systems and networks.

Penetration testing | The act of simulating an attack on an organization's resources to assess an infrastructure's true vulnerability. A penetration test simulates an actual attack. Penetration testers use a variety of methods including social engineering, software hacking, and physical intrusion.

Perimeter security | Any method that restricts access to a defined area, such as a military base, corporate campus, infrastructure facility, or office building.

Personally identifiable information (PII) | Any information that can be used to identify, locate, or contact a specific individual. Also includes any information that can be combined with other information to piece together a specific individual's identity. A Social Security number is an example of PII. Several laws and regulations specify that PII must be protected.

Phishing | Creating legitimate-looking websites or e-mails that trick a user into entering sensitive information such as passwords, Social Security numbers, or credit card numbers.

Physical security | The process of ensuring that no one without the proper credentials can physically access resources.

Piggybacking | Refers to when employees regularly hold open doors and allow each other to enter without swiping their ID badge, which may cause an information leak.

Point-to-Point Protocol (PPP) | A protocol for communication between two computers. Typically, the connection from the client to the server is over a telephone line.

Point-to-Point Tunneling Protocol (PPTP) | A protocol that sets up a point-to-point connection between two computer systems over an Internet Protocol (IP) network.

Policy | *1.* A document that describes specific requirements or rules that must be met in a given area. *2.* A formal statement of management intent regarding the business practices of an organization. A policy is binding upon all affected individuals.

Port scan detector | Software that monitors network ports to detect a port scan attack. These attacks are usually the precursor to a more serious attack.

Port scanning | A technique designed to probe a network's open ports looking for a weakness.

Pretexting | A technique where the attacker lies about his or her own identity or intent in order to persuade the victim to reveal sensitive information.

Prioritization | Regarding log files, the process of determining which log files and/or entries are important and may require action versus which are less important or informational only.

Privacy impact assessment (PIA) | A comprehensive process for determining the privacy, confidentiality, and security risks associated with the collection, use, and disclosure of personal information. It also describes the measures used to mitigate, and if possible, eliminate identified risks.

Private key | The encryption key that is held privately by the user.

Probability of occurrence | The likelihood that an attack will occur.

Procedures | A defined series of steps or actions for achieving an objective or result. For example, a defined workflow used to enforce policies is considered a procedure or a set of procedures. Procedures are often written to ensure that tasks are completed in the same way each time, preventing unexpected problems.

Process control system (PCS) | A mechanism used to control the output of a specific process.

Programmable logic controller (PLC) | A programmable electronic device used in industrial automation to provide logic and sequencing controls for machinery.

Protected EAP (PEAP) | Similar to EAP-TTLS, which uses TLS to provide network authentication but differs in technical implementation details.

Protected health information (PHI) | Any information that concerns health status, health care, or any payment for health care that can be linked to the individual. This is interpreted very broadly and includes all of an individual's medical record and payment history.

Psychological acceptability | Security mechanisms should be as nonintrusive as possible, providing security while minimizing disruption to user activity.

Public key | A public key is used to communicate with the private key. This key is publicly available.

Public key infrastructure (PKI) | A framework that consists of programs, procedures, and security policies that employs public key cryptography and the X.509 standard (digital certificates). It is a hybrid system of symmetric and asymmetric key algorithms.

Q

Qualitative risk assessment | A method of risk assessment that assigns a subjective label (usually "high," "medium," and "low") to a risk scenario.

Quantitative risk assessment | A method of risk assessment that assigns a dollar value to every data point.

R

Radio Frequency Identification (RFID) badge | An ID badge with an embedded radio frequency identification chip. This chip can store information about the badge holder, such as authentication information and security access levels.

Red team | In a penetration test, the red team consists of penetration testers who have been given some background knowledge of the infrastructure.

Registration authority (RA) | An entity that is responsible for the registration and initial authentication of certificate subscribers.

Relational database (RDB) | A database that stores data in tables and provides for relationships between various data.

Relational database management system (RDBMS) | The system stores the claim files and the pricing information.

Remote access server (RAS) | A server that provides an authentication service for users that are dialing into a network or accessing it from the Internet.

Remote Authentication Dial In User Service (RADIUS) | A client/server protocol that provides authentication, authorization, and accounting for a remote dial-in system.

Remote terminal unit (RTU) | A microprocessor-controlled electronic device that interfaces with objects in the physical world to a distributed control system or SCADA system by transmitting telemetry data to the system and/or altering the state of connected objects based on control messages received from the system.

Retina | A graphically intensive vulnerability scanner.

Risk | The probability that a particular threat will exploit an IT vulnerability causing harm to an organization. Risk is measured in terms of probability and consequence.

Risk acceptance | Simply accepting the risks and doing what you need to do anyway.

Risk assessment | The process of identifying and prioritizing risk.

Risk avoidance | Choosing to avoid an activity that carries some element of risk.

Risk mitigation | A strategy that combines attempts to minimize the probability and consequences of a risk situation.

Risk transference | Shifting responsibility for a risk to a third party.

Risk-adaptive access control (RAdAC) | Policy changes dynamically based on the risk environment.

Role | Allow you to generalize and separate a subject's function from its identity.

Role-based access control (RBAC) | Access control system where rights are assigned based on a user's role rather than his or her identity.

Root | The superuser in Linux and UNIX systems.

RSA asymmetric encryption algorithm | A public key cryptosystem based on factoring large numbers that are a product of two prime numbers.

Rule-based access control (RuBAC) | Policy defined by a set of rules determined by the system administrator.

S

Sandbox | A security mechanism for isolating programs running in a shared environment.

Sarbanes-Oxley (SOX) Act | Created to protect investors by improving the accuracy and reliability of corporate financial disclosures. SOX accomplishes this by strengthening existing penalties and making corporate officers personally responsible for the disclosures.

Secret | Information that would cause serious damage to national security if disclosed. This is the most common national security classification level.

Secret key | Key used to encrypt and decrypt messages.

Security Assertion Markup Language (SAML) | An XML-like markup language that allows web applications to pass a security token for user identification.

Security association (SA) | Records the configuration the computer systems need to support an IPSec connection.

Security identifier (SID) | A variable that identifies a user, group, or account.

Security information and event management (SIEM) system | A software package that centralizes and normalizes log files from a variety of applications and devices.

Security through obscurity | The security of an access control mechanism should depend on the secrecy of its design or the secrecy of details of its implementation, which is the opposite of open design.

Self-signed certificates | Issued when CAs are internal to an organization, which allows the organization to have complete control over the distribution and life of the certificate.

Sensitive information | Information that is not widely known or available.

Separation of privileges | The practice of dividing essential steps of a task between multiple individuals.

Separation of responsibilities | Authentication system in which two conditions must be met in order for access to be granted. If one condition is met but not the other, access is denied.

Service level agreement (SLA) | An agreement between an organization and a third party that describes availability levels, security protection levels, and response times to a breach.

Service provider | The organization that depends on those identities in a federated identity system.

Service set identifier (SSID) | An access point's ID on a wireless LAN.

Shadow password | An encrypted password database used in Unix and Linux operating systems.

Shared secret | Something only the subject and the authentication system know. A shared secret can be a piece of data that is known only to the parties that are communicating with one another. A shared secret is used for encryption.

Simplicity of design | Access control mechanisms should be as simple as possible, using as few components and procedures as necessary to meet the requirements.

Simultaneous Authentication of Equals (SAE) | Secure password-based key exchange mechanism used in the WPA3 wireless standard.

Single loss expectancy (SLE) | The cost you expect to incur in one loss incident.

Single sign-on (SSO) | A method of access control that allows a user to log on to a system and gain access to other resources within the network via the initial logon. SSO helps a user avoid having to log on multiple times and remember multiple passwords for various systems.

Single-factor authentication | The act of identifying a user as authentic with a single authentication factor.

Smart card | An ID badge or other card with an embedded RFID chip that stores basic identification and authentication information.

Social engineering | The use of manipulation or trickery to convince authorized users to perform actions or divulge sensitive information to an attacker.

Software as a Service (SaaS) | A model of software distribution. Instead of simply selling an application, a SaaS vendor hosts the applications and offers access for a small subscription fee.

Spear phishing | A phishing attack targeted at specific, usually high-level individuals within an organization.

Standard | A collection of requirements that must be met by anyone who performs a given task or works on a specific system.

Subject | The user, network, system, process, or application requesting access to a resource.

Super Administrator | A user with full rights on a system.

Super user do (sudo) | A command that allows an administrator to run processes as root without actually logging in under the root account in a Linux or UNIX system.

Supervisory control and data acquisition (SCADA) process control systems | Systems utilized to monitor and control telecommunications, water and waste control, energy, and transportation among other industries and utilities.

Supplicant | Software running on the client that wishes to connect to the network that interfaces with the 802.1x environment.

Symmetric encryption | A form of encryption where the sender and the receiver use the same key for encrypting and decrypting an object.

System access control list (SACL) | A system-created access control list that handles the information assurance aspect of access controls.

Systematic declassification | Any document that is less than 25 years old but of significant importance to the historic record of the United States can be reviewed for early declassification. Once identified, these documents go through the same procedures as automatically declassified documents.

T

Tailgating | Refers to when one person uses the successful authentication of another to gain access to a facility.

Target | Any system or network that contains valuable data and has attracted the notice of the hacker.

Temporal Key Integrity Protocol (TKIP) | Encryption used for WLANs.

Terminal Access Controller Access Control System (TACACS) | A remote access client/server protocol that provides authentication and authorization capabilities to users that are accessing the network remotely. It is not a secure protocol.

Terminal Access Controller Access Control System Plus (TACACS+) | A remote access client/server protocol. It is a Cisco proprietary protocol and provides authentication, authorization, and accounting.

Threat | A potential attack on a system.

Threat assessment | The process that deals with the potential for weaknesses within the existing infrastructure to be exploited.

Three-factor authentication | The act of identifying a user as authentic with three authentication factors.

Ticket-Granting Service (TGS) | A server or service that is authorized to issue tickets to the client after the client has already received a Ticket-Granting Ticket. A Ticket-Granting Service verifies the user's identity using the Ticket-Granting Ticket and issues the ticket for the desired service. A ticket-granting service is part of the Key Distribution Center.

Tiger team | In a penetration test, a tiger team is composed of testers who are given no knowledge of the infrastructure and are attacking a target that is unaware of their existence until the attack is made.

Token | Something the subject has that no one else does. Smart cards and challenge-response devices are commonly used tokens.

Tool | A technical method or control used to complete a task or achieve a goal, such as enforcing policies.

Top Secret | The highest level of information sensitivity in the National Security classification scheme; it is defined as any information that would cause grave damage to national security if disclosed.

Trade secrets | Information that is a kind of valuable asset and if disclosed, could harm the controlling organization.

Transparency | Being open and honest about the infrastructure. Not hiding any data from the users.

Transport Layer | Methods and protocols for encapsulating application data.

Transport Layer Security (TLS) | A secure protocol that supports a number of different cryptographic algorithms, relying on digital certificates and public key encryption.

Two-factor authentication | The act of identifying a user as authentic with two authentication factors.

Two-person control | The concept that two authorized individuals must be available to approve any sensitive activity.

Type I error | A false rejection in a biometric access control system.

Type II error | A false acceptance in a biometric access control system.

 U

Unclassified information | Information that has not otherwise been assigned a sensitivity level under the national security classification scheme; unclassified information is generally subject to public release under the Freedom of Information Act (FOIA).

Unicast | The sending of messages to a single network destination. The opposite of unicast is broadcast, where data are sent to all network destinations.

Uninterruptable power supply (UPS) | A device that supplies backup power to servers and other devices.

Unit testing | A method of testing that ensures that a specific function or module works as designed.

UNIX | A multi-processing, multi-user family of operating systems originally developed by Bell Laboratories. Most often used for servers.

Verification mode | The mode in which a biometric system makes a simple one-to-one comparison and returns a binary result.

Virtual private network (VPN) | A system that uses a public network (usually the Internet) to transmit private data securely. Users on a VPN can exchange data and share resources as if they were directly connected via a LAN.

Vulnerability | An unintended weakness in a system's design that makes it possible for attackers to take control of a system, access resources to which they are not authorized, or damage the system in some way.

Vulnerability detection | The stage after information gathering in the penetration test, which helps the team choose specific attack vectors and target systems during the penetration attempt.

Ward | A metal projection in a warded lock that must line up with the grooves on the key in order to unlock.

Whitelist | A list of known approved behaviors that should be automatically allowed.

Wide area network (WAN) | A network that connects several smaller networks. For example, a large corporation with offices in New York, Chicago, and Los Angeles might have a LAN in each local office and then connect those three LANs via a wide area network.

Wireless mesh networks | A networking scheme based on a distributed network mesh topology. Each node in the network connects to multiple nodes; each node also acts as a router for the nodes it connects to, allowing traffic to hop along multiple paths to a destination.

World Intellectual Property Organization (WIPO) | A group of 188 nations that have signed treaties to protect intellectual property across national borders.

References

Adams, Carlisle, and Steve Lloyd. "Core PKI Services: Authentication, Integrity, and Confidentiality" (Microsoft TechNet, 2009). http://technet.microsoft.com/en-us/library/cc700808.aspx (accessed May 16, 2010).

Adams, Carlisle, and Steve Lloyd. *Understanding PKI: Concepts, Standards, and Deployment Considerations*, 2nd ed. New York: Addison-Wesley Professional, 2002.

Allsopp, Wil. *Unauthorised Access: Physical Penetration Testing for IT Security Teams*. Hoboken, NJ: John Wiley & Sons, 2009.

Austin, Thomas. *PKI: A Wiley Tech Brief*, 1st ed. New York: John Wiley & Sons, 2001.

Barman, Scott. *Writing Information Security Policies*. Indianapolis: New Riders Publishing, 2002.

Bosworth, Seymour, M. E. Kabay, and Eric Whyne, eds. *Computer Security Handbook*, 5th ed. Hoboken, NJ: John Wiley & Sons, 2009.

Britton, Chris, and Peter Bye. *IT Architectures and Middleware: Strategies for Building Large, Integrated Systems*, 2nd ed. Indianapolis: Addison-Wesley Professional, 2004.

Center for Internet Security. http://cisecurity.org/en-us/? (accessed April 14, 2010).

Cole, Eric. *Network Security Bible*, 2nd ed. New York: Wiley, 2009.

Deluccia IV, James J. *IT Compliance and Controls: Best Practices for Implementation*. New York: Wiley, 2008.

Ferraiolo, David F., D. Richard Kuhn, and Ramaswamy Chandramouli. *Role-Based Access Control*. Norwood, MA: Artech House Publishers, 2003.

"FFIEC Releases Supplemental Guidance on Internet Banking" (FFIEC.gov, Press Releases section, June 28, 2011). https://www.ffiec.gov/press/pr062811.htm (accessed March 19, 2020).

Fry, Chris, and Martin Nystrom. *Security Monitoring*, 1st ed. Sebastopol, CA: O'Reilly Media, Inc., 2009.

Gregg, Michael, and David Kim. *Inside Network Security Assessment: Guarding Your IT Infrastructure*, 1st ed. Indianapolis: Sams, 2005.

Harris, Shon. *CISSP All-in-One Exam Guide*, 3rd ed. (All-In-One Certification). New York: McGraw-Hill Osborne Media, 2005.

Harris, Shon. "Cryptography." In *CISSP All-in-One Exam Guide*, 3rd ed. New York: McGraw-Hill/Osborne Media, 2005, 587–683.

Institute of Electrical and Electronics Engineers (IEEE). http://www.ieee.org/index.html (accessed April 11 and 14, 2010).

International Organization for Standardization (ISO). http://www.iso.org/iso/home.htm (accessed April 14, 2010).

Internet Engineering Task Force (IETF) Web site. http://www.ietf.org/ (accessed April 14, 2010).

"Introduction to RBAC" (HISSA, January 9, 1995). https://csrc.nist.gov/CSRC/media/Publications /Shared/documents/itl-bulletin/cslbul1995-12.txt (accessed March 19, 2020).

Kelley, Jay. *Network Access Control for Dummies*. Somerset, NJ: Wiley, 2009.

"Kerberos: The Network Authentication Protocol" (MIT, April 8, 2010). http://web.mit.edu /Kerberos/ (accessed April 11, 2010).

Krawetz, Neal. *Introduction to Network Security (Networking Series)*, 1st ed. Rockland, MA: Charles River Media, 2006.

Lam, Kevin, David LeBlanc, and Ben Smith. *Assessing Network Security*. Redmond, WA: Microsoft Press, 2004.

Landoll, Douglass J. *The Security Risk Assessment Handbook: A Complete Guide for Performing Security Risk Assessments*. Boca Raton, FL: Auerbach Publications, 2005.

Lemos, Robert. "Microsoft Warns of Hijacked Certificates" (CNET News Technology News, January 2, 2002). http://news.cnet.com/2100-1001-254586.html&tag=tp_pr (accessed May 16, 2010).

Manzuik, Steve, Ken Pfeil, Andrew Gold. *Network Security Assessment: From Vulnerability to Patch*, 1st ed. Burlington, MA: Syngress, 2006.

McCabe, James D. *Network Analysis, Architecture, and Design, Third Edition* (*The Morgan Kaufmann Series in Networking*). San Francisco: Morgan Kaufmann, 2007.

Mel, H.X., and Doris M. *Cryptography Decrypted*, 1st ed. New York: Addison-Wesley Professional, 2000.

MIT Kerberos Consortium. http://www.kerberos.org/index.html (accessed April 11, 2010).

Mitnick, Kevin D, and William L. Simon, and Steve Wozniac. *The Art of Deception: Controlling the Human Element of Security*. Somerset, NJ: John Wiley & Sons, 2003.

"National Information Assurance (IA) Glossary," CNSS Instruction No. 4009 (Committee on National Security Systems, April 26, 2010). https://www.hsdl.org/?view&did=7447 (accessed March 19, 2020).

National Institute of Standards and Technology (NIST). http://www.nist.gov/index.html (accessed April 11, 2010).

NIST: Computer Security Resource Center. "An Introduction to Role-Based Access Control" (NIST Computer Security Division—Computer Security Resource Center, December 1995). http://csrc.nist.gov/groups/SNS/rbac/documents/design_implementation/Intro_role _based_access.htm (accessed April 19, 2010).

Oram, Andy, Anton Chuvakin, and John Viega. *Beautiful Security*, 1st ed. Sebastopol, CA: O'Reilly Media, Inc., 2009.

Requirement, Legal. "NIST.gov–Computer Security Division–Computer Security Resource Center." http://csrc.nist.gov/ (accessed April 14, 2010).

"RFC 1492—An Access Control Protocol, Sometimes Called TACACS" (Internet FAQ Archives, July1993). http://www.faqs.org/rfcs/rfc1492.html (accessed April 27, 2010).

"RFC 1994—PPP Challenge Handshake Authentication Protocol (CHAP)" (Internet FAQ Archives, August1996). http://www.faqs.org/rfcs/rfc1994.html (accessed April 27, 2010).

"RFC 2138—Remote Authentication Dial In User Service (RADIUS)" (Internet FAQ Archives, April 1997). http://www.faqs.org/rfcs/rfc2138.html (accessed April 27, 2010).

"RFC 2284—PPP Extensible Authentication Protocol (EAP)" Internet FAQ Archives, March 1998). http://www.faqs.org/rfcs/rfc2284.html (accessed April 27, 2010).

"RFC 2637 (rfc2637)—Point-to-Point Tunneling Protocol (PPTP)" Internet FAQ Archives, July 1999). http://www.faqs.org/rfcs/rfc2637.html (accessed April 27, 2010).

"RFC 4120—The Kerberos Network Authentication Service (V5)" (IETF Tools, July 2005). http://tools.ietf.org/html/rfc4120 (accessed April 11, 2010).

"Role Based Access Controls" (NIST Computer Security Division, Computer Security Resource Center, 1992). http://csrc.nist.gov/nissc/1992/Role_Based_Access_Control-nissc-1992.html (accessed April 19, 2010).

Schneier, Bruce. *Secrets and Lies: Digital Security in a Networked World*. Somerset, NJ: Wiley, 2004.

Schultz, E. Eugene, and Russell Schumway. *Incident Response: A Strategic Guide to Handling System and Network Security Breaches*. Indianapolis, IN: New Riders Publishing, 2001.

"TACACS+ and RADIUS Comparison" (Cisco Systems, January 14, 2008). http://www.cisco.com/en/US/tech/tk59/technologies_tech_note09186a0080094e99.shtml (accessed Apri 27, 2010).

"US Coast Guard, Hawaii Improve Port Safety, Security and Commerce Through CIBER's Web-Based System" (CIBER, n.d.). http://www.ciber.com/ciber_overview/stories/search_results_single.cfm?id=coastguard (accessed May 15, 2010).

US Department of Commerce, Office of the Chief Information Officer. "Electronic Transmission of PII Policy" (n.d.). https://www.osec.doc.gov/opog/privacy/pii_bii.html (accessed March 5, 2010).

Vacca, John. *Network and System Security*, 1st ed. Burlington, MA: Syngress, 2010.

Von Clausewitz, Carl. *On War*. Brooklyn, NY: Brownstone Books, 1909.

Whitman, Michael. *Principles of Information Security*. Florence, KY: Course Technology, 2007.

Wiles, Jack, et al. *Techno Security's Guide to Securing SCADA: A Comprehensive Handbook on Protecting the Critical Infrastructure*, 1st ed. Burlington, MA: Syngress, 2008.

Wilhelm, Thomas. *Professional Penetration Testing: Creating and Operating a Formal Hacking Lab*. Burlington, MA: Syngress, 2009.

"Wireless Deployment Technology and Component Overview," Microsoft TechNet: Resources for IT Professionals. http://technet.microsoft.com/en-us/library/bb457015.aspx (accessed May 11, 2010).

Wright, Craig. *The IT Regulatory and Standards Compliance Handbook: How to Survive an Information Systems Audit and Assessments*. Burlington, MA: Syngress, 2008.

Index

Note: Page numbers followed by *f* and *t* indicate figures and tables, respectively